Paths to a Middle Ground

ATLANTIC CROSSINGS

Rafe Blaufarb, Series Editor

Paths to a Middle Ground

The Diplomacy of Natchez, Boukfouka, Nogales, and San Fernando de las Barrancas, 1791–1795

CHARLES A. WEEKS

THE UNIVERSITY OF ALABAMA PRESS
Tuscaloosa

The University of Alabama Press
Tuscaloosa, Alabama 35487-0380

Manufactured in the United States of America

Typeface: Minion

∞

The paper on which this book is printed meets the minimum requirements of American National Standard for Information Sciences—Permanence of Paper for Printed Library Materials, ANSI Z39.48-1984.

ISBN: 978-0-8173-5645-3 (pbk. : alk. paper)

ISBN: 978-0-8173-8522-4 (electronic)

A previous edition of this book has been catalogued by the Library of Congress.

Library of Congress Cataloging-in-Publication Data

Weeks, Charles A., 1937–

Paths to a middle ground : the diplomacy of Natchez, Boukfouka, Nogales, and San Fernando de las Barrancas, 1791–1795 / Charles A. Weeks.

p. cm.

Includes bibliographical references and index.

ISBN 0-8173-1210-2 (cloth : alk. paper)

1. Natchez Region (Miss.)—Ethnic relations. 2. Mobile Region (Ala.)—Ethnic relations. 3. Tombigbee River Region (Miss. and Ala.)—Ethnic relations. 4. Indians of North America—Government relations—1789-1869. 5. Spaniards—Mississippi—Natchez—History—18th century.
6. Spaniards—Louisiana—New Orleans—History—18th century. 7. Colonial administrators—Mississippi—Natchez—History—18th century. 8. Colonial administrators—Louisiana—New Orleans—History—18th century. 9. Political culture—Mississippi—Natchez Region—History—18th century—Sources. 10. Political culture—Alabama—Mobile Region—History—18th century—Sources. I. Title.

F349.N2W44 2005

305.8'00976226—dc22

2005002043

Contents

Maps and Diagrams

Preface

This book represents a blend of older borderland histories, which emphasize the role of the Spanish during the sixteenth through the early nineteenth centuries in the broad area stretching from California to Florida, and more recent work that portrays the same region as one of encounter among its most numerous peoples, Native Americans, and other European and African newcomers in addition to the Spanish. Benefiting from the work of archaeologists, anthropologists, and social historians, these newer studies present a much fuller and more complex picture of place and time. While still maintaining a Hispanic perspective, this work endeavors to further an appreciation and understanding of a region that was not so much a frontier or borderland but rather a place of mixing and melting, where politics and diplomacy often sought the impossible: the creation and maintenance of "walls"—or boundaries—to make good neighbors where, to borrow more words of the poet Robert Frost, there was always "something that doesn't love a wall."

In the course of working on this project, many people and institutions have contributed much to it and to my education. I would like to thank them for their help and encouragement and absolve them from any of the book's shortcomings. The people who played an especially important role in its creation include, first, Patricia K. Galloway of the University of Texas at Austin, who called my attention to the existence of Spanish materials in the Mississippi Department of Archives and History when she was associated with that institution and encouraged me to become familiar with them and to read them carefully. I continue to benefit from her scholarship and wisdom. Sarah J. Banks, a professor of modern languages at Jackson State University, and I collaborated in the preparation of a reader consisting of Spanish documents from the late fifteenth through the eighteenth centuries to illustrate Mississippi's Spanish heritage. She approached that project with great enthusiasm, which encouraged me to continue working with eighteenth-century Spanish documents and ultimately produce the translated documents included in this book. While working in Spain, I benefited much from the knowledge of G. Douglas Inglis—now director of the The Texas Tech University Center in Sevilla—about Spanish archives generally and the Archivo General de Indias in particular. His interest in the same region and period and his enthusiasm for eighteenth-century history have been a continual source of encouragement. Colin G. Calloway, head of the Native-American Studies department in Dartmouth College, took an interest in the project and offered many good suggestions about an earlier version of the text. Jack D. Elliott, Jr., has been a most helpful source of knowledge about Spanish Natchez, particularly the house its Spanish governor built. A good friend and former colleague, the late Robert L. Smith, entered the lists late and provided generously of his talent and time to translate a number of French documents and edit an earlier version of the narrative portion of the book. Thanks to him and Pat Galloway I was reminded constantly of the continued importance of people of French or French Canadian descent in the life of a region that became only nominally Spanish during the second half of the eighteenth century. Finally, I appreciate very much the many good suggestions offered by anonymous readers of the manuscript.

The book prepared by Sarah J. Banks and me, *Mississippi's Spanish Heritage: Selected Writings, 1492–1798* (1991), came about with the help of the Mississippi State Department of Education and grants from the National Endowment for the Humanities and the Hardin Foundation. At the time of its preparation, I was benefiting from a National Endowment for the Humanities–Reader's Digest "Teacher-Scholar" award that made possible a year-long sabbatical to work with documents from which many were selected for the book. The "Recovering the U.S. Hispanic Heritage" program of the University of Houston provided a small grant in 1996 that allowed me to assemble in translated form documents pertaining to the Nogales controversy of the early 1790s and the subsequent presentation and publication of a short paper on that topic. The grant also encouraged me to travel for the first time to Spain to work in such Spanish archives as the Archivo Histórico Nacional in Madrid and the Archivo General de Indias in Sevilla. During one of my many visits to Sevilla, the Escuela de Estudios Hispano-Americanos, in addition to providing lodging, offered an opportunity during one of its weekly Mesas Redondas, or roundtable discussions, to share some preliminary thoughts on the subject of the cultural dimension of late eighteenth-century Spanish-Indian diplomacy in the lower Mississippi valley. The staffs and collections of the Historic New Orleans Collection, the State Historical Society of Wisconsin, the Library of Congress, the Bancroft Library of the University of California at Berkeley, the New York Public Library, the Baker-Berry Library of Dartmouth College, the Ohrstrom Library of St. Paul's School, and the Mississippi Department of Archives and History have offered me pleasant and valuable places to work.

Paths to a Middle Ground

Introduction

An Argument

Piomingo, the astute and able Chickasaw chief, when invited by the Spanish to participate in a major assembly in 1793 with other Chickasaws, Choctaws, Creeks, and Cherokees, responded by saying he would follow a "straight path" to Nogales, the site chosen for the meeting.[1] In using the word *path*, Piomingo invoked perhaps the most common symbol used by Indians in their highly metaphoric language, especially in diplomatic discourse.[2] Its meaning and significance derived from the numerous physical paths or trails connecting villages and making possible frequent and remarkably fast communication. Such practical importance enhanced the word's symbolic or metaphoric meaning, for in Indian rhetoric *path* connoted a range of human relationships from the difficult or even bellicose—conveyed by such modifiers as crooked, dark, obstructed, bloody, or red—to the amicable or peaceful when described as straight, clear, or white.[3] In this particular context, Piomingo expressed a preference for the latter, and it is the one sought by local Spanish officials as they endeavored through diplomacy to forge closer ties with chiefs such as Piomingo and the people they represented.

The essay and documents that follow will attempt to offer some insight into the diplomacy associated with establishing and maintaining such paths in the Gulf South during the last few years of a century of imperial rivalry in North America. It was a diplomacy that was defined principally by Native Americans but also one that eighteenth-century Europeans could understand and employ. Despite differences of culture and interests, Europeans and Indians found that they shared a diplomacy with similar assumptions and characteristics. Both knew the ways of diplomatic negotiation: missions to convey important messages or engage in talks, full-scale councils or congresses accompanied by elaborate protocol, interpreters, and eloquent, often highly metaphoric language.[4] That diplomacy contributed much to break down barriers and boundaries and define the region as one of mingling and exchange, perhaps even "the world's first multicultural society."[5]

The focus here will center on the end of the century, particularly the first half of the decade of the 1790s. Then both local Spanish officials and representatives of the major Indian groups in the region concluded that they needed to be more active in finding ways to deter what they saw as serious challenges coming from the newly independent United States. Although Piomingo, in spite of his words of 1793, continued to follow paths to the Americans, many other chiefs and factions, who had begun to feel more insecure as they experienced increasing pressure from an expanding American population, found it more advantageous to respond to such Spanish invitations as that extended to Piomingo in 1793.

This story begins in early 1791 with a Spanish decision to establish a post at the mouth of the Yazoo River some eighty-five miles north of Natchez.[6] Both the governor-general in New Orleans, Estevan Miró, and the governor in Natchez, Manuel Gayoso de Lemos, had concluded that such a post, which Gayoso hoped might eventually become a city, was needed to deter a projected American settlement there, backed by the South Carolina Yazoo Company.[7] Dubbed earlier by the British "Walnut Hills" because of a stand of black-walnut trees, the site lay at the western end of what the Spanish regarded as the northern boundary of the Natchez district within their province of West Florida.[8] Miró appointed a member of the Louisiana Infantry, Elías Beauregard, as commandant of the new post, to be called "Nogales," the Spanish plural of "walnut," and he provided Gayoso a copy of the instructions he had prepared for Pedro Foucher, commandant of the recently created post of Nuevo Madrid, to serve as a model for Beauregard's instructions. They reveal that, although the Spanish saw the post as a way to deter a similar American one, emigration by Americans willing to take an oath of allegiance to the Spanish king should be encouraged, and the commandant was instructed to discharge his office in such a way as to demonstrate the advantages of a community ordered by good government. After a difficult trip up the Mississippi River from New Orleans, Beauregard took charge of construction work on a fort and other buildings for what Gayoso described as "the most important [post] of this province because of its location with respect to our neighbors and its land."[9]

Gayoso joined Beauregard's expedition to Nogales and spent most of April there. By means of a diary, he provided a rather detailed and sanguine report of his activities, which included entertaining a delegation of Indians.[10] Shortly after his return to Natchez, however, he received a letter, written in English, containing the names of two chiefs of the Choctaw Nation, Franchimastabé and Taboca. The letter had been carried to Nogales by Itelegana, one of the Choctaw chiefs Gayoso had met during his stay at Nogales, and delivered to

Beauregard to send down to Natchez. It protested what the authors described as a usurpation of lands belonging to the Choctaws and their "brothers" the Chickasaws. The letter was short and blunt. Not only did it accuse the Spanish of taking the land by force; it said that it was not theirs to occupy, that fifteen villages "of our nation" wanted it, and that the Chickasaws and the Choctaws were united in their opposition to the Spanish initiative. They begged the Spanish to leave and, as others repeated in later communications to Spanish officials, "let the cane grow again."[11]

More than a year of active diplomacy followed, involving principally Gayoso and a number of Choctaw and Chickasaw chiefs, aided by traders and interpreters. Gayoso tried to meet the objections raised by Taboca and Franchimastabé so that the Spanish could build their post in a way that would strengthen the bonds of "friendship and commerce" agreed upon in 1784 meetings with the Choctaws and Chickasaws in Mobile and deter American expansion. Culminating with a major congress in Natchez in May 1792, Gayoso's diplomatic efforts produced a treaty in which the principal Indian chiefs in attendance agreed to the post.

This success, encouraged by subsequent events including a visit to New Orleans later in the year by a large delegation of Indians that included a group of Cherokees, led late in the next year to another major council or assembly at the site of the new post at Nogales. This meeting supported other measures to check what all agreed were threats coming from the north. For the Spanish, these measures included creating a squadron of naval vessels to patrol the Mississippi River, establishing additional posts, appointing resident diplomatic agents or commissioners, and, for those Indians meeting in New Orleans, forging some kind of confederation to include Choctaws, Chickasaws, Creeks, Cherokees, and other groups. Finally, in the spring of 1795, the diplomatic efforts of Gayoso and the Chickasaw chief Ugulayacabé secured enough support from the Chickasaws to enable the Spanish to create farther north the post of San Fernando de las Barrancas along the east bank of the Mississippi River on bluffs like those of Nogales and Natchez. A few months later, however, other diplomats in Europe undid this work by means of the Treaty of San Lorenzo between the United States and Spain, which required Spain to withdraw from all these posts and turn them over to the United States. San Fernando de las Barrancas soon became the city of Memphis, Tennessee.

Both the Spanish, in terms of what their officials set out to accomplish in this region, and the great majority of the people living there—the Indians—lost by this 1795 treaty. The Spanish were forced to give up the posts their local representatives had worked so hard to achieve, and they eventually gave up all claims to a political presence in the region. In the context of their withdrawal, many Indians felt betrayed, sensing they had lost a major ally in their struggle to hold at bay an ever more aggressive and expansionist United States. More important perhaps was the loss of a significant participant in the political culture of the region. With the absence of the Spanish, politics became less competitive and hence less diplomatic. There were fewer opportunities for chiefs such as Piomingo to bargain in the context of pressures from what historians Arthur Whitaker and Frank De Fina characterize as the "insatiable voracity of [American] frontiersmen and speculators" and others who concluded that the region could no longer accommodate Indian ways of life.[12] The paths open to the Indians, in other words, diminished and for many ultimately came to mean paths of egress.

Hence, a particular significance of the focus of this essay and accompanying documents. A consideration of the diplomatic process centering on Natchez, the Choctaw village of Boukfouka, the new post at Nogales, and San Fernando de las Barrancas can add to an appreciation of a century in which European newcomers and Indians created and sustained diplomatic paths as one way to live together. Despite strains and lapses, these paths helped define here, as elsewhere, a "middle ground"—an economy and culture of exchange involving goods, people, and language.[13] Both Spanish officials and their Indian counterparts had a very real sense of what might be described as a kind of eighteenth-century *realpolitik* that reflected a remarkable sensitivity to power relationships and native traditions enabling them to resolve problems through diplomacy. Indian participants in this process—notably such leaders as Franchimastabé and Taboca of the Choctaws, Bloody Fellow of the Cherokees, Piomingo and Ugulayacabé of the Chickasaws—were shrewd politicians and diplomats. Like their European counterparts, they had developed formal ways of dealing with one another, many of which could be easily understood by Europeans. To such chiefs, historian John Alden has pointed out with regard to the 1760s and 1770s, "the strategy of balance of power had not the slightest mystery."[14]

Other historians after Alden have done much to bring out more about the active and important role these chiefs and others played in a multicultural diplomacy that to a considerable extent integrated European newcomers into the life of the region during the eighteenth century. Greg O'Brien's recent history of the Choctaws during the last quarter of the eighteenth century and the early part of the nineteenth portrays the important role of the two Choctaw chiefs, Franchimastabé and Taboca, in the politics and diplomacy of their time.[15] Claudiò Saunt's study of changes among the Creeks in the eighteenth and early nineteenth centuries devotes considerable attention to such chiefs as Efau Hadjo and Hoboithle Micco to balance what he sees as too much emphasis in earlier literature on Alexander McGillivray, a Creek chief of Scottish and Creek ancestry.[16]

In addition to directing attention to other chiefs, Saunt writes about how power should be seen to expand over the century to include warriors and women. Others have explored this dimension of power in the Indian world. Theda Perdue and Kathryn Braund provide additional insight into the important role of women as agents of change by describing how Cherokee and Creek women through marriage to traders integrated them into the kinship structure of their societies. They also educated the traders in native ways. Hence, traders, their wives, and their children played valuable roles as diplomatic agents and cultural intermediaries. Many of the male children became chiefs.[17] These various people and practices made Indians "facilitators of the many multicultural accommodations essential for survival on a colonial frontier."[18]

Although limited to what Europeans or Americans recorded and interpreted in documents—in this case Spanish documents—the discussion that follows will endeavor to sustain an emphasis on the contribution of these Native Americans and their culture to the political life of the eighteenth-century Gulf South. Recent historical literature has done much to establish their deserved place in histories of the region; more still is needed to make their voices and actions better known and understood. Despite changes resulting from a century of interaction between Native Americans and the European newcomers, their culture remained strong and influenced substantially the procedure and substance of the diplomatic agenda of the early 1790s. Ceremony, symbolism, and—what often seemed to Spaniards and other Europeans who had been raised in a culture of written as well as spoken language—long, repetitious talking set much of the agenda. Those elements created and sustained the paths of communication that defined much of life and made possible resolution of issues.[19] Through such practices, Spanish officials and Indian elites at the end of the century overcame the difficult terrain of multiple centers of power to create and sustain paths, which, while never straight, did facilitate the peaceful resolution of such issues as Nogales and for a few years enabled Indians to find more common ground with the Spanish.

As will be seen, the diplomacy creating such paths was neither easy nor always successful. The documents that record the talk and activities of Piomingo provide an example of the challenge to local Spanish officials and ultimately, in his case, failure. During the American Revolution, Piomingo and his faction supported the English against the Spanish. In the period following the Revolution he shifted his allegiance to the Americans, developed close ties with American settlers who were settling in Tennessee along the Cumberland River, and became a good friend of a leader of those settlers, James Robertson, whom he referred to with another common metaphorical term deriving from the importance attached to kin as "my Brother Colonel Robertson."[20]

Given the Spanish orientation of this book, some irony accompanies its initial focus on Piomingo's metaphor of "straight path" in his talk of June 1793 saying he would follow such a path to the assembly called by the Spanish. Securing his support had become an important goal of Spanish officials, but in the end it failed, for he continued to follow the paths between his town, Tchoukafala, and Cumberland and other points north, where there seemed to be, in his view, more for him and his "nation." "I often go to Cumberland to See my Friends there," he said in 1789, and "the Spaniards . . . are people we niver loved they have Sent to us often to come to them but we will not if we can help it."[21]

He did not waver in the 1790s, and the Spanish had to look to and cultivate other chiefs. Competition to create paths and connections fed the politics and diplomacy of the time, making the paths neither straight nor one-directional. It was a complex politics, but for a time it worked to sustain both the Spanish and the Indians. Spain's eventual retreat, beginning in 1795, left only the United States as an increasingly aggressive and unified external power that proceeded to behave as Spanish officials and some Indian chiefs said it would. The insatiable demand for land by Americans supported territorial expansion as an important object of public policy, which found support in an ideology of republicanism to support an agrarian "empire for liberty."[22]

Despite the failure to secure the allegiance of Piomingo and his faction of Chickasaws, the diplomacy making possible the resolution of the dispute over Nogales and the achievement of other agreements marks a high point of Spain's presence in the lower Mississippi valley. Indian diplomats, too, could regard the moment as a good one, particularly in view of what happened when they found their position significantly weakened by the Treaty of San Lorenzo of 1795, which required the withdrawal of Spain from most of the region. In Gayoso's view such an achievement was not easy; it required much tact and patience. He and others realized they had to pay close attention to the many interests, traditions, and values present among those with whom they dealt and which, while perhaps changing, nevertheless remained strong. Aptly characterized as "an astute Indian diplomat," Gayoso seemed particularly successful in securing whatever goals he and his superiors in New Orleans and Havana agreed were important.[23]

Indian leaders, it must once again be emphasized, brought to these proceedings as much diplomatic savvy as Gayoso and his colleagues; they need to be seen as players, and not mere pawns, in the political games of the century.[24] A number of them had already many years of experience dealing with Europeans and even Americans. Taboca, one of the two whose names were on the May 1791 letter to Gayoso, had participated in a congress with the British in Mobile in 1765 and twenty years later, in the fall of 1785, led a delegation of Choctaws to meet with American commissioners at Hopewell in South Carolina. There he impressed observers as one who expressed forcefully Choctaw interests, and he and others did much to educate Americans as to Indian expectations. In the summer of 1787 he led a delegation of Choctaws to Philadelphia to press Americans to honor the Hopewell agreements, particularly with regard to trade. "By the 1790s," notes O'Brien, "Taboca possessed greater knowledge about Euro-American people than any other Choctaw. He had traveled to more non-Indian centers of power and had met more Euro-American officials than any other Choctaw of his generation."[25]

The other name or title on the protest letter sent to Gayoso was that of the war chief Franchimastabé, who had actively assisted the British during the Revolutionary War. During that time he apparently agreed to the cession of the Nogales lands to the British, and he led Choctaws in a joint British and Choctaw war party to Natchez in search of American rebels and, later, led another force of Choctaws to assist the British during the siege of Pensacola. As a consequence of these activities, he received the sobriquet "the English chief."[26] Both these Choctaw chiefs, Taboca and Franchimastabé, had established themselves as forces to be reckoned with by the time the Spanish displaced the British.

As indicated, comparable figures can be found among the Creeks and Cherokees, and, among the Chickasaws, the chief known to the Spanish as Ugulayacabé emerged in their eyes as a prominent leader and the one most friendly to their interests. "Ougoulayacabe's importance in his nation is great," wrote Gayoso to Governor Carondelet in New Orleans in the summer of 1793; "he has declared himself on our side, and because of his talents and his influence, I believe he is capable of counteracting the machinations of Piomingo."[27]

The experience and position of leaders such as these simply reinforced to the Spanish the fact that Indians were the most numerous and powerful presence in the region.[28] Deference to their numbers, their skill as negotiators, and their traditions was a sine qua non of successful relations; the Spanish had to understand and accept the import of such words as those expressed by the Chickasaw chief Taskietoka to Juan Delavillebeuvre, the first Spanish commissioner to the Choctaws and Chickasaws: "you are in a borrowed land."[29] As such, the Spanish, as had the French and British before them, needed to honor the value Indians throughout the century continued to attach to exchanges of all kinds, especially those enhanced by ceremony and gifts, as a way to seal social and political relationships.[30] And, to take issue with the view of Arthur Preston Whitaker, the Spanish, as had their predecessors, did gain some understanding, as did the Indians of them.[31]

Such understanding may have been imperfect, or, if acquired, not always liked. Often, early in the century, the French misread Indian ways, and after the French some Spanish and American officials found it particularly difficult to accept the importance they attached, for example, to gifts. At Hopewell in

1785, Americans described the Choctaws as being "the greatest beggars, and the most indolent creatures we ever saw." Similarly the Spanish commandant in Mobile in 1793, Manuel de Lanzos, described a talk of Franchimastabé during a visit to that post as "about nothing but the poverty which his Indians are suffering" and concluding with "the usual begging position." Indians resented such views. They explained and justified gifts in terms of their kinship system or, as Taskietoka put it, that Europeans and eventually Americans should see themselves as guests. They were ways fathers and children and brothers supported one another, and, because to a large extent Europeans had been accommodated by this kinship system, encounters such as these required the exchange of gifts as symbols of generosity, friendship, and hospitality.[32] Furthermore, it has been observed that Indian chiefs came to depend on such gifts as evidence of their capacity to secure desired goods and therefore these gifts became a source of power for them.[33]

These and other points will emerge more extensively in the two-part discussion that follows. The first part highlights how Indians and Europeans interacted with one another to form what might be called a culture of diplomacy, or ways of talking and acting that blended Indian and European elements to make possible the identification and advancement of common interests. That process began with the arrival in the region of the British and the French in the late seventeenth century and continued with more activity by the Spanish as they replaced both the French and the British as the major European presence in the region after the American Revolution. The second part will then examine how this culture of diplomacy operated to make possible the resolution of the Nogales conflict and the achievement by the Spanish of additional posts and closer ties with members of all the major Indian groups in much of the lower Mississippi valley and Gulf South in the early 1790s.

Part I

1
Initial and Sustained Contacts in the Gulf South
From Violence to Diplomacy

Sixteenth-century Native American and European encounters in the Gulf South contrast markedly with those of the eighteenth. Beginning with the arrival of a number of Spanish expeditions from islands in the Caribbean and the Gulf of Mexico, there was little of a diplomatic nature about them: they were ephemeral, often violent, and certainly disruptive. With the exception of the Florida peninsula, the Spanish did not establish any permanent residency in the area until the late seventeenth century when they decided to locate a post and eventually a city at Pensacola. That initiative was a response to La Salle's Mississippi expedition of the 1680s, which led to his claim of the region for the French king, and the expansion of the English into the interior of the Carolinas. With the Spanish still a peripheral presence, the British and the French found themselves rivals in this part of the world as well as farther to the north and in Europe and Asia. In the middle of the century the Spanish replaced the French as the principal European rival to the British, and then, as a consequence of the American Revolution, Americans challenged the Spanish. Despite changes of players, North America became a setting for the great geopolitical games of the eighteenth century, an ongoing competition that, because Europeans occupied only tiny settlements, required the political and economic support of Indian groups, often achieved only after careful respect for native diplomatic protocol.[1] This marginal presence of competing European groups and their dependence on Native Americans help explain much of the contrast between sixteenth- and eighteenth-century encounters. The discussion that follows will elaborate further on how political relations between Europeans and Indians came to be defined by diplomacy rather than violence in the eighteenth century.

For Native Americans, or "Indians," as European and later American documents referred to them, the first contacts of the sixteenth century proved to be momentous, for they set in motion forces that altered significantly—and often for the worse—their ways of life. Disease brought by the Europeans inflicted havoc on their societies and influenced population decline, movement, and amalgamation and, in so doing, contributed to the decline of southeastern chiefdoms.[2] New goods and new plants and animals were introduced, not all of them benign. The most significant of these contacts in the lower Mississippi valley came with a Spanish enterprise, that of Hernando de Soto and his expedition of 1538–43. It began in the general area of Tampa, Florida, moved north into what is now Georgia, then turned west, and—among other things—left a legacy of disease-bearing pigs in the region.[3] Soto's *entrada* was in the grand tradition of all such expeditions of that age of the conquistador; there was little time for the "tact and patience," as Gayoso later put it, of diplomacy, little regard for native life and liberty.[4] It perhaps can be best understood and appreciated as an extension of its leader, described by a recent biographer as "a colossal paradox," "grim and engaging, fascinating and contemptible, pious and hypocritical, prudent and reckless, at once enterprising, destructive, arrogant, bold, and savage," a "megalomaniac."[5] Hardship, violence, destruction, death for all concerned accompanied the expedition from start to finish. Soto himself suffered; he lost both fortune and life.[6] Although not devoid of diplomacy, encounters between Indians and Soto, the *conquistador* and *adelantado,* stand in marked contrast to those of Gayoso, the governor and diplomat of over two hundred years later.

Sustained contact among Indians and competing European newcomers created a different kind of political environment. European monarchs and their governments sought to strengthen their respective states through the establishment of empires in North America and elsewhere. Whatever success they achieved with regard to establishing at least the symbols of empire in the form of towns and military posts occurred only after securing the cooperation and support of the always far more numerous native peoples.

This endeavor began in the lower Mississippi valley and Gulf South toward the end of the seventeenth century with the expansion of the English into the western Carolinas and Georgia and the establishment of permanent French settlements along the Gulf coast and in the lower Mississippi that followed La Salle's somewhat pretentious claim of the whole of the Mississippi valley for the French, a type of gesture that Canadian historian William Eccles has characterized as having about as much substance as that of the kings of England to the crown of France.[7] Sometimes, interaction between newcomers and natives could be violent, as in the case of the slaving expeditions of the late seventeenth century, the Yamasee and Natchez wars of the first two decades of the eighteenth, and the war of the 1730s between the French and their Choctaw allies and the Chickasaws. Yet, because no European power ever possessed enough strength to dominate, each found peaceful relations in the form of trade and the formalities and compromises of diplomacy essential. Cooperation and negotiation were required for Europeans to sustain their limited presence in the region.[8] Over time miscegenation further broke down barriers to produce what has been characterized as a heterogeneous social order.[9]

The French required the agreement of resident Indian groups to establish a presence along the Gulf coast and in the Mississippi valley, and they continued to maintain it only through Indian sufferance.[10] They established posts on the coast at Biloxi in 1699 and Mobile Bay in 1702 and on the Red River at Natchitoches in 1714. In 1716 they built a fort where present-day Natchez, Mississippi, is located, and founded New Orleans two years later. In these endeavors they and their Indian counterparts established precedents and examples for their successors to follow.[11] As the dominant European group until the end of the so-called French and Indian War in 1763, the French, concludes ethnohistorian Patricia Galloway, developed an interaction with Indians that was "exceptionally fruitful and non-exploitative by colonial standards."[12]

During this time, some Choctaws, seeing advantage in sustaining close relations with the French to help them ward off the English and their Indian allies, entered into a gift-alliance system with the French. The system failed, however, to sustain peace or to make the Choctaws "pliant tools," in the view of Richard White; rather, suggests Mary Ann Wells, they proved to be "elusive." In the 1730s and 1740s Choctaws went to war with Chickasaws, who were more under the influence of the English and other nations, and the emergence of a pro-English chief and faction among the Choctaws led to civil war in that nation.[13] Even though it did not always work, this gift-alliance system, forged early in the century by French officials and their Indian counterparts, continued to be used during the British and Spanish periods. Indeed, with the exception of Piomingo and his faction of Chickasaws, it seemed to function particularly well in the context of the Nogales question and its aftermath. In balance, its reaffirmation seemed to produce benefits for all concerned.

The French withdrew as an imperial power from North America in 1763, to be replaced by the British and the Spanish. In the so-called Family Compact or Treaty of Fontainbleau of the previous year, the French transferred New Orleans and Louisiana to the Spanish; with the exception of New Orleans, the British replaced the French east of the river.[14] Louisiana's first Spanish governors, however, sustained the diplomatic practices of their predecessors with the help of many French people who remained in Louisiana.[15] The British began to reorganize administratively their much-enlarged North American empire and to develop closer and more amicable relations with the many Indian groups who had aligned themselves with the French, especially those who, like a group of Iroquois, Loups, and Shawnees at Fort Pitt in 1763, affirmed their resolve to carry on the fight against the English. "The English have killed us; they started the war, and we shall finish it," they said.[16] The British created a southern district for Indian affairs and created the post of superintendent of Indian affairs, which was occupied during much of the time with some degree of success by John Stuart, whom many Indians came to use as an intermediary to resolve conflicts. Because the British wanted the support of both the Creeks and the Choctaws during the American Revolution, Stuart intervened to end an eleven-year conflict between the two groups.[17]

The British furthered these efforts by means of a number of congresses with various Indian groups to clarify boundaries, to establish the basis for conducting trade and the distribution of gifts, and to provide a forum for the discussion of grievances and problems. For the Choctaws, the most important of these occurred in 1765 at Pensacola, in 1771–72 at Mobile, and, again at Mobile, in 1777. The last-named meeting produced the agreement that established boundaries for a Natchez District within what had earlier been created as the province of West Florida and which the Spanish later assumed to include the site of their projected fort at Nogales.

The Spanish displaced the British from Florida during the American Revolution as a consequence of the successful military campaigns of the governor-general of Louisiana, Bernardo de Gálvez, directed against the British posts of Baton Rouge, Mobile, and Pensacola between 1779 and 1781.[18] During this two-year period the British and Spanish fought each other on another front, namely, the Indian. Both sought the favor and support of Indian peoples, with the British requesting aid in the form of warriors to help with their military defenses. Two years before Spain's entry into the war in 1779 and less than a month after taking office as governor of Louisiana, Gálvez wrote to his uncle, José de Gálvez, the Spanish minister of the Indies, about the importance of cultivating the good favor of neighboring Indians so that they could be counted on as allies in the event of Spain's involvement in the war. He recommended ways of doing it and, like his predecessors beginning with Ulloa and O'Reilly, proceeded to court their friendship through gifts, trade, and numerous meetings in New Orleans and elsewhere.[19]

The peace settlement of 1783 concluding the American Revolution, by which Britain acknowledged the Mississippi River to be the western boundary of the newly independent United States, began a radical process of change in the demographic and ultimately political character of the trans-Appalachian region of the new United States—a nation-state in name only—south of the Ohio River. With little regard for people already living in the region (the Indians), Americans—"audacious and independent men," in the words of historian Sánchez-Fabrés Mirat—began moving in ever-increasing numbers to settle in such areas as the Tennessee and Cumberland River valleys.[20] To establish some semblance of legal claim to these lands, they used pliant state governments to secure land cessions from those Indian chiefs willing to agree to the grants.[21]

They thereby created a complex political challenge to Spanish officials, who found they had to deal with a weak central government in the United States (one Alexander Hamilton described in the context of the debate on a proposed new constitution in 1787 as "destitute of energy," whose representatives were "mere pageants of mimic sovereignty"), to individual state governments, and to a citizen body that attached little value to any kind of government.[22]

Despite its weakness, the new Confederation government took some steps to satisfy the interests of those Americans eager to move west by securing cessions of land from Indians. It took the position that those Indian tribes siding with the British during the American Revolution had forfeited their right to soil. On the basis of this conquest theory, it proceeded to negotiate treaties—some of them fraudulent, according to Anthony Wallace—with Indians both north and south of the Ohio River that gave the Indians peace in exchange for cessions of land. In so doing, however, it challenged an assumption of such states as Georgia, the Carolinas, and Virginia that their governments had jurisdiction over the region and its population, including Indians. That laid the basis for confusion and conflict between the two centers of authority. Employing the same conquest theory as the Confederation government, these states often seized the land of Indians, contending that those Indians who had helped the British during the Revolution—notably the Creeks and the Cherokees—had forfeited their property as had the Loyalists. In some cases they negotiated treaties with Indians—most of them with those few open to such initiatives—and authorized sales of land. Conflict between the central government in the United States and these states continued even after ratification of the 1787 constitution strengthening the central government. Adding to this confusion, frontier people often went it alone and independently settled or purchased land.[23]

Efforts by the Confederation government to assert the primacy of its authority in this area reached a high point in 1785 when Congress appointed commissioners to negotiate treaties with southern Indians and passed an ordinance for the regulation of Indian affairs. The commissioners proceeded to conduct assemblies late in that year and in early 1786, at Hopewell in South Carolina, with the Cherokees, the Chickasaws, and the Choctaws, events that produced treaties with each group, collectively known as the Hopewell treaties. The Confederation congress followed the negotiation of these treaties by passing an ordinance stating that it had "the sole and exclusive right and power of regulating the trade and managing all affairs with the Indians not members of any of the States," limited by the caveat "that the legislative right of any State within its own limits be not infringed or violated." Following the British model, it divided the "Indian department" into northern and southern districts, with the latter including all the Indian nations residing south of the Ohio River. It appointed a superintendent for each.[24]

Although the United States government seemed to want to assert its authority over Indian affairs, and in so doing limit the actions of both state governments and individuals and thereby ameliorate Spanish concerns, it seemed to the Spanish to challenge their position in the region in two ways. First, based on the 1783 treaty with Britain acknowledging American independence, the United States claimed the Mississippi River and the thirty-first parallel as its boundary with Spanish possessions in North America. Second, it acted on behalf of those Americans rapidly settling the trans-Appalachian west by demanding free navigation of the Mississippi River and a right of deposit in New Orleans. Spain's position on the boundary derived from the absence of any statement about boundary in its separate treaty in 1783 with Britain and from Miró's view that the land was Spanish after the Spanish commandant of the Arkansas River had crossed the Mississippi River and claimed the entire region during the American Revolution after Spain had joined France on the side of the Americans.[25] Assuming validity in such a claim, the Spanish minister of state, the Count of Floridablanca, proceeded in 1784 to establish a border as "a line running from the Flint River to the Hiawasee, thence down the Hiawasee, the Tennessee and the Ohio to the Mississippi."[26] Beginning in 1785, a long diplomatic process to resolve these two questions began and encouraged the parties to exercise some restraint in the territory in dispute—a task made difficult by the independent actions of Americans who continued to take full advantage of weak and divided government to move and settle on their own. That diplomacy, conducted on both sides of the Atlantic, concluded ten years later with the 1795 Treaty of San Lorenzo, in which Spanish diplomats accepted the American position on the boundary.[27]

These diplomats thereby undid the work of local Spanish officials of about thirty years to forge good relations with Indians and eventually establish new posts. Furthermore, the diplomats in Philadelphia and Madrid did not consult Indians with regard to issues of boundary. Many Indians felt betrayed, deserted, and abandoned, as they had in the context of French withdrawal in the 1760s. They feared the ravenously expansionistic Americans who blithely ignored efforts by their government to provide some protection for Indian lands and interests. Some Choctaws even turned on their own and used the moment to plot the assassination of Franchimastabé. Many more Indians threatened to disrupt the work of the boundary commission.[28]

The sale of Louisiana to the United States by France in 1803 and the cession of Florida by the Spanish in 1819 marked the end of European political presence and left only one major power confronting the various Indian groups in the region—the United States. Such a state of affairs proved detrimental to the Indians, to put it mildly. Above all it weakened a political and diplomatic culture characterized by many competing interests and centers of power that worked well to respect and protect the many diverse groups and interests in the region. In this world, as in other parts of North America, Native Americans had been able to play the various competing European powers against one another.[29] As the century progressed and as French and English mixed with Indians, values and interests emerged at odds with more traditional Indian ways—a state of affairs that tended further to weaken native groups. With just one external power—and that one increasingly energetic and effective in supporting the restlessness and avarice of its citizens—the system of competition or playing off no longer worked. What followed was what was predicted by Stephen Minor, Gayoso's adjutant who undertook two missions to the Choctaws to try to resolve the dispute over Nogales, and Bloody Fellow of the Cherokees: the forcible removal of Indians to areas west of the Mississippi River.

2
Forging Diplomatic Paths
Native Participants

By the end of the eighteenth century, Indians and newcomers had encountered one another and mixed in a variety of ways. Europeans competing with each other sought Indian allies, and this political objective blended with an active trade involving the exchange of deerskins and pelts for a variety of European goods. An ability to provide goods, whether in the form of trade goods or gifts, proved essential to secure political support. The exchange of goods required traders, who settled where they worked and became part of the native societies when they married Indian women and, through them, part of the clan structure. A process of physical and cultural miscegenation began that altered the cultural and physical landscape significantly.[1] All of these changes influenced the politics and diplomacy of the region.

The arrival of these few newcomers did not significantly alter native traditions until late in this period of sustained contact; even then traditions remained sufficiently strong so that European and American officials had to honor Indian expectations and practice to be successful in their work. While a full discussion of Choctaw, Chickasaw, Creek, and Cherokee culture, particularly as it evolved and changed over the course of the eighteenth century, is neither possible nor appropriate here, a brief summary—albeit overly synchronic—of how it has been represented in contemporary accounts and secondary literature can be useful toward an understanding of the politics and diplomacy of this period. That will be the purpose of the discussion in this chapter.

Indians remained throughout the dominant people of the region as they did throughout other parts of what Americans viewed as "the West," a fact acknowledged by the American official most responsible for Indian affairs in the 1790s, Henry Knox; and their leaders learned how to manage the outsiders with remarkable skill. When outsiders arrived to talk and deal, they could use meetings like the ones at Hopewell with the Americans in the 1780s to try to educate them as to Indian ways and expectations.[2] Skilled European and American diplomats needed to heed such instruction in order to pursue successfully any negotiation. The Spanish commandant in Pensacola seemed to understand that when he told the minister of the Indies in 1787 that the Spanish must understand and honor Indian culture, particularly the nature and significance of clans, in order to maintain loyalty among Indian groups.[3]

It needs to be emphasized at the outset that throughout the period, native life centered around villages, clans, and moieties, and, as a consequence, political power tended to be diffused and weak. Understanding this fact along with knowing something of such common institutions and practices as councils, blood revenge, reciprocity, and matrilineality as well as particular individuals and their relationships with one another proved to be crucial for the success of any diplomatic undertaking.[4] Europeans might use such terms as "Choctaw Nation" or "Creek Nation," and Indians might themselves employ such categories; nevertheless, they disguised a far more fluid and complex political and social reality than those names suggest. Their use by Europeans reflected a desire for a more centralized and orderly world than in fact existed. To the extent that these terms described any kind of reality, suggests a recent work, they describe what might be best understood as "coalescent societies" that had taken the place of older chiefdoms and confederacies.[5] The argument advanced by Richard White that "the various ethnic and village groups" of the world of the *pays d'en haut* of the Great Lakes region "took on a common identity only when they opposed other groups" has some relevance to an understanding of the world south of the Ohio River. Indian leaders such as Franchimastabé and Taboca may have talked about themselves as Choctaws, but their behavior and that of many other chiefs often did not transcend their villages or the factions that supported them. Such localism contributed to the failure of attempts during the Spanish period to create a "great Indian confederation."[6] Indian country, Colin Calloway concludes, "was a world of villages, bands, and clans," a world that probably in the course of the eighteenth century became even more disparate as more and more mixed bloods, competing allegiances, and external economic and political forces emerged—all challenging older sources of authority and cohesion.[7]

And yet, scholars have found, there were cohesive elements that gave some reality to those categories. As noted, there were common cultural institutions and expectations. While there were distinctive ways of speaking—dialects sufficiently varied to allow for a differentiation by the Spanish of the Choctaws into those of the Large Party, the Small Party, and the Six Villages—still they found ways to communicate among themselves as Choctaws or Creeks or with other Indian groupings, as Europeans learned, through symbolic gestures, common metaphors, objects, stories, and rituals.[8] Clan or kin groupings linked people of different regions and could and did provide a unity where there was no political unity as Europeans might have wanted or understood at the time. Indeed these kin linkages could even transcend "national" boundaries; a Creek, Mistilebeck, was identified as a nephew of the Chickasaw chief Ugulayacabé.[9] Furthermore, people moved about: the Natchez people early in the century were compelled to move after their defeat and dispersal by the French, and, as will be noted, some Cherokees moved into a region that put them in greater proximity to the Chickasaws and Creeks. People exchanged news and goods continually, all sustaining paths, albeit ones that were not always straight or clear or understood by Europeans and Americans. Finally, despite linguistic differences and the importance attached to village and clan, Indian leaders, as suggested, did refer to themselves, at least when talking to the outsiders, as Choctaw or Chickasaw or Creek or Cherokee. Certainly Franchimastabé and Taboca did in their letter to Gayoso protesting the Nogales enterprise. From their perspective, they wanted the Spanish to see and appreciate a degree of unity.

Of the two "nations" mentioned in that letter, the Choctaws were the more numerous and occupied a region "of crucial strategic significance" throughout the century.[10] Although counts vary according to time and source, Choctaw villages numbered at one point more than seventy, and although they had changed and moved, they tended in the course of the eighteenth century to cluster in four groups.[11] The western Choctaws lived at the head of the Pearl River; the eastern Choctaws could be found in the vicinity of the Tombigbee River; the Six Town Choctaws were to the southeast of the Pearl River and along streams that flowed into the Chickasawhay River; and finally a small group of Chickasawhay lived farther south still on the river of that name.[12] As had the French and the English before them, the Spanish in the last quarter of the eighteenth century saw the Choctaws divided into three groups: the Large Party, which corresponded to the western Choctaws; the Small Party, corresponding roughly to the eastern group; and the Six Towns. Each of these groups encompassed a number of villages headed by a chief and some assistants and advised by a council of elders. Each village had or could appoint a "red" or war chief when the occasion demanded, and the groups could and did choose one of their prominent chiefs to lead them. European officials, including Gayoso, tried to designate one chief as the principal one for the entire nation but generally with little success.[13] For him, as for European officials before him, political relations required dealing with the many rather than the few. Little had changed since the French governor of Louisiana, Vaudreuil, observed in 1744 that "each village has its own chief, who, with his warriors, follows the course that seems good to him, so that they are so many small republics."[14]

The Chickasaws were less numerous than the Choctaws, numbering about three thousand at the time of the American Revolution and living in seven autonomous towns or villages in the general area of present-day Tupelo, Mississippi.[15] Although a slave trade encouraged by the English had led to war with the Choctaws in the 1730s, by the end of the century Choctaws often referred to them as "brothers" in the diplomatic discourse of 1791–95. The American secretary of war, Henry Knox, noted a close relationship in terms of character and language. "Both the Chickasaws and the Choctaws are represented as candid, generous, brave, and honest, and understanding each other's language," he told President Washington in 1789.[16] Like the Choctaws, they often divided, divisions caused primarily by competition for their trade and political allegiance rather than geographical or ethnic separation. Chickasaw leaders such as Piomingo often saw these divisions as sources of weakness, compelling a need to deal skillfully with such outsiders as the Americans or the Spanish. During a congress in Mobile in the 1770s, Chickasaw spokesmen complained that their "nation" was "distracted and split in parties by the jarring interests of traders" and "vagabonds that resort to it [and] who are only suffered to live because they are white men and British subjects."[17] Two principal factions seemed to make up the nation in the early part of the 1790s: a pro-American faction headed by Piomingo and a pro-Spanish faction headed by Taskietoka (often referred to as the Chickasaw "King" in Spanish documents) and Ugulayacabé.[18]

The Creeks and the Cherokees became involved in the diplomacy related to an effort to create a "grand Indian confederation," a project that had solid roots in the Indian world by the end of the American Revolution, and to augment the number of Spanish posts in the region.[19] Like the Choctaws and Chickasaws, they divided into factions according to personal loyalties, geographical location of villages, or trade ties, and some played a major role in the diplomacy that is the focus of this book. Therefore, it is useful to have some sense of how contemporary accounts and the historical literature portray them so as to understand better their participation.

That literature does not provide any clear consensus as to the genesis or degree of Creek identity and unity. Using the writings of Benjamin Hawkins, the American commissioner or agent to the Creeks in the late eighteenth century, anthropologist Robbie Ethridge describes the emergence of a coalescent Creek political entity, towns and their locations, and the nature of the population that had absorbed other Indian peoples such as Shawnees and Natchez.[20] Historian Verner Crane found the Creeks of the late seventeenth and early eighteenth centuries to be the most numerous of all the four major Indian groups in the Gulf South, numbering about twenty thousand, and characterized them as "the shrewdest politicians." At this time, according again to Crane, the Yamasee War brought about the forced migration from South Carolina of a number of Indians hostile to the British, followed by further amalgamation. Although widely dispersed and loosely organized, some semblance of a Creek collective—if not a political—identity emerged by the early eighteenth century as they tried to balance living with the colonial powers surrounding them and maintaining their own land and independence.[21] The basic political unit was the town or township. Creeks towns were scattered over an area drained by three major river systems: the Coosa-Tallapoosa-Alabama, the Occonee-Ocmulgee-Altamaha, and the Chattahoochee-Flint-Apalachicola.[22] The nucleus of the Creeks consisted of people who spoke a common language, Muskogee, but what eighteenth-century observers William Bartram and Benjamin Hawkins described as a Creek confederacy had come to include other groups and languages, an aspect noted by Ethridge.[23] One of the most important of these towns in the late eighteenth and early nineteenth centuries, Tuckabatchee, developed when Shawnee refugees entered the region in the last quarter of the seventeenth century after Iroquois expansion into their homeland, and it became the principal town of the Upper Creeks.[24] The newly appointed Spanish commissioner to the Creeks, Pedro Olivier, held an important meeting there with chiefs of most of the principal towns in June 1793 after the important meeting in New Orleans of Choctaws, Cherokees, and Chickasaws to endorse the creation of a confederation of all Indians groups in the region.[25]

While Ethridge has concluded that Creeks had coalesced to achieve a degree of unity by the late eighteenth century, some historians have disagreed about the kind or degree of unity. Michael Green has emphasized a particularistic and factional nature of what others have called "a confederacy." He describes the Creek Nation at the time of the American Revolution as "an alliance of semi-sovereign, semi-autonomous groups scattered throughout the region that has since become Georgia, Alabama, and northern Florida." These groups, he has argued, "were united by neither language nor a common history." Although, according to Green, they "often combined in temporary coalitions for defense" and avoided "internecine conflict," they "rarely united for a common long-range purpose."[26] On the other hand, according to Kathleen Braund, the Muskogees or Muscogulge peoples shared a common language, history, and culture, and "were linked by a network of related clans, and claimed and defended certain lands as their own." She argued that they "had become a nation by the times the Europeans discovered them," "were more like each other than they were different," and "were distinct from their neighbors: the Cherokees, the Choctaws, and the Chickasaws."[27] The British used *Creek*, she says, to refer to a group living on Ochese Creek, which flows into the Ocmulgee River in Georgia, who found ways to collaborate when threatened by external threats.[28]

To complicate matters further, the Spanish sometimes referred to the residents on the Chattahochee-Flint rivers as the Uchizes and those on the Coosa-Talapoosa as Talapusas or "Talapuches." Much of the time their use of the term *Talapuche* in documents simply meant all Creeks and was so indicated with a parenthesis to that effect.[29] The English used the terms *Upper Creeks* to describe the former group and *Lower Creeks* to describe the latter, and that terminology continued with the Americans, a categorization that gave real meaning, according to Braund, to the term *Creek Confederacy*.[30] Another related group or nation, the Alabama or Alibamones, resided along the Alabama River. A Suluche Mastabé put his mark on the treaty signed at Nogales in 1793 for the "Creek, Talapoosa and Alibamon nations."[31]

The Cherokees lived farthest from the Spanish and for that reason were the last to be courted by them.[32] They did not seek ties with the Spanish of either a political or an economic nature until the early 1790s. Then, along with the Shawnees, one faction, the Chickamauga Cherokees, sought Spanish help to advance the cause of Indian unity.[33] Like the other major Indian groups, they were divided into towns, regions, and factions, and they moved. At the time of European contact they lived in an area of about forty thousand square miles crossed by headwaters of streams flowing east, west, and south from the southern Appalachians, but that area had contracted substantially by the end of the century.[34] One count puts the number of their towns at forty or fifty in the eighteenth century; yet another, more systematic study found 160 town names in documents taken from three periods in the eighteenth century.[35] According to anthropologist Charles Hudson, these regions coincided partly with sufficient varieties of dialect to make it difficult for the speaker of one to understand the speaker of another.[36] He describes these regions as chiefdoms and largely independent of each other, although there were ties of kinship that provided important links, as they did among all the other groups of the region.

In what has been described as "a fatal step," the Cherokees sided with Britain during the American Revolutionary War. In retaliation against Cherokee raids on behalf of their Tory allies, American frontier people launched a number of raids that so devastated the Cherokees that they were forced to sue for peace and surrender a substantial amount of land. Those chiefs who dissented from this settlement moved west, allied themselves with Creeks, and established the Chickamauga towns southeast of present-day Nashville. From there they continued to raid Americans living in Georgia, Tennessee, and the Carolinas.[37] Some Cherokee chiefs signed one of the treaties at Hopewell with the United States in late 1785, and in 1791 some Cherokee chiefs signed another treaty, the Treaty of Holston, also with the United States, in which they agreed to the cession of more land.[38] That cession dismayed a number of other chiefs, particularly those of the Chickamauga group including Bloody Fellow,[39] and in early 1792 they traveled to Philadelphia where American officials attempted to placate them by entertainment and ceremony and an increase in the annuity to the nation.[40] Continued opposition among Cherokees to concessions to Americans and active cultivation of them by John McDonald, a friend and collaborator of William Panton eager to expand his commercial operations, led to McDonald's appointment as Spanish commissioner to the Cherokees and success on his part in persuading some Cherokees to seek closer ties with the Spanish; his efforts culminated with a journey by Bloody Fellow and other Cherokee chiefs in late 1792 to Pensacola and New Orleans, there to align themselves with the Spanish. That major tour occurred just few months after Bloody Fellow and others had returned from Philadelphia.[41]

This too brief and all-too synchronic overview of the principal population groups of the region will provide a framework for further discussion of their characteristics that very much affected the diplomacy of the entire century and particularly the first part of the decade of the 1790s. That part of the discussion can bring out more of the fluid character of these societies and note changes they underwent during this very important century of interaction with foreign groups, beginning, again, with the French and the British and continuing with the Spanish and the Americans.

The century was one of both change and continuity. Euro-Americans came into the region and stayed, and, despite changes of government, many continued working as traders or interpreters. Many of them married Indian women and became thereby members of Indian societies. The Creek leader Alexander McGillivray was perhaps the best-known product of the mixing of peoples and cultures in the course of the century, for he used his linguistic skills and kin relations to full advantage. The arrival of newcomers brought about changes in Indian societies that probably made them more amenable to diplomatic relationships. Franchimastabé, the Choctaw war chief and cosigner of the 1791 letter to Gayoso protesting the Nogales establishment, found diplomacy a more useful strategy for achieving his objectives. Both he and Taboca provide what might be cited as two of many examples of how such categories as "Choctaw" or "Chickasaw" and even "Spanish" or "American" disguise a far more complex and fluid reality.

3

Forging Diplomatic Paths

Emergence of a Culture of Diplomacy

Sustained contacts between natives and Europeans in the eighteenth century brought about change for all and gave added meaning to the phrase *new world*.[1] In the course of this change, a diplomatic culture emerged that reflected many of these changes and no doubt encouraged them. While it incorporated elements of what the new people brought, perhaps most important the written word, it sustained and even expanded native traditions. The treaty became a written document; indeed, it assumed the characteristics of a distinctive literary form, but it also retained the connotation and the importance of a meeting or council.[2] At such meetings, the spoken word (often very metaphoric as in the case of Piomingo's response to the invitation to Nogales), symbolic objects such as wampum to represent, for example, ways to maintain contact, and elaborate protocol long characteristic of Indian diplomacy remained more important than any piece of paper produced at the conclusion. With varying degrees of success Europeans—especially those like Gayoso, who had been a member of a diplomatic family—could understand and appreciate many of these traditions, for they accorded with their own understanding of what diplomacy required. They too had developed a special language of diplomacy and protocols to be followed in formal diplomatic exchanges, and they could appreciate the role of peace chiefs like Taboca, who undertook missions to resolve problems—to sustain open and white paths.[3] The discussion that follows will endeavor to provide further insight into the characteristics of this diplomacy as it came to define a dimension of European and Indian interactions in the course of the eighteenth century, important for the resolution of the Nogales controversy and further initiatives in the early 1790s.

Diplomatic practices among Native Americans reflected larger political and social realities, which, it should be kept in mind, could and did change over time.[4] As noted, the government and social organization of all the major Indian groups—Choctaws, Chickasaws, Creeks, and Cherokees—helped shape the diplomacy of the period and thereby create the paths of communication with similar characteristics. Decentralization, localism, individualism, and egalitarianism characterized what might be regarded as the political culture of the region, as they did, according to foreign observers, the newly independent United States in the 1780s and 1790s, where political power was minimal and largely local.[5] Where there were no states, individuals and small groups reigned supreme, but perhaps without the kinds of power present in the so-called stateless preliterate societies discussed by Pierre Clastres for Indian South America.[6] Village groups were autonomous and were led by chiefs who had to earn their status.[7] Each village had one or two chiefs corresponding to the division of tribes into moieties representing war and peace. While these chiefs were subordinate to a great chief, they could for the most part govern independently. The arrival of Europeans in the region added another ingredient to this mix, but Indians proved remarkably adept at employing diplomacy to deal with them, and Europeans proved equally able to adjust to native expectations.[8]

Historical evidence from the eighteenth century records attempts by Europeans to instill more hierarchy and order and thereby create a system more akin to theirs and hence easier to influence; through their practice of awarding medals and patents to chiefs in an effort to simplify their political relations, however, they probably ended up reinforcing a dispersal of chiefly power. Even though government operated on the level of the village, clan, and tribe and through multiple chiefs or headmen, a great chief nominally headed the tribe or "nation," as Europeans wanted to see the larger units and as they talked about them in their documents. Gayoso reported that during the Nogales assembly of 1793 he announced he would regard Franchimastabé as both principal chief of the "Large Party" of the Choctaws and principal chief for the entire nation. Choctaws apparently played to European preferences, at least in a verbal sense, by using the term *king*. Regardless of title, chiefs often found their power limited and challenged, as evidence for this particular diplomatic episode amply demonstrates. Needless to say, throughout the eighteenth century this political structure proved often frustrating to European and American officials, who continued to see Choctaw polity consisting of what Vaudreuil described in the 1740s as "so many little republics."

Like their French and British predecessors, Spanish officials tried to make this dispersal of political power work to their advantage in much the same way as Indian elites often manipulated competing foreign interests in ways to benefit themselves. As Gayoso resignedly put it in a letter to Carondelet, "those who have to deal with them [Indians] have to follow their system or better not to undertake any business."[9] With some understanding and respect for this system, the French began the practice of bestowing medals, uniforms, *bâtons* (staffs of office), and other objects on various chiefs in the hope that these objects would enhance the "chiefly authority" of their possessor. The practice worked up to a point; at any rate, it became an integral part of the culture of diplomatic exchange and intercourse that both the British and the Spanish practiced as well.[10]

The conferral of these objects—particularly medals—often provided occasions for ceremonies full of ritual and pageantry that elicited much approval from the recipients, if the reports are accurate, and, they hoped, deference to the authority represented and expressed. A significant part of a report submitted by Alejandro O'Reilly shortly after his arrival as Louisiana's new governor in 1769 contains an elaborate description of the meetings held in New Orleans with nine Indian chiefs and their retinues whom he had asked to come. With some detail it describes the protocol—the ceremonies, dress, and objects—associated with such encounters. The chiefs appeared "with the trappings of the greatest respect and ceremony," accompanied by interpreters and "quite a number of Indians, singing and playing upon their military instruments." After the governor entered the hall and seated himself, each one of the chiefs saluted him with a little flag, which was described as a small pole decorated with feathers. The salute consisted of waving the flag in a circle over the governor's head and touching him on the chest four times, then giving it to him. The smoking of pipes, an action symbolizing peace, then followed. Each chief presented O'Reilly with his burning pipe and held it while the governor smoked, which, as the report notes, "His Excellency did as he was not ignorant of its significance." Finally each chief gave him his hand, "the Indian's greatest sign of friendship."

Speeches followed. O'Reilly began by extending to the Indians the greetings and friendship of the king of Spain. Then the chief of the Bayagoulas asked permission to speak, which was granted. Referring to the governor as "Father and great chief," and himself and the other Indians as "thy children," he requested that the same favors and benefits that had been enjoyed under the French would be continued. The other chiefs assented by raising their voices, beating on their chests, and making signs of approval. O'Reilly "surprised and pleased" them by agreeing, and they—in the words of the report—"looked at each other as if they could not believe the news."

Then the governor took a medal bearing the royal effigy, kissed it, and placed it around the neck of each of the chiefs present. He touched both shoulders of each chief with a sword, made the sign of the cross on his forehead, and embraced the chief and shook his hand. They, according to the report, "again showed such admiration that it was evident how pleasing to them was the ceremony and that it was the first time they had seen it." O'Reilly said that he reinforced these good feelings by delivering to them the presents which he had promised and providing them an opportunity to see the troops under his command maneuver.[11] All of these gestures supported later assessments of O'Reilly as the person who established the bases for Spanish policy toward Indians in successive years.[12]

One might see the use of medals on the part of Europeans as a new form of wampum that for Indians could take a variety of forms: beads, linked together in strings or belts; collars; or even the calumet pipe. Wampum seemed universal among Indian groups. It often served as money, but it also played a very important role in diplomatic encounters and negotiations. The pipe and objects associated with it represented peace. Some types of wampum in the form of red beads, like red paths, represented quite the opposite. When Indian chiefs spoke, they often elaborated on the importance and meaning of these objects so as to educate Euro-Americans, as did the Chickasaw chiefs Piomingo and Mingatushka at a major congress held by Americans with the Choctaws and Chickasaws at Hopewell in 1786. "The period has arrived that I have visited you to see you," said Piomingo, "and to regulate everything that respects us. These beads are our credentials of peace and friendship, and two of us have come to bring the talks of the nation. These white beads are of little value but in our nation, where they are kept by even our children with veneration, as tokens of peace and friendship." "When we red people talk," said Mingatushka in his talk, "we give beads as a proof of friendship, and I give these." The talks were interspersed with the presentation of the beads in the form of strings and belts.[13] As we shall see, the link Mingatushka made between beads and talk extended to other objects as well. All meetings of this sort required the presentation of gifts, for talk had no meaning without gifts. What historian Daniel Richter has observed of the Iroquois applies to other Indian groups: "Gifts made words true and legitimized the position of the person who conveyed them." Belts and strings of wampum, he points out, "were prepared in advance to accompany each 'word' to be presented at a treaty conference."[14]

Many Indian chiefs and their followers came to see these ceremonies and the medals and other objects associated with them as expressions not just of friendship or kinship but of power, both secular and spiritual, as they certainly were in the case of wampum. In a secular sense, it has been observed, the medals came to represent access to outsiders and all they might provide—notably, desired trade goods. A fondness for medals and the European willingness if not eagerness to confer them may only have made an already loose political structure even looser and hence difficult to engage and manipulate. The distribution of medals often tended to foster jealousy among chiefs and thereby exacerbated rather than diminished discord.[15] Officials in the field, such as Juan Delavillebeuvre, complained that there were too many chiefs who, simply because they had been awarded a medal or a patent or had been the recipient of a gift, thought themselves privileged and important.[16] Nevertheless, the practice of receiving such objects became an integral part of eighteenth-century diplomatic culture and further evidence that the French and their Euro-American successors were perceived as occupants of "borrowed land," as Taskietoka of the Chickasaws put it.

In order to sustain presence and influence, Europeans had to learn the importance of the gift-kinship system of the Indians, an important unifying force among them and a means to accommodate outsiders. That task proved sometimes difficult for Europeans, at least early in the century: it assigned roles to mothers, fathers, and brothers unlike those with which they were familiar, living as they did within patriarchal societies. Socially, Indians lived in matriarchies in which kinsmen traced relationships to one another through women.[17] That meant that the head of a woman's household was her brother, not her husband.[18] Husbands and fathers of children were regarded as guests more than relatives. They had little authority over the children; indeed, they were expected to indulge them. The system generalized that expectation by attaching high value to generosity, a characteristic expected of a good father.

Generosity required the ability to provide gifts. It also required the commitment and ability to protect. If Indians came to regard Europeans as "fathers" and themselves as "children," then Europeans had to demonstrate a willingness and capacity to help them defend themselves from perceived enemies. In a political sense, that could, and often did, work to the advantage of a particular European group. Many examples from throughout the century might be cited, but for the Spanish, who found themselves with an expanded presence in the region after the American Revolution, the ones that are most pertinent come from that time. Here, we might note briefly just one. In August 1784, a large group of Iroquois, Cherokee, Shawnee, Chickasaw, Choctaw, and Loup Indians came to St. Louis to ask for help. Addressing the commandant, Francisco Cruzat, as "our true Father," they asked him "to deign to concede an open road" so that they might come and solicit his and all the Spaniards' protection—"as brothers"—from Americans who "like a plague of locusts" were coming to settle in "the territories of the Ohio River, which we inhabit."[19]

Although the century brought changes, the system continued to function as an important part of native culture and often led to the success or failure of commercial or political relations. Diplomatic intercourse early in the century revealed some confusion in the minds of Europeans, particularly with regard to the use of the terms *father* and *mother.* What outsiders had to understand is that the father within the conjugal family had little authority over his children; rather, as noted, he was perceived as one who should be indulgent and kind toward them. Indians used the language of this system in their talk with the French or British or Spanish, often as a way to excuse behavior or gain advantage. When, for example, the governor of Pensacola, Manuel de Zéspedes, reported on the visit in 1761 of a large number of Alabama, Talapuche, and Chickasaw Indians asking for peace, he observed that one of the principal chiefs had directed his comments to the then French governor in New Orleans, with whom the Spanish were allied, and told him he should regard himself as the father of a family with many children whom he has educated well. When some of them behave badly, Zéspedes reported the chief as saying, he should not regard it as his fault, nor should he generalize the behavior to all of his children. Rather he should forgive and expect that in the future they would behave well.[20] Many years later the letters between Gayoso and various Indian chiefs contain similar language. In an exchange early in the Nogales dispute, Indians referred to Gayoso as "father" and themselves as "sons" or "children" and defined the relationship with one another, particularly if they were Choctaws and Chickasaws, as a sibling one, with Choctaws describing the Chickasaws as "brothers."[21]

Although Europeans may never have understood fully the nuances of this kinship system, they did seem to understand from even the first encounters one of its central values, the importance of being generous and understanding. Indians of the region saw gifts as an expression of affection, not obligation, Michael Morris points out.[22] Beginning with the French, Europeans tried to capitalize on the importance attached to gifts by using them, as they did medals and other objects, to create a hierarchy of chiefs with which they could work. Chiefs quickly learned that their skill in extracting goods from competing Euro-Americans could enhance their status, for it meant they would have goods to distribute and fulfill the expectation that they be generous. The competitive nature of this practice often meant, however, that Euro-Americans could not always count on the full loyalty and support of those to whom they awarded gifts and patents. The behavior of Franchimastabé in the late eighteenth century provides an example of what the French had experienced earlier when they competed with the British for the favor of the Indians.[23] The award of annual presents to chiefs continued, however, and made the expense of their stay in the region a substantial one. European officials often complained that the expectation of gifts was little more than extortion. Nevertheless, they knew they had to be generous to secure the friendship and allegiance of Indians, and they knew enough from their own culture of the importance of gifts and the good feelings engendered by their exchange.[24] Before any personal encounter with natives during his 1699 reconnoiter of the Gulf coast, Iberville deposited at a campsite "two axes, four knives, two packages of glass beads, a little vermilion," confident, as he later wrote, that the "two Indians who came at sunrise to watch me from a distance of 300 yards would come there after we had left."[25]

Subsequent encounters, certainly among people of importance, always required the exchange of gifts, an expectation that to European officials, particularly those in charge of colonial treasuries, often seemed to be excessive. Indeed, after the costly French and Indian War, the British tried to reduce their gifts to Indians, a policy that put in serious jeopardy their success in dislodging the French from North America.[26] Demands on resources for gifts, along with supplies, were especially acute during major congresses, particularly during the English and Spanish periods. Such meetings sometimes attracted over two thousand Indians, all expecting to be fed and certainly, in the case of chiefs, to be provided gifts. Securing and maintaining friendly relations required the award of annual gifts to each Indian group. Louisiana's first Spanish governor, Antonio de Ulloa, understood quite clearly what had become local expectations. Provision must be made, he told the Marqués de Grimaldi in Spain, for two types of gifts: annual gifts and extraordinary gifts demanded by the occasion. In addition, budgets must allow for the maintenance of Indians at meetings called by local officials.[27] Government budgets acknowledged these recommendations; indeed, the one for 1767 said that Indians living in areas ceded by the English required gifts for 1761 and 1762 and warned that if they did not receive them they might very well resort to war.[28] When Indians referred to governors, who regarded themselves as the personal representatives of the king, as fathers, they verbally incorporated these officials into their kinship system and their societies. In so doing they imposed an obligation associated with fathers, namely, the need to be generous and to demonstrate that trait before any important discussions. As a Spanish governor of Louisiana noted much later, "Indians never listen to propositions that are not supported by presents."[29] Above all, European officials from early on knew that they were occupying and using native land and that gifts served as a kind of tribute for the use of that land.[30]

Parsimony on the part of Europeans could prove costly in terms of lost good will and even support. As part of an effort to impose limits on all categories of expenditures, the British continued during the American Revolution to cut back on what they saw as the staggering expenses associated with Indian affairs. This attempt to limit expenses may have been a reason for the failure of the British to "pay" for the land at Nogales which they agreed to include in the Natchez District during the Mobile congress of 1777.[31] Historian James O'Donnell argues that penury on the part of officials in London may have lost Pensacola to the Spanish. The general in charge, John Campbell, had requested as much assistance as could be provided by Indian warriors but asked that each one bring his own weapon. Almost 1,500 Creek, Choctaw, and Chickasaw warriors responded by April 1780, enough to prompt the approaching Spanish commander, Bernardo de Gálvez, to request an agreement so as " 'to avoid reciprocal hostilities by allied Indians'."[32] Later, however, when there were about seven hundred Choctaws on hand to help in the defense of the post, the general canceled his request when he learned that help was coming and sent about half of the Choctaw warriors home with few supplies or gifts. During the attack on Pensacola by the Spanish, a Choctaw sally led by Franchimastabé broke through Spanish lines, but the British apparently failed to support it. This neglect produced an angry letter from Franchimastabé complaining about lack of support and failure to make good on promised gifts.[33]

An understanding and respect for these expectations on the part of Spanish officials, particularly Gayoso, became an important element in the diplomatic successes of the early 1790s. Gayoso knew the importance of gifts and what they symbolized, although he realized their cost and took measures to try to regularize and thereby limit their distribution. The appointment of commissioners to represent Spain in the various Indian nations was seen as one way to reduce the number of extraordinary occasions that might require gifts. Yet, when the occasion demanded it, every effort was made to have gifts on hand or on the way. During the Nogales negotiations he and his adjutant made every effort to assure the Indians with whom they dealt that there were gifts available for them either in Natchez or in New Orleans. One of the provisions of the 1792 treaty with the Choctaws and Chickasaws read that the governor "hands over at the present time to the mentioned chiefs the keys to these warehouses in which the goods are [stored] so that they may take from them whatever they wish to be satisfied." His generosity as a father included a willingness to take "sons" of chiefs to further their education and apparently won him much esteem. All of these gestures worked well as expressions of understanding of and respect for Indian approaches to matters of law and peace.[34]

The goods of trade and the people involved in their exchange became an important part of native life and over time altered it significantly. Trade goods and traders assumed an important status in the diplomatic culture of the time in part because chiefs increasingly saw traders as vital links to goods they so much wanted to enhance their status.[35] When European traders arrived in the area, they quickly found themselves integrated into native societies by establishing kinship ties and then becoming agents for change. They facilitated a demand for new goods—not all of them salutary—and helped to link Indians to a global economy with values different from those that had sustained them in the past.[36] As noted, many traders settled in Indian villages, married Indian women, and had children. Jean de la Villebeuvre (Juan Delavillebeuvre) found over forty traders or people associated with them living in Choctaw villages during his diplomatic mission to the Choctaws on behalf of Governor Estevan Miró in late 1787.[37] As husbands of Indian women, traders became members of their wives' kin groups, and they acquired some valuable linguistic skills by learning local languages. When understood and respected, those relationships and skills proved valuable to traders and eventually made the traders useful in a political sense. Regarding the trader Ben James as a "Choctaw mestizo," Governor Miró found him to be important in Spanish-Choctaw diplomacy in the late 1780s. Other Spanish officials continued in the 1790s to see him as valuable, along with the author of Franchimastabé and Taboca's letter to Gayoso, Turner Brashears, and others.[38]

Spanish officials recognized the importance of traders and trade as they attempted to expand their influence and forge alliances. When the British withdrew from the region after the American Revolution, the Spanish knew it was very important to sustain the commerce to which the Indians had become accustomed. Because many British traders wanted to remain and continue their trade, the Spanish government decided to take full advantage of their knowledge and their connections. After the congresses with Indians in Pensacola and Mobile of 1784 that committed the Spanish to sustain the trade of their predecessors, Miró and the Spanish intendant, Martín Navarro, recommended that two veteran traders in the area, William Panton and James Mather, be engaged to maintain the trade. "These men," observed Miró and Navarro, "know the English traders settled among the Indians who have been united with them by friendship and family ties for many years and through whom this trade is carried on; they know the language, and it would be difficult to substitute others from any other nation whatever."[39] Governor Carondelet, Miró's successor, valued the importance of one of the traders who had come to the region during the British period. Early in 1793, he instructed Gayoso to enlist the help of John Turnbull and "the sons he has in the Chickasaw Nation" in the Spanish effort to locate a fort at Chickasaw Bluffs.[40] At times, however, traders with their special interests and connections could be added obstacles in the way of securing policy objectives, as will be seen in the case of Brashears. More often, however, the diplomacy of the early 1790s worked because of the assistance of such people, for these traders played roles of what recent literature calls cultural brokers or mediators.[41] By the time the Spanish arrived, many of the male children of these traders had become chiefs, notably the sons of a British trader among the Chickasaws, James Colbert.

The linguistic and cultural skills acquired by traders meant that they could often serve as interpreters during any diplomatic encounter. Indeed, Indians often insisted on having people present specifically designated as interpreters; they preferred to choose them, and for that reason the interpreters assumed a major political role. The French policy of sending young boys to live in Indian villages to learn the language and ways of life provided a cadre of interpreters, many of whom remained in the region as traders and eventually served both the British and the Spanish as interpreters.[42] One member of a French family who came to be highly regarded for his expertise in the Choctaw language was Simon Favre, and Indians often insisted that he should be on hand during any serious discussions to make sure that meanings were communicated accurately. Because of his competence in the language, he acquired a certain status among the Choctaws, a quality highly valued and respected in diplomatic exchanges. Favre attended major assemblies and often found his name attached to written treaties.

Favre proved to be an able assistant to the first Spanish commissioner to both the Choctaws and Chickasaws, Jean de la Villebeuvre, another Frenchman who had come to the region in the 1760s in the context of the transfer of Louisiana to Spain. He remained in the service of the Spanish as a member of the Louisiana Infantry organized by the Spanish and in 1779 took possession of Natchez for them, where he then served as that post's first Spanish commandant. Usually signing his correspondence to Spanish officials as "Juan Delavillebeuvre," he learned some Spanish and Choctaw, and both skills enabled him to be perhaps the most important person of the many involved in ongoing dealings with the Indians, particularly the Choctaws. It was he who, in the capacity of Spanish commissioner to the Choctaws in 1793, negotiated the Treaty of Boukfouka that ceded the Spanish the site of the former French fort Tombecbé on the Tombigbee River for the creation of a new fort.[43] When Delavillebeuvre was appointed commandant of the new fort and moved there from Boukfouka, a Dutchman who had come to the region and lived among the Choctaws and Chickasaws as a trader, Benjamin Fooy, assumed the position of Spanish commissioner to the Chickasaws.[44]

These people—government officials, traders, interpreters, and others—kept the diplomatic paths cleared and used. Decision-making was not limited to the few, however; native tradition did not allow for that. Again, the newcomers, the Europeans and Americans, deferred to the egalitarian nature of Indian society that required the solicitation of many voices and ultimately their assent, usually in the context of a council meeting such as the one that occurred before Chickasaw chiefs agreed to the cession of their Chickasaw Bluffs to the Spanish in 1795 for the new post of San Fernando de las Barrancas. Indeed, the term *treaty* in this context included council or meeting as well as any document that might result, and the proceedings took on a sacred significance.[45] During a "treaty," hours and hours of speech-making took up much of the time but at the same time honored the belief that negotiations should be consensual and that everyone—at least every chief—had a right to be heard. During times of transition from one European power to another—as in the 1760s when the British replaced the French in the lower Mississippi valley and in the 1780s when British presence gave way to Spanish—these meetings took the form of large congresses. As Estevan Miró put it to the Marqués de Sonora in June 1787, "the repetition of the Congress from time to time is almost necessary, whenever there is a Power that intends to work against us; as the French and English did, who, when at war drew to themselves the Nations referred to." Miró then quoted his predecessor, Bernardo de Gálvez, who had suggested that annual congresses might be in order at designated places, during which presents could be distributed as the circumstances dictated.[46]

The congresses acknowledged the oral nature of communication and served as a way to assure continuity of trade and gifts and to affirm that Indian favor and support were important. When agreements were formalized by treaties, they were read out loud, article by article, so that Indians could understand and respond. British and Spanish officials often found themselves hosting upward of two thousand Indian chiefs, warriors, women, and children at such meetings.[47] Two such events highlighted the period under consideration here: the Natchez congress of 1792 followed in 1793 by a similar large gathering at Nogales. Indians reveled in these large formal assemblies and meetings, in part because they were often occasions for much ceremony and the distribution of gifts. On occasion, ceremonies of adoption could occur, whereby a governor, such as the French governor Kerlérec in the 1740s and Gayoso during the 1793 Nogales assembly, would be given a name or title and thereby incorporated into an Indian group. All meetings required smoking the calumet, an important symbol of peace, as was the presentation of beads of certain colors. Adoption, naming, and smoking the calumet all expressed deeply held beliefs about people, their relations with one another, and even with the spiritual world and thereby integrated diplomatic encounters into the ongoing social life of Indian people. Interpreters played key roles during these events, working with scriveners or secretaries to record everything that was said.[48] While often there was much ceremony and high rhetoric, much of the talk could be quite practical and blunt, as during the congress between the British and Choctaws at Mobile in 1771 and between the Spanish and Choctaws and Chickasaws at Natchez and Nogales over twenty years later.

The British held three major congresses, and these established a model for the Spanish to follow. After the conclusion of the French and Indian War that resulted in the withdrawal of French political power in North America and of the Spanish from Florida, John Stuart, the newly appointed British superintendent of Indian affairs for the southern district of the continent, met with Creeks, Choctaws, and Chickasaws in Pensacola and Mobile in 1765. The Spanish conducted assemblies with the same groups in the same places almost twenty years later. Here the Indians exchanged their French medals for English ones, thereby giving the British superintendent a voice in the selection of Indian leaders. The British also secured rather substantial cessions of land. To achieve that objective they had to assure that both the practice of trade and gifts introduced by the French would continue. With regard to trade and gifts, Stuart tried to emphasize trade over gifts and to be very specific as to what rules should be followed by traders. He issued a list of nineteen guidelines for those engaged in the Indian trade that included a prohibition on the use of liquor, rifles, and ammunition as items that could be sold or exchanged. He also put limits on the quantity of undressed skins traders could purchase and on credit to be extended, and he established a uniform set of weights and measures and a list of fixed prices for goods to be sold to Indians. Almost twenty years later, Spanish officials did the same and in the same places.[49]

Two congresses involving the Creeks, Choctaws, and Chickasaws took place six years later in Pensacola and Mobile. The Pensacola meeting between British officials and Upper Creeks dealt mainly with trade issues and land. After some initial resistance, the Creeks agreed to cede some land along the Alabama River to the British. Shortly afterwards, British officials met with Choctaws and Chickasaws in Mobile. Here the British attempted to secure the continuation in power of chiefs friendly to them. They distributed new medals, because most of the chiefs who had received medals in 1765 had died. In addition, the congress produced an agreement whereby the Choctaws agreed to assist in the survey of a boundary between their land and the province of West Florida.[50] Despite attempts by British authorities—in particular Stuart—to limit the number attending and hence the expenses, a detailed accounting of gifts distributed listed by name or title and village over seven hundred chiefs and warriors who received them. The principal and most contentious topic of discussion was trade. The superintendent told the traders in attendance that, because "they understood the Indian languages," they "should listen attentively" to the words of those Indians who spoke. The pipe of friendship was lit and smoked. Afterward Stuart opened the sessions with a speech in which he defended the British emphasis on trade by telling the Indians that "instead of annual presents," as was the custom during French rule, "we have given you a plentiful trade." Then he chided them by saying "if you are not industrious to reap the benefit of it in its full extent you must blame yourselves." He then went on to detail "some of the most flagrant insults, which your people have been guilty of," accusing Indians of such things as "plundering the store of Mr. Bradley" and "insulting the other inhabitants at that place [Natchez]." Telling them he had not broken a promise to invite them to a congress, he exempted the Chickasaws present from his list of indictments. He then went on to invite their response to complaints of "some riotous people among you" for having broken into houses of traders and insulting them.[51]

The next day, after the ritualistic smoking of the pipe, the calumet, which the superintendent pointed out was the gift of an Arkansas chief as a token of friendship, various Indian chiefs aired their complaints very bluntly, as interpreted and recorded by scribes. They complained of lack of honesty on the part of traders in adhering to the tariff agreed upon at the 1765 congress, failure to enforce the standard of weights and measures despite the appointment of a commissioner to make sure traders adhered to it, and the presence of unlicensed traders. As the Spanish also experienced among the Quapaws in Arkansas, complaints included failure on the part of the British to send "a doctor of guns" to repair those out of order. They even complained about being provided with "such narrow flaps, they do not cover our secret parts" and causing them to be put "in danger of being deprived of our manhood, by every hungry dog that approaches us." In talk enriched by metaphors of kinship, the speakers told Stuart "you are a good and a just father, and have not forgotten your children." They described him—if the accuracy of the translator and recorder is to be trusted—as "a great doctor who can cure all distempers, the sight of whom comforts and chears the spirits of this patient." Perhaps mixing metaphors a bit, they said he was "like a turkey perched on the top of a high tree" and they were like the brood of chickens, eagerly looking up at him, but unable to reach him. "At our return to our houses, our young, our old, our fathers our wives our children will all rejoice and be happy in having their wants supplied." They perhaps had in mind the gifts provided the chiefs.[52]

Well before the loss of Pensacola, lack of goods to distribute as gifts during meetings hampered British officials in their diplomatic efforts during the American Revolution. Stuart and his successors were instructed to be more frugal in the matter of expenditures on gifts and other items; at the same time, they were told to court the Choctaws and Chickasaws more assiduously to counter American and Spanish initiatives to enlist them on their side.[53] With the latter object in mind, British officials held a congress in May 1777, again in Mobile, with Choctaws and Chickasaws.[54] The meeting produced a treaty with the Choctaws that established a boundary for the Natchez District. Sufficient gifts were not available, however, to distribute, because, according to one report, the supply ship carrying the presents for the congress failed to arrive. Stuart bought some items from local merchants to distribute. Whatever the reason—failure of the ship to arrive or economy—Franchimastabé, who attended the congress and affixed his signature to the agreement, took the position later that payment had not been received for the land at Nogales.[55]

Two years later, traders may have helped British officials avoid the consequences of a shortage of gifts, at least among the Choctaws of the Six Towns. At that time the Spanish, now at war with the British, were actively competing with them for the favor of the Choctaws by offering gifts. Pousuhama of "English Town" wrote to "the acting commissary," Captain Cabert, to assure him continued loyalty because of the generosity of "our white people." He confessed that "altho we have not Behaved lately as we ought; we have not thrown your talks away. We went astray and received presents from the Spaniards but on our Return there was our own white people with their goods to support us by which we have no right to throw you away, we still Listen and hold our Brethren the English by the hand."[56]

When the Spanish replaced the French in Louisiana, their first governors took certain measures to secure the friendship of Indians. They met with varied success.[57] We have noted the initiatives of the first governor, Antonio de Ulloa, particularly with regard to the matter of gifts, and the very impressive ceremony of greetings and introduction of his successor as governor, Alejandro O'Reilly. More substantial meetings took place after the retrocession of Florida to Spain at the end of the American Revolution, for Americans now took the place of the British as competitors with the Spanish for the supply of Indian goods and the good will they might bring. On the other hand, the Americans even more than the British, who by means of the celebrated Proclamation of 1763 prohibited settlement beyond the Appalachian Mountains, sought Indian land.[58] Achievement of independence removed the 1763 barrier, and Americans began to look for land west of the Appalachians. Here were both a challenge and an opportunity for the Spanish.

The peace settlement of 1783, while ambiguous with regard to the American-Spanish boundary on the continent of North America, left Spain as the preeminent European power in the Gulf of Mexico, making that body of water in effect a kind of Spanish Mediterranean. With Florida and Cuba clearly in Spanish hands, the homogeneity of this region became a major geographical, political, and economic force influencing Spanish policy makers. To preserve their position, the Spanish could and did, as indicated, count on two important groups of people: Indians and traders. Both had over the years developed economic ties that they very much wanted continued. As the decade progressed, Indians became increasingly uncertain about the motives of Americans with respect to their land. Interest in preserving land and trade, then, became something the Spanish could use toward the end of preserving their limited presence in the Mississippi valley and Gulf South.[59]

Reports of events in 1783 seemed particularly ominous with respect to the security of that land and trade. Spanish officials in New Orleans were therefore easily persuaded to respond favorably to a visit, in September 1783, by Alexander McGillivray, the son of a Scottish trader and a Creek woman, whose father had been a Frenchman, to Arturo O'Neill, the Spanish governor in Pensacola. Referred to as a "*mestizo*" by O'Neill, McGillivray, because of his maternal link to the Wind Clan of Creeks, could and did regard himself as a Creek. He presented himself to both the Spanish and the Americans as the head of the Creek nation, although in many ways he was, in the words of Saunt, "deeply alienated from most Creek traditions and the vast majority of the Creek people." To the extent he wielded any chiefly authority, it was probably limited to the Upper Creeks where he lived. In terms of dealing with outsiders, he had an advantage in language, for he had been educated in English schools, and as a trader he had developed close ties to William Panton and his firm in Pensacola. Because of pressure put on the Creeks by Georgia to cede land in the context of British withdrawal, he and some other Creek chiefs came to seek the trade and friendship of the Spanish. A letter from McGillivray followed this visit in which he asked for "the beneficent protection of Spain" for Creeks and their lands. He specifically urged the Spanish to continue the English trade by making sure there were enough goods available and that it consider him for an appointment as the Spanish agent among the Creeks.[60]

Indeed, there seemed to be an urgency to his request, for by this time two states of the new American confederation, North Carolina and Georgia, had moved aggressively to secure Indian lands on the premise that they were sovereign states and that Indians who lived within those states and had supported the British could be regarded as conquered nations and compelled to surrender their land. Unlike other states, they did not surrender their western land claims until 1790 and 1802, respectively.[61] In 1783, North Carolina confiscated all but a small portion of Cherokee lands within its bounds, and later that year Georgia secured a cession of land from some Creeks by means of the Treaty of Augusta. Only two Creek chiefs signed that treaty, however, and it was quickly repudiated by McGillivray and other chiefs. Even the congress of the Confederation, which began to challenge assumed state prerogatives in matters of land and Indian affairs by appointing commissioners to the southern Indians and negotiating agreements with them, proceeded to award a large grant of land to the land speculator William Blount, a man whom the Creeks, because of his avarice with regard to acquiring Indian lands, dubbed "'the dirt king.'" In 1790, he became the governor of the Territory of the United States South of the Ohio River.[62]

Reports of migrations of large numbers of Americans across the Appalachians were received on a regular basis by Spanish officials in America and in Europe.[63] McGillivray devoted a considerable portion of his letter to O'Neill to emphasizing that for this reason his people and the Spanish needed each other. He said that many inhabitants of the thirteen states were leaving their homes and moving west to look for new ones in the forests to avoid being assessed taxes by the states in order to service the debt incurred during the Revolutionary War. A few weeks before that letter the Spanish ambassador in London, Bernardo del Campo, warned the minister of state, Floridablanca, that waves of discontented Americans were crossing the mountains and heading toward the Mississippi valley and very quickly could become a danger for neighboring Spanish possessions. Other letters arrived in Spain reporting alarming news about the rapid growth of the American west and suggesting a need to take more action to secure the friendship of Indians.[64]

That such friendship might not be difficult to secure seemed apparent in reports and complaints from Indians themselves about a major invasion of their lands by Americans. During the summer of 1784 the Spanish commandant in St. Louis, Francisco Cruzat, agreed to a major council with a party of 260 Iroquois, Cherokee, Shawnee, Chickasaw, Choctaw, and Loup Indians. There he heard them compare the invasion of their lands in the Ohio River valley to "a plague of locusts." They implored him "to concede an open road" so that they might come "to clasp your hand." They promised to be "always ready to shed our blood for the Spanish flag."[65]

Yet, south of the Ohio River many Indian leaders revealed uncertainty as to whether to pursue closer relations with the Spanish or the Americans. Concern about trade, gifts, and land loomed large in their thinking. Geographical proximity to settled parts of the United States provided another influence. The trader and interpreter, Simon Favre, reported in November 1783 that two important Choctaw chiefs of the Large Party, Taboca and Franchimastabé, had gone to Savannah with a "significant number" of the Small Party. He said that "the savages do not want to go to Gálveztown to receive gifts" and that both Franchimastabé and Taboca had refused to see him and had prohibited their warriors "to listen to the message." Because continuing gifts and trade seemed so important, Favre said he had decided to go immediately with four great-medal chiefs to Bay St. Louis to see the veteran Louisiana trader, "Mr. Maxent [Gilbert Antoine de St. Maxent]," who had just returned from Spain after completing a mission begun in 1781 on behalf of his son-in-law, Bernardo de Gálvez. There he had made recommendations for postwar Indian policy, secured a contract to procure goods for the Indian trade, and been appointed a lieutenant governor to trade with the Indians.[66] Georgians' failure in the end to satisfy the Choctaws helped him and other Spanish-sponsored traders.[67]

In the first half of 1784, Spanish officials on both sides of the Atlantic began to respond to these challenges and opportunities. A royal order of June 1784 ordered the closing of the Mississippi River to all non-Spanish ships. It was followed, as mentioned, by Floridablanca's assertion of the Ohio River as Spain's northern border.[68] In Florida, in the meantime, O'Neill accepted McGillivray's request for Spanish protection of the Creeks. To formalize the relationship, Governor Miró and his principal associate, the intendant, Martín Navarro, then invited the Creeks to attend a congress in Pensacola in May 1784 and the Chickasaws and Choctaws to one in Mobile a month later to formalize a commitment to friendship and commerce.[69]

In the middle of April, Miró emphasized to Martín Navarro the importance of these congresses as a way to establish friendship by assuring the Indians that trade would continue and admonished the intendent to be present. "The difficulties that present themselves to establish the friendship of so many nations—the sole object of such congresses—are greater today because of the lack of goods to establish commerce, which is the principal encouragement of these provinces and that provides what these nations need in exchange for their pelts." That, he said, was "a constant clamor of the speeches of the Indian chiefs who during the war came to this Capital."[70] Navarro decided that he should accompany the governor to the congresses in both Pensacola and Mobile, for he concluded that the importance of securing commerce and a general peace required his attendance, despite the current state of his health and other inconveniences.[71] McGillivray, described by Navarro as a "mortal enemy of the Americans," quickly acknowledged notification of the congress and told Miró that he had told his most important chiefs to be ready to go and to take as few warriors as possible with them. He warned Miró, however, that, "notwithstanding such needfull caution, there will be a good many that will go."[72]

The congresses met in Pensacola for a week beginning in late May and in Mobile for about the same length of time in late June. Navarro provided a short report of their proceedings, referring to the Creek delegation in attendance at Pensacola as the Talapuches. The opening session there took place on May 30, presided over by Miró, O'Neill, and him, during which they expressed a desire to establish the basis for a permanent peace and friendship "with all the Indian nations." In contrast to the report of O'Reilly's meetings with Indians in New Orleans in 1769, Navarro did not describe ceremony associated with any of the meetings. He reported that on the next day the thirteen articles of a treaty of peace and trade and prices expressed in terms of pounds of peltry for various trade goods, as well as regulations to guide traders, were read, interpreted, and approved, a proceeding that took up all of that day and the next. The treaty document recognized the complex political reality of the Creeks by listing McGillivray as the "principal representative" of the "upper, middle, and lower" villages of the Talapuches and the individual chiefs of different towns or groups of towns. On June 3 and 4, gifts were distributed according to the number from each village, followed on the next day by the bestowal of large medals on eight chiefs and small medals on six. The Indians departed on June 6 with enough *aguardiente* and powder for ten days of travel, "full of thanks and affection for our nation," after experiencing arrogance (*soberbia*) and haughtiness (*altivez*) at the hands of others, according to the intendent.[73] Following these meetings, Governor Miró appointed Alexander McGillivray as Spain's commissioner to the Talapuches, charging him to maintain the "dependence and subordination" of his villages to "Our Sovereign" and to monitor traders to make sure that they adhered to the prices established at Pensacola.[74] McGillivray thereby assured himself access to goods to distribute to the Creeks, and in so doing he would enhance his power. To assure continuity of trade, the firm of William Panton, based in Pensacola, was eventually allowed to keep its store at St. Mark's at the mouth of the Apalachicola River and to send a shipload of goods to Pensacola to supply the immediate needs of that trade. Eventually, the Spanish gave Panton's firm responsibility for the trade with the Creeks and, in 1789, the trade with the Choctaws and Chickasaws.[75]

From Pensacola, the Spanish officials went immediately to Mobile, where, again, according to Navarro's report, "from our arrival the Indian nations did not cease in arriving." In the end, according to the detailed reports on the congress, over two thousand Choctaws from fifty-eight villages, over four hundred Chickasaws from seven villages, about as many Alabama Indians from nine villages, and some Talapuche Indians from one village attended. Although some concern arose as to whether the Chickasaws would respond to the invitation, in the end most of them came. Despite the large numbers in attendance, according to Navarro, gifts were provided "that gave them much satisfaction." Agreements were reached similar to those of Pensacola with the Creeks. Navarro found the Choctaws concerned about disruptions in trade and characterized the Alabama Indians as "a nation of bad faith, bellicose, and fearful" who inhabited the headwaters of the Alabama River near Mobile. Nevertheless, he reported, after hearing the proposals of friendship, they agreed to them and offered to fulfill them "in the most exact manner."[76] In response to the concerns about trade, the Spanish decided to work with traders who had been in the region and awarded the privilege of supplying the Choctaws and Chickasaws to James Mather and Arthur Strother, two New Orleans merchants who agreed to use Mobile as an entrepôt.[77] Four years later, in response to complaints coming from Indians about the failure of traders to supply goods at the agreed-upon prices, both Miró and Navarro told the minister of the Indies, Antonio Valdés, that the integrity and continuity of traders must be upheld and the warehouse in Mobile maintained. "If it happens that the Indians change the Merchants with whom they trade . . . we will undoubtedly lose them, and they will be very difficult to regain once the United States is able to attract them to its friendship and trade."[78] To sustain this continuity, they decided in 1788 to withdraw the Choctaw and Chickasaw trade from Mather and Strother and award it to Panton, the veteran Scottish trader in Pensacola with many contacts among Indians.[79]

These congresses and the treaties that resulted provided the framework of what the Spanish saw as an alliance between them and the Creeks, Choctaws, and Chickasaws, expanded in 1793 to include the Cherokees. Yet such an alliance required that the expectations set down on paper in Pensacola and Mobile be met by the regular provision of gifts and trade goods. Some Indian leaders saw the Americans as an alternative source for both, especially after the Hopewell meetings between Americans and Cherokee, Chickasaw, and Choctaw chiefs and warriors in late 1785 and early 1786. During several days of elaborate and formal meetings with hundreds of people from these groups, American commissioners and state agents were able to take advantage of some doubt and dissatisfaction regarding the ability of the Spanish to provide desired goods. Two chiefs not recorded as present at the Mobile congress with the Spaniards, Taboca and Piomingo, led their respective delegations of Choctaws and Chickasaws, and they agreed to put their nations under the protection of the United States and to cede some land. They also made clear their desire for trade goods and an expectation that Americans would supply them.[80]

For a time, however, the Creeks, particularly those most under the influence of McGillivray, continued to regard the Americans as untrustworthy people—indeed, as enemies—and did not take part; they had in mind Georgia's success in persuading small groups of Creeks to cede land by means of three treaties.[81] Indeed, McGillivray told Miró shortly after the meetings that a grant of land ceded to Americans by "the Chickesaws deputy" who was "influenced by the large bribes Made him" was Creek land—Muscle Shoals on the Tennessee River—but that since then the Creeks had driven off the pretended proprietors. He also reported to Miró that he had instructed chiefs to collect enough warriors to drive out any American settlers they might find on Creek lands but in the process to shed blood only "where Self Defence Made it absolutely Necessary." In 1789 the trader Ben James reported that the Creeks had decided to attack American settlements on the Tombigbee "from its source to its mouth." In partial defense, McGillivray said the Alabama Indians were the ones responsible, but he told Miró that the problem was that the Indians could not determine whether the settlers—many of whom like him were *realistas* or loyalists during the American Revolution—were subjects of Spain.[82]

Finally, in 1790, Americans persuaded several Creek chiefs, including Alexander McGillivray—who was still serving as Spain's commissioner to the Creeks—to journey to New York to be entertained in grand fashion, meet with President Washington, and agree to a treaty of alliance with the United States acknowledging its sovereignty over those Creek towns within American boundaries. Furthermore, McGillivray and the other chiefs agreed to the cession of land to Georgia, although it was not enough to satisfy Georgians. Finally, a secret agreement awarded McGillivray a stipend three times greater than what he received from the Spanish. Georgians, many Creek chiefs, and Spanish officials denounced it, and, in the end, few of its provisions were implemented. Furthermore, McGillivray found his reputation among Spanish officials tarnished.[83]

Power in this world continued to be dispersed and the politics associated with it competitive and personal. The players in the game—particularly Indian chiefs—could continue to play off the different competing interests by following many and not very straight paths. Some could lead to the Spanish, others to the Americans, which, after 1783, could mean Georgians or Virginians or commissioners representing the American government. In this complex mix, there were many opportunities for "vagabonds" or "imposters," or opportunists—forerunners perhaps of the "confidence man" portrayed in Herman Melville's nineteenth-century novel set in the Mississippi valley—people who developed great skill at playing many roles.[84] As represented in both Spanish and American documents, the most notorious of this period was William Augustus Bowles, a former loyalist from Maryland who posed as both a Creek and a Cherokee and attempted to wean both away from the Americans and the Spanish and align them with the British in the Bahamas.[85] Treaties and agreements, to be at all meaningful, required careful nurture through gifts, trade, and much talk. The Americans and the Spanish might want to think that their treaties covered all Choctaws, Chickasaws, Creeks, and eventually Cherokees as if they were sovereign unified nations; the reality at this time was otherwise. Americans could not agree as to what "sovereignty" meant; for Indians, the concept had ambiguous meaning at best. As a consequence, for both Euro-Americans and Indians, almost constant talk supported by gifts and trade goods seemed to be required. The events of 1791–95 suggest the Spanish seemed to have the advantage over those they saw as their rivals.

Part II

4
The Nogales Dispute, 1791–1792

Some Immediate Antecedents

In the years following the American Revolution, local Spanish officials endeavored to find common ground with Indian elites and local traders in an effort to check what all increasingly saw as challenges coming from the United States. Responding to overtures from the Creek chief Alexander McGillivray, these officials held the 1784 congresses in Pensacola and Mobile to negotiate treaties of friendship and commerce and thereby assure the continuation of the trade that had come to occupy an important place in the political and economic life of the region. In what seemed to be a policy at odds with efforts to check American expansion and protect Indian lands, these same officials encouraged the immigration of Americans into the region by offering land grants to those willing to take an oath of allegiance to the king of Spain. As further enticement, they sought modification of Spanish trade regulations. In addition, they established a naval squadron on the Mississippi River and military and trading posts, and expanded civil administration to Natchez, where in 1789 Manuel Gayoso de Lemos—as governor rather than commandant—became the principal Spanish official.[1]

The establishment of new posts by the Spanish began with San Estevan (St. Stephen) in 1789 about sixty miles upstream from Mobile on bluffs overlooking the Tombigbee River. The relative ease of its creation contrasts with that of Nogales two years later, but its genesis did expose a problem confronting the Spanish as they sought good relations with Indians. The Spanish had encouraged immigration as a way to expand Spanish presence, and they found many willing immigrants among former Loyalists who were eager to leave an inhospitable United States. They found the requirement to take an oath of allegiance to the Spanish king to be no obstacle whatsoever. Local Alabama Indians and Choctaws viewed these former Loyalists as Americans, however, like those who had begun to pressure them to cede land. Responding to reports that the Alabama Indians threatened "to burn, lay waste, and destroy" the settlements of Tinzas and Tombecbé, Governor Miró hastened plans to establish the new post. At the same time he recognized in this liberal immigration policy a significant problem with regard to maintaining good relations with the Indians. He realized, as did others afterward, that the Alabama and other Indians must be convinced that the Americans who had settled north of Mobile and elsewhere had become Spanish subjects through their oath of loyalty, so this immigration policy did not contradict a general commitment to check American expansion and respect land the Indians regarded as their own.[2]

The establishment of the Nogales post provided the Spanish with an opportunity to persuade Indians that the establishment of new posts and limited immigration did not threaten their land or trade. The strong opposition expressed by Franchimastabé and Taboca's letter made it clear that the task would not be easy. Both of these Choctaw chiefs were veterans of dealing with outsiders for many years and saw advantages in keeping their options open about who might best serve their interests. Taboca, for example, had just led a delegation of Choctaws to meet with American commissioners in South Carolina in an effort to secure favorable trade arrangements. Both chiefs had risen to prominence during the time the English had sustained a political presence in the region, and they and others still required more evidence that their interests would best be served by alignment with the Spanish.[3] Led by Gayoso, the new Natchez governor, they did just that by means of almost continuous talk on many levels after the expression of opposition to the Nogales post. An examination of that complex diplomacy will be the subject of the next chapter; this one will review some of the events leading to the decision to establish Nogales.

What Spanish officials saw as a provocative series of actions directed against their interests, culminating with the project of the South Carolina Yazoo Company to put a settlement at the mouth of the Yazoo River on land they considered Spanish, led them to establish a post there. These actions began overtly with the creation of Bourbon County by the State of Georgia in early 1785. Responding to a petition from Thomas Green, allegedly on behalf of other Natchez residents, the Georgia assembly created the new county on the east bank of the Mississippi River, stretching from the mouth of the Yazoo River south to the thirty-first parallel—the line the American government regarded as the southern boundary of the United States, according to the terms of its 1783 treaty with Britain. The legislature then proceeded to appoint Green and three others as justices or "commissioners," as they came to be known, to organize a county government. They set out for Natchez to begin their work, but the affair quickly became a fiasco. Green demanded the surrender of the Spanish garrison and spread rumors of an imminent invasion from the north led by the western hero of the American Revolution, George Rogers Clark.[4] Another of the so-called justices or commissioners, William Davenport, began to solicit the support of Choctaws and Chickasaws in the Georgia venture. The creation of the county moved a Georgia judge in the same year to say that he looked "'forward to a time, not very far distant, when . . . the whole of [Georgia] will be settled and connected to the banks of the Mississippi'."[5]

Estevan Miró took decisive action to try to derail the scheme. He ordered the Natchez commandant, Francisco Bouligny, to report promptly the arrival of any Americans there and to regard Green as "a fugitive resident of Natchez."[6] Davenport's proselytizing among the Choctaws and Chickasaws caused Miró to ask Alexander McGillivray to pressure Chickasaw chiefs to "make the said Davenport retire from their Nation, and to admit no other American." He told McGillivray that such action should be seen by those chiefs as in their interest and "in conformity to what was agreed upon in the Congress held with me at Mobile." Finally, in the summer of 1786, he told the commandant in Natchez, Carlos de Grand-Pré, that the demand of Green and others for the surrender of the fort and district of Natchez was an act of "imposters" that warranted their arrest. He then instructed Grand-Pré that should he be in the position to capture him "or any of the pretended Commissaries in that vicinity," he should do so and send them to New Orleans.[7]

These challenges to Georgia's attempts to establish a county did not deter land speculators whose desire for land to sell provided the principal motive for the creation of the county. In 1786 a trader by the name of John Wood secured a grant of two to three million acres of land from the Choctaws. Posing as an agent of the American government, he had come to Franchimastabé's village of West Yazoo in the summer of 1785 with an invitation from that government to meet with its representatives. He then led the Choctaw delegation, which included Taboca, in the arduous two-month trek to the meeting with American commissioners in Hopewell in present-day South Carolina.[8] Wood turned his land over to a Thomas Washington, who, in 1789, associated himself with three South Carolina partners. With the addition of other partners, they then purchased a quantity of goods, part of which were to be used to satisfy Choctaws, the rest to help in the settlement of people at Walnut Hills (Nogales). Other speculators, among them Patrick Henry of Virginia, became active—all at a time when the new American constitution provided for a stronger central government, which, through its secretary of war, Henry Knox, attempted to implement an Indian policy that would secure peace for the American frontier. Three companies came into existence and asked for and secured from the Georgia assembly enormous grants of land Georgia considered its own. One of the companies, the South Carolina, received a grant enclosed by the thirty-third parallel on the north, the Mississippi River on the west, and a line running east from the mouth of Coles Creek to the Tombigbee River, which formed the eastern boundary. Included in this tract were the mouth of the Yazoo River and

Nogales, where the goal became the establishment of a town and a trading post. The company appointed James O'Fallon as general agent to treat with the Indians and the Spanish.[9]

All of these actions took place without any kind of formal consultation with or authorization from the American congress, the Spanish government, or the Choctaws or Chickasaws whose land was encompassed by Bourbon County and the grants made to the Yazoo companies. Much celebrated later in literature and film in an emerging mythology of the American frontier, individualism and localism reigned supreme in the new United States, encouraging individuals to pursue vigorously—and even illegally—their own interests. Government was minimal and so celebrated by the likes of Thomas Jefferson.[10] Under the Articles of Confederation, as noted, the United States was no more than a confederation of states, each one often acting independently of the others.

Even after the ratification of the new constitution and the establishment of a new government under it in 1789, central power remained very limited and even more vague with respect to Indian affairs than it had under the Articles of Confederation.[11] Where government did exist, it often served as a way to advance private interests, as in the case of the Yazoo affair. States like Georgia and South Carolina chartered companies and awarded them grants of land in Indian country in defiance of the central government.

Nevertheless, the congress under the Articles of Confederation did act to assert some authority over Indian affairs and thereby check such actions as those of Georgia, although with little success.[12] Congress appointed Benjamin Hawkins, Andrew Pickens, and Joseph Martin as commissioners to treat with "the Cherokees, and all other Indians southward of them." Those commissioners convened the meetings that took place in Hopewell in late 1785 and early 1786 with Cherokees, Chickasaws, and Choctaws. As those meetings were taking place, the Confederation congress formally repudiated the act of the Georgia assembly creating Bourbon County. Then, asserting that it had "the sole and exclusive right and power of regulating the trade, and managing all affairs with the Indians," the congress passed in the summer of 1786 an ordinance for the regulation of Indian affairs. It created an Indian department and divided it into two districts, southern and northern, and appointed a superintendent for each.[13] By the end of 1786 the Confederation government could consider the project to create a Bourbon County scuttled and the land speculators foiled, at least on paper. The Georgia assembly continued to assume, however, that it wielded sovereignty over the land in question, and the Yazoo speculators and many others relentlessly continued to practice what the Declaration of Independence affirmed as a natural right to pursue happiness. For them, that meant seeking land grants and moving into the region. Utilizing the expertise of William Davenport, Yazoo speculators influenced the Georgia assembly to appoint him a commissioner to the Choctaws and Chickasaws and win them over to their interests. By February 1791, they had formulated plans to send a band of "militia colonists" to the mouth of the Yazoo River.[14]

From the perspective of both Spanish officials and Indian leaders, American individualism and localism provided, at the same time, challenges and opportunities. While the Spanish minister to the United States, Diego de Gardoqui, worked in New York to effect some kind of resolution to the question of boundary and navigation privileges on the Mississippi River and open commercial opportunities, some Americans on the other side of the Appalachian Mountains—unhappy with governmental response to their land and commercial interests—sought close relations with the Spanish and even threatened to secede from the United States and create some kind of Mississippi Valley republic. They found a particularly enthusiastic advocate in a merchant and former Revolutionary War general, James Wilkinson. The Spanish governor in New Orleans, Miró, proceeded to develop a limited friendship with him and to consider sending the newly appointed governor of the Natchez district, Gayoso, on a fact-finding mission among Americans living in the area to determine the sentiments of the people with regard to Spain.[15] Something of an opportunist and confidence man, Wilkinson persisted in telling the Spanish of the dissatisfaction of Americans living in the West and that they suspected that in 1792, Miro's successor, the Baron de Carondelet, was encouraging the Cherokees to attack them. Then, in early 1794, he wrote Carondelet that "it is beyond doubt that the Western inhabitants of the united States must become tributary to the Power which controlls the navigation of the Misisipi."[16]

Providing substance to the agreements made at Pensacola and Mobile in 1784 became an ever more important priority of Spanish policy, especially as some chiefs, including Taboca and Franchimastabé of the Choctaws and Piomingo of the Chickasaws, remained uncertain in their views as to who might best serve their interests. For Franchimastabé, a veteran at playing many sides, Georgians, Americans, and Spaniards continued to offer three alternative sources of gifts and trade goods and the power and prestige they represented. Creek chiefs, particularly McGillivray, seemed secure in their disposition toward the Spanish, but they remained flexible. In 1787, he and other Creek chiefs met with the newly appointed American superintendent of Indian affairs for the Southern Department at an assembly in Coweta; three years later, in 1790, he led a delegation of Creek chiefs to New York, where they were entertained in high fashion by President Washington and other officials and signed a treaty with the American government. Miró found no harm in the earlier "reconciliation" with Americans as long as it remained clear that the Creeks remained under Spanish protection and did not admit American traders.[17] The 1790 trip and resulting treaty caused some concern and probably became one of the reasons for the appointment of Pedro Olivier as resident commissioner to the Creeks in 1792. McGillivray, who has been characterized as a Talleyrand of the South because of suspected duplicity, may have concluded that the new national government of the United States could provide needed additional protection from states that continually pushed for more cessions of land.

In this particular context, events in early 1787 encouraged Miró to intensify his diplomatic efforts to buttress the allegiance of Choctaws and Chickasaws by pledging to fulfill Spain's commitment to provide gifts and trade goods. As the agent of Georgia among the Choctaws and Chickasaws, William Davenport sought to exploit complaints among Choctaws, particularly those of the Large Party headed by Franchimastabé, about the Spanish trade agreements of 1784. By 1787 the Mobile traders Arthur Strother and James Mather, who had been given a provisional monopoly of the Choctaw and Chickasaw trade, were finding it increasingly difficult to adhere to the 1784 price schedule as prices for deerskins declined in Europe. Indeed, the Choctaws and Chickasaws said that traders associated with Mather were rejecting their pelts. As a consequence, the Indians seemed especially willing to turn to others for more favorable trade arrangements.[18] A "talk" to the "Kings, headmen, and Warriors of the Choctaw Nation" provided Davenport by the governor of Georgia sought to exploit this willingness. The talk expressed determination on the part of Georgians, which included establishing a company to carry on trade with the Choctaws and Chickasaws, "to have a path through the Creeks where goods ammunition and Everything Necessary shall brought to supply your Nation with goods." Georgians sought thereby to enlist Choctaw and Chickasaw support against the Creeks, who continued to resist their actions to acquire Creek land.[19]

In March, Davenport, along with Benjamin James, a licensed Spanish trader who also served as an agent for Georgia, and Pedro Juzan, the Spanish commissioner based in Mobile, met with Choctaws and Chickasaws in Franchimastabé's village of West Yazoo. Fully part of Choctaw society since his arrival in the region in the late 1760s and marriage to a Choctaw woman, James, like Brashears and many other traders, assumed an almost chameleon-like identity. Although a Georgia agent, James had notified Juzan and the interpreter Simon Favre of this meeting to allow a forum in which Choctaws and Chickasaws could express their grievances to the Spanish. But when the meeting took place, Juzan angered James by refusing publicly to shake his hand, an act that embarrassed and humiliated James before the Indians in attendance, for they attached much importance to such acts of greeting. After hearing James complain about this snub, Juzan listened to various Choctaw and Chickasaw chiefs speak. They complained that traders were rejecting a large number of deerskins and were not honoring prices agreed upon in 1784. In the end, Juzan seemed to make progress in convincing the Chickasaw chief—identified in his report as the "King of the Chickasaws," who was the most direct of all the speakers—and Franchimastabé that Governor Miró would listen carefully to their complaints.[20]

Juzan's representation of the meeting suggests that the Spanish seemed to convince the Indians of their sincerity. Apparently his presence and words persuaded Franchimastabé to favor the Spanish. Juzan told Franchimastabé that Miró was aware of the Choctaws' grievances and had sent him "to listen to them, to know them, and to carry them to New Orleans, because his intention is to maintain peace among the red men, Chickasaws, Choctaws, and Talapuches." Juzan reported that his questioning of James's reliability caused the trader to take off his hat and, "full of rage," to deny accusations that he was collaborating with the Americans and affirm that he was present only to observe.[21] Then, according to Juzan, "the American commissioner"—probably Davenport—said that the Americans had no intention of taking land, that they wished only to ask for "the white and open way so that the blood of red men or white men never will be shed." Seeing an opportunity to enlist the Choctaws and Chickasaws against the Creeks, he went on to admit Americans had disputes with the Talapuches but said that the Talapuches were to blame, for "these people have lost their minds." "They have killed our women and children" and "done us all possible harm, which has been the reason we take up arms." Furthermore, "these evil men" have also interfered with the delivery of trade goods that "you had lost from our fathers, the English."[22]

The two Choctaw chiefs spoke, Yaganehuma first, by order of Franchimastabé, and then Franchimastabé. Yaganehuma said that the words of both sides seemed fair: "I being a red man, poor, and not knowing what to do, extend my arms to the South and to the North to receive the hand of both in the hope of seeing which one will be the first who will say the truth." To that, the American commissioner Davenport said some of his people might prefer the Spanish, others the Americans; regardless, the Americans could receive both. Franchimastabé then spoke words that favored the Spanish. Directing his first comments to Davenport, he said very briefly that "not knowing you nor from where you come, I cannot respond to you." Then, addressing Juzan as his "brother" and Favre as his "nephew," he said he would entrust his words to them to carry to their chief and would remain calm in his village until Juzan should return. As he said later during the discussions about Nogales, he emphasized the unity of the Choctaws and the Chickasaws and the importance of speaking as one. Saying that he did not want to act alone, he insisted that his "elder brothers" the Chickasaws should speak first and that if the Choctaws and Chickasaws should ask, he "would not be so reluctant to travel" and that it (their word) would transport him over the land that is the "galleries of my ancestors."[23]

Although Juzan indicated that Franchimastabé—still in possession of medals awarded by the British—was leaning now toward the Spanish, two events following this meeting at Yazoo suggested that conditions remained very fluid and even dangerous. First, the Creeks, led by Alexander McGillivray, continued to oppose American meddling, sometimes with violence, as befell Davenport in June. A band of Coushatta Creeks came upon Davenport and other Americans and killed him and three of his companions. McGillivray told Miró that he had sent the Creeks in response to information that Davenport "was about building a fort for the reception of Americans near to the Chickasaw nation." He noted that "the fall of Davenport will greatly weaken American influence among the Choctaws & Chickasaws, a number of whom appear much in that interest." He identified James, who had also reported the killing of Davenport, as one who "was greatly instrumental in establishing Davenport's influence."[24] Although he may have agreed with some of what McGillivray said, Miró condemned the action for its violence and potential threat to Spanish-American relations at a time when diplomatic negotiations were under way in New York to try to resolve the boundary and navigation issues.[25] Second, and more positive, was Piomingo's and Taboca's dissatisfaction with the failure of Americans to live up to promises made at Hopewell. Piomingo directed his complaints to one of the commissioners of the Confederation government, Joseph Martin, and Taboca led a delegation of Choctaws to persuade the American congress to comply with the terms of the Hopewell treaties.[26]

To assure the Choctaws and Chickasaws that their trade complaints had been heard and that Spanish traders would adhere to the agreements of 1784, Miró decided to send Juan Delavillebeuvre on a mission to meet with the chiefs of both nations to convey this message and secure their understanding and support. Miró saw qualities in Delavillebuevre that made him particularly able to undertake this mission, for, as noted in the last chapter, Delavillebeuvre had already established credentials as an Indian diplomat. He had gained some knowledge of the Choctaws and their language, and during the American Revolution he worked to secure their support for the Spanish. In 1784 he went on a mission to persuade the Choctaws to attend the Mobile congress.[27] Hence the governor thought he was the most qualified person to undertake this mission, for he had "an acquaintance with the old chiefs."[28]

Miró provided Delavillebuevre with detailed instructions that outlined a challenging mission. He told Delavillebeuvre to meet with both Chickasaw and Choctaw chiefs and deliver a talk in which he would explain to them that the depressed market for deerskins in London had caused genuine trouble for the traders in Mobile. Then he was to assure them that these traders had promised him they would honor his wishes to adhere to the terms of trade outlined and agreed upon in Mobile three years earlier. Miró then told Delavillebeuvre to warn the Indians about the dangers of trafficking with any white people other than those authorized by the 1784 treaties. Referring to the death of Davenport, Miró stated such people should be sent back to their land. He then asked Delavillebeuvre to expose the fraudulent nature of the Hopewell treaties of the previous year by pointing out that the chiefs who agreed to them did not represent the major chiefs of their nations. Finally he told Delavillebeuvre to persuade those chiefs who still held British medals and patents to come to New Orleans to exchange them for Spanish ones.[29]

Delavillebeuvre set out for Franchimastabé's village of West Yazoo in September 1787 and returned to Bay St. Louis on the Gulf coast in late November. There he prepared a journal, which he sent on to Miró along with some notes and a list of Choctaw villages with the names of traders attached to many of them.[30] Those documents and transcripts of speeches submitted by Juzan form the principal record of the mission. Delavillebeuvre reported that he and his party set out from New Orleans on September 24, traveled by water along the coast to Bay St. Louis, and then up to West Yazoo. They arrived at Yellow Canes, one of the Six Villages, on October 7 and remained there until the tenth. Delavillebeuvre reports that while in Yellow Canes he admonished the chiefs of the Six Villages to be present at the meeting in Franchimastabé's village of Yazoo for an assembly of the entire nation. From Yellow Canes the mission then traveled to West Yazoo "with the utmost difficulty," arriving there on October 13 after a journey of four days.[31]

Delavillebeuvre devoted a very long paragraph of the journal to his meeting with James, who had arranged the March meeting in West Yazoo. Seen as a "Choctaw *mestizo*" by Miró, James's ambivalent position as both a licensed Spanish trader and a Georgia agent had raised concern among Spanish officials. James seemed eager to atone for any past indiscretions.[32] He told Delavillebeuvre he had come from his village expressly to see him; Delavillebeuvre then told him that he had to be present at the assembly. Delavillebeuvre also told him to go to New Orleans, for the governor wanted to speak with him. James replied that he was afraid to go because the strong words he had directed to Juzan might provide cause for his arrest. He apologized for making them but then said Juzan was really at fault "by refusing in front of the entire assembly to shake his hand" and, as a result, embarrassing him. He told Delavillebeuvre he had already returned his commission as an agent for Georgia because of his oath of loyalty to Spain. Delavillebeuvre assured him that the Spanish government was very benevolent and for that reason he should not be afraid to go to New Orleans. He then encouraged James to do all he could to persuade those Choctaw chiefs of his party still holding English medals, especially Franchimastabé, to accompany him to New Orleans and exchange the medals for Spanish ones. Although James failed to appear at the meeting, his influence apparently persuaded a number of chiefs of the Small Party to come with great eagerness, according to Delavillebeuvre, to surrender their English medals. James acted, however, in a way that seemed best to serve his interests and those of his Indian friends and relatives. He sought the confidence of William Panton and perhaps even Alexander McGillivray while maintaining contact with William Blount, the American land speculator who became governor of the Territory South of the Ohio River when it was organized.[33]

The formal meetings in West Yazoo, or "Grand Yazoo," as Delavillebeuvre referred to it in his journal, did not begin until November, in part so that the Chickasaws could be notified. Juzan reported the speeches given there: Delavillebeuvre spoke first and conveyed Miró's message to the Indians and was followed by three Choctaw chiefs. Franchimastabé's response expressed forcefully the point that the Spanish needed to honor their commitments with regard to trade. "We have believed that the traders should follow the price schedule established in Mobile, but we have seen with pain [instead] that [the prices] of the merchandise have increased." He promised, nevertheless, to give up "the English banner" in exchange for a Spanish one but insisted that he should be regarded "as a strong tree" that no wind could uproot. He then offered, according to Juzan, a white necklace and a white wing, describing them as "symbols of our friendship" and asking for a banner longer and larger than the one Delvavillebeuvre had brought.[34] Speaking on behalf of the Small Villages, Mingo-huma underscored Franchimastabé's remarks about trade and emphasized that trade should supply the Indians what they needed, particularly powder and balls, and be carried on according to the price schedule agreed upon in Mobile.[35] Chetonaque of the Six Villages affirmed that he and the others of his party were genuine friends of the Spanish, free from the taint of ever "going to see the Americans." He even offered, as had Mingo-huma, to assist in the apprehension of white men reluctant to leave if told: "We shall have them tied up and sent to Movila."[36]

Although Franchimastabé was not among them, protesting that he had a daughter at point of death and a "flux" that caused his joints to swell, a number of chiefs did go to New Orleans to meet with Miró in January and to exchange English medals for Spanish. Described as the second to Franchimastabé in the Large Party, Yaganehuma attempted to explain what had happened at Hopewell. Alluding to the fact that Americans had been active in soliciting both friendship and cessions of land, Yaganehuma admitted he had gone to the Americans but not with the intention of introducing them into the Nation or giving them land, only to ask for gifts. He said gifts and drink had been bestowed upon him and those who had accompanied him—enough drink to inebriate them. In that condition they had been given a paper to sign. In addition, he said, "they then gave us a flag of their nation, the very one that I now deliver to you, my father." He said he took the paper and later burned it. He asked Miró to understand that the poverty of the red men sometimes brought about these indiscretions. "Today we take your hand, you are our father and we your children. I ask you to forget all and that you never ask me again to speak about the imagined matter," he concluded. Then Taskietoka, the "King of the Chickasaws" and one to whom Franchimastabé often deferred, delivered Franchimastabé's medal and requested a Spanish one and said that Yaganehuma carried with him English and American flags to be surrendered. Those gestures, Taskietoka said in his speech before Miró, persuaded him that Franchimastabé "will be steadfast" from then on in his support for the Spanish.[37]

Taskietoka's assessment of Franchimastabé proved to be a bit too sanguine. Franchimastabé, along with Taboca, remained detached and flexible. Indeed, in telling Miró that all Chickasaw chiefs and warriors "have given our word and our heart to the Spanish Nation and intend to remain steadfast in our promises," Taskietoka had to exclude Piomingo, leader of "the American party," who had accompanied Taboca to Philadelphia in the summer of 1787 to urge American compliance with the Hopewell treaties Miró had characterized as fraudulent. According to Delavillebeuvre's journal, Taboca found, after having reached the Choctaws—perhaps just back from Philadelphia—that he had "to leave shortly to rejoin the Americans at La Belle Rivière [the Ohio River]."[38] Taboca and Franchimastabé sent the letter to Gayoso in May 1791 protesting the Nogales enterprise, and, despite Spanish efforts, Piomingo remained steadfast in his allegiance to the Americans.

In the context of this diplomatic activity, Spanish officials moved to enhance the importance of Natchez by replacing the system of military commandant in Natchez with a civil administration and appointing Manuel Gayoso de Lemos as the first governor. Son of a Spanish diplomat and educated in Westminster College in England, Gayoso brought valuable linguistic and political skills to this new post. Shortly after his arrival in Natchez in 1789, he strengthened the newly created civil administration for the district by laying out a full-fledged town or city, as evidenced in documents referring to the place as a *ciudad* and even authorizing the creation of a *cabildo* or town council. As suggested, Gayoso was a happy choice on the part of the Spanish, one who fulfilled the requirements outlined by the Spanish minister of the Indies who sought for Natchez one "skilled in prudence and diplomacy and who spoke fluent English."[39]

While Miró pursued closer ties with Indians, both he and Gayoso listened to some of the Americans who were moving westward and settling in areas north of Spanish territory, particularly on the south side of the Ohio River in what became the states of Kentucky and Tennessee. Gayoso talked to a number of inhabitants of Kentucky, Cumberland (Tennessee), and some of the settlements on the Ohio and contemplated some sort of mission to Cumberland and Franklin.[40] Some Americans, particularly after the Spanish closed the Mississippi River, concluded that it would be in their interests to open paths to the Spanish. They even supported projects to detach the whole region from the United States.

Perhaps the best known of these people, who saw his interests and those of the South Carolina Yazoo company better served by establishing good relations with both the Spanish and the Indians, was James Wilkinson. He had fought in the American Revolution, then moved west over the Appalachians, and eventually became involved in the Yazoo schemes. Unflatteringly characterized by one historian as making "a career out of deception and double-dealing," Wilkinson sought to pursue his own interests as well as those of the South Carolina Yazoo Company by offering his services as the company's agent, just two weeks after its formation.[41] He told the directors that it was important for the success of their enterprise that they seek the friendship and support of both Governor Miró and the Indians. The job of agent went, however, to another enterprising fellow, an Irish doctor by the name of James O'Fallon, whom historian Thomas Abernethy describes as being "endowed with an uninhibited tongue and a vivid imagination." Wilkinson was not happy with the choice and tended thereafter to play more to the Spanish opposition to the company's schemes by sending many letters to Miró with information about its activities and others to people associated with the land schemes to seek the support of the Spanish. Wilkinson even provided Miró with maps of the grants made to the Yazoo companies. Yet Wilkinson continued to work on behalf of the company; indeed, he came to see himself as a crucial intermediary. He wrote the South Carolina directors and told them that it was important that they seek the friendship and support of the governor as well as of the Indians. O'Fallon ultimately agreed with Wilkinson. Miró found it advantageous to maintain good relations with both men. In late 1789, he advanced a sum of money to Wilkinson and recommended to the minister of the Indies that Wilkinson be granted an annual pension. At the same time, he continued to be sensitive to attempts to resolve the boundary and navigation issues. The communications of both Wilkinson and O'Fallon provided added reinforcement to Miró's concerns about the ambitions of the Americans and the need for the Spanish to establish a more substantial presence in the region.[42]

Having received the reports of Wilkinson and others about the plans of the Yazoo company, Miró decided by the spring of 1790 to act to scuttle the Yazoo projects. He saw that best accomplished by establishment of the post at the mouth of the Yazoo River. In May, he wrote to his immediate superior, Domingo Cabello, the captain general in Havana, to report on the Yazoo challenge and ask for instructions. He told Cabello, however, that if the Yazoo schemes went forward before he received such instructions, he would proceed to establish the post at the mouth of the Yazoo. He enclosed Wilkinson's letter and the letters Wilkinson had sent with it.[43] Luis de Las Casas succeeded Cabello in Havana and agreed that something should be done. In November 1790 he told Miró that no one associated with the South Carolina Yazoo Company should be allowed to settle at the mouth of the Yazoo River.[44] Then, in January 1791, Gayoso received a letter from one John Williams, who told about plans by the South Carolina company to establish a settlement at Walnut Hills. Gayoso forwarded this letter to Miró, who later in the month gave Gayoso permission in the form of approval from Luis de Las Casas in Havana to proceed with the project.[45] In the meantime, Gayoso had visited the site and prepared a plan for a fort.[46]

Miró chose Elías Beauregard, a member of the Louisiana Infantry, to undertake the establishment of the post at Nogales and serve as its commandant under Gayoso. He provided Beauregard with some general instructions as to how he should conduct himself and his government. "Your conduct," he wrote, "should uniformly conspire to secure respect for the territory of the King." Then, perhaps with an eye to attracting immigrants, he told Beauregard that his administration should be so fair and "amiable" that any foreigners passing through for the first time could readily see the "notable differences" deriving from the "advantage" and "tranquility" that they might enjoy under "our government."[47] To serve as official interpreter for the new post, Gayoso recommended the appointment of the Choctaw trader Ebenezer Fulson.[48]

In late March, Gayoso set out for Nogales to assist in the preparation of the site.[49] On the way he experienced a prelude to things to come with regard to how the Choctaws were to view the project. From on board his galiot, *La Flecha*, he wrote to Miró from Bayou Pierre on March 27 that he had received information from "Pedro Bruin" (Peter Bryant Bruin, an Irishman who had secured a large land grant on Coles Creek) that in the previous week a number of Choctaw Indians "who were in that capital" had told a neighbor of his, "who spoke Indian perfectly," that they were very unhappy, for they had not received the gifts they had expected. At the same time, they had learned of plans to establish a post at Nogales, and they expressed displeasure with regard to it. Gayoso told Miró that "these people have no right to object to such projects in territory that legitimately belongs to 'Our August Sovereign.'" Nevertheless, he continued, it was important that in the present circumstances they should be kept happy and "that in a material sense they know that no other nation favors them more than ours." He suggested that the way to convince them was to bestow gifts opportunely and that such a time was now and an appropriate place Nogales. After his return to Natchez in early May, Gayoso concluded that the plans of the South Carolina Yazoo Company for a settlement there had been effectively

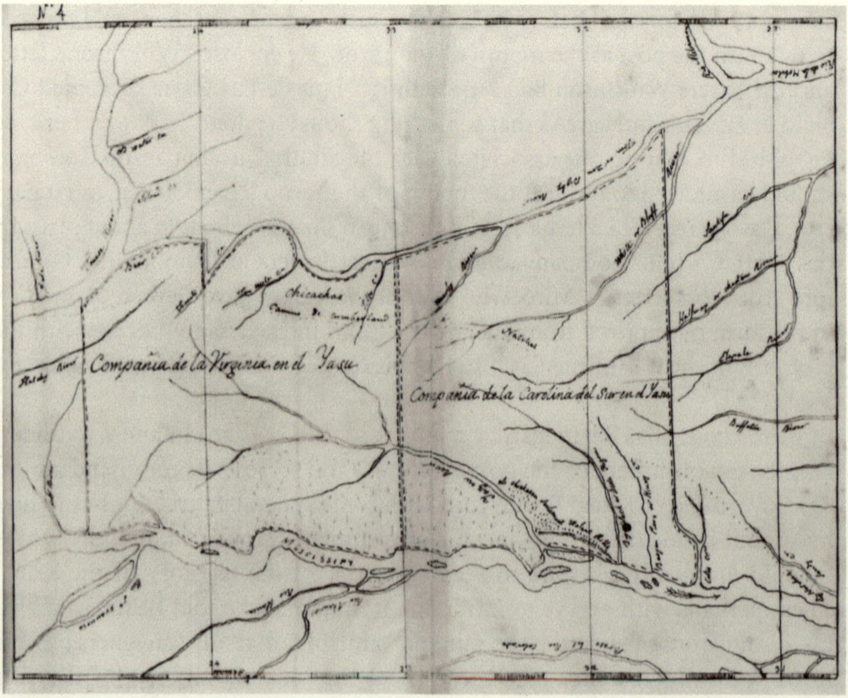

Figure 1. Land claims of the Virginia and South Carolina Yazoo Companies (1790). The map was provided by James Wilkinson to Estevan Miró along with other documents related to the activities of the two Yazoo land companies that had obtained the land grants from the legislature of Georgia. Miró forwarded these documents to Spain with his recommendations on the matter. Estevan Miró to Antonio Valdés, New Orleans, Aug. 10, 1790, transcript copy in MDAH, RG 26, SPT, ledger 3, reel 3, following 456. Courtesy of the Mississippi Department of Archives and History.

killed and that, as a consequence, the Spanish need not establish the practice of regular gifts at Nogales or any other place in the district or provide all the Indians might ask. Rather, he thought that in an opportune way some might be "showered with attention." Above all, he thought they should be managed in such a way as to preserve their friendship. Those views were shortly to be tested and revised.[50]

Gayoso spent most of April at Nogales, and during that time he once again examined the site, this time with the help of John Girault, and entertained visiting Indians.[51] After the trip, he submitted a report to Miró in the form of a diary with his observations about the site and its relation to the river and to the hinterland.[52] The descriptions were reinforced by two additional documents: the map provided by Wilkinson showing the grants by Georgia to the Virginia and South Carolina Yazoo companies accompanied by instructions

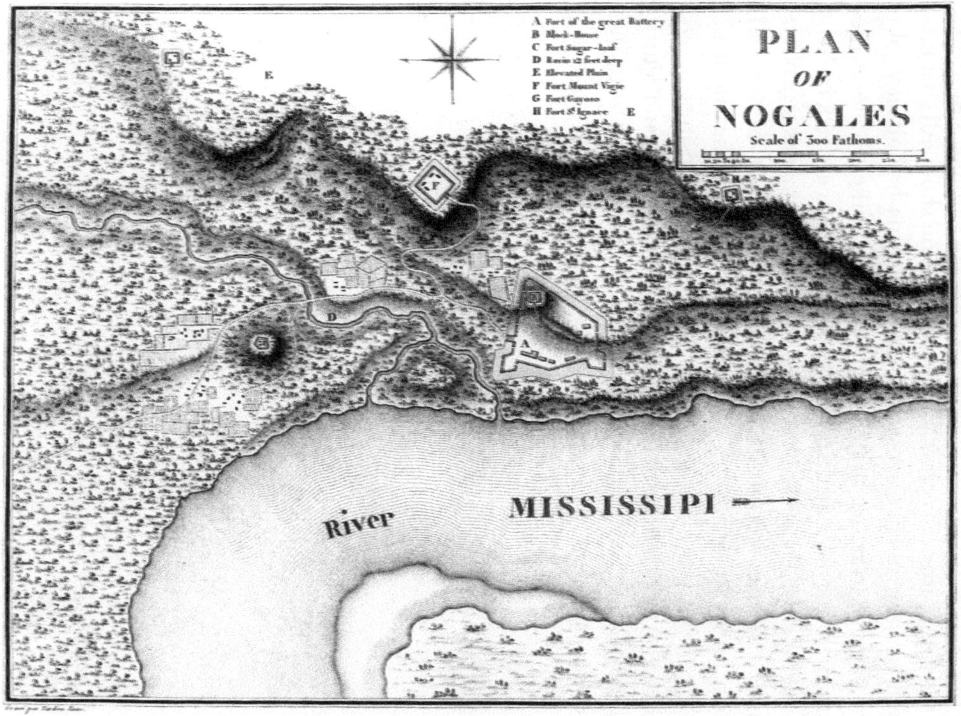

Figure 2. Plan of Nogales, ca. 1796. This depiction of the Nogales site as developed by the Spanish is one of several maps and drawings prepared for Victor Collot's account of his journey down the Ohio and Mississippi rivers in 1796 on behalf of Pierre Adet, the French minister to the United States. The account was first published by A. Bertrand in 1826. An English edition, translated by J. Christian Bay, was published as *A Journey in North America* (Firenze: O. Lange, 1924; repr. New York: AMS Press, 1974), 3 vols. Courtesy of the Mississippi Department of Archives and History, Accession No.: MA/81.0002 (a).

prepared by Gayoso for the new commandant, and a drawing, bearing the governor's signature, of a fort.[53] Gayoso describes how he played the role of host for a group of Choctaws consisting of the chief Itelegana from the village of Boucfouka and six other warriors from different villages. He extended hospitality to the visiting Indians in a variety of ways that included entertaining Itelegana with a ride on his galiot.[54] They traveled about a league upstream and then returned to a ceremony that consisted of the firing of cannons and shouts of "Long live the King!" from the crew and from people on shore. All that impressed the Indians very much, Gayoso recorded. Itelegana had already told Gayoso that he planned to return to his nation to inform others there of the Spanish settlement. A few days later, another group of Indians arrived, including the small-medal chief Panto Tistabe and one identified only as a nephew of Franchimastabé. Gayoso reported that they presented themselves "with all the pomp of which they were capable," which included "dancing the calumet," an important gesture of peace and good will.[55] None of these visitors manifested any evidence of opposition to the Spanish project. Gayoso could return to Natchez at the end of the month confident that the project met with the approval of the Choctaws.

5
Diplomacy of the Nogales Dispute, 1791–1792

Given his experience with Choctaw visitors during the April visit to Nogales, Gayoso no doubt received Franchimastabé's letter—bearing also the name of Taboca—with some surprise shortly after his return to Natchez. One might speculate that had the two chiefs been with Itelegana and Panto Tistabe and the other Choctaws at Nogales and been entertained by Gayoso, they would have thought differently, but probably not, for their motivation was complex, as the events of the next year revealed. Late in May their letter to Gayoso was delivered to the commandant Elías Beauregard at Nogales to be forwarded to Natchez, thus beginning a year that tested the ability of many to sustain amicable talk, to keep paths open and white, and ultimately to enable the Spanish to have their fort. In late May, Gayoso informed Miró of the letter protesting the establishment of the post, claiming that it was an invasion of land that did not belong to the Spanish. The letter opened with language that defined at the outset an important parameter of discussion, that of the Spanish governor as father and the Indians as children: "I have heard that my Father, the Father of the Choctaws and the Chickasaws, without knowing the reason why takes our lands."[1] The following discussion will focus on how Spanish officials, particularly Gayoso, responded and thereby made possible the major council or assembly in Natchez in May 1792 that produced a treaty document formally ratifying the work of the previous year.

Although he said he was not bothered by the letter—dismissing it as the probable work of some white rogue (*pícaro blanco*) in the nation—Gayoso concluded that he must respond by collecting gifts for the Indians and writing a letter of response. He furthermore decided that out of respect to the authors the letter should be carried to Franchimastabé by someone of importance and ability, someone who could provide him with more insight into the nature of the opposition. He settled on his adjutant, Stephen Minor (Estevan Minor), an Anglo-American born in Pennsylvania who had come down the Mississippi

River during the American Revolution and joined the service of Spain. In 1781 he was appointed adjutant for Natchez after its surrender to the Spanish. There he had begun to acquire much of the land on which the later town or city of Natchez was established as well as some facility in both Spanish and Choctaw. Demonstrating unwavering loyalty to Gayoso, he came to be admired, according to historian Jack Holmes, by both Spaniards and Americans in Natchez. The governor chose two others to accompany him, Richard King and the interpreter Ebenezer Fulson.[2] Gayoso told Governor Miró that both Minor and King had some understanding of Choctaw and could therefore be in a position to assess whether Fulson was interpreting "faithfully." He said his letter to Taboca and Franchimastabé would be written so that it could be easily interpreted. The main object of the trip was to assure the Indians of the good intentions of the Spanish.[3]

Minor departed Natchez on May 30 and returned on June 13, when he submitted to Gayoso a report in the form of a diary. Following a route that roughly corresponded to much of what is identified on the map of the Virginia and South Carolina Yazoo grants that accompanied Gayoso's instructions to Beauregard as the "Camino de Cumberland"—later the Natchez Trace—Minor headed north by northeast to Franchimastabé's village of West Yazoo. It was there the 1787 meetings between Governor Miró's emissary, Delavillebeuvre, and Choctaw and Chickasaw chiefs and others had taken place. Along the way he stopped in a village near what he calls in his diary the Halfway River, which appears on the same map by that name or Choctaw River. There he met the son of a chief by the name of Sulusmastabé or Red Shoes, who welcomed him, he recorded, and agreed to accompany him to Franchimastabé's village and provide whatever assistance he could in the talks.[4] When the father arrived, he, too, expressed delight at seeing Minor and agreed also to accompany him.

The party arrived in Yazoo, and, when they first met, Franchimastabé made it clear to Minor that talks would be on his terms and not those of Gayoso. Responding to Minor's request for an audience the next day, Franchimastabé said Minor would have to wait until other chiefs were notified, for when he (Franchimastabé) would go to see white people he would have to wait until they wanted to speak. Minor, he said, would have to do the same in his country.[5] Minor took advantage of the delay to meet with others.

Minor reports that among those he met were white men of importance living in the country—people who, he learned, had achieved importance by means of both trade and marriage to Choctaw women. Because of these ties and the influence they represented, Minor told Gayoso that winning their support was crucial for winning Indian approval of the Nogales post. From them he learned that it was the trader Turner Brashears, a native of Bladensburg, Maryland, who was the author of Franchimastabé and Taboca's letter. Indeed he learned that Brashears had become very important to Franchimastabé through both trade and marriage. He had come into the region sometime during the American Revolution and had worked as a trader and married a daughter of Taboca, who was also probably a niece of Franchimastabé. Within matriarchal Choctaw society, those familial ties made Franchimastabé responsible for any of Brashears's children. Brashears and other traders living among the Choctaws, Minor learned, were concerned that Nogales might become another trading post for the expanding operations of William Panton, whose company had assumed from the Mather-Strother firm of Mobile the exclusive privilege of supplying the Choctaw-Chickasaw trade in 1788 after Delavillebeuvre's mission.[6] After learning of a conversation in which Brashears told Franchimastabé that if Nogales were ceded and a settlement allowed there they would "all become slaves," Minor had to conclude that the task of persuasion would involve traders as well as chiefs.[7]

One of these traders, Malcolm McGee, who, like Brashears, had lived in the nation for many years, provided some explanation of Franchimastabé and Taboca's position that the land on which the Spanish wanted to put their post was not Spanish. He told Minor that the English had failed to pay for the land ceded them by the Choctaws when a boundary was established between the Natchez District and the Choctaw Nation in 1777. According to McGee's account, John Stuart, the English superintendent of Indians, promised that goods would be provided to pay for the cession but that they had not been delivered. Franchimastabé and others repeated that point in subsequent discussions. What became clear at that point is that the Spanish would have to arrange for some kind of payment.[8]

Meetings that followed involving both Franchimastabé and Minor were both private and public; they tended to follow this pattern during all such major councils or assemblies, as they did in Europe. Much formality and ceremony characterized the public events, but the difficult political work occurred during the private sessions. Minor described a conversation between him and Franchimastabé that went beyond the Nogales question. After the conversation between Franchimastabé and Brashears, overheard in part by McGee, Franchimastabé came to his lodge at about eight in the morning, and the two of them discussed not only Nogales but what Minor saw as another problem: horse theft. When Minor raised that issue, Franchimastabé sent for another trader living among the Choctaws, one Philip Hayes. Minor accused him of possessing stolen horses and demanded that they be brought to him immediately. Eventually, Minor and Franchimastabé agreed on a way to deal with this particular problem.

In contrast to such encounters, the formal public meeting assumed the dimensions and characteristics of an assembly or congress replete with much protocol and symbolism, all of which Gayoso, when he received Minor's account, interpreted as confirmation of an "inclination to our nation."[9] It took place in a *glorieta* or public space specifically constructed for the speeches and discussions. A Spanish flag was placed in each corner. Franchimastabé seated Minor in front of him "more or less in the middle of his chiefs and warriors, who numbered about two hundred." During this meeting, Minor executed the principal charge of his mission by presenting Gayoso's letter in response to the one of Franchimastabé and Taboca. Franchimastabé then asked McGee to read it in what Choctaw the trader could muster. The chief asked the others to respond; when they did not, according to Minor, Franchimastabé turned to him and said they would not speak unless they were drunk and then they would do so in an insolent manner. The Choctaw chief then proceeded to deliver a speech in which he said that the Choctaws and Chickasaws should be regarded as "brothers and the same people" and that they were united in opposition to the cession of land, a portion of which was identified as "An Old Chickasaw Settlement" on the map of the Yazoo claims (see Figure 1). He repeated what Minor had already learned from McGee: the English had not paid for the land ceded to them by the Choctaws. Minor responded by saying that the Spanish leader desired only "to protect the land of his beloved red people so that it would not be taken by the Americans."[10]

After Minor explained that the Spanish king wanted no more than to build a fort at Nogales "to protect the lands of his beloved red people" from Americans, who, in contrast, wanted not only the land but the destruction and expulsion of all red people in its vicinity, Franchimastabé asked that there be no further discussion of the Nogales question. Minor then proceeded to bring up the other issues he had raised in private conversation with Franchimastabé that seemed more amenable to some kind of resolution. He pointed out that the Choctaw nation had become a sanctuary not only for stolen horses but also for runaway or stolen slaves. Franchimastabé agreed that indeed there was a problem of theft, and he asked Minor to draft a statement both could sign to be the basis for resolving it. Minor happily agreed and then proceeded to secure a promise from Franchimastabé that people from Natchez traveling through his nation carry an appropriate passport identifying them as residents of Natchez and authorizing their travel.

After this public meeting, events tended to move in favor of the Spanish position on Nogales. Before Minor's departure for Natchez, Franchimastabé came to him and said that he would send two of his chiefs, Itelegana and Taboca, to see the governor, along with three men for each chief "to serve as witnesses." He said his sending of Itelegana should be seen as equivalent to his own going, for "he would trust and approve of whatever he did." On his return,

Minor stopped at the village of Red Shoes, who told him he had no objections to the Spanish post.[11]

Following Minor's return to Natchez in the middle of June, Gayoso proceeded to translate the diary into Spanish and then send a copy of it with a long letter describing meetings that took place in Natchez between Minor and two Choctaw chiefs, Itelegana and his brother, Stonahuma. Judging from the length and detail of the letter, which follows Minor's diary in Part III of this book, those meetings assumed the dimensions of a veritable congress, although with perhaps not as many present as those who attended the 1784 affair in Mobile. Gayoso reported the major speeches given in the public meetings and describes the ceremony associated with them. He also reported to Miró what took place in what he considered to be more frank and more positive private discussions between him and Itelegana, who, Minor learned during his second mission the following spring, was being discussed as a possible successor to Franchimastabé. Gayoso had, as had Minor by means of his diary, enabled Choctaw voices to become part of the historical record. The governor expressed optimism about achieving an amicable resolution of the issues raised by Taboca and Franchimastabé in their letter and suggested a meeting attended by only the principal chiefs and some warriors living in the vicinity of the Natchez district as a way to resolve "all our differences."

Gayoso's letter merits attention for what it reveals about his thinking and how he engaged in diplomacy and recorded it. He began by discussing what he regarded as the very successful mission accomplished by his adjutant. He drew attention to the way Minor was received, noting that the Choctaws seemed to be pleased to have a Spanish official in their country and so expressed their pleasure by the formality of the public assemblies in the *glorieta* decorated with Spanish flags. From that he concluded that if they expressed dissatisfaction with the post at Nogales, it was, as he had suspected, the work of someone else, whom Minor, of course, identified as Turner Brashears, the trader who lived in the nation—indeed, in the very house of Franchimastabé, where, in Gayoso's words, he rewarded the chief "with a thousand trinkets that flatter" his ambition and influence. Gayoso might regard him as a white rogue; nevertheless, he and other other traders who had established themselves among the Choctaws and Chickasaws now had to be somehow persuaded of the rightness of the Spanish position.

In the letter, however, Gayoso focused his attention on the meetings between him and the Choctaws who came to Natchez shortly after Minor's return. On the day of their arrival, the Choctaw delegation insisted on the usual protocol of extending greetings, in this case by shaking the governor's hand. Gayoso says he supplied them with rations and made sure they were "content in every possible way." On the next day, formal ceremonies took place during which both warriors and chiefs presented themselves "painted in peace with a very happy countenance." As recorded by Gayoso, Itelegana did most of the talking for the Choctaws and was the spokesman for Franchimastabé. He argued eloquently that the site should be free of a Spanish post or town—that the trees and cane should be allowed to grow again at Nogales so that the game upon which the Choctaws depended for their living would not be jeopardized. There should be no Spanish settlement, and, by implication, no American. He repeated that, although the land had been ceded to the English, whom in general the Choctaws admired, payment had not been received, and for that reason the Spanish could not regard it as theirs.[12]

Stonahuma then spoke and repeated Itelegana's points. He too posed as a spokesman for Franchimastabé by displaying the large medal given to Franchimastabé by the Spanish and saying his principal chief had given it to him "to confirm whatever I might say." He pointed out that the Chickasaws and Choctaws were "the same people, the same interest, and the same will" and that both were opposed to white settlement on their land. In response to both these speeches, Gayoso said that the "Great King" of the Spanish wanted merely to protect "his vassals and friends throughout the extent of his dominions that in this country begin at the mouth of the Yazoo." In contrast to the public discourse, the talk in private meetings between him and Itelegana seemed encouraging to Gayoso, for Itelegana seemed to speak there not as the voice of Franchimastabé but as his own person. In that role he said there was merit in the Spanish position, leading Gayoso to suggest another meeting with several chiefs and as few warriors as possible as a way to resolve the issue. He said he would be willing to offer a portion of his salary, if necessary, to help defray expenses. As evidence that he had gained the confidence of at least two of the chiefs, Gayoso reported that Itelegana was going to leave with him "a son" to be educated.[13]

Subsequent encounters with Itelegana and other Choctaws and Chickasaws led to a strengthening of good feelings and additional relationships. In late October, Red Shoes visited Natchez and talked with Minor. Minor reported that Red Shoes complained about treatment at the hands of "Mr. G-P," probably Charles de Grand-Pré, who sometimes acted for Gayoso in the governor's absence. Minor apparently succeeded in making amends for ill feeling resulting from that treatment. He went personally to Red Shoes' camp "near the hospital" and there learned that Franchimastabé, sometimes referred to by both Minor and Gayoso as "the Old Friend," was not in good health, indeed, may even have died. Minor said that Red Shoes came to regard him as a "man of truth" and his friend. He reported that the chief told him that the Choctaws, Chickasaws, Creeks, and Cherokees "had made a firm and lasting peace to stand by each other in defence of their rights and their lands." Minor said he thanked Red Shoes for that information and that the chief then pledged to send a runner to give him any information worthy of notice that should come to his attention.[14]

Red Shoes seems to have been won over. He eventually asked Gayoso, as had Itelegana, to take one of his "sons"—probably a nephew—also to be educated. In April 1792, just after Minor returned from his second mission to the Choctaws, Itelegana's thirteen-year-old boy arrived. Gayoso found him to be "of excellent disposition" with an eagerness to learn. In time, both Gayoso and other Choctaw chiefs extended and widened this particular path to understanding through the learning of languages and living together. A large-medal chief, Tanquapa of the Choctaws, and a group of Choctaws and Chickasaws accompanied the boy. They asked for medicine for the king of the Chickasaws, "who finds himself with leg sickness," wrote Gayoso, who interpreted all of these encounters and gestures as evidence of "positive" feelings toward the Spanish. "If they did not put faith in us," he told Miró's successor, Carondelet, "then they would not leave in my power sons of the first chiefs, nor would they come asking for medicine." Gayoso used the presence of the two Choctaw boys in his house to begin the process of educating David Urqhart and Enrique Vaucheret in Choctaw.[15]

Other visits by other Choctaw delegations sustained Gayoso's optimism about eventually winning the support of the Choctaws and Chickasaws for the Spanish project, but they also underscored a need for patience. Shortly after the letter to Miró, Gayoso reported to Beauregard, the commandant at Nogales, a visit from another Choctaw great-medal chief, one Chafale, along with a small-medal chief and some warriors. They came to Natchez to express support for the Spanish project. "Both he and many other chiefs of their nation are infinitely happy to see our establishment at Nogales," Gayoso told Beauregard. Many more delegations came to Natchez in the course of the year to express their views and to test Gayoso's diplomatic skills and stamina. These meetings continued into the next year and finally included a visit by some eighty Choctaws led by Franchimastabé when Gayoso was in New Orleans to meet the new Louisiana governor, Carondelet. Dealing with so many strained one's patience and resources, Gayoso told Carondelet, for one needed always to be gentle and have on hand an ample supply of gifts. Only in that way could they eventually be brought to reason. Once again, however, he expressed confidence in the outcome by pointing out that Itelegana, along with the chiefs and warriors who came in the name of the lower Choctaw villages, supported the Spanish initiative.[16]

While in New Orleans in January 1792, Gayoso briefed Carondelet about the important events of the previous year relating to Nogales and asked for instructions. He described his trip with Beauregard to begin work at the site in April and his first encounter there with Itelegana, who had come to greet him "as a friend of Spain" and impressed Gayoso as a "person of talent and understanding." He went on to report the letter of Franchimastabé and Taboca expressing opposition to the post on the grounds that it was on land not Spanish and would disrupt the hunt. He then said he had decided to send Minor to get more information and to deliver a response to Franchimastabé and Taboca. Minor, said Gayoso, was treated very well and received a pledge of friendship for the Spanish from Franchimastabé and a commitment to send Itelegana and other chiefs to Natchez to continue discussions. Gayoso pointed out to Carondelet that Minor had found many Americans living among the Choctaws. Among them he noted Turner Brashears as one who was especially close to Franchimastabé. Gayoso identified him and the other traders as the major source of opposition. In contrast, he mentioned Itelegana's support, which was reinforced by a group of chiefs and warriors of the Lower Villages giving their support and telling him that only Franchimastabé opposed it. As in his earlier correspondence, Gayoso said he thought those meetings and others had gone very well, that the Indians had been well treated and appropriate gifts distributed. He concluded that Itelegana could be regarded as a friend of the Spanish and that they could count on him even against the "advice of Franchimastabé." In requesting instructions, Gayoso did say, however, that opposition to the project remained strong and that therefore he and others needed to be flexible and resourceful. "One must take advantage of the moment the Indians are in good humor; they must not be given time to change their minds." He reiterated the importance of gifts and asked that some be sent to Natchez so that he would have them to distribute when the Indians arrive.[17]

The visit of Franchimastabé and some eighty Choctaws, many of them chiefs, to Natchez while Gayoso was in New Orleans required a response from the Natchez governor. That became one of the objectives of a second mission of Minor to the Choctaws. As in the case of the first mission, Gayoso prepared a letter for Franchimastabé in which he apologized for his absence from Natchez when the chief came with his retinue and explained that he had gone to New Orleans to speak with the new governor about matters of great importance, many pertaining to Franchimastabé and his nation. He repeated, however, the view that the Spanish had legitimately inherited the land at Nogales from the British and reminded him that the Spanish had made a regular gift to him. On the matter of gifts, he counseled patience "with the expectation of gaining more," for, Gayoso said, the new governor deemed the matter of such importance that he had determined to do nothing on his own until receiving permission from the king. To underscore Minor's stature as one who had his full confidence, he said he was returning by Minor the white beads that the Choctaw chief had sent to him.[18] The Natchez governor wrote shortly thereafter a more general letter to be delivered to Taskietoka of the Chickasaws, whom Minor had identified as one to include in the diplomatic process, for, said Minor, "the Old King [Franchimastabé] will do nothing without consulting him." Gayoso conveyed his affection and that of the king of Spain and urged unity among the Chickasaws, Choctaws, Talapuches, Cherokees, and other "Indian nations that are in our vicinity." He invited Taskietoka and Franchimastabé to Natchez and asked that he be told in advance so that they could be received appropriately.[19]

In addition to the letter and white beads for Franchimastabé, Gayoso prepared rather detailed instructions as to what Minor should attempt to accomplish on this mission. With resolution of the Nogales matter still the main goal, Gayoso asked Minor to get as much information as he could about the politics and geography of the Choctaws. He told Minor to go to Franchimastabé's village and deliver his letter, a copy of which was given to Minor to read. In addition to delivering the letter, Gayoso instructed Minor to do all in his power to assure the Indians of the friendship of the Spanish and to tell them once again that the purpose of the fort was to help them defend their lands from incursions from the Americans. Gayoso admitted that the British had not made good on their promise of payment, and he said that the Spanish would provide a remedy by means of gifts to the various chiefs and by allowing the Choctaws to continue hunting on the other side of the Mississippi River. With regard to hunting, he instructed Minor to tell the Choctaws that the Spanish at Nogales would provide a means for the Indians to exchange their pelts for whatever they might need and thereby obviate the need to go to Mobile or Pensacola. He told Minor to repeat the apology expressed in his letter for not being in Natchez when Franchimastabé and the other chiefs came in January and to explain the importance of his going to New Orleans to greet and confer with the new governor. He also repeated the invitation to come to Natchez.

Gayoso included more specific requests, one of which could be read as weakening his repeated assertions that the Spanish did not desire land. He told Minor to suggest that the border between the Choctaw Nation and the Natchez District be set at the Pearl River, not because the Spanish wanted the land but because it would be a way to make clear to the Americans that they should stay out. As Miró had done earlier in his instructions to Delavillebeuvre in 1787, Gayoso told Minor to observe the white men living among the Choctaws, the influence they had, and the way they operated. No doubt with Turner Brashears in mind, Gayoso told Minor to determine whether any of these people had particular influence on Franchimastabé and, if so, to try to attract them to the Spanish side. Gayoso asked for geopolitical information: the number of villages, the distance between them, their population, and the most influential chiefs. He even asked Minor to try to identify the chief most likely to succeed

Franchimastabé. On a more personal level, the governor asked Minor to tell Itelegana that he was taking good care of his son and giving him a good education. Furthermore, he told Minor to inform Sulusmastabé that if he would send him his son, the boy would receive the same care. In general, Gayoso told Minor to reassure the Choctaws that he was determined to bring about a prompt and mutually satisfactory resolution of the problem of Nogales and to strengthen ties with the Indians.[20]

With letter, beads, and instructions in hand, Minor set out for Franchimastabé's village of West Yazoo on March 15. Weather delayed his trip at Bayou Pierre. While there he learned of a meeting between Americans and Choctaws, Chickasaws, Creeks, and Cherokees at Muscle Shoals on the Tennessee River. He sent that news to Gayoso, who may already have learned of the possibility of the meeting.[21] Gayoso reported it to Carondelet along with news of Minor's trip. Both officials responded. Gayoso sent additional instructions to Minor telling him to "do all you can to determine what occurs at the mentioned treaty, which is your object, who is behind it, the companies or some of the inhabitants of the west, and what Indians attend it." He even told Minor to go there immediately if he should find out that Franchimastabé should be one of the Choctaws in attendance and persuade him not to sign any treaty with the Americans by reminding him and the others of existing agreements with the Spanish.[22] Carondelet decided to send Juan Delavillebeuvre there as the "King's commissioner," with money and an interpreter or secretary to observe the proceedings and report back.[23] Perhaps in response to Gayoso's report of Minor's mission, Carondelet also prepared a letter for Franchimastabé in which he stressed the importance of peace among all Indian groups and pledged the friendship of Spain to all, especially the Choctaws, Chickasaws, and Cherokees. He told Franchimastabé of the possibility of a war between the Creeks and the Americans if the Americans did not get what they wanted in a treaty. All that led up to a warning to Franchimastabé to be wary of the Americans—"these [Americans] may usurp their lands, kill the hunt, and reduce them to nakedness and misery"—and, once again, to see the value of a Spanish fort at Nogales.[24] Citing communications from the minister of state in Spain and the captain general in Cuba as expressions of the determination of the king to secure the Nogales post, Carondelet told Gayoso to negotiate secretly with Franchimastabé and other principal chiefs of the Choctaw nation solely "to conserve for the Choctaw Nation that territory that Americans have occupied to the number of two thousand families."[25]

Accompanied again by Richard King and Ebenezer Fulson, Minor left Bayou Pierre and arrived in Franchimastabé's village on March 22. There a series of meetings occurred, which consisted, as in earlier encounters of this nature, of public events, characterized by much ceremony and oratory, and private discussions, principally between Minor and Franchimastabé and Minor and traders. Again Minor provided a record in the form of a diary, which he submitted to Gayoso on his return to Natchez. In it Minor records that the first public assembly afforded an opportunity for many chiefs to speak.[26] As host and principal chief, Franchimastabé began. He repeated his opposition to the cession of Nogales, but he talked about other things, too, beginning with an account of a recent trip to the Chickasaw Nation. There, he said, he had learned that his "oldest brothers, the Talapuches and the Cherokees," had come to express a desire for union, and, as proof of their friendship, they had given him a package of white beads to show to his nation. He then proceeded to distribute the beads to the principal chiefs. After that gesture, he asked his guest, Minor, to speak, whereupon Minor presented Gayoso's letter, which was read—to the apparent satisfaction of all—by Benjamin James, the trader who had played such a prominent role in the 1787 mission of Delavillebeuvre. Minor then proceeded to express the Spanish position regarding the value of a post at Nogales, to which, according to his account, there was little response, although an unidentified chief did express support for the Spanish view. Franchimastabé had the last word, and he chose to stress the importance of the views of the Chickasaws on the matter and the need to stop the trade at Nogales, a point that traders with whom Minor spoke also emphasized. Minor said that if people opposed the trade at Nogales, then he should not talk further about "reclaiming those lands." On that note, he reported, the assembly concluded.[27]

Minor's summary of the private conversations that followed indicates that Franchimastabé's principal concern was his standing among the other chiefs, particularly the younger ones, some of whom, he said, had already threatened his life. The chief made it quite clear that to maintain his status—perhaps even his life—he needed gifts. In response to that point, Minor told Franchimastabé that he could appropriate the greater part of the gifts "destined for the chiefs" without the others' knowledge—a gesture that apparently pleased Franchimastabé immensely, for Minor records his saying, "I always thought that at the end you would find the true path to my heart."[28]

Minor judged his trip a success, but for Gayoso it was clear that more talk must occur. Still elusive, Franchimastabé revealed he had interests and concerns other than the Spanish plan to build a military post at Nogales. He needed gifts to buttress his status. Gayoso's view that a meeting between him and several chiefs should occur with him as host seemed to be confirmed. To assist in such future discussions, Minor provided Gayoso with a good bit of useful information—an estimate of the total population of the Choctaws; the importance of Brashears and James; and Franchimastabé's apparent willingness to sell land west of the Pearl River—all of which Gayoso relayed to Carondelet in New Orleans.

An event that Minor regarded as most productive in terms of sustaining diplomatic momentum occurred the day before the final council. It consisted of a meeting with Taboca, "a man of much influence" and a "great speaker."[29] Minor and King went to meet him in his village of Conchitó. There the chief entertained the two visitors, Minor reports, with "a good meal, while the Spanish flag was waving over us." Taboca took from a small box evidence of his role as a principal Choctaw diplomat, particularly as an emissary to the Americans: letters from an Englishman and an American that apparently served as recommendations, portraits of George Washington, Washington's wife, Governor Penn and others—all tokens of friendship, Minor concluded. Minor invited Taboca to Natchez, and the chief said he would not take sides during any formal session planned to conclude the Nogales diplomacy.[30]

Events, epistolary and other, underscored the importance of Minor's mission and led to Gayoso's submission of Minor's diary and a report to Carondelet in late April. Together they suggested that the matter of Nogales could be regarded as concluded with payment of compensation the Indians expected and the cessation of the commerce at Nogales to which the traders living among the Choctaws and Chickasaws objected.[31] Just before Minor's return, Gayoso responded to a request from Taskietoka for some medicine to alleviate what a delegation of Chickasaws had described as swelling in his knees. Not knowing precisely what to send, he provided some camphor in a paper marked with one cross. In addition, he sent coffee, sugar, two kegs of *tafia,* a quilted piped tomahawk, a piece of tobacco, and some paint "as a remembrance of my Friendship."[32] On the day of Minor's return to Natchez, Gayoso sent a message to Carondelet telling him that Minor had fulfilled his commission to deliver a letter to Franchimastabé and to secure from him and the other chiefs consent for the Nogales post. All that was required was a gift not to exceed two thousand pesos. He said Turner Brashears would arrive shortly with a letter from Franchimastabé. Gayoso said that as soon as Brashears—already identified by Gayoso as someone very important to win over to the Spanish side—arrived with the letter, he would write again and send along both a copy of the letter and Minor's diary. Obviously pleased and excited, Gayoso provided Carondelet in another letter of the same day a description of the site and the locations of certain structures. "It is not possible to find along the Mississippi a better place to establish a post for the defense of this Province," he wrote. Four days later Carondelet forwarded these letters as attachments to one of his own to the Spanish minister of state, the Count of Floridablanca, informing him of success in securing Nogales.[33]

A letter of April 14 from Gayoso to Carondelet reported in detail what obviously the Natchez governor regarded as a most important event: the visit of Taboca to Natchez. Understanding the import of Minor's description of him, Gayoso described him as "an old man who has had much influence at all times in his nation" and one who had been courted by both the English and the Americans, who through their letters, which the chief carefully retained, "nourish his ambition to know and to intervene in public matters." Taboca told Gayoso that American officials, including President George Washington, continued to court him and the Choctaws along with other Indian groups south of the Ohio River. Taboca brought with him to Natchez someone Gayoso described as his older son, "another who follows him," and "three relatives." He provided them lodging in his house, for, as he said, he knew that Taboca had been accustomed to being treated very well by both the English and the Americans. As the governor noted, the last time Taboca was in New York, General Washington had "treated him with great intimacy, having his house open at any hour and even recommending to him that he should frequent it often." Taboca and his retinue spent three days in Natchez.[34]

During his visit Taboca reassured the governor that both he and his nation supported the Spanish acquisition of the territory of Nogales but on condition that trade there be stopped. Gayoso told him that it would and later explained his action to Carondelet by pointing out that "all the traders of his nation are married to their [the chief's] daughters and through this means have influenced them with this idea." Gayoso concluded—perhaps a bit too optimistically—that, because the Panton stores in Pensacola and Mobile supplied all the traders, ending the trade would not be so difficult.[35]

The conversations between Gayoso and Taboca—again using the services of the trader Ebenezer Fulson as interpreter—touched on persistent competition from the Americans and the British. To counter overtures from those quarters, Gayoso said he endeavored to impress on Taboca the value of close association and cooperation with the Spanish. They discussed the activities of the Yazoo companies, and Taboca assured Gayoso that the Choctaws would never allow Americans to occupy their land. Furthermore, Taboca supported a close, defensive alliance, and Gayoso said they could count on the Spanish for help even to the extent of providing munitions should they be required. Taboca reported to the governor that General Washington had written to Franchimastabé and the whole nation to say that the United States did not need their land and that anyone who should suggest that view should be regarded as bad. Washington apparently had admitted that some people in fact did want to come to settle but then said that was not his will.[36] With regard to the Yazoo companies, Gayoso said that he told Taboca that they thought they had a right to some of their land because of a concession made to John Wood, who owed his success in securing the land grant to Taboca. The chief emphatically denied that suggestion. He explained that Wood had accompanied him to Philadelphia, but because he did not have an interpreter and was not able therefore to understand, it was not possible to make any such agreement. Taboca then went on to say that on the way to Philadelphia, Wood had given him some used breeches and other gifts to make him happy. After their arrival, Taboca said he had "scornfully" returned the breeches and gifts to Wood and even vowed that at some time when he had returned to his country he would "tie him up and scourge him for the tricks he had played."[37]

Finally, with regard to real or rumored British influence and in response to Taboca's general query as to whether "their old friends" the British might return, the two discussed the activities of one often described in the Spanish documents as the "adventurer Bowles." William Augustus Bowles, who claimed to be a Creek by virtue of marriage to a Creek *mestiza*, had appeared among the Creeks to challenge the position of Alexander McGillivray and the commercial monopoly of the Panton-Leslie traders based in Pensacola. Usually characterized in Spanish documents as an "adventurer," Bowles pursued many interests throughout the world. In the 1790s, posing as "Director General of the Creek Nation," he promoted the creation of some kind of Indian confederation under his leadership and tied commercially to traders based in the Bahama Islands.[38] Taboca admitted that he was aware of the activities of Bowles, particularly the recent sacking of a Panton store in St. Mark's at the mouth of the Apalachicola River. Reference to that event enabled Gayoso to impress on Taboca the view that Bowles was up to no good and that he was doing all he could to agitate the Talapuche Nation. Even Fulson became involved peripherally in this matter of British influence by telling Gayoso that there were some people still "who had direct correspondence with England." Furthermore, said Fulson, one Turnbull, an old inhabitant of this district, right now was in England and had written to a brother of Fulson recently to say that before long the English would return and that some Americans were working with them. Gayoso described Fulson as a man of integrity and as one attached to the Spanish government even though the brother was not.[39]

Carondelet included this letter as an attachment to his own to the Count of Floridablanca in Spain. In his letter, Carondelet provided an assessment of the general disposition of the Choctaws and then recommended, as Gayoso had earlier suggested, that a commissioner be appointed to the Choctaw Nation. He went further and suggested termination of the monopoly on trade enjoyed by the Panton, Leslie firm and the establishment of free trade between New Orleans and the various Indian nations. He recommended the appointment of Juan Delavillebeuvre as commissioner, "a sagacious and prudent man with knowledge of the Choctaw language" and one who had done much "to unite all the nation to the cause of Spain." He said the commissioner should reside in the nation, in this case at "the side of Franchimastabé, the chief of the nation." By September, Delavillebeuvre had arrived in the Choctaw Nation and established a residence in Boukfouka, a short distance from Franchimastabé's village of West Yazoo. Floridablanca and the Council of State approved the appointment at the end of the year and set his salary at just over eight hundred pesos.[40]

Given what seemed like a major diplomatic offensive from the United States, aided by Piomingo of the Chickasaws, the appointment of a Spanish commissioner to both the Choctaws and the Chickasaws and some sort of assembly to bring to a formal conclusion the Nogales matter assumed particular importance, indeed, urgency. Quite possibly the same letter to which Taboca referred as from President Washington, Henry Knox, the American secretary of war, wrote to "the chiefs and warriors of the Choctaw Nation" in February expressing the desire of President Washington "that peace shall be as firm and enduring as the mountains." Through Knox, Washington extended an invitation to four or five of them to visit him in Philadelphia, where they "will be graciously received, well treated, and sent away enriched with presents which will evidence the goodness of his heart and the friendship of the United States." About two months later, in April, William Blount, the governor of the territory of the United States south of the Ohio River, wrote to the chiefs and warriors of the Choctaw Nation affirming the friendship of the United States and inviting them to a "treaty" at Nashville. Piomingo urged Choctaws, including Franchimastabé, to attend the meeting. Although he included Franchimastabé among those he hoped would go, he did record that he had heard that "the Choctaw nation is displeased with the old chief [Franchimastabé], and they have threatened his life in consequence of his conduct with the Spaniards." Then in words that made any prospect of the Spanish winning his favor seem most unlikely, Piomingo asserted, "My advice is they shall leave Louisiana. Pay attention to my words and proceed to the treaty." Knox especially wanted to revive the spirit of Hopewell and reassure the Choctaws that, although military means might be needed to subdue some "bad Indians" in the north, peace had been achieved with the Creeks, Cherokees, Choctaws, and Chickasaws.[41]

Franchimastabé and many others seemed to take the initiative at this point. Responding to the invitation to come to Natchez, Choctaws and Chickasaws began to arrive on May 10. In the end, over three hundred met to conclude in a formal way the many months of discussions on Nogales as well as to reaffirm the commitments made at the Mobile Congress of 1784 and subsequent meetings. Some remained for more than a week filled with activities that, as described by Gayoso, sustained Indian diplomatic traditions. There were formal public meetings devoted to such rituals as smoking together, speeches, and, on the final day, a slow reading of the treaty article by article and then its signing. Many private meetings enabled key chiefs and Gayoso to work out details of the final agreement. Finally an event that always had a very important place in the social and ceremonial life of Indians, a lengthy and "splendid" ball game, as Gayoso described it, brought the proceedings to a satisfactory conclusion.[42]

Some of Gayoso's long account of the proceedings might be highlighted for what it reveals about his representation of a diplomatic process that owed much of its success to a careful respect for Indian traditions and expectations that attached much importance to gifts, ceremony, and talk.[43] Furthermore, the account reveals much about Gayoso himself and his view of such key Choctaw and Chickasaw leaders as Franchimastabé and Taskietoka. (Taboca is not recorded as being present or as a signatory of the treaty.) As Minor said he would, Franchimastabé deferred to Taskietoka, who played the principal role in securing assent to the Spanish position.[44] At the beginning, Franchimastabé went so far as to say that not only he and all the Choctaws Nation were under Taskietoka's orders, but all the Indian nations—the Cherokees, Talapuches (Creeks), Chickasaws, and Choctaws—had just made an alliance and had accepted his leadership. As a consequence, Franchimastabé said, it was Taskietoka's will that would be accepted as final.[45] Almost a year later Delavillebeuvre played on this deference to the Chickasaws and the affirmation of some kind of alliance as he worked to try to end a conflict between the Creeks and the Chickasaws by referring to the Choctaws as the "Younger Brothers" of the Chickasaws when he reported that he had asked the Choctaws to act as mediators in the conflict.[46]

Taskietoka expressed determination to conclude the matter of Nogales but, like Franchimastabé, "counted on being thanked for it," meaning that he expected gifts sufficient for payment. In a conversation with this Chickasaw leader, Gayoso reviewed the history of the question and acknowledged the failure of the English to pay for the site. Taskietoka said he was aware of the issue. He went on to offer some explanation of Franchimastabé's deference to him by telling Gayoso that it was he who was responsible for advancing the career of Franchimastabé. He said he had secured a large medal from the English for the Choctaw chief and then—with reference to Delavillebeuvre's mission of 1787—persuaded him to exchange it for a Spanish medal. For that reason, concluded Gayoso, the Chickasaw leader "considers Franchimastabé his creation." Despite the overtures from the Americans, Gayoso found Taskietoka disposed to see the Spanish as his true friends and, after this conversation, took him to the royal warehouse to show him what was available there for gifts. He pledged to turn over to him and Franchimastabé its keys in return for their compliance—a commitment that became one of the articles of the treaty. "He agreed to this," wrote Gayoso, although he insisted later on the addition of "nine kegs of powder and much brandy to satisfy the warriors."[47]

The matter seemed settled, and all that remained was the reading and signing of a treaty drafted by Gayoso and the conferral of beads and gifts in a major ceremony. Gayoso reported that he worked very hard the night before the assembly met. He arranged strings of beads for each of the chiefs, with the two longest ones signifying "the paths to peace between this country and the Chickasaw and Choctaw nations, with an equal number of pieces of tobacco" for each chief—all signs of peace. He also formulated the articles of the treaty to be read out loud and signed. Because of inclement weather the day of the gathering, Gayoso requested the use of the recently built parish church. There, he arranged chairs and a table and made sure the artillery was ready for a triple salute upon completion of the treaty. He invited the principal people of the community and surrounding area to attend. After seating the various chiefs and warriors, Gayoso delivered the opening speech in which he reviewed the Nogales matter. Taskietoka responded by saying both the Chickasaws and the Choctaws were now ready to accept the cession. Gayoso called up the quartermaster of the garrison and ordered him to hand to Taskietoka the keys of the royal warehouse and then said to the chief, "These are the keys to the warehouses where the goods belonging to His Majesty are to be found, take them, and whatever is in them divide among your chiefs and warriors until they are satisfied." "In this way," he continued, "[I am] putting at your disposition whatever I have, [so that] you will not be able to say that I have treated you with stinginess" and "that neither the Chickasaw nor Choctaw nations will have the least wish to demand from Spain another thing for the disputed lands." Gayoso reviewed the precise boundaries agreed upon, and the various chiefs and warriors concurred. Thereupon the governor presented the white beads "as the sign of purest friendship." Pipes were smoked and the cannons fired. After a reading of the treaty article by article, the important Indian chiefs, Spanish officials, certain residents of Natchez, and even some Americans who were passing through—all in the hope that they could testify as to the "legality," as Gayoso put it, of the proceedings—signed the document. This treaty "of friendship" clarified boundaries in such a way as to establish clear Spanish title to the Nogales site. Three articles then stipulated that the Spanish would provide the Indians with substantial gifts, including the privilege of taking from the royal warehouses "whatever they wished to be satisfied."[48]

Gayoso reports that at the end Franchimastabé sounded a sour note and thereby provided him with an opportunity for a reprimand—a gesture that, he reported, won the approbation of other chiefs. After a meal provided by Gayoso for the principal participants, Franchimastabé questioned openly whether the commitment to provide gifts would be honored. With a "firm and dry air and fixing on him," Gayoso told him that he had been scrupulous in keeping his word with regard to all that had been agreed and that Franchimastabé contradicted himself and "the knowledge of everyone." Gayoso describes Franchimastabé as humiliated by these words and the other Indian chiefs, including Taskietoka, openly angry with the chief. Franchimastabé thereupon apologized, and Gayoso concluded that it was more Turner Brashears who was the snake in the grass. It "was Brashears, who surely had advised his chief to speak in those terms, since it was known that it did not proceed from the heart of Franchimastabe," wrote Gayoso.

After that, all went well. The participants used the two following mornings to pass out the gifts. Taskietoka distributed his by hand. Afternoons were devoted to the ball game that Gayoso described "as one of the most splendid that has ever been seen." Both Franchimastabé and Taskietoka and several other chiefs remained as guests in his house; at the same time, the governor provided much drink in the Indian camp and kept Ebenezer Fulson there every night so that he might overhear all the conversations. As he put it in his report, "when these people enjoy their drink they speak their feelings without disguise." Fulson reported no words of discontent. Taskietoka had to be placated with an additional gift of some one hundred pesos arranged privately, and both he and Franchimastabé were given "a quantity of trifles"; several Indians were given some seventy pesos each to compensate for horses that were either lost or stolen. It was not until the nineteenth of the month, nine days after the meetings began, that the last Indians left Natchez.[49]

Some measure of the success of the Natchez assembly can be seen in the response to the American governor's invitation to the Choctaws and Chickasaws to come to Nashville for a similar meeting in the summer. William Blount sent an emissary, Anthony Forster, with his invitation. Forster met in council with chiefs of both groups in June. He reported that the Chickasaws generally supported participation. "Mountain Leader" (Piomingo) took an active role and "appeared to embrace the view of the United States, and exhibit unequivocal marks of his attachment to the United States." Other chiefs seemed to go along with him. The one exception was the "Hair-lipped King" (Taskietoka). On the other hand, the Choctaws seemed more divided, and the council that met in one village with Forster ended on a discordant note when "a mob of drunken Indians" broke up the assembly and "tore the peace belt in pieces." Forster reported that "one Brassheart" had given a talk that dissuaded most Choctaws from accepting the invitation by suggesting that the red ink in the American letters meant that Americans intended to kill Choctaws at the assembly. "Brassheart" was no doubt Turner Brashears, who now actively promoted "the Spanish interest." Blount saw him as the principal reason why so few Choctaws came to Nashville: "This Brassheart was the only man who had any taffia in the town where the council assembled, and it was no doubt he who made the party drunk, and induced them to tear the belts."[50] The author of Franchimastabé and Taboca's letter now seemed firmly on the side of the Spanish, a fact not too pleasing to Blount who, in addition to getting Foster's report, had just received news from the trader Ben James that "every white man in this nation must be dependent to the Spanish government."[51]

6
Paths to Boukfouka and the Tombigbee, 1792–1793

Gayoso portrayed the Natchez assembly and treaty as a success in concluding a process to foil the American settlement at Nogales and secure better relations with both the Choctaws and the Chickasaws. Four key people—the Choctaw chiefs Franchimastabé and Taboca, the trader Turner Brashears, and the Chickasaw "king" Taskietoka—seemed now on the side of the Spanish. These people continued to play significant roles as Spanish officials sought to build on the success of this assembly to strengthen ties with Indian groups. They were joined by others, and their efforts resulted in two more events of some importance within the year that followed: a November assembly in New Orleans to propose a confederation of Indians aligned with the Spanish and a treaty the following May ceding to the Spanish the site of the former French Fort Tombecbe for a new Spanish post. The discussion in this chapter will focus on the diplomacy associated with preliminary efforts to create a confederation and the May treaty at Boukfouka ceding land on the Tombigbee to the Spanish.

Building on the experience and successes leading to the 1792 Natchez congress, Gayoso continued to play the major Spanish role in pursuit of these objectives. Shortly after submitting his report on the Natchez assembly, he prepared an analysis of "the political state of Louisiana" to inform the new Spanish minister of state, the Conde de Aranda, about the "Plaza and District of Natchez" and to recommend measures to make the entire province, of which his jurisdiction was part, a more effective barrier "against the ambitious intentions of the United States."[1] His observations about the United States in this essay reflected an awareness of ongoing diplomatic negotiations between Spanish representatives and American officials over the issues of boundary and navigation of the Mississippi River and evidence of a desire on the part of United States officials to achieve more pacific relations with Indian groups south of the Ohio River as a way to avoid the consequences of the more bellicose north of the river. Almost constant warfare between Americans and Indians had characterized those relations since 1789, and in November 1791 an American army suffered a major defeat in the Maumee country.[2]

The year before that military setback, the United States had created a "Territory South of the Ohio River" out of land ceded by North Carolina and appointed William Blount its governor.[3] The American secretary of war, Henry Knox, who was in charge of relations between his government and Indians, then appointed three commissioners to the major nations of that jurisdiction: James Seagrove for the Creeks, James Robertson for the Choctaws and Chickasaws, and Leonard Shaw for the Cherokees.[4] As Gayoso prepared his report for the Conde de Aranda, Blount was making preparations for his major assembly with Choctaws and Chickasaws in Nashville for August 1792, but he met a setback when Brashears intervened to discourage Choctaws from attending during the council held by Blount's emissary, Anthony Forster.[5]

In his essay, Gayoso described the United States as divided into two bodies, one that was "submissive to the government" and one that was not. The latter body, he wrote, was permeated by "the private associations of persons who are nourishing new projects," specifically the companies of North and South Carolina on the Yazoo River and of a Virginia company on the Tennessee River. Although deterred with regard to establishing a settlement at Nogales, the Yazoo speculators remained alive and well and eager to hatch new schemes adverse to the interests of Spain, he noted. Furthermore, these speculators, along with those who had populated the settlements in Kentucky, Cumberland, and Franklin, had interests, he said, that were "directly opposed to those of the rest of the United States." He noted that their agents continued to court the Indians actively and put pressure on their national government to secure navigation rights on the Mississippi River by making free use of the river the central diplomatic issue in talks between the United States and Spain.[6]

Gayoso praised the actions already taken to strengthen Louisiana, but he recommended that more be done. He lauded the creation of "a respectable squadron of galleys" for the Mississippi River and other measures to improve what he had described to Carondelet, shortly after the latter's arrival as governor-general in late 1791, as the poor state of provincial defense. To build on those accomplishments and sustain more effectively the very important treaties of friendship and commerce negotiated with the Indian nations after the American Revolution, Gayoso placed particular emphasis on one measure others had recommended: the appointment of resident commissioners to the Indian nations. The Spanish governor in Pensacola, Arturo O'Neill, who came to have major reservations about the reliability of McGillivray, had proposed such a measure in late 1786, and Delavillebeuvre had done the same after his 1787 mission to the Choctaws.[7] Up to this point, Spain had relied on only a few traders, such as Benjamin James, and chiefs like Alexander McGillivrary, all of whom proved of limited or dubious worth, even though McGillivray—still the official Spanish commissioner for the Creeks—had traveled to New York in 1790, participated in the negotiation of a treaty of friendship and commerce with the United States, and agreed to accept an annual stipend from the American government.[8]

Resident commissioners directly responsible to the governor of Louisiana, Gayoso observed, would live in the various nations as representatives of the king and work to keep the Choctaws and others "perfectly inclined toward our government." No doubt with William Augustus Bowles in mind, he suggested that such individuals would be in a position to prevent others from the outside, such as those "English of the island of Providence [*Providencia*] and Canada . . . to intrigue among them and to separate them from our side." While McGillivray seemed to be of somewhat questionable reliability, Gayoso recommended continued working with him. He even suggested that James Wilkinson be brought back into the fold, even though that person was of doubtful reliability.[9] Primary emphasis should be placed, however, on resident commissioners. "There is no other way," Gayoso repeated later, "to keep the Indian Nations friendly to our interest than to have in them our own Commissaries, persons of ability, who will put in practice the instructions you send them, winning one by one the influential Chiefs." Commissioners, by acquiring influence over the body of the Nation, "through opportune gifts, proportionate to these people," concluded Gayoso, can introduce to the diplomatic process an element already present in the management of affairs among "the civilized Nations."[10]

Gayoso's call for the appointment of resident commissioners came, however, after Carondelet had begun to act on the matter. Although Gayoso had in mind Turner Brashears for such a post among the Choctaws, Carondelet decided to appoint Juan Delavillebeuvre to be the Spanish resident commissioner in the Choctaw and Chickasaw nations and Pedro Olivier to assume that position for the Creeks. With encouragement from William Panton, who was eager to expand his trade to include Cherokees, he appointed John McDonald, a trader and former British agent who had established a Cherokee family, to represent the Spanish among the Cherokees.[11]

Although supportive of the appointment of Delavillebeuvre and delighted that there would now be a resident commissioner among the Choctaws and Chickasaws, Gayoso was also aware that he had suggested to Brashears the possibility of his assuming such a position. The Natchez governor told Carondelet that the Spanish must continue to rely on Brashears. "He is an intimate friend of Franchimastabé and married to the daughter of Taboca," he observed in a long letter of July 1792, reporting a visit of Taboca to Natchez with a letter from Brashears. Gayoso pointed out that Brashears had been successful in dissuading Franchimastabé and Taboca from going to Cumberland the next month when Americans there hoped to secure another treaty.[12]

Careful cultivation of such important chiefs as Taboca continued to be a major priority for Gayoso. When Taboca came to visit him in Natchez, he extended to this venerable chief and those close to him maximum hospitality and consideration by lodging him, his "son," and another warrior in his house. Taboca, he wrote, "is accustomed to this consideration and it is important to keep him friendly to us, for it is public knowledge that Englishmen and Americans alike always pay him court, and now more than ever it would be most prejudicial for the Americans to win him over."[13]

Both Gayoso and Carondelet recognized the importance of commissioners and traders in sustaining good relations with chiefs such as Taboca, especially now with the new American national government's placing similar people among the major Indian nations with elaborate instructions to establish good relations.[14] In this competition for Native American support, American officials often found their efforts undercut—despite the creation of some semblance of territorial government and the appointment of commissioners—by actions of state governments and the continuing "almost ungovernable nature of the frontier whites" and their constant pressure on Indian lands and encouragement to violence. Knox recognized this situation in his instructions to Blount, saying that "the Indians have constantly had their jealousies and hatred excited by the attempts to obtain their lands" and that somehow all such designs should be suspended for a long period.[15] Blount himself told Piomingo that "the United States do not want to take land from any red people; they have land enough."[16] Such words meant little to the Creeks, however, who had come to distrust Piomingo and dubbed Blount as "the dirt king" because of what they regarded as his insatiable quest for cessions of land.

The Creeks and other Native Americans were not passive in this context. They, as much as Gayoso, Carondelet, and others, worked actively to protect themselves more effectively. In 1792, Shawnees and Cherokees joined Creeks, Choctaws, and Chickasaws in this endeavor.[17] Led by Bloody Fellow of the Cherokees and Taskietoka and Ugulayacabé of the Chickasaws, these people assumed an especially important diplomatic role particularly in the effort to create what Carondelet endorsed and promoted: a confederation with some real political clout.

Indeed, the whole idea and practice of confederation had long been a part of Native American political life and was seen as a way to deal with the European invasion that began in earnest in the seventeenth century and had, by the end of the American Revolution, "solid roots."[18] Stephen Minor became aware of this fact during his second mission to the Choctaws in the spring of

1792 when he learned that Cherokees and Creeks had made overtures to Franchimastabé to effect some kind of confederation. South of the Ohio, Shawnees, joined by Chickamauga Cherokees and Creeks, had done much to maintain communication and promote unity between southern and northern Indians at a time when pressure on Indians north of the Ohio River increased with relentless ferocity, resulting in open warfare in the late 1780s and early 1790s. At that time, these groups launched a major effort to promote Indian unity as a way to thwart the American invasion.[19] Sometimes these efforts took the form of violence—as an attack on Buchanan's Station south of Nashville in September 1792—but sometimes they assumed a diplomatic character in such form as the missions of Bloody Fellow and other Cherokees, first to Philadelphia at the beginning of the year to meet the president and his secretary of war and secure a commitment to honor the treaty commitments of Hopewell (1785) and Holston (1791), then to Pensacola and New Orleans later in the year.[20]

These chiefs apparently left Philadelphia pleased with what the Americans offered, although it has been suggested that Spanish envoys then in the city "intrigued" with them and persuaded them to seek collaboration with the Spanish.[21] Regardless, their satisfaction was limited, and forces were at work supporting action to resist the Americans. According to a report submitted by David Craig in early 1792, Shawnees endeavored to persuade both Cherokees and Creeks to help them against the United States. He noted that Alexander McGillivray expressed hope that "a general confederacy should take place among the Indians" and that he, despite the fact he was now receiving an annual stipend from the American government, had sent the Cherokee chief Dragging Canoe to the Chickasaws in an effort to persuade Piomingo and his party to join.[22] In June Cherokees met in council and prepared a letter to the Spanish commandant in Mobile lamenting pressure on them from "the Virginia people" for their land. They requested all the help the Mobile commandant could give them.[23] What other American documents describe as younger chiefs and warriors found a more militant approach appealing. During a Cherokee council attended by the newly appointed American commissioner to hear reports of those who had been to Philadelphia, militants expressed concern about continued threats to their land and continued to commit random violence. They resolved to respond with violence that took the form of the attacks on Willstown and Buchanan's Station in September. Bloody Fellow argued vigorously against this course of action, however.[24]

For American officials Bloody Fellow had defined himself as a major voice in favor of peace. They concluded that role should be recognized and encouraged. One way to accomplish that was through a change in title. During a meeting with Blount at Coyatee in late May, the governor informed Bloody Fellow that the president of the United States had determined that he should from henceforth "be known and distinguished by the more honorable name of General Eskaqua."[25]

William Panton in Pensacola began to play a major role in encouraging both Cherokees and Creeks to align themselves more closely with the Spanish. At this time he was eager to expand his trading business to include the Cherokees, and he found that his economic interests blended well with both Spanish and Cherokee political interests. He therefore found receptive ears in both the governor in Pensacola, O'Neill, and Carondelet when he suggested the appointment of John McDonald, who, like Panton, had been a loyalist during the American Revolution, to be the Spanish commissioner to the Cherokees. Noting that McDonald had a family among the Cherokees and "maintains considerable influence among these people," Panton recommended that those ties be buttressed by making available "generous presents" for the new commissioner to distribute. In the fall of 1792, McDonald reported success to Panton in bringing about "an alteration in the Nation in favour of Spain." He identified Bloody Fellow and other chiefs "of the first rank" who came from different parts of the nation and could therefore be regarded as representative of it as disposed to align themselves with the Spanish. He said he would come down to Pensacola with them.[26]

At about the same time McDonald complimented himself on effecting "an alteration" in the Cherokee Nation, Delavillebeuvre sent a report to Carondelet in which he described Taskietoka as the most effective advocate of closer ties with the Spanish. After arriving as resident Spanish commissioner among the Choctaws and Chickasaws, he sought to carry out what Carondelet had given him as one of his assignments: persuading Choctaws and Chickasaws to support the formation of "a league." Despite reservations about the possibility of accomplishing such an ambitious project, in view of "the distance, dissension and the meager harmony that prevails among our neighboring nations," he reports calling an assembly after Taskietoka had come to the Choctaws about a month earlier "with a discourse and a string of beads on behalf of the Talapuche, Chauanone [Shawnee], Cheraquí, Abenaquie, Hou, Quayatonone, Mascuca nations" for the Chickasaws and Choctaws. Taskietoka's speech and work encouraged Delavillebeuvre to tell those at the assembly that because "the Americans were misleading them" and "had taken lands from the Cheroquis," they "must unite and combine their interests under the protection of the Spaniards." Delavillebeuvre urged Carondelet to give Taskietoka "a great medal of gold and a good present." "Your Lordship cannot imagine how much the king of the Chickasaws has done for us since his arrival in the Chacta nation," he concluded.[27]

The Cherokees continued on to New Orleans at the invitation of Carondelet, and there, in November, they were joined by over one thousand Choctaws, Chickasaws, and Shawnees with the intent, as Carondelet described it, to enter into a "confederation of all the Indian nations that inhabit the region enclosed by the Ohio and Mississippi Rivers, the Appalachian Mountains, and the Gulf of Mexico."[28] Carondelet included in his correspondence describing the meeting speeches made by Bloody Fellow and Taskietoka in support of the undertaking. Bloody Fellow inveighed, "with much force and energy," against "the incessant usurpations" of the Americans, and Taskietoka, citing the recommendation of the Shawnees and other Indians to the north for the creation of a confederation, urged strong support for the project.[29] Capitalizing on an awareness among those present as to what their brethren north of the Ohio River were experiencing, Carondelet offered to solicit the mediation of the king of Spain to resolve the disputes between them, whom he described as their "allies to the North," and the United States.[30] With regard to a confederation, he proposed the establishment of a permanent congress with three representatives from each of the four principal nations and urged these nations—Choctaws, Chickasaws, Creeks, and Cherokees—to refrain from conflict.[31] Responding to the advice of William Panton, who described the Cherokee chiefs as "well known" and whose talk "will have a favorable effect," Carondelet urged Bloody Fellow and his colleagues to travel to the Choctaws and Chickasaw to promote a confederation.[32]

In the following year Carondelet made the establishment of such a confederation a major goal of Spanish policy. In the end, however, his views about how such a union might be established proved too strange, perhaps too European, for the Indian world which had to accept and support it. He saw his newly appointed commissioners as means to his ends. Employing language as metaphoric as that of Piomingo and other chiefs, he told the Choctaws and Chickasaws to heed the "great chief" he had sent to them (Juan Delavillebeuvre) "to keep all the roads amongst yourselves white in order to make one strong, powerful family which, under his protection should have nothing to fear from its enemies." He also recommended that an Indian congress meet to consider the establishment of "a confederation of the Creek, Cherokee, Choctaw, and Chickasaw nations, purely defensive, under the protection of Spain." He suggested that such a congress consider at least three important issues for both Spanish and Indians: war and peace, boundaries and gifts, and the creation of a permanent congress.[33]

Carondelet saw a close relationship between the issue of war and peace and and that of boundaries. In his mind, boundary issues involved the United States, the Indian nations, particularly the Cherokees and Creeks, and Spain. On their resolution depended the achievement of peace. Of all the major Indian groups in the region south of the Ohio River, the Creeks, along with the

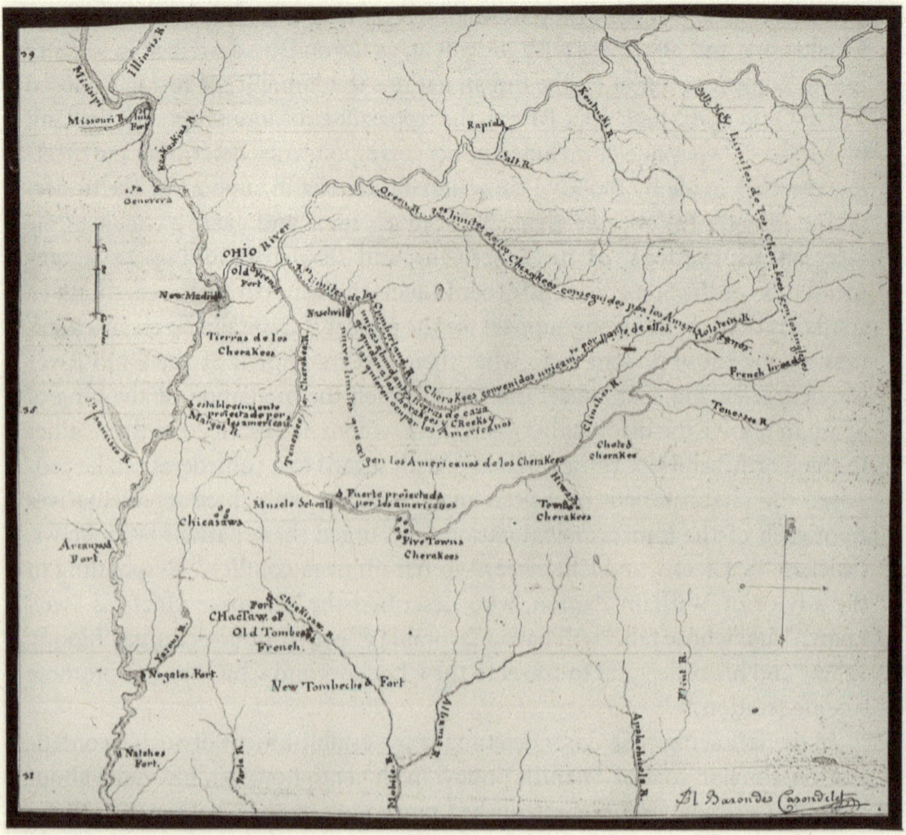

Figure 3. Confederation of Indian tribes of the Appalachian Mountains, Ohio and Mississippi rivers, attack on Cumberland by the Cherokees and Creeks (ca 1792). Courtesy of Ministerio de Cultura, Archivo Histórico Nacional, Madrid, Sección de Estado, *Legajo* 1998, *Sig.* 20. Also represented as "Map of Cherokee boundaries with the English, those secured and those assumed with North Americans to the east of the Mississippi valley." [1793–1797]. AGI, Mapas y planos de la Florida y la Luisiana, 152; Baron de Carondelet to the Conde de Aranda, New Orleans, Jan. 8, 1793, AHN, *Estado, leg.* 3898, *Reservada,* N.° 26; and in MDAH, RG 26, SPT, ledger 4, reel 4, following 612.

Chickamauga Cherokees, were the most hostile to American advances, and for that reason many Creeks turned against the Chickasaws, whom they saw as too friendly with the Americans. As a consequence, Creeks and Chickasaws tended to be in what Spanish officials saw as a state of war during most of the late 1780s and early 1790s. No confederation could be established until that conflict was resolved. Carondelet saw the creation of a permanent congress as a way to resolve conflicts, and, assuming the role of a kind of eighteenth-century Woodrow Wilson, he called upon the four nations to defer to its authority any decision for war. Such a decision would therefore be a collective one and not one made without the knowledge and consent of its members.[34]

The third issue Carondelet hoped could be resolved was that of gifts—their frequency and distribution. Like so many of his European predecessors he saw them as a major cost of empire that needed somehow to be contained. He proposed that gifts be distributed on an annual basis and in accordance with what the congress determined to be the needs of the various nations. Such an assessment, he thought, should be made after the harvest when specific needs would be clear. He suggested appropriate places for the distributions: the Barrancas de Margot (Chickasaw Bluffs) for the Cherokees and the Chickasaws; Pensacola and Apalache for the Creeks; and the Yazoo for the Large Party of the Choctaw and the Tombigbee River for those of the Small Party. With these procedures Carondelet hoped that the expectations of the Indians could be limited and that they would not travel to New Orleans or to Natchez in the expectation of receiving gifts—a habit about which Gayoso, Delavillebeuvre, and others had often complained.[35]

With these proposals, Carondelet went much further than the initiatives Gayoso had discussed in his report to the Conde de Aranda, but he saw Gayoso as the best person to bring Choctaw, Chickasaw, Creek, and Cherokee leaders together to discuss them and in the end see them as means to achieve the unity so enthusiastically promoted in New Orleans. Beginning in April 1793, Gayoso began the dissemination of news of such a congress, to be held at the ball court of Nogales at the end of June. The task of achieving those objectives proved a daunting one, as Delavillebeuvre had suggested the previous October, given problems of distance and divisions and conflicts among those to be included. A major division took the form of ongoing hostilities between Creeks and Chickasaws. In the end, the congress had to be postponed to the fall.

In his role as resident commissioner in the village of Boukfouka, a short distance from Franchimastabé's West Yazoo, Delavillebeuvre proved an important supporter for Gayoso and Carondelet. His diplomatic mission had already contributed to the attendance of about one thousand at the November New Orleans meetings with Carondelet, and in the following spring he was able to secure from a number of Choctaw chiefs a treaty allowing the Spanish to build a fort on the site of the former French fort of Tombecbé. He thereby achieved at least one of Bloody Fellow's goals of two new Spanish posts on the Tennessee and Tombigbee rivers. On his return home from New Orleans and with encouragement from Carondelet, Bloody Fellow had visited both Chickasaws and Choctaws, and he made a stop in Boukfouka. There he impressed the new resident commissioner, Delavillebeuvre, very much—"I have seen very few Savages as civilized as Bloodyfellow."[36]

Delavillebeuvre and his reports from Boukfouka to Gayoso and Carondelet provide additional valuable insight into the complex politics in this very fluid and particularistic region of villages and clans, one that eluded the kind of neat categorization implicit in Carondelet's use of the phrase "four nations." Furthermore, it was a place where the Spanish had to depend significantly on the services of traders and other people who had their own special place and interests in this world to serve as interpreters, commissioners, or brokers. Nevertheless, many of them continued to function quite effectively as promoters of Spanish interests. Delavillebeuvre perhaps stands out in this regard. Because he had done so much to advance good relations between the Spanish and the Choctaws and in the process gained much skill and knowledge during the American Revolution and the decade of the 1780s, he seemed then to be the best person to serve as resident commissioner among the Choctaws and Chickasaws. Just before his appointment, he undertook in the spring of 1792 a mission for the Spanish to Muscle Shoals, where American commissioners planned to meet with representatives from the major Indian nations of the Southeast. His instructions directed him to try to deter any American offers by inviting the Indians to either Natchez or Pensacola. As Gayoso told Brashears, who had been suggested as a possible commissioner, "it is much better that one of our principal warriors live in your country," a man "of such familiarity and probity that whatever he should tell you should be as though I were to speak it." This background, in the view of historian Jack Holmes, enabled him to achieve his greatest success at Boukfouka.[37]

The instructions given Delavillebeuvre reveal what both Gayoso and Carondelet saw as the nature and importance of this office. Both men expressed concern about the reported presence of a large army in Kentucky and the prospect of a congress in Cumberland (Nashville) to distribute gifts and secure a treaty. The instructions began by stating that the interests of the king required peace among "all the Indian nations that surround us." Then they enjoined the Indian nations not to cede any land to the United States and not to allow into Indian country anyone who was not a licensed Spanish trader or who was without a passport. With specific reference to the continued persistence of Yazoo speculators looking for land in spite of the recent Natchez Treaty and the securing of Nogales, Gayoso told Delavillebeuvre, "the United States may help them." Finally, the instructions admonished Delavillebeuvre to discourage the Indians from living in idleness and to "apply themselves to hunting or agriculture so that they can live independently and not in reliance on gifts that we might provide."[38]

Gifts, however, could not be avoided; Gayoso especially realized their continued importance and that of other objects and gestures as essential for the preservation of diplomatic paths and the creation of new ones. Gayoso told

Carondelet that Delavillebeuvre must have gifts to secure his position: "it is the first *entrada* of a commissioner, he is going to live among them and therefore needs something to distribute among friends." Gayoso noted again, however, the danger of having too many gifts and thereby encouraging Indian dependence on them. He also observed that the commissioner needed a flag for his house and said he had supplied Delavillebuevre with the one from his galiot, *La Viglilante*.[39]

Again, revealing sensitivity to other native customs, namely that an official person "speak through the mouth of someone else," interpreters were appointed for Delavillebeuvre. Gayoso first appointed yet another non-Spaniard to that position, Benjamin Fooy. Dutch by birth but, like McDonald, Brashears, James, and so many other traders, part of Indian society through marriage, Fooy had come to America and eventually settled as a trader among the Chickasaws and Choctaws. Gayoso described him as one "who speaks perfectly French, English, Chickasaw, and Choctaw." Fooy later assumed the position of Spanish commissioner to the Chickasaws. Delavillebeuvre continued as commissioner to the Choctaws, and Simon Favre, who had worked with Delavillebeuvre during the 1787 mission to the Choctaws, served as his official interpreter. "He [Favre] is the best one in the province, with a great influence over the Indians, and he knows how to lead them firmly," Delavillebeuvre commented.[40]

Delavillebeuvre received news of his appointment as commissioner in Atacapas where he was serving as commandant and arrived at his new post in late August "at point of death," he recorded. His debilitated condition did not, however, impede his getting to work immediately and submitting some lengthy and opinionated reports. During the trip, which took six days from Bayou Pierre, he reported suffering an attack of fever "more virulent than ever." Lacking "spiritual or temporal aid," he told Carondelet that he had managed to pull himself "out of danger with much hot water." After visiting Franchimastabé's village and making his first speech, he went to the area of the Small Party, where he decided to settle. Delavillebeuvre told Carondelet that when Favre learned of his coming as commissioner, he had a "comfortable hut" built for him. He said he decided to live there because he would find life "simpler." Furthermore, he seemed to want to maintain some detachment from Franchimastabé, whom he found about to leave for Mobile with Turner Brashears in response to an invitation from the commandant there, Manuel de Lanzos. "He is being spoilt by being asked everywhere," commented Delavillebeuvre; "he will become more and more troublesome." Delavillebeuvre did report, however, that Franchimastabé had given two American medals he had to Brashears to send to Gayoso. Furthermore, the newly arrived commissioner found Franchimastabé's village an unpleasant place—perhaps because he was still recov-

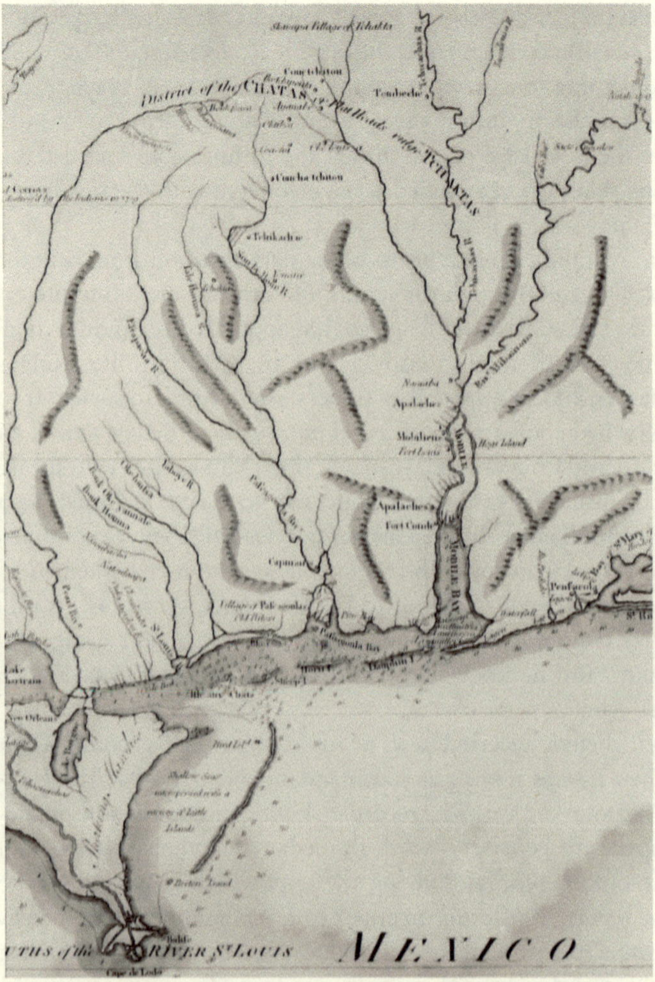

Figure 4. Detail from Map of Louisiana from D'Anville's Atlas showing a "Boukfouca" and "Tombecbe," 1788. The location of Boucfouca has support in written documents, including the correspondence of Delavillebeuvre, but Tombecbe, where the Spanish located their Fort Confederation, should be on a latitude with the mouth of the Yazoo River and Nogales. Courtesy of The Historic New Orleans Collection, Accession No. 1949.22 i, ii.

ering from his trip and illness—filled, he wrote, with "nothing but drunkards who expose one all the time to the risk of being insulted and molested." On a more positive note, he found Brashears "trustworthy" and therefore able to keep him informed about what was going on in Franchimastabé's village, a place he said was only two hours away. His finding West Yazoo to be a place filled with drunkards reinforced his recommendation to Carondelet that everything be done to forbid the introduction of liquor into the Choctaw Nation. "It is coming from everywhere and is making the Indians nasty and insolent. Those who are obliged to live among them suffer from this fact," he concluded.[41]

Delavillebeuvre set out to secure as much information as he could about Blount's assembly in Nashville, which occurred at about the time he took up residence as commissioner. Relying principally on information of a trader in the Chickasaw Nation he identified as "Naquânse," who accompanied the Chickasaws there and served as an interpreter, Delavillebeuvre reported that over five hundred Chickasaws led by Piomingo and Ugulayacabé and just over one hundred Choctaws went and remained there eighteen days. Perhaps reflecting the influence of Brashears, only two Choctaws went from the western division, or Large Party; the others came from the Small Party and included Tloupoue Nantla, a chief who possessed a large medal given by the Americans, and thirteen captains, including a son of Benjamin James. Delavillebeuvre reported they were led by "Jean Pchiline" (John Pitchlyn), a trader, whom Blount described as "a warm active man, and a friend to the United States" with substantial influence over the Choctaws. Probably because Pitchlyn had taken an oath of allegiance to Spain and was perceived to have violated it by going to Cumberland, Delavillebeuvre decided he should be arrested. Gayoso concluded, however, he should be pardoned. During the assembly the Americans distributed "twenty-two commissions" but no medals and to the chiefs and warriors a quantity of gifts consisting of limburg and woolen blankets, powder, and—in the absence of ball—lead ingots. He said that they were not given any scissors, knives, vermilion, or kettles "and only three rifles to the principal chiefs." Other than expressing a resolve to "destroy the Kickapoos," the Americans did not mention war. The Americans proposed to begin trading with the Chickasaws and Choctaws on a bayou of the Cherokee (Tennessee) River known as Bear Creek. Although the prospect of trade seemed pleasing, the Chickasaws apparently told Blount that the proposed site would probably not survive attacks by the Talapoosas (Talapuches), who "killed their men even in the midst of their towns, and stole all their horses." They suggested Cumberland as a better place, for, as reported by Delavillebeuvre "the young men who went in that direction to hunt could sell them their furs." Finally, Delavillebeuvre reported, Blount named four Chickasaw chiefs—Payemingo (Piomingo), Ugulayacabé, Mongoulachamingo, and Tchinabé—to go to Philadelphia the next spring to meet President Washington, "where once there they might expect to be fully compensated for their troubles."[42]

The meetings in Nashville, according to Delavillebeuvre, pleased both the Choctaws and the Chickasaws who attended, and they made it clear the Spanish would have to respond with something better. The Choctaws and Chickasaws were immensely satisfied with the gifts received, he said, and the Chickasaws in particular "are praising the Americans to the skies, saying they did not speak harshly to them and did not ask to buy land of them as they had been told." Eventually a regular trade did begin between the Americans and the Choctaws of the eastern division, or Small Party. A Choctaw chief, Tloupouyenantla (Ilepoonenaatla), who along with three Chickasaw chiefs had been given an American medal, expressed pleasure with this meeting with Blount at what he described as a "middle ground, where we hope to meet often."[43]

Reacting to these reports, Gayoso emphasized to Carondelet "the necessity of our treating the same Indians with generosity and skill to check the Americans." He then supported what Carondelet had recommended about the distribution of gifts: that they be provided at one place and one time. "The continuous gifts that are given to the Indians are not of much consideration," he pointed out, "but as we distribute them to each individual in proportion to how they present themselves it does not enlarge the total of the gift." Providing the gifts all together at one time and place, he concluded, would dramatize the generosity with which "we treat them"; besides, "it would discourage them from bothering us between times" and, in addition "to leaving the Indians more content," it "would be beneficial to the royal treasury."[44]

Delavillebeuvre began and sustained something of a diplomatic offensive of his own that might be interpreted as a response to the American initiatives culminating in the Nashville meeting and certainly deriving encouragement from Taskietoka's speech and its advocacy of alliance with the Spanish. He called a meeting in the "Large Part" and delivered a talk on behalf of Carondelet. He told the Choctaws that, rather than being deceived by "isolated white men" and drawn into a war along with other Indians, "it was their duty to join the Chickasaws, the Talapoosas, and the Cherokees in order to prevent these same whites from invading their lands, which they covet."[45] He conveyed similar thoughts to members of the Small Party in an address delivered in the village of Atchontchouba on the third of September. There he reminded them of promises they had made at the Congress of Mobile always to be "faithful to the Spanish nation" and "never enter into any treaty, either of friendship or trade, with any foreign nation without first consulting your Father the Governor." The Spanish, he said, had promised "to care for the chiefs, warriors, women, and children, to furnish villages with traders and with necessary merchandise at a fair price to clothe your women and children" and "to support you against your enemies." Chiding them for admitting "several bad characters" who spread false promises and caused ill will, he emphasized the importance of not allowing any white foreigner into the nation without a passport from the Spanish governor or one of his commandants. Once again he urged union with the Chickasaws, Cherokees, and Tallapoosas "from whom you should never be separated" so that they might be able to drive away any "ill-mentioned white man" who might attempt to seize their lands or to prevent any armed foreign nation to pass through their territory to attack neighbors or friends. Delavillebeuvre found somewhat later the Choctaws of the Small Party to be those closest to the Spanish.[46]

Manuel de Lanzos, the Spanish commandant in Mobile, reinforced these points when he met with a large group of Choctaw chiefs and warriors at San Estevan on the Tombigbee River or possibly farther north at the site of the former French Fort Tombecbé in late September. Franchimastabé may have been among them, for Delavillebeuvre had reported that chief about to set out for Mobile with Brashears. Lanzos reported that in addition to fifteen chiefs, just over two hundred warriors, ten women, and seven children came to that meeting. Speaking on behalf of "the general chief of the province" to assure them of the friendship and protection of "the great emperor of Spain," he urged them not to be seduced "by any foreigners who under the guise of friendship might introduce themselves and end by appropriating your belongings and territories." He cited the Shawnee, Cherokee, and Abenaqui nations as people who had been "seduced by the bait of a first present in the hope of receiving another like it." Lanzos pointed out that, unlike other nations, "our great emperor does not desire to take over your lands." Furthermore, he "does not desire that other nations should take them, as for instance, the Americans, who covet them as they have shown and still show as regards their neighbors, being always desirous of encroaching." Lanzos ended by saying that their "Great Father" above all wanted to maintain peace, and he urged that they "treat gently all the whites who reside in your village unless you suspect them of being inimical to your interests." Above all, he said they should not kill anyone except in self-defense. Harmony, he concluded, should be the great objective.[47]

Spanish officials such as Lanzos certainly were important in conveying the sentiments of Carondelet and helping the new commissioner by so doing. For Delavillebeuvre, however, the Chickasaw king Taskietoka proved to be a more effective voice. He repeatedly described him a strong advocate of Spanish interests, continuing the role he had played during the Natchez assembly of the previous May where he proved instrumental in persuading Franchimastabé finally to give his assent to the treaty. Delavillebeuvre found that Taskietoka had refused to go to Cumberland in August and that he had quarreled with both Ugulayacabé and Piomingo over the matter. Instead, he set out for the "Talapoosa" Nation and returned accompanied by beads and tobacco with the message from them for the Choctaws to warn them to beware of the Americans, who sought only "to seize their lands and enslave their women and children."

The king of the Chickasaws "is carrying you in his heart," Delavillebeuvre told Gayoso.[48]

Delavillebeuvre sought to emphasize continued strong support for the Spanish among both the Chickasaws and the Choctaws. He reported in one letter to Gayoso information that Ugulayacabé's attendance at the Cumberland meeting was solely for the purpose of finding out what happened "to make a report of it to our governor," a representation that contrasts with that of the official minutes. They depicted a rather impressive and flamboyant Ugulayacabé, who participated actively in the proceedings. Characterizing him as "a great man," the minutes said that "in council, he ranks among the first of his nation; has a considerable property, is a large man, of a dignified appearance; he appeared at the conference in scarlet and silver lace, and in the heat of the day with a large crimson silk umbrella over him."[49] Trade may have developed between the Choctaws of the Small Party and Americans, but Delavillebeuvre—perhaps too optimistically—told Carondelet that its chiefs, particularly "Mingopouscuche" of Conchak, "all have our interests at heart."[50] His conclusion that the Talapoosas were warning the Choctaws "to beware of being deceived by the Americans seeking to seize their lands and to enslave their women and children, as was the case of the Cherokees" found further credibility in Taskietoka's information that the Talapoosa Creeks remained very hostile to American interests.[51]

Helped by the positive views expressed in these reports, Gayoso remained sanguine about prospects of continued success in good relations with the various Indian nations. With regard to the large number of gifts the Americans handed out at Cumberland, he told Delavillebeuvre that he could easily convince the Indians "that we give them much more and more timely, they can carry them to their houses, and they don't have to go as far as Cumberland." To Delavillebeuvre's list of chiefs favorably disposed to the Spanish, Gayoso added Franchimastabé, Taboca, Itelegana, Sulesmastabé, and Stonahuma. He then mentioned two traders "upon whom I have the greatest confidence," Turner Brashears and Benjamin James.[52]

In separate letters he added two more to the list of friendly and valuable traders, Hardy Perry and John Turnbull. Perry, like so many other traders, had settled among the Chickasaws, married, and had children and even grandchildren there. After lengthy conversations with Perry, Gayoso concluded that although this trader had always adhered to the interests of the country of his birth, he had "never opposed ours." He was an "intimate friend" of Piomingo and promised to bring this chief to Natchez after the latter's visit to the Americans, an offer that Gayoso said flattered him very much "because I want to understand the way of thinking of said chief."[53] Gayoso assessed him as "a fine man and one of importance in the Chickasaw nation."[54] Like Perry, Turnbull had established kinship ties through his Chickasaw wife and their children. Carondelet recognized his importance by granting him a concession to establish a store in Mobile in spite of objections from William Panton, who accused him of trading illegally with both Choctaws and Chickasaws and encouraged him to establish one at the Ecors à Margo, or Chickasaw Bluffs, a site then coveted by both Americans and Spaniards.[55] With a Turnbull store at the Chickasaw Bluffs, the Spanish position would be much enhanced. "If the Americans try to eject us from that place to which they have no more right than we," Carondelet argued, "the Chickasaws will oppose them because Turnbull has children in that nation; and we shall in that way unite all the nations against them."[56] Although he had participated in the 1781 Natchez uprising against the Spanish, Turnbull eventually returned to Spanish territory, worked for a short time in the Mobile trading firm of Mather and Strother, then settled on a plantation near Baton Rouge. Coker and Watson suggest that, along with Gayoso, he may have developed an interest in trade based in Nogales. In time Turnbull's influence with the Chickasaws came to be seen as crucial for the establishment of the post at Chickasaw Bluffs that became the Spanish San Fernando de las Barrancas.[57]

Of all the chiefs who seemed important to both Delavillebeuvre and Gayoso, Bloody Fellow continued to loom especially large in their correspondence of late 1792. After the November assembly in New Orleans where they had asked help of the Spanish to check "the usurpations of American settlements west of the Appalachians," the Cherokees headed by Bloody Fellow did as Carondelet and Panton had urged and went first to Natchez and then to the Choctaws and Chickasaws.[58] They remained in Natchez for about two weeks in December, after which Gayoso provided a lengthy account of their conversations, emphasizing what he did to make the chiefs happy and impress them "with respect to the Spanish nation." He said that he lodged them in the Hospital and told them that they might come every day to have breakfast with him. For their other meals, he said he provided "ample rations." The governor's house served as the venue for the discussions, where, wrote Gayoso, after their arrival on December 18, "they behaved with the greatest discretion without speaking a word about their business until after eating." Talks centered on how the Cherokees, by accepting the protection of the Spanish king, could assure themselves assistance. Gayoso suggested that the Spanish serve as mediators between them and the United States with regard to the questions of lands wrongly taken and the establishment of permanent boundaries. They apparently welcomed that commitment and warmly endorsed the idea of calling a congress of the chiefs of the neighboring nations to be presided over by a commissioner of the king. Bloody Fellow urged, however, that it be held at a place called the Hickory Ground below the falls on the Mobile River rather than on the Yazoo.

Additional comments of Bloody Fellow as recorded by Gayoso suggested that much work of a diplomatic nature needed to be accomplished before such an assembly might meet. Bloody Fellow offered some observations about the New Orleans meeting that undercut somewhat Delavillebeuvre's fulsome praise of Taskietoka. He told Gayoso he had met both Franchimastabé and Taskietoka and had talked with them but found he could not rely much upon what was said "because they were always drunk." More important, he found that they were not keen about joining a league or confederation that would include the Cherokees because of the great distance between them. Gayoso saw an opportunity to break down barriers between the Cherokees and at least these particular Choctaw and Chickasaw leaders by encouraging the chief and his companions to pursue more diplomacy by returning to their country through both the Choctaw and Chickasaw nations. There Gayoso told Bloody Fellow he could talk again with Franchimastabé and others because, as Gayoso put it, "the Choctaw Nation greatly enjoyed hearing words and were accustomed to forget them if they were not repeated often." With regard to a visit to the Chickasaws, Gayoso suggested that, given divisions among them, Bloody Fellow try to meet separately with Piomingo "to win him to the side of reason and to re-establish the King of that Nation in all his power."

Finally, Gayoso proposed that Bloody Fellow, because he had with him "a son of good age to be educated," leave the boy with him for that purpose. The chief said that had been his wish, but he had not dared to tell the governor because it might be imprudent to ask without the means to pay for the expenses. Gayoso said he would take care of the education of the boy, for, as he wrote to Carondelet, "I believe it very important that those young men who some day should govern our friends the Indian Nations have a Spanish education and heart." Bloody Fellow accepted Gayoso's offer on condition that the boy would be treated "in the same way that we are accustomed to treat the sons of noblemen." He asked that the boy go to New Orleans to "learn to speak, to read, and to write" and then to Spain for further education—an education he thought might take seven or eight years to complete. He even asked that he might bring another son in the course of the year for the same reasons. Gayoso agreed and handed Bloody Fellow a passport for that purpose. Both agreed the boy should assume the Christian name of Charles.[59]

After leaving Natchez, Bloody Fellow and the other Cherokees then passed through both the Chickasaw and the Choctaw nations. The governor had asked Bloody Fellow to carry with him two letters, one addressed to Piomingo and Ugulayacabé and the other to Hardy Perry. The first included one from Carondelet. Both expressed in general terms Spanish friendship for the Chickasaws. "Come be my Friends, my arms are opened to press you to my heart; and give you proof of my sincerity," intoned Gayoso. He wrote Perry because he saw that trader as a means to reassure both Governor Blount and Governor Telfair of Georgia of his desire to reconcile the interests of everyone and thereby achieve peace and to persuade both Piomingo and Ugulayacabé to come to see him. "My policy is entirely bent towards bringing peace about," he assured Perry.[60]

Bloody Fellow stayed with Delavillebeuvre in the house of "the beloved man," as he described Delavillebeuvre, and was "well-received" there. The two discussed the plan for a congress to consider the formation of a confederation and agreed that the site of the former French Fort Tombecbé should be the place for the meeting. As mentioned, Delavillebeuvre found him to be one of the most civilized and delightful people he had met and preferable to many white men.[61] Like Gayoso—who had asked Bloody Fellow to do what he could to bring about peace between the Chickasaws and the Creeks—Delavillebeuvre deemed him valuable as a mediator, in this case for the purpose of effecting some kind of reconciliation between the two Chickasaw chiefs Taskietoka and Piomingo.[62]

After spending twelve days with Delavillebeuvre, Bloody Fellow and his entourage traveled to Piomingo's village of Tchoukafala. While there they provided Carondelet an assessment of the conflict between the Chickasaws and the Creeks. Bloody Fellow agreed with Piomingo's view that the Creeks had started it. "You desire to have all roads white," he wrote, "but the Creeks have just stained them with blood spreading the blood of the Chickasaws which fact will spoil our way and consequently our talk." He accepted what Piomingo himself had told Carondelet in a letter dated the same day: that Creeks, using ammunition supplied by the Spanish, had killed one of Piomingo's warriors and, as a consequence, Piomingo seemed bent on making trouble. Bloody Fellow said he would "spare no Paine in talking to Piomingo," whom he described as "my old friend" and able to speak his tongue. The Cherokee chief repeated his recommendations that the Spanish should place forts on the Tombigbee and Tennessee rivers and—despite the conflict between Creeks and Chickasaws—once again endorsed the idea of a "general meeting with all Nations." He said that even Piomingo had proposed such an idea.[63]

Delavillebeuvre's letters to both Carondelet and Gayoso from Boukfouka during the winter and on into the spring of 1793 continued to discuss all these matters and others. The letters project the image of a commissioner working very hard entertaining frequent visitors, gathering information, writing letters, and always handing out gifts. Indeed, the time required to prepare correspondence seemed so great that Delavillebeuvre asked Gayoso to send him a soldier "who writes a beautiful hand" to relieve him. He said his eyesight was failing and that perhaps his writing was not too clear. He sent out frequent requests for specific items to have on hand for presents, commenting that the commissioner must always have merchandise for such a purpose on hand. "The English and American Commissaries have spoiled the Indians by giving presents in great profusion, without which they do not respond," he wrote Gayoso. "The most rhetorical and beautiful talks scarcely cause any attention unless adorned with red and blue blankets." He asked Carondelet to understand that his frequent visits to the Choctaws, all requiring gifts to distribute, did not mean that he had become "a beggar like they are." Rather, he said, "they are "simple folk whom presents move more than all speeches adorned with much rhetoric." Delavillebeuvre specifically requested limburg, blue silk shirts embroidered in vermilion, silk handkerchiefs, powder and balls, rifles, and white summer blankets. He identified certain goods as appropriate for the summer: limburg, Indian shirts, taffy, vermilion, knives, *bucheson,* red and white flannel cloth, little black and white beads, powder, balls, and some guns. He suggested that the best place to distribute gifts to the Choctaws would be the Tombigbee district, possibly the site of the former French fort.

He continued to make forthright assessments of individuals and groups and recommend ways to advance Spanish interests. He saw the Chickasaws as quite different from the Choctaws. The former he found "much more cunning." Of the less cunning Choctaws, he characterized the Large Party as "cowards of the first order, Franchimastabé being first, on whom the French never relied." He concluded that Franchimastabé had little sympathy for the Cherokees; indeed, he and other Choctaws accused them of stealing their horses every time they went hunting in the north. As noted, he concluded that the Spanish could rely more on the Choctaws of the Six Villages and the Small Party, even though many of the latter came away from Cumberland very happy with their treatment there and had proceeded to develop trade relations with the Americans. The Creek-Chickasaw conflict took much of his time, and he devoted some attention to Carondelet and Gayoso's desire to establish an additional post on the Mississippi River at Chickasaw Bluffs—what he referred to as the "Margot River project." All of these activities he found challenging and at times frustrating. He admitted that he had a great desire to see his family but concluded, "the Zeal that I have for the king's service will always be more important."[64]

While Delavillebeuvre often found himself weighed down by activity that seemed to achieve little, an event of May 1793 pleased Carondelet and provided the commissioner with reward. He was able then to report to both the Louisiana governor and Gayoso the accomplishment of one of Bloody Fellow's recommendations, one much encouraged by Carondelet. By means of a treaty with a group of Choctaw chiefs, Delavillebeuvre secured thirty square *arpents* of land on bluffs along the Tombigbee River—the site of the 1730s French fort—for the Spanish to build a fort of their own and establish a store. Taking advantage of the generally favorable disposition of chiefs of the Small Party of the Choctaws, he reported that he had quickly assembled twenty-six large and small medal chiefs on May 12 to agree to the cession of land and a reaffirmation of the Choctaw-Spanish alliance. To help persuade the chiefs, Delavillebeuvre promised the establishment of a store there to supply the Choctaws with trade goods. The negotiations, which Delavillebuevre characterized as difficult because of probable opposition of Americans in Cumberland, the unreliability of some Choctaws, and the known opposition of such Chickasaw chiefs as Piomingo and Ugulayacabé, occurred in his residence and took only one day. Delavillebeuvre sent the signed document posthaste to New Orleans "by two-mounted young men who are to travel day and night to announce this news to the Baron," he told Gayoso. He went on to note that the Choctaws (probably referring to those Choctaws such as Franchimastabé who did not attend) did not know anything of this until two days before the meeting when "it was necessary to inform them." Delavillebeuvre expressed hope that news would not reach the Chickasaws for some time and that therefore the Americans might not "create any obstacles." He noted that the governor general had said that he would send workmen to begin work on the fort as soon as he received news of the treaty, a commitment not fulfilled.[65]

Quite understandably, Carondelet greeted this news with enthusiasm, for securing the site provided him with much encouragement with regard to the project for an Indian confederation.[66] He interpreted the event as one of major geopolitical significance. Commenting on the news to the captain general in Havana, Luis de Las Casas, his father-in-law, the governor emphasized the strategic position of the site, noting that it would provide more security to land drained by the major rivers of the region, the Mississippi, the Tombigbee and Mobile, and the Yazoo. He observed that it tied the Choctaws more firmly to Spain and undercut some of the "intrigues" of Governor Blount to enlarge American influence among the Chickasaws. With regard to the latter, he emphasized the value of the establishment of a store there by the House of Panton. No doubt with Bloody Fellow and the Cherokees in mind, he noted that with this additional post the Spanish would be in a better position to assist the Cherokees as they sought to defend their lands between the Tennessee and Cumberland rivers. He recommended the use of the "soft stone" (probably limestone) for the construction of a fort that "will be eternal." Because of what he saw as a signal accomplishment on the part of Delavillebeuvre carried out under very difficult circumstances during a year in which he suffered often from lack of supplies, he recommended that the commissioner be promoted to lieutenant colonel and receive an appropriate increase in salary. He did not forget the importance of Simon Favre as interpreter and proposed a salary increase for him.[67]

Delavillebeuvre could well feel some sense of accomplishment with the achievement of this agreement, but as time passed he expressed frustration over delays in building the fort. He repeatedly told both Gayoso and Carondelet that the post needed to be built promptly so as to provide substance to the Spanish commitment to expanded trade and protection and to assure that the Choctaws would not regard him "as the greatest liar there ever was." Work finally began the following spring of 1794, several months after the major assembly to create the framework of a confederation of Chickasaws, Choctaws, Creeks, and Cherokees. When completed, the fort was called "Confederation," in honor of the Nogales treaty's provision for the establishment of an "offensive and defensive alliance of all four Indian nations under the protection of Spain." As such it aspired to be a kind of capital of the new confederation—"a symbol of Spain's commitment to the Southern Indians," in the words of historian James Pate. And, appropriately, Delavillebuevre became its commandant.[68]

7
Tangled and Twisted Paths to Nogales

As they did in other parts of the world, forts in this region often turned out to be much less than their creators intended or expected, or as people later wanted to see them.[1] Like the earlier French Fort Tombecbé, the Spanish "Fort Confederation" might be so regarded. Much to Delavillebeuvre's dismay—for he saw his credibility with the Choctaws threatened—the building of it was delayed, as was the holding of the assembly to create the confederation in honor of which it was named. Contrary to Carondelet's recommendation, the fort was built of wood and not stone, and the confederation turned out to be one in name only.[2] One can find much of the explanation for these differences in the vagaries of politics and diplomacy—all of which enrich the irony in the inscription that appears on a plaque installed on the site by the Colonial Dames of Alabama in 1935 on the two-hundredth anniversary of the establishment of the French fort: "Here Civilization met Savagery, and the Wilderness beheld the Glory of France." The "glory" of France in this region, if there was any, proved transient, as did the later Spanish.

A somewhat more accurate text would somehow endeavor to summarize the complexities associated with the diplomacy and politics associated with it, which, in this case, led to Spanish withdrawal. Too many words that don't lend themselves to commemorative plaques would be required, however, and they would not lend themselves to heroic notions of glory. Continued factionalism and conflict among Indians, exacerbated by the diplomatic and commercial initiatives of Americans, challenged both the Spanish and Indian efforts to achieve an order that such a fort appropriately symbolize. For those like Gayoso, Taskietoka, and Bloody Fellow who thought such goals might be achieved by means of additional Spanish posts and a confederation, such obstacles had somehow to be met and surmounted. They were not daunted by sustaining persistent talk and negotiation. As a consequence, another major assembly gathered, this time near the site of the new Spanish post at Nogales, to

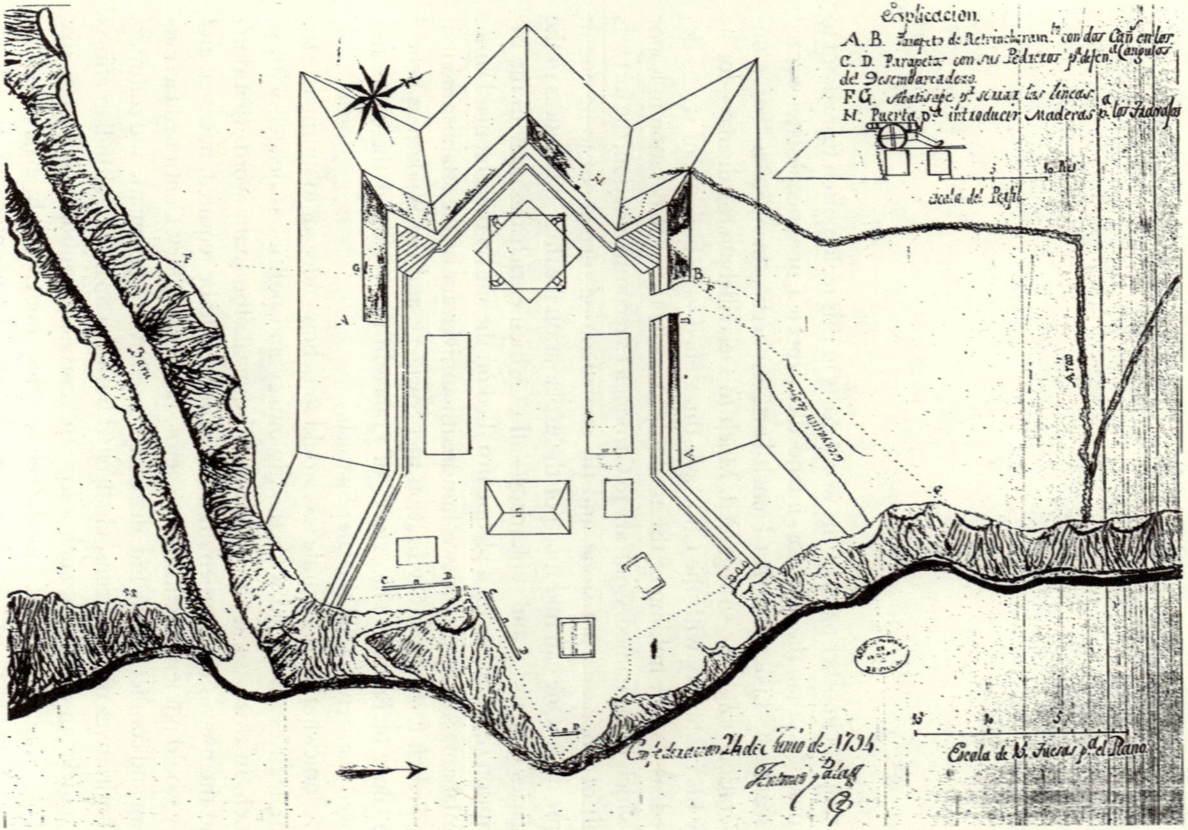

Figure 5. Plan for a Fort Confederation, signed by Antonio Palau, June 24, 1794. Courtesy of the Ministerio de Educación, Cultura y Deporte, AGI, Mapas y planos de la Florida y la Luisiana, 163.

produce a treaty calling for confederation. A discussion of that talk and of the obstacles it sought to overcome provides the substance of the narrative that follows.

Factionalism and feuding involving principally Creeks and Chickasaws continued to pose one of the major impediments in paths to the assembly. The Creeks, particularly the Talapuche faction associated with McGillivray, continued to regard the Chickasaws with suspicion and hostility. They saw them as willing to ally themselves with Americans against the Creeks. One manifestation of that hostility occurred in October 1792 just a month before the New Orleans meeting. A group of Talapuche Creeks, who had just visited Delavillebeuvre in Boukfouka, set out to kill those they believed were Americans living in the Natchez District. As part of that campaign, they murdered and mutilated several members of the McFarlane family living along the Big Black River, an event that prompted Gayoso to warn Delavillebeuvre to be wary of his safety in Boukfouka. After learning more about the affair from Taboca during a visit of that chief and some eighty warriors, women, and children, Gayoso told Carondelet that everything should be done to prevent the Talapuches from continuing "their forays into this district."[3]

Spanish officials confronted problems west of the Mississippi River, problems that were sometimes exacerbated by Indians living to the east. The Osages continued to be perceived as a threat to the kind of order they sought. They challenged Spanish efforts to cultivate good relations with the Quapaws of Arkansas and other groups. Sometime in late 1792 or early 1793, a group of northern Indians complained to the lieutenant governor in St. Louis that the Spanish had failed to keep roads white; instead, they said, "they are strewn with our bones." The reason? The Osages and the failure of the Spanish to "prevent them from killing our horses," among other things.[4] In late 1792, "war" broke out between the Ayches and Adayes of east Texas and some Choctaws. According to the Spanish commandant in Natchitoches, the Choctaws not only comported themselves badly with Indian groups there during their hunting expeditions; they also inflicted harm on people living under his jurisdiction. They robbed "them of their labors, turning their horses loose in their crops, killing cattle secretly in the woods, and stealing horses in all parts to take to their villages," he reported.[5] Gayoso considered sending Itelegana and Stephen Minor to try to work out these problems so that they would not endanger his efforts east of the Mississippi River.[6] All of these matters—and many more—took the time of both Gayoso and Carondelet; some of the problems had to be settled before there could be an assembly and an agreement to confederate.

The most substantial challenge, however, consisted of the hostilities between Chickasaws and Creeks that seemed to intensify as the consequence of the killing of some Creeks by Chickasaws about the time of the McFarlane raid in late 1792. A long history of conflict between the two groups lay back of that affair, nourished by suspicions on the part of both the Creeks and the Spanish that Americans moving into the valley of the Tennessee River were using the Chickasaws, particularly that faction headed by Piomingo, to pursue their expansionist goals. The murder of Davenport and his companions in the vicinity of Chickasaw Bluffs in 1787 came about in part because of such suspicions. In 1789, McGillivray, the same Creek leader who had apparently encouraged that act, saw a connection between Piomingo's attempt to open trade with the United States and the decision of American leaders to establish a post at Muscle Shoals. He opposed both. A year later, an American detachment set out to begin the project at Muscle Shoals but was compelled to withdraw when attacked by a group of Cherokees and Creeks. Then there was the McFarlane raid and an attack by pro-American Chickasaws on some Creeks. In that attack three Creek youths were killed, including the son and the nephew of Efau Hadjo (Mad Dog), the Creek war chief who, in the spring of 1793, had emerged as a contender to succeed McGillivray after the latter's death in February in Pensacola at the house of his friend, William Panton. Following this event, sporadic fighting continued, which included an invasion of Chickasaw country by a large war party acting on orders of Louis Milfort, another Creek leader seen by some as more deserving than Efau Hadjo to be principal chief of the Creeks. With these ongoing altercations, there could be no assembly with a good representation of Chickasaws and Creeks in attendance.

Gayoso's call for a congress in April 1793 set the end of June as a time for its meeting, but very quickly he expressed doubt as to whether this goal could be met. He worried about the lack of a clear successor to McGillivray. Certainly Gayoso hoped, as did others, that someone would emerge in whom the Spanish could place more confidence than in McGillivray, who, although apparently opposed to American interests, had been willing to accept an annual payment in 1790 from the Americans after agreeing to the Treaty of New York, and, as Gayoso put it, began to sustain more "intimate correspondence with American chiefs." He agreed that if the Chickasaws and Creeks did not resolve their differences, the Americans would take advantage of disunion, and it would be necessary to postpone the assembly. "We should not waste any time," he wrote, "to reconcile the two warring nations and bring together all our Indian friends and thereby provide by means of our conduct proof to the Americans that we are not exciting the Indians against them." Yet he seemed rather pessimistic about prospects for accomplishing this goal: "All the Indian nations that surround us are inconsistent and for the same reason difficult to manage." He seemed especially frustrated with the Creeks, whom he described as having an unreliable character. He found that they would go to extremes in insulting not only their neighbors the Americans "but also all who live in the Choctaw and Chickasaw nations and even the vassals of His Majesty residing in the territory of this government."[7]

Even though the challenges seemed at times overwhelming, Gayoso continued to work hard to bring about the congress. Carondelet had designated him as the official primarily responsible for planning the assembly to promote his February 1793 proposal for a confederation, which would include a permanent congress representing the major Indian nations of the Gulf South.[8] Beginning in April, the Natchez governor sent out letters to several key people to disseminate news of the congress. One of the letters went to the Chickasaw trader John Turnbull, outlining a talk to be delivered to Chickasaw leaders. The talk, Gayoso said, should begin by a reaffirmation of the friendship of the Spanish. Then it should stress the need to end hostilities with the Creeks so that a meeting of the principal chiefs of the Cherokee, Chickasaw, Choctaw, and Creek nations could be held at the ball court on the Yazoo River. Finally, Gayoso asked that the end of June be set as the time. He asked Turnbull to explain the advantage of the site by pointing out its proximity to the governor's sources of provisions. He was well aware of its traditional significance to both the Choctaws and Chickasaws and that it had not been included in the agreement with the British establishing a boundary. In addition to establishing a plan for peace, Gayoso told Turnbull to say that an agreement as to how gifts might best be distributed would be considered.[9]

Similar letters went to other chiefs and traders. Preoccupied with the need to settle the Creek-Chickasaw conflict, Gayoso sent letters to the three major Chickasaw chiefs, Taskietoka, Piomingo, and Ugulayacabé, and to two other traders who lived and worked among the Chickasaws, Benjamin Fooy and Hardy Perry. As in the Turnbull letter, he emphasized the need to resolve differences between Chickasaws and Creeks. He reassured Taskietoka that the governor in New Orleans had taken steps to stop the "bad proceedings of the Creeks" and that by means of the assembly "all the differences between your Nation and them" would end. He asked Fooy to inform him as to the cause of the misunderstanding between the Chickasaws and the Creeks, and he requested that Perry assist Turnbull in his efforts, specifically those aimed at "reconciling Paye Mingo [Piomingo] with the King" and with the Creeks and the Chickasaws. One letter went to Bloody Fellow to emphasize the importance of a Cherokee presence at the assembly. Gayoso even encouraged him to bring to the meeting "some people of the Northern Nations so that they may observe and be witnesses of my way of thinking & of the protection our Great King gives to all the Indians." Describing Franchimastabé as "my dear Friend and Brother," he told Bloody Fellow that Delavillebeuvre would call an assembly of chiefs of his nation "to express to them my intentions for the welfare of all the red people upon whom I look as my Children." He said that he expected to see him at the ball ground.[10]

The letters seemed to have some good effect. Several Choctaw and Chickasaw chiefs assembled in Piomingo's village of Tchoukafala, or Long Town, on the first of June for a meeting during which Piomingo said he would follow a straight path to the assembly called by Gayoso. Benjamin James attended and recorded many of the speeches. They provided evidence that the Choctaws had already done some good work as mediators between the Chickasaws and Creeks and could continue in that role. James reported that one of the Choctaw chiefs, Tuscoonopoy, devoted his speech to an explanation of the belt of wampum he carried from "my elder brothers the Creeks." He said the wampum had been sent by way of Pensacola and Mobile with the help of William Panton and delivered to two "beloved men" of the Choctaws and then by means of them or someone else to the Chickasaws. Two Creek chiefs, Peomingo of the Cowittas (Cowettas) and Offey Hago of the Tuckabatches, had sent the wampum as an expression of their desire for "continual friendship," after they had been informed by Panton that a "large army was coming against them." They asked that an answer to the wampum be sent as soon as possible. Hoping to restore peace between the Chickasaws and Creeks—a state of affairs very much desired, according to another chief, Tuscoonopoy, by "our fathers and beloved white people the Spaniards"—Taboca of the Choctaws had undertaken that mission. Mucklasso Mingo of the Chickasaws accepted the belt of wampum, telling those present that "with such Belts as this, my forefather Pyomattohah used to declare peace." He then went on to comment optimistically that even though "the day has been very dark and cloudy for some time past, now the sun is getting out of the clouds" to shine on their women and children and allow them "to prosper and replenish."[11]

The wampum was presented to Piomingo of the Chickasaws, who then commented that by "seizing [it] with both hands" and holding it fast, he declared his desire for peace, even though he had "put up with Creek insults for six years past," actions he described as the murder of both his people and "our white people" and the theft of horses. For these reasons, and the fact that the Chickasaws were "but a handfull of people" and therefore could be laid "desolate in a little time" by the growing number of Americans nearby, he and others had sought the friendship and help of the Americans. They had responded in a generous way by sending some corn, building forts, and now sending a peace talk. He complained that the Creeks did not understand these conditions and had therefore made light of them. Nevertheless, he affirmed his desire for peace so that "the dark cloud that has been over us so long be blown off, and the Sun shine clear on us." Finally, Piomingo gave his support to the meeting at the

Yazoo ball court requested by Gayoso and promised that he would attend. "I will go the straight path to the Assembly," James recorded him saying.[12]

Despite Piomingo's statement in June, the path to an assembly was anything but straight or clear. For someone like Gayoso it no doubt looked still very much twisted, overgrown, and not just a single way but many. Furthermore, other paths continued to take on a red coloration. Chickasaw and Creek blood continued to be shed. Given the persistence of violence among bands of Creeks and Chickasaws, the time proposed by Gayoso—the end of June—proved to be unrealistic. For many, reflecting once again the many centers of power defining the political landscape of the region, the proposed location was not satisfactory. Political power among these groups continued to be dispersed among villages. Some village chiefs, to be sure, had more influence than others, but despite efforts of Europeans to center power in one, the local culture dictated otherwise. The Indian world remained one of "so many little republics," a condition that was complicated by the near anarchic world of the Americans, who, despite some efforts of the central government to rein them in, continued to put pressure on the Creeks, the Cherokees, and, increasingly, the Chickasaws and Choctaws. Franchimstabé of the Choctaws and, perhaps less so, Piomingo among the Chickasaws seemed to have a certain edge in terms of influence, but it was a soft edge, for both were constantly challenged by other chiefs. As for Piomingo and what seemed to be a commitment to follow a straight path to an assembly at Nogales, he continued to be an elusive quarry for the Spanish, and in the end the American connection proved for him to be the more attractive one.

A council held by the recently appointed commissioner to the Creeks, Pedro Olivier, at about the same time as the meeting of Choctaws and Chickasaws reported by Benjamin James in Tchoukafala, revealed to that Spanish commissioner opposition to both the time and place for the assembly. Shortly after his arrival in Creek country, Olivier extended an invitation to Creek chiefs to meet with him in Tuckabatchee, the village of an old ally of Alexander McGillivray, Efau Hadjo, more commonly referred to in English or Spanish documents as "Mad Dog" or "Perro Rabioso."[13] A close associate of Alexander McGillivray, this chief, the father and uncle of two victims of American violence in 1791, served as the chief Creek representative to the United States after McGillivray's death in Febraury 1793.[14] Olivier asked that all Creek chiefs be summoned to "Tokepatche" (Tuckabatchee), and, with the exception of some Lower Creeks and Seminoles, a large number came. There, according to Olivier, they received "warmly" the plan of Carondelet for a confederation of the four nations but found the time and place of the proposed assembly to approve such a confederation "impossible." They liked neither the proposed site, because of its distance, nor the time, "because," as Olivier wrote, "they cannot leave their towns until after the fiesta of the maize and the renewal of the ball game, which are now on the eve of taking place and to which they are attached by their laws and customs, with no possibility of failing in them." They proposed as an alternative site the one ceded by a group of Choctaws to the Spanish in the Treaty of Boukfouka, the old French fort on the Tombigbee, and as a more propitious time the middle of September. They all—including Efau Hadjo—inquired as to whether Piomingo of the Chickasaws would attend, saying that they "were anxious to see that man with whom they had much to discuss."[15]

Olivier reported having several discussions with Efau Hadjo and another chief, Kiskilasky, about these matters and others. He found all the meetings of the council useful as a way to learn more about the Creeks, particularly their relations with Americans, the influence of white traders among them, and the relative importance of the various chiefs. He noted that the traders who had been "among them since infancy" were gaining more and more influence and that many Creeks seemed especially attached to a Joseph Cornell who, they insisted, should be their interpreter. He described the Creeks as divided into the Talapoosas, Abecuches, Upper Creeks, Alibamons, and Lower Creeks, with a principal chief for each part and each as deserving of the good words he had used to describe Efau Hadjo and Kiskilasky. Olivier told them that Carondelet had suggested the latter two be given some special rank and an annual pension should they join in the effort to establish a confederacy. He said they were flattered by that gesture but that Efau Hadjo had agreed with Olivier that there were others who were just as worthy of special recognition. Olivier's report suggested more support among the Creeks than the other groups for attending a congress and establishing a confederation, a disposition helped perhaps by McGillivray's earlier advocacy of close ties with the Spanish and continued widespread Creek suspicion of and even outright hostility toward Americans.[16]

Although he had indicated to Benjamin James that he would support an assembly and attend, throughout the summer and fall Piomingo remained suspicious of the Creeks and loyal to his American friends. By means of a message to Efau Hadjo and other Creeks, which he sent in September through the American commissioner to the Creeks, James Seagrove, he provided in effect a response to what these chiefs had discussed with Olivier and in so doing established more clearly his position than he had at Tchoukafala. He lamented the ongoing conflict of Creeks and Chickasaws but put the blame on the Creeks: "We was [*sic*] as brothers, and by your own conduct caused to be otherwise . . . by spilling the blood of both Indians and whites." In so doing, the Creeks, he said, had talked and behaved differently from "our forefathers": "Our forefathers and our great men that used to talk is Dead and Gone. On both sides we are a new Set that has Grown up Since and I think that you seeme as if you Did Not wish to Eemetate [imitate] them but to speake as if you had two tongues to speake with." Piomingo went on to criticize the Creeks for dealing with the Americans in the wrong way, saying that he "always thought the only way to keep my land was to keep at peace with all my Neibours." He asked for a response, suggesting once again that the guilt of any continued shedding of blood would be the responsibility of the Creeks.[17]

Since the previous autumn at least, groups of both had been shedding blood and thereby staining paths. Ending "the war," however, was not so easy, but efforts continued so that the goal of holding an assembly by the end of June could be met. In the minds of Gayoso and Carondelet, Americans, particularly Blount, seemed to be encouraging the conflict as a way to divide the Indians, thereby weakening them and making it easier to possess their land.[18] Furthermore, what the documents refer to as a "war" certainly was not that in the contemporary European sense of the word. The conflict often consisted of retaliation carried out by relatives of a victim—the operation of a "law of blood"—and such matters eluded any kind of final resolution.[19] The longer the war continued, some believed, the greater the danger it might widen. Such a development would devastate any plan for an assembly or a confederation.

As noted, the Choctaws, particularly Taboca, had begun to try to straighten and whiten paths to make possible a June assembly. Others encouraged Gayoso to be more active in the efforts to achieve peace. In April 1793—the same month in which he began to disseminate plans for an assembly—Gayoso met with a son or nephew of Ugulayacabé, several other Chickasaws, and a Choctaw chief identified as Red Shoes. They provided more insight into the origins of the conflict and urged him to serve as a mediator. The Chickasaws had come to deliver to the governor a letter from Taskietoka and a petition from Ugulayacabé asking for food and war matériel. As to why the conflict began and continued, they explained that, when a group of Creeks found themselves "on the frontiers of Cumberland" the previous fall, one of them saw an opportunity to take a gun he wanted from another member of the group. To get it, he killed the man without the others knowing and to cover up the crime said that a Chickasaw had done it.[20]

The "law of blood" then went into operation. The relatives of the Creek victim accepted the story of the murderer and avenged the death of the member of the Creek party by killing a Chickasaw identified as "the first warrior of Piomingo." Others became involved. A group of Creeks attempted to secure vengeance near Hardy Perry's house, according to the story told Gayoso, but were foiled. A short distance from Perry's house, they encountered a woman they believed to be a Choctaw. In fact she was a Chickasaw, who slipped away at night and warned some of her brethren. When the four Creeks arrived the next day at Perry's house, the Chickasaws killed three of them. Echoing words of Piomingo, these Chickasaws went on to tell Gayoso that, because they were a small nation compared with the Creeks, they had "to look in all directions."

They had been successful in getting some help from both Governor Blount and James Robertson, but, according to Gayoso, they had not "closed their ears to the Spanish."[21]

In the same letter to Carondelet, Gayoso said that Sulushemastabé (Red Shoes) of the Choctaws—probably the same Red Shoes mentioned by Minor in his first journal and then later in Natchez—implored him to act as a peacemaker. Describing himself as "not the first chief of his Nation" but one "as important as Franchimastabé," because of the latter's neglect of "all the business that interested them," Sulushemastabé said he was expressing the desire "of all of his nation." Employing the language of kinship, he told the governor he should view the Indian nations as his sons and himself as a father. A father should do what all fathers must do when one of the brothers "strives unjustly" with another. He does not abandon the errant sibling; rather, he corrects him "so that he will return to be in harmony with the rest." Sulushemastabé urged Gayoso to avoid acting as "some English governors" had previously done. As he put it, those governors "had split a ball in two, giving one half to the Creeks and the other to the Chickasaws," thereby leading them to think that they were supporting war between themselves under the guise of friendship.[22]

Gayoso responded to these points with words of his own and some action. He pointed out to the Chickasaws that one of their major problems was lack of unity caused by a small faction who listened to and followed Piomingo rather than adhering to the talks of their "true King." According to Gayoso, "without difficulty the Chickasaws agreed that what I said was true, and even let it be known that they disapproved of Piomingo's conduct." He then told them that since it was the desire of the nation to have peace, the governor-general had wisely pursued a policy of withholding arms and should continue to do so.[23]

Knowing, as he put it, that he would be compared to the Americans in this regard, he sent them away with gifts that included some munitions. He sent the "King's boat" to the Chickasaws with five hundred bushels of corn, some limburg, vermilion, and "some other bagatelles." He went further and gave them what arms he had "left at the time, which I could not very well refuse," explaining that action to Carondelet by saying that his position would be enhanced "with powder and ball" when the king of the Chickasaws distributed the munitions. He expressed the hope that he might even win the support of Piomingo's followers. Describing these Chickasaw visitors as the first Chickasaws who had come to see him, he said he added "a nice present" and told them to go by water to a place called "Yakony Patafan," or "Yagaono Patasadye (the flat grounds, according to Delavillebeuvre), on the Yazoo River, where the Chickasaws had allowed John Turnbull to establish a store. There, he said, they should await the shipment of corn and other items. He told the commandant at Nogales, Elías Beauregard, to send an interpreter and one other with the boat. According to Gayoso, some of the Chickasaws went on "to advise the Nation," and the others remained. He said they "were most happy for the gift of corn, which was deposited on land."[24]

Gayoso reported in this long letter of June 8 that Turnbull had secured the agreement of many Chickasaw chiefs, including Taskietoka, to come to the assembly. According to the governor, Turnbull, while on his way to the Chickasaws, had heard that their king (Taskietoka) and other chiefs were coming by another route. He met them and returned to the site of his store and brought together other chiefs "of greatest importance who were nearer." There he read them the "word" about the proposed assembly; they liked it very much and agreed to come. Assuming that it would meet as planned on the last day of June, Turnbull charged Mongulachamingo, "the man of most importance with distributing in the Nation the sticks that would indicate the day the Assembly would meet." He then went on to Baton Rouge, where he had a house, bringing along the king of the Chickasaws and two other chiefs "to pass the time" until the meeting of the assembly.[25]

Pressure from the Chickasaws on the Choctaws to join them in resisting the Creeks compelled other Choctaw chiefs besides Taboca to promote a peace process. They encouraged Gayoso to mediate it so that the goal of the June assembly and perhaps even confederation could be achieved. Gayoso reported to Carondelet in this same communication of June 8 that two weeks after Red Shoes and the Chickasaws saw him, two Choctaw chiefs, Mistichicó of the Six Villages and Itelegana of the Large Party, had also asked him to serve as a mediator. Both said they had received red knives from the Chickasaws, a way to ask them to join in the war with the Creeks. Gayoso reported that Itelegana apologized for bringing so many people with him but said the importance of the matter would excuse their number. As a way to stress the importance of mediation and emphasize the need for Gayoso's services, Itelegana presented to the governor strings of beads with trimmings representing the Cherokee, Choctaw, Chickasaw, and Creek nations and their different paths. Itelegana explained the symbolism in the strings by pointing out that three of the strings were white and the fourth red and broken. He asked Gayoso to present the governor-general with these strings and to make white the path joining New Orleans with their nations. Gayoso expressed some displeasure with all this detail and symbolism, commenting that had Itelegana remained in his nation he would have learned from Delavillebeuvre that both he and the governor-general were working to achieve peace among the nations. Still, he regarded Itelegana as "a man of influence and capable of taking revenge by causing a revolution in the minds of the Choctaws." He provided him a gift, one he said was his due following the Natchez Treaty. He also provided some things for his people.[26]

Taboca and Pedro Olivier seemed to be especially important in working to achieve peace in the spring of 1793. Of all the Choctaw chiefs who became involved in this process, the peace chief Taboca once again impressed Gayoso. "I can do no less than inform you that Taboca has comported himself perfectly on this occasion, traveling very much to reconcile the Creeks and Chickasaws, having gone himself to the Creek Nation," he wrote.[27] Acting on instructions from Carondelet, Olivier made a trip to the Chickasaws "to make arrangements so that the Creeks can make peace with the Chickasaws," according to a letter of Creek chief, Louis Leclerc de Milfort, a brother-in-law of McGillivray.[28] Working through Delavillebeuvre, Olivier attempted to get chiefs of the Choctaw Nation to make the trip to Mongulacha. There he hoped they would help to "negotiate the peace between the Creeks and the Chickasaws" as well as to check the "bad conduct of the Alibamons and Creeks toward the whites established in the lands of the Choctaws and Chickasaws."[29] Olivier's effort turned out to be a vain one, according to him. Apparently Taboca was the only Choctaw chief who came to the Creeks.[30]

Gayoso realized that the meeting at the ball court at Nogales at the end of June was impossible, and he sent out a letter to the various parties setting early August as the time.[31] Gayoso's reason: another outbreak of hostilities between the Chickasaws and Creeks.[32] Nevertheless, a number of Choctaw and Chickasaw chiefs and warriors arrived at Nogales in late June, and, when he heard of their coming, he hastened to meet them, despite the fact that he expected Piomingo to arrive any day in Natchez. Piomingo, however, had apparently gone to Chickasaw Bluffs to receive a quantity of arms and corn from Americans. Gayoso met some Chickasaws and Choctaws at the ball court, and he proceeded to have a private conference with the Chickasaws during which he scolded them for being ungrateful and deceptive by taking presents from both the Spanish and Americans. He decided in the end, however, "to mix severity with sweetness" to win their support and sent by water a shipment of food to offset the American gift of corn. He thought that if he did not, then they might heed the suggestion of a chief identified as "Lobo" (possibly Wolf's Friend or Ugulayacabé), who had come to Nogales with a group of Chickasaws with news about Piomingo, to turn back because they now had food (from the Americans). Furthermore he was afraid that the Creeks were not serious about making peace.[33]

While at Nogales, Gayoso said he received a letter from Delavillebeuvre in Boukfouka telling him that it would be impossible to have the Chickasaws and Creeks meet at the end of June. Repeating what the Mobile commandant had learned, he said the Creeks thought the assembly should be after the green corn festival.[34] That letter and one from Ugulayacabé in July urging a fall meeting—a healthier time of year, according to this Chickasaw chief whom Gayoso had by now come to regard as very important—brought about another change in date, to the fourth moon, or October 19. Gayoso proceeded to send out messages to that effect, including one to Delavillebeuvre.[35]

Communication often broke down. In late August, a "surprised and embarrassed" Delavillebeuvre reported from Boukfouka that his courier, taking a message to the Creeks asking that the assembly be postponed, had met Mistilebek Chaty, identified by Gayoso as a nephew of Ugulayacabé, and a group of Creeks. Mistilebek Chaty said he had been commissioned by all the Creek chiefs to lead the group. He expressed surprise about the postponement for "three moons," for, according to him, as reported by Delavillebeuvre, that "would be the very time the Americans would attack their homes." He said they did not want to wait for such an attack "but expected to go with the Cherokees and attack the Americans on the way"; therefore, "they could not attend the Assembly at that time, nor could the Cherokees." Delavillebeuvre said he "was constrained to agree to their proposition" if Gayoso also would agree. He provided the group—forty-seven in all—with "two beeves," one of which was eaten during their stay in the Choctaws and the other for their journey to Nogales, where they asked to remain until the others could arrive. Delavillebeuvre further reported that the Choctaws demanded that Favre be the interpreter at the assembly and not Gayoso's interpreter, Jean Baptiste Trenier, and that Mistilebek Chaty had told the Creeks in speeches "around the camp fires" that he (Gayoso) had asked the nations to meet and that "the Red Men" are not obligated to work together.[36] Because of the early arrival of these Creeks at Nogales, Gayoso sent his galiot, *La Activa,* to Nogales with supplies and a message to Mistilebek Chaty inviting him and four of the chiefs to come to Natchez to talk so that he could learn their intentions.[37]

The postponements enabled Gayoso to send another letter to the American governor in Nashville, William Blount, to clarify Spanish objectives with regard to the Indians and to give vent to some unhappiness at reported American activity, particularly the sending of arms to the Chickasaws. He told Blount that in all their dealings with the Indians, the Spanish were exercising restraint and seeking a way to bring peace and stability to the region. He said both he and the governor-general had been working hard to reconcile differences between the Creeks and the Chickasaws and thereby prevent a general war. Despite his gift of some arms to the Chickasaws who had visited him in April, he told Blount he had taken particular care not to supply the Chickasaws—the weaker of the two nations—with ammunition when they asked. Instead, he had sent only a "sufficient quantity" of corn to Piomingo. Gayoso directed Blount's attention to the treaties of friendship and commerce between the Spanish and the Choctaws, Chickasaws, and Creeks after the conclusion of the American Revolution and asked why the Americans challenged those agreements with treaties of their own. In particular, he cited those of Cumberland of 1789 with the Choctaws and Chickasaws and of New York the following year with the Creeks. With regard to the New York treaty, Gayoso told Blount that it really was no more than an agreement between the American Congress[1] and Alexander McGillivray, who was guided by personal interests by maintaining a "double correspondence" and by receiving a stipend from both Spain and the United States. Most Creeks, Gayoso pointed out, concluded that McGillivray had betrayed Creek interests and was an "imposter" and therefore had repudiated the treaty. Ending on a more conciliatory note, Gayoso suggested that neither the Americans nor the Spanish "should manage Indians as slaves to our Politics." Rather, both should strive "to make them happy, quiet, and as useful a People as possible, and not perplex their minds with notions, that will make them miserable, troublesome, and a useless set of men, on the face of the earth."[38]

Gayoso continued to move ahead with plans for the congress and tried to limit the number attending but in the end found that effort futile. Through various channels he said that the purpose of the meeting was not to distribute gifts but to transact business and that therefore only the principal chief from each village and some small medal chiefs and captains should attend. Some indication of ultimate failure to limit numbers came from Delavillebuevre, who wrote in late May that even though he had informed the Choctaws as to Gayoso's wish, they "do whatever they like." They "are capable of going 100 leagues merely to get something to eat. We are not their masters: they do whatever they like, always saying yes; and although they always agree to what I tell them, always do as they please." A couple of weeks later Delavillebeuvre said he had tried but failed to persuade some chiefs visiting him why it was important to limit the number. He said he "did not know how to make them understand that only two chiefs should go from each large village and one from each small village," to make a total of eighty-four.[39] Ugulayacabé told Gayoso to see virtue in numbers and to accept Indian practice, which was that, when white people call on the principal people of a nation to go to a meeting, the "inferiors are free to go." Otherwise, the chief pointed out, it would appear that the chiefs were seeking their own benefit and not that of that nation.[40] Gayoso seemed inclined to accept Ugulayacabé's arguments, for he described him as "the person of most influence in the whole [Chickasaw] nation" and one therefore "capable of counteracting the machinations of Piomingo."[41] Indeed, he had even "declared himself on our side." Gayoso accepted his role as father; those so viewed must be prepared to be accommodating and generous. Indians "do not evaluate or appraise things in the same way of civilized nations, neither in time or circumstance," he noted. Furthermore, given the presence and competition of Americans, the Spanish had to be as generous as they. As he told Carondelet,

Indian expectations had to be honored; otherwise there could be no effective relations. They had to be treated in the manner to which they had become accustomed in the matter of presents, "and more particularly at the present time because of what the Americans are doing with the Chickasaws and are meditating doing with the Choctaws."[42]

8
The Nogales Assembly, 1793

By the time the assembly called by Gayoso in April for late June finally got under way almost four months later in October after one more delay, over two thousand Indians had arrived, most of them (about fifteen hundred) Choctaws—far more than Gayoso had wanted. Its proceedings, while replete with formality and ceremony and successful in the end to the extent of producing yet another treaty document, continued to reflect the messy nature of the region's politics. As such, however, it can provide significant insight into the diplomatic culture that supported the resolution of issues and the achievement of limited goals.

Although October 18 had been set for the beginning of the assembly, the late arrival of most of the Choctaws required Gayoso to postpone the opening ceremony to October 26. A large delegation of Chickasaws attended, led by Ugulayacabé, but despite his promise to come, Piomingo was not among them. He remained angry with the Creeks for spilling blood and identified "the mad dog and the other head men" as those who should receive his talk. Furthermore, he was still inclined to turn to Americans for help.[1] No Cherokees appeared until after the adjournment of the assembly and Gayoso's return to Natchez; then over ninety of them appeared in Nogales. When two of the chiefs in the group continued on to Natchez to meet Gayoso, they found no one there who could speak or understand their language. Gayoso did not submit his final report to Carondelet until early December, a delay occasioned, he said, by a need to deal with other business that included sending "assistance" to New Orleans and then to the "upper reaches of the river." Both he and Carondelet feared the possibility of an invasion of some sort down the river by Americans, now with French backing. Along with other major European powers, Spain found itself in late 1793 at war with the radical republican government in France, and France's new minister to the United States, Edmond Genêt, had been active soliciting support for the cause in America, which included dislodging the

Spanish from Florida and Louisiana. A letter Gayoso sent from Walnut Hills (Nogales) on October 18, however, anticipated much of what he put in the final report.

Despite the absence of a Cherokee delegation when the others were present and the failure in the end to establish a confederation with institutional expression in the form of a permanent congress, Gayoso represented the meeting as another diplomatic success. It produced a treaty "of friendship and guaranty" that—at least on paper—added the Cherokees to Spanish "protection" and defined the relationship among all as an "offensive and defensive alliance." The alliance would supposedly check the American threat, aided and abetted by the spring of 1793 by the appeal of Edmond Genêt, representing the French government in the United States, to many Americans, particularly those living west of the Appalachians, to unite and expel the Spanish from the region. Such Americans found the cause of French republicanism an appealing one, certainly to the extent of offering them a useful ideology to justify expansion under the guise of creating "an empire for liberty." Furthermore, Gayoso might hope that the treaty, supported by the good feeling emanating from the assembly, would discourage such conflicts as the ongoing one between Creeks and Chickasaws that had so delayed and even jeopardized the assembly. It secured more support for the cession of land for a second Spanish post on the Tombigbee River and provided for more order and control in the distribution of annual gifts to the nations, with the Chickasaws agreeing to receive theirs at Chickasaw Bluffs, thereby enhancing the possibility of an ultimate Spanish occupation of the site. Finally, it established a more formal status for commissioners by stating that all the nations would admit such persons as the official representatives of the king through whom communication should take place and judgment made as to which whites had a right to be in the respective nations.

The words in the treaty expressed all of these changes, to which the attendees responded with enthusiastic approval by shouting "good" after the reading of each article, according to Gayoso's long report. In accounts of similar assemblies or councils, the Americans, the British, and the French relate similar procedures to secure approval of agreements. One might even regard the reading aloud of the text article by article followed by a shout of "good" to indicate approval as more important than the text itself; indeed, for the more than two thousand Indians attending, just the fact of the meeting and their presence provided a stamp of legitimacy to whatever document might emerge. That fact enlarged the meaning of "treaty" to embrace "meeting." For both Indians and Europeans, the talk, the language, the ceremony associated with such proceedings were the keys to keeping paths clear and open—much more than a paper document labeled "treaty."[2]

And, as with any such major undertakings, certain people played especially crucial roles. Gayoso identified in his letter of October 18 and the December report a number of people he thought contributed to the success of the meeting and who would continue to be valuable. He praised the contributions of Juan Delavillebeuvre, who "has great knowledge of the Indians and consequently knows how to manage them," and Simon Favre, perhaps "the most eloquent man there is in [the use of the] sterile [*esteril*] Choctaw language." Gayoso observed that the Indians depended upon Favre to use the language, and "they listen to speeches made by him with more pleasure than [those] from the mouth of any other." He recommended the appointment of Benjamin Fooy as commissioner to the Chickasaws. Fooy "knows the Chickasaw Indians and has the esteem of Ugulayacabé and other individuals of rank," Gayoso commented, "and without an individual of this kind, I believe our affairs may not go so well in the Chickasaw nation." By the time of the Nogales assembly, Fooy was serving as de facto commissioner. With regard to keeping paths open to make possible a stronger alliance with the Indians and the achievement of at least one more post on the Mississippi River, at Chickasaw Bluffs, Gayoso noted two more individuals: the Chickasaw chief Ugulayacabé and the trader John Turnbull.[3]

In his October letter Gayoso told Carondelet that "you can count on the blind adherence of Ougoulayacabe to our interests." That view, in light of Ugulayacabé's noteworthy presence in the 1792 Nashville assembly and as shown by the letters of the next year and a half, was perhaps too sanguine. Nevertheless, Gayoso represented him to be the most enthusiastic adherent of Spanish interests during the Nogales assembly. He also saw him as perhaps the most important of the Chickasaw chiefs in view of what he saw as the demise of Piomingo and his party with the defection of the two sons of James Colbert, the most influential of Chickasaw chiefs. Ugulayacabé responded to Gayoso's opening speech with enthusiasm and gave his full support to the proposals. Even after returning to the Chickasaw camp, removing the suit that Gayoso had given him, and donning his native dress so " 'that the white men's clothing would not disturb my understanding,' " he concluded that Gayoso's proposals deserved the full support of all present. Using figurative language similar to that of the biblical St. Paul in a call for his kind of unity, he said the four Indian nations should be likened to the four fingers of a hand that, when a thumb is added, "in this case the Spanish nation, then the power of all is united." By the summer of 1793, Gayoso had concluded that Ugulayacabé's importance among the Chickasaws was substantial and that, by investing in measures to support and even augment that influence, he could promise Carondelet that the formation of an American settlement at Chickasaw Bluffs could be prevented.[4]

Ugulayacabé preferred, however, not to make any decisions without first consulting Turnbull—evidence of the status of that trader among the Chickasaws and the increasingly important role played by such peoples in Indian affairs. Gayoso found his attendance at the assembly "opportune" in that he could assist in discussions of trade matters, and he relied heavily on both Turnbull and Ugulayacabé during this assembly and the period immediately following as the Spanish moved to secure Chickasaw Bluffs. Turnbull served as an interpreter when Ugulayacabé and Gayoso talked and pledged that he would do all he could to destroy the influence of Piomingo and promote a Spanish post at Chickasaw Bluffs. As a gesture to both the Spanish and Turnbull, Ugulayacabé agreed to try to secure support among the Chickasaws for Turnbull to operate a store at the same location, an action that then might facilitate the location of a military post there. Gayoso said he would use Turnbull as the person to provide Ugulayacabé with his "annual reward" of five hundred silver pesos and that Ugulayacabé would be responsible for the distribution of the annual Spanish gift to the Chickasaws.[5]

Gayoso devoted attention in his report to three Choctaw chiefs who had been instrumental in the diplomacy leading to the resolution of the Nogales controversy: Franchimastabé, Taboca, and Itelegana. Although he sometimes found Franchimastabé's behavior annoying, Gayoso employed him to foil what he saw as an attempt by Taboca and Itelegana to use the assembly as a way to diminish that old chief's "interest"—his ability to extract and redistribute goods—and in so doing unsettle the kind of order Gayoso wanted. Gayoso said that when Taboca stepped ahead of Franchimastabé and others of the Large Party as they presented themselves, he ignored him and gave his hand first to Franchimastabé, then to the rest, leaving both Taboca and Itelegana as the last of the chiefs to be greeted. Then, to balance his snub of these two, he both praised and scolded Franchimastabé. He commended him "for his good conduct" and told him that if he had strayed occasionally it was not his fault. Rather, he said, it was the work of "some evil chiefs in his nation" who not only advised him badly but forcibly compelled him to do what he did not plan. On the other hand, he criticized him for delaying his arrival so as to bring with him as many Choctaws as possible. He said his tardiness had caused "serious damage to the Chickasaws and Creeks who had waited long [and] consumed many supplies." Nevertheless, at the conclusion of the assembly, he announced that he would regard Franchimastabé as not only principal chief of the Large Party but of the entire nation as well.[6]

Like so many Europeans before him, Gayoso desired very much an order or hierarchy of chiefs who ideally would communicate with him through such commissioners as Delavillebeuvre and Fooy. Such a state of affairs would obviate the need to have expensive assemblies. In addition to identifying Franchimastabé as principal chief both of the Large Party and of the entire nation, he selected a chief who had supported the Boukfouka treaty, Mingo Puscus, to be principal chief of the Small Party, and Mistichicó for the same position in the Six Villages.[7] Of the Creek chiefs present, Gayoso accorded special recognition to the chief identified as a nephew of Ugulayacabé, Mistilebek, or Red Shoes, of Tuckabatchee, a village that seems to have assumed something of the status of a diplomatic center or capital of the Creeks, much as Franchimastabé's West Yazoo had for the Choctaws. All the other chiefs, he said, should unite in their respective divisions to contribute to the general good of the nation and thereby facilitate the opening and maintenance of straight paths to peace and harmony. In identifying these people as major chiefs, he repeated what many others had said before him, among them Delavillebeuvre: that there were too many chiefs "who believe they no longer should obey or even that they are subjects of a principal chief of each group."[8]

In the end, however, the plurality of chiefs with strong loyalties to their villages contributed to the failure to achieve a grand confederation under Spanish guidance and protection and institutionalized in the form of a permanent congress. Although Ugulayacabé had vividly endorsed the idea of unity through the metaphor of the hand—four fingers with the help of a thumb can enable a hand to lift a great weight—he and the other chiefs told Gayoso "unanimously" that it would be impossible to implement a permanent congress. They thought the idea a good one but said no red man, even though he might be chief, could be persuaded to live a year without going to his village. Gayoso proposed, as an alternative to a permanent congress, that the chiefs meet whenever the "King's commissioner" should request such a meeting. They agreed to that suggestion.[9]

And they agreed to all of the various articles of the treaty after each one was read. That reading and ratification took place on October 28, two days after elaborate opening ceremonies directed by Gayoso but incorporating important Indian objects and formalities. His account describes a kind of moveable ceremony done apparently to impress the Indians as to the importance of the new post at Nogales. It took place at various sites such as *El Gallo* and *Pan de Azúcar*, accompanied by the firing of artillery. Most significant—in terms of the emphasis he gave it in the report—seemed to be the ritual of presenting beads and smoking a pipe, in this case "a rich pipe of black stone" given to the governor by northern Indians and filled with tobacco mixed with wine. Each article was ratified by a shout of "good." The report notes a moment of tension with regard to Article 12, which proposed the site of the old Fort Tombecbé as the place for the Choctaws to receive their annual gift. Gayoso had learned that there was opposition among the Large Party, either because some of them did not approve the recent cession of the site to the Spanish or because they saw an opportunity through delay in ratification to extract an "extraordinary gift." He said that that he forced a decision by threatening to leave the following day. That strong stand, he reported, won the support of the other nations present.[10]

The Gayoso of this report emerges as an effective leader of the proceedings. Although the late arrival of Choctaws delayed the opening, he finally set the time for the official opening as the twenty-sixth of October. He delivered the lengthy opening speech, skillfully deflated whatever opposition there was among the Choctaws to certain terms of the treaty and the Tombigbee cession, and limited—out of necessity, apparently—the amount of gift giving. Furthermore, he took advantage of—or perhaps contributed to—a steady weakening of traditional functions of leaders. Expressing concern for ongoing disorders, he made a selection of principal chiefs for the largest delegation of Indians present, the Choctaws.

Throughout he continued to respect and to use the history and traditions of the overwhelming number of Indians present, representing the population of the region. Acknowledging the preponderance of Choctaws present, he made Choctaw the lingua franca of the proceedings. As in all such events, the calumet and the act of smoking assumed great significance as a way to make possible harmony among parties and peaceful negotiations. Most impressively, he invoked the memory of the Natchez Indians to underscore the importance of the meetings. On the day after the opening speeches he displayed before the assembly a very large two-pound stone pipe that the Natchez Indians had smoked at the Temple of the Sun, "when they used to gather together to discuss serious matters." Describing the stone as similar to the kind found in the mountains of the Escorial, he said the pipe had been discovered "in the district of Bufalo some twelve leagues from the village in one of the mounds [on which] they used to place their temples." He asked Simon Favre to light the pipe. After smoking it, he passed it to the representatives, "telling them that since the ancient Indians of Natchez were the most renown among those of their color and were consulted by all their neighbors on matters of great significance, they all used to smoke the same pipe on [such] occasions."[11]

Gayoso reported that the Choctaws liked what happened, and to show their approbation they asked whether they could confer on him an Indian name or title and thereby sustain the tradition of conferring names or titles on colonial officials responsible for the execution of treaties. The Choctaws had bestowed this honor before on French and British officials. He told them he "had no hesitation about receiving proof of their esteem, especially if from this it might result that they might be more punctual in carrying out what I advised them for the well being of their nation." An elaborate ceremony then took place in which Taboca, wearing a special collar placed around his neck by Franchimastabé, conferred on Gayoso the title of *Chactimataha*, or "King of the Choctaws," a title that Ugulayacabé used in many of his future letters to Gayoso. Gayoso replied with what he described as a comic speech "with allusion to the nature of the Choctaws, which made them laugh a lot." That ceremony, he observed, pleased them all, and many chiefs remained to eat with him.[12]

With Gayoso's departure from Nogales on the twenty-ninth, the congress might be regarded as concluded. For those enamored of power and order, it should have been. The life of politics and diplomacy, however—certainly in this region and at this time—was not so tidy. The assembly's end was as indefinite as was its beginning.

The group identified in the text of the treaty as responsible for convoking the assembly—the Cherokees—did not attend. The reason? They found "themselves involved in a campaign against the American States," according to the text of the treaty.[13] A few days after its conclusion and Gayoso's departure, however, a large group of Cherokees and one Creek chief appeared in Nogales. In a letter dated November 5, the commandant of Nogales, Elías Beauregard, informed the governor that six Cherokee chiefs, ninety warriors, and a Creek chief had just arrived. After Beauregard told them the assembly had just ended and that they had been represented there by an Alabama chief, they gave him two letters for the governor of Natchez from John Thompson, an interpreter, and John McDonald, the Spanish commissioner to the Cherokees. Two of their chiefs said that they wanted to come down to Natchez to explain the late arrival. According to them, they had been obliged to sell their arms and munitions to the Chickasaws to get food, since they had been robbed of most of their horses. They said they were tired and expected presents.[14]

Gayoso said the two chiefs came to Natchez but found they could not communicate with him or anyone else, for the only member of the delegation who spoke Choctaw remained in Nogales. Nevertheless, he extended his hospitality. To do so he had to purchase something from private stores for them, for he had nothing left after the Nogales assembly. In a letter the next day he scolded Beauregard for allowing the two to make the trip without an interpreter. Because they could not communicate, he did not know whether they were chiefs or warriors. He told Beauregard to gather all the chiefs together to explain that the assembly had ended and to tell them that he did not know they had planned to attend it. For that reason he had no presents available for them. He did tell Beauregard to suggest that they return to their nations by way of New Orleans, where they could receive presents. One of the letters identified one of the chiefs as "Little Turkey" and said he came with power to represent his nation. Because Gayoso could not tell whether one of the chiefs who came to Natchez was Kanitta (Little Turkey), now a "beloved man" among the Cherokees, he told

Beauregard to make sure that chief received a copy of the treaty. He also instructed Beauregard to give Little Turkey a carbine he was sending.[15]

In the end the Cherokees and the one Creek did not go to New Orleans. Gayoso wrote to Carondelet two days later and said that because he could find no one who understood Cherokee, he had decided to send the two chiefs, or warriors, back to Nogales. He sent the carbine for Little Turkey, an item that he said cost twenty-five dollars.[16] Later, Carondelet expressed disappointment that Little Turkey and the others did not receive some present more than the carbine. Still expressing hope for some kind of confederation, Carondelet recalled for Gayoso how much the Cherokee chief had talked about the subject: "Respecting Bloody Fellow, he talked to me much about the propriety and convenience of the four nations being united for their mutual defence and the protection of Spain."[17]

9
Paths—River and Other—from Nogales to San Fernando de las Barrancas

While the Nogales congress did not achieve in the end all that Spanish officials and some of the Indian participants may have wanted, it did provide an occasion for more ongoing talk, ceremony, and interaction that in the end proved more important than a specific treaty document. The treaty that came out of the assembly assumed and claimed too much. After reaffirming all previous agreements beginning with those of 1784, it added the "Cherokee Nation" to those under the protection of the Spanish king. Neither Bloody Fellow nor any other Cherokees were present for the reading and approval of the treaty, and those who finally appeared after the fact represented only a portion of the "Cherokee Nation" listed in the text as one of the parties. The treaty verbally changed the nature of the alliance of Indian nations with the Spanish from a vague association of friendship and commerce to "an offensive and defensive alliance." As a way to check such conflicts as the Creek-Chickasaw war, it pledged "all and each one in particular" not to act unilaterally on matters that might affect "the security and preservation of the other." Furthermore, it identified specific locations for the distribution of gifts to the various nations, and it pledged each nation to accept commissioners sent by the king and to use them as a means of communication and as judges of the legitimacy of whites residing in the nations. While Carondelet and the Cherokees identified with Bloody Fellow did not get a confederation institutionalized by means of a permanent congress, both could regard the commitment to consult as a kind of collective security arrangement that, if used, might hold the Americans at bay and check internal conflicts. Above all, the process associated with achieving the treaty sustained and perhaps even strengthened diplomatic paths.[1]

Yet the treaty, like the fort named in its honor, embodied aspirations that in the end proved ephemeral. And so it was with the next project: the establishment of another post on the Mississippi River at a place known in English as the Chickasaw Bluffs, where today one finds the city of Memphis, Tennessee.

The Spanish called the post there San Fernando de las Barrancas in honor of Fernando, the future king of Spain. Although they did not occupy it long, the diplomacy undertaken for its acquisition benefited from earlier diplomatic successes and provided thereby further insight into those elements that contributed to a political culture capable of sustaining peace and coexistence.

As evidenced by their talk leading to the Nogales assembly, both Carondelet and Gayoso had already begun to see the need for enhanced Spanish presence farther north on the Mississippi River. Given continued pressure by Americans on Indian lands, their views resonated well with many Indian leaders. The most obvious place for a new Spanish post: the site referred to by the French as the Ecors à Margot, a place with high bluffs along the eastern bank of the Mississippi at the mouth of the Margot River. The British called the place Chickasaw Bluffs, and the Spanish converted the French to "Barrancas de Margot." During his visit to New Orleans in late 1792, Bloody Fellow encouraged Carondelet to pursue its acquisition and development, along with the site at Muscle Shoals on the Tennessee River, to deter what he described as imminent American occupation. Carondelet concluded that Chickasaw Bluffs, the one site of several in the vicinity identified by the commander of Spain's Mississippi River fleet, had greater strategic importance than Muscle Shoals. Sharing Bloody Fellow's concern about American designs on the place, he observed in the spring of 1793 that, should the Americans succeed, they would become in a short time masters of the river. These two were not the first, however, to reach such conclusions.[2]

Spanish experience during the American Revolution influenced significantly their thinking about Chickasaw Bluffs. Like those of both Natchez and Nogales, the bluffs provided a strategic site overlooking the river and were therefore valuable for the protection of river traffic. During the Revolution, a strongly anti-Spanish and pro-British faction emerged among the Chickasaws, led by James Colbert, a Scottish trader who had settled among the Chickasaws and acquired three Chickasaw wives. Shortly after the Mobile congress of 1777, in the words of historian James Atkinson, he "initiated significant and official Chickasaw participation in the war when he raised Chickasaw parties to patrol the Mississippi, Tennessee, and Ohio Rivers." In these activities Chickasaw Bluffs served as a place from which to intercept, search, and even sometimes fire on Spanish vessels.[3]

After the war, Chickasaw country, as Calloway puts it, "remained a thorn in Spain's side." Colbert, who found it difficult to accept the British defeat in the American Revolution, continued to lead raids on Spanish vessels on the Mississippi River. During one of these raids, in 1782, he and his band seized the boat carrying the wife of the lieutenant governor of Spanish Illinois, Francisco Cruzat, and her four children. They were held as prisoners for nineteen days. That event dramatized further to the Spanish the importance of the site and a need to secure wider influence among the Chickasaws despite the fact that all Chickasaw villages sent numerous delegates to their 1784 Mobile assembly.[4]

Spanish interest intensified in 1787 when Piomingo, who by then had emerged as the principal leader of an American faction among the Chickasaws, agreed to allow Americans to build a fort there—a move that brought about violent reactions from Creeks, including the killing of Davenport and others and the beginning of what came to be referred to as the Chickasaw-Creek War.[5] The November 1792 meeting in New Orleans with Chickasaws, Choctaws, and Cherokees and reports of increased American military and diplomatic activity led Carondelet to conclude that the Spanish needed not only a stronger alliance with Indians but additional posts, including one on the bluffs of the Margot River.[6] In May 1792, he told the captain general in Havana that "if the Americans succeed in settling on Chickasaw Bluffs, not only will they be in a short time masters of the navigation of the Mississippi through the advantage of being in a situation above Walnut Hills, Natchez, and New Orleans, to which by means of the rapid current they could arrive in a few days . . . but they will force Spain to desist from her right of collecting duties, which come down to our settlements in Illinois, New Madrid, etc." In this same letter he pointed out another particular advantage of the site enhancing the value of the bluffs: "a whirlpool which forces boats to pass within pistol shot of the hill which dominates the river, and on which they would erect the fort."[7]

Americans, particularly those established in the Cumberland region, had indeed cast covetous eyes on the site. Like the Spanish, they recognized its strategic importance and certainly could agree with Carondelet's assessment of its military value. They also saw value, as did the Spanish, in suggesting the possibility of locating a trading post there. Each competed with the other to secure Chickasaw permission to establish such a post. Still playing something of a dual role as he did in the context of Delavillebeuvre's 1787 mission to discuss trade matters with Choctaws and Chickasaws, Benjamin James told Blount that if "you want the Indians to pitch on a place for you to send your goods; no place suits as well as the Chickasaw Bluffs, or say the mouth of Wolf river." He then went on to tell Blount that, although he felt his life threatened, he would be happy to assist in the distribution of the goods he recommended should be sent: "2,000 pounds of powder, and 4,000 pounds of lead . . . and other things equivalent, such as flints, knives, and arms." He characterized every white man in this nation as "dependent on the Spanish."[8]

Events in Europe associated with the French Revolution began to play a role in the diplomacy and politics of the Mississippi valley by the time of the New Orleans meetings in late 1792 and strengthened Spanish interest in establishing a post at Chickasaw Bluffs. During the summer of 1792, a new, more radical government—one committed to abolishing the monarchy and establishing a republic in France and to making the revolution an international one—came to power in what has been called the second French Revolution. France was already at war with Austria and Prussia, countries where many who feared the revolution had fled and where they began to work to end it, especially as it became more and more radical. In January the war expanded when the new French government declared war on Britain and Spain. For radical revolutionaries, the war transformed the Revolution into a veritable worldwide crusade.[9]

French people living in Louisiana followed the events in Europe closely. Many of these people supported the cause of the revolution and hoped that it might bring about a restoration of French authority in Louisiana. Named after the most radical group in the first National Assembly in France, Jacobin clubs came into existence. In February 1793, Carondelet expressed concerns about these people and their activities to the captain-general in Havana: "The minds of these people, already excited by the news brought by some vessels of the great advantages secured by the Republic, have been disturbed." Wine from Bordeaux, he said, had been received by one of the richest merchants in New Orleans and used "to be drunk with the good patriots" at a dinner at which "the victories and progress of the French arms" were toasted. Carondelet went on to suggest to Las Casas that the Spanish government might return Louisiana to the French in exchange for the French portion of Hispaniola.[10] Influenced no doubt by recollection of the uprising some thirty years earlier of the French inhabitants of New Orleans against the new Spanish governor, he issued, at the same time as he called for the creation of an Indian confederation, a proclamation greatly limiting talk and meetings in any way sympathetic to the events in France.[11]

Outside New Orleans, much happened to intensify these worries. The new French government's minister to the United States, Edmond Genêt, became an energetic promoter of French republicanism in America after he landed in Charleston, South Carolina, in the spring of 1793. His instructions told him to work to establish some kind of pact between France and the United States whereby both would work to extend "the empire of liberty." That required both "to punish the powers still retaining colonial systems," an injunction that sanctioned working actively to end British rule in Canada and Spanish rule in both North and South America.[12] Knowing of widespread sympathy in the United States for the revolutionary cause, Genêt began to work toward these ends as he journeyed north from Charleston to New York to present his credentials to President Washington. He began arming privateers for use against the British and by so doing violated American neutrality and law. In general he seemed to be appealing over the head of the government to the American people for support.[13] These actions posed an immediate challenge to the American government, which by means of a presidential proclamation in March had declared itself neutral with respect to the war in Europe.[14] Because of Genêt's behavior, the American government demanded his recall. By the time that happened, his popularity had declined in the United States, and a new government in France disavowed his activities and revoked his commissions. Rather than returning to France to face probable execution, he married the daughter of Governor George Clinton of New York and settled on a farm on Long Island.[15]

For a brief time, however, Genêt's cause found enthusiastic adherents west of the Appalachian Mountains among those who remained disgruntled with failure of the U.S. government to secure navigation rights on the Mississippi River and pursue a more aggressive Indian and land policy to open the area for their settlement and exploitation. In the words of historian Arthur Whitaker, "when Edmund [*sic*] Genêt proclaimed a holy war against the Spanish tyranny he found a ready response among the frontiersmen from Georgia to Kentucky."[16] Consistent with the general object of promoting republicanism and liquidating colonialism, his instructions called upon him to promote unrest in Louisiana, and he was authorized to assemble expeditions against Louisiana and Florida. Before doing anything to carry out those instructions, however, he found George Rogers Clark, the hero of the American Revolution in the west, and James O'Fallon, the Yazoo speculator who promoted a settlement at Nogales, ready to put together an expedition to march against New Orleans.[17] In 1793, Clark had accepted a French major general's commission to assist Genêt in a plan to move against the Spanish. Learning of that initiative, Gayoso sent a letter to Beauregard at Nogales in early November urging him to "live with the greatest care, for the French refugees in the United States plan an invasion of this province from the upper reaches of the [Mississippi] River." He then outlined measures Beauregard should implement, including the identification of suspicious activities and people, naming three he would like arrested. He followed that letter with a long one to Carondelet reporting information, gathered by an American, confirming Clark's appointment and the creation of an expedition of five thousand men to move the following spring.[18] Ugulayacabé repeated that number to Gayoso the following March in a letter written by Fooy: "I have found out the truth there is the Number of five thousand going against you."[19]

Throughout 1793 and early 1794, Carondelet continued to receive such reports, many of them much exaggerated. They all reinforced his fears of invasion not only from the north down the river but also from the south.[20] The American commissioner to the Creeks, James Robertson, who had been among those who sought the help of the Spanish in late 1780 and had named a district of the Cumberland settlements after Estevan Miró, informed the commandant in New Madrid of a projected invasion of Spanish settlements by people from Cumberland and Kentucky operating under French commissions.

In a letter of February 1, 1794, Robertson tried to assure Gayoso that his "government is far from promoting their Measures, but on the contrary have constantly opposed them." Robertson admitted limits, however, as to what the U.S. government could do. "The Nature of it [the government] however," he told Gayoso, "is such, that every man under it is at liberty to go where, and when he pleases." Then, from Pensacola, William Panton reported French privateers off the coast of Florida.[21] Finally, in the spring of 1795, a major slave conspiracy and insurrection centering on the estate of Julian Poydras in Pointe Coupeé (Punta Cortada) added more evidence in the mind of Carondelet to the dangers of sedition deriving from the French Revolution, its ideas, and its partisans in America.[22]

Yet, well before the activities stimulated by the French Revolution and the Genêt mission, the acquisition of Chickasaw Bluffs had become a priority of Spanish policy in the Mississippi valley, at least in the mind of Carondelet. A beginning could be made, he thought, through the trader John Turnbull, who, Carondelet knew, had established a Chickasaw family and, through it, ties to the nation. In December 1792, he told Gayoso that the Chickasaws had asked him to permit Turnbull to establish a trading post on the Yazoo River. Aware that William Panton might object, Carondelet at first dissented, whereupon, as he told Gayoso, "the king of that nation was so annoyed with my objection that he threatened to go over to the Americans and leave my table." Carondelet then decided to allow Turnbull to place a trading house "on the Mobile [River]," but he wrote a letter to Panton explaining the action and suggesting that because Panton could import goods without paying a tax, he could probably put Turnbull out of business. He told Gayoso, however, that "if we can induce him [Turnbull] to place one [a store] on the Margot River, the territory of which belongs to the Chickasaws, it will be very easy to make use of it to furnish arms and ammunition to the Cherokees in the guise of a present, and take away from the Americans the means of establishing themselves in the same place, as they have planned." "The Chickasaws," continued Carondelet, "will consent to the raising of a small fort by us to protect Turnbull's storehouse providing that he should ask for it; and we shall make him ask for it in exchange for some privilege in his commerce or some presents." Should the Americans object, thought Carondelet, the Chickasaws would oppose them because of the fact of Turnbull's place in the nation by virtue of his marriage and children.[23]

Given Turnbull's kinship ties to the Chickasaws and the Chickasaws' preference to have him as their trade contact, both Carondelet and Gayoso continued to see him as a means to help secure the site. Panton, however, stood in opposition to any expansion of that trader's commercial business, and a challenge for these officials—as Gayoso's letter from Chickasaw Bluffs of August 1795 so well reveals—was at least to postpone as long as possible any definitive resolution of this commercial rivalry.[24] Despite a reminder by Panton of his firm's exclusive privilege to the Choctaw and Chickasaw trade, Carondelet told the Natchez governor in 1793 to consult with Turnbull—then in Baton Rouge—to determine how that trader might work through his sons in the Chickasaw nation to secure permission to build a store.[25]

Carondelet also solicited the aid of Juan Delavillebeuvre in Boukfouka. In March 1793, Delavillebeuvre reported that the Chickasaws had consented "for Turnbull to put up a trading post at a place not exactly on Chickasaw Bluffs" but about thirty leagues from his house on the Yazoo River.[26] Taskietoka and several other Chickasaw chiefs includng Piomingo asked that Turnbull "supply us in our needs" but that he do so not at Chickasaw Bluffs, as Delavillebeuvre had asked, but at the place on the Yazoo River.[27]

Panton objected strenuously to these concessions and did his best to discredit Turnbull. "By some subterfuge or another [Turnbull] was permitted," he wrote Carondelet in June 1793, "to carry large quantitys of Taffia and other goods up the river Yassou into the heart of the Choctaw & Chickesaw hunting grounds, where he fleeced us out of a great many skins that would have been brought to us at Mobille but for this unexpected intrusion." He went on to tell Carondelet that if Turnbull or any other person should be permitted to interfere with the Chickasaw, Choctaw, Creek, and Cherokee trade, he would cease business. Finally, after John Joyce, a partner of Turnbull, agreed in early 1795 that he and his partner would relinquish any claim to "the trade, traffic or commerce with the Chickasaw and Choctaw Nations," Spanish officials decided the concession to build a store at Chickasaw Bluffs should go to Panton, a fact Gayoso did not want to reveal, however, to those Chickasaws he met in the summer of 1795.[28]

The ongoing conflict between Creeks and Chickasaws seemed to make acquisition of the site even more imperative, for, if the conflict continued, then Spanish officials thought it could be manipulated by Americans as an excuse to take the place and thereby challenge the Spanish position in the lower Mississippi valley. They viewed with great skepticism Piomingo's willingness to seek trade and gifts from Americans and to cede land to them at such places as Muscle Shoals and Chickasaw Bluffs for the purpose of establishing trading and military posts. Delavillebeuvre saw the Chickasaw-Creek conflict, the plan for an assembly at Nogales, and the future of Chickasaw Bluffs in early 1793 as closely related. "If, as you have observed," he wrote Carondelet, "the Americans gain the Margot River at the Chickasaw Bluffs as a result of it [war between Creeks and Chickasaws], they will control the whole area, they will inject themselves into the Chickasaws, and will make themselves masters of all that part, doing to us all the injury they wish, hindering the meeting of the Nations as you have planned."[29] Carondelet found those words useful two years later when he wrote the captain-general in Havana, Luis de Las Casas, to recommend improvements in "Fort Tombigbee" (San Estevan). He argued that the outbreak of war between the Creeks and the Chickasaws and the establishment of an American post at Muscle Shoals on the Tennessee River required improvements in that Spanish post downstream from the newer Fort Confederation. The Creek-Chickasaw conflict and the American position at Muscle Shoals would give the Americans an excuse and a position "to capture Chickasaw Bluffs" and thereby gain control of "passage and navigation on the upper part of the River."[30]

In this context Carondelet and Gayoso began to employ actively the Mississippi River galley fleet, created in January 1792, and its commander, Pedro (Pierre) Rousseau, as a way to strengthen the Spanish presence along the river and ultimately deter possible invasions from the north and the occupation of Chickasaw Bluffs by Americans.[31] In late 1792, when word came of a possible American attack, Carondelet ordered Rousseau to take several vessels up to New Madrid with reinforcements. Carondelet told Rousseau to reconnoiter the Bluffs to determine a suitable place for a fort. By the time of his arrival at New Madrid, the threat of an attack on that post had diminished, and Rousseau began the return voyage almost immediately. He paused at the Bluffs and in his diary of the expedition waxed eloquent about the site "almost at the entrance of the River à Margot" and "a superb place to build a fortification." "One cannot see any finer lands, with small hills in some places, and very level in other places," he concluded.[32]

For the balance of 1793, threats seemed to diminish, although Carondelet did become preoccupied with the possibility of a French attack from the south and for that reason directed Rousseau to take the galleys downstream in June. Toward the end of the year, however, he began to receive news of more activity to the north related to the machinations of Clark and Genêt and therefore decided that another expedition under the command of Rousseau was in order. Again, the destination was New Madrid and the object to provide reinforcements, but this time Rousseau's orders included the requirement that he stop at Chickasaw Bluffs to deliver there the annual presents to the Chickasaws, as specified in the Nogales treaty. The fleet left New Orleans on January 21, 1794, and reached Natchez on February 18. It remained there for a week and then proceeded to Nogales and then Chickasaw Bluffs, where it arrived on April 8 to deliver the presents to the Chickasaws before proceeding to New Madrid. No Indians were present then, further delaying Rousseau. Ugulayacabé finally arrived, however, with one identified as his son, and reported that the rest of the nation had been delayed. Rousseau entrusted the gifts to him for distribution to his people. Then, before departing, he ordered the galleys to assume a combat formation and fire a general salute of the artillery. Despite receiving news that the Franco-American expedition had failed, he continued on April 26 to New Madrid, the principal object of his trip. Rousseau prepared quickly to take advantage of high water to return, achieving at least the objective of delivering gifts to the Chickasaws and reassuring the people living in the area of New Madrid.[33]

Events in late 1794 and early 1795 reinforced the resolve to secure the site by use of the fleet and the services of certain key people. In defiance of the American government, Georgia awarded more than thirty million acres of land bordering the Mississippi River well to the north of Chickasaw Bluffs to four different land companies.[34] Carondelet responded to that action by advising the Chickasaws of it and again telling Rousseau to prepare to take an armada of naval vessels to New Madrid and be prepared to seize the Bluffs.[35] In late December, Ugulayacabé visited Gayoso and reported a trip by Piomingo to meet with President Washington. That report, combined with resumption of war between Creeks and Chickasaws in early 1795 and the prospect of a new American post at Muscle Shoals, raised the specter of American involvement and use of the war as an excuse to seize the Bluffs. Delavillebeuvre had already suggested that possibility in 1793. Now, in 1795, John Forbes, an associate of Panton, in effect repeated what Delavillebuevre had written but linked the outbreak of war to the Georgia land schemes, when he told Panton in March that Georgians "have already begun their operations by raising a War between the Chickasaws & the Creeks."[36]

As Rousseau and the fleet moved upriver toward Natchez, Ugulayacabé headed downstream to Natchez by pirogue with one of his "sons" and from which he planned to return in a similar vessel belonging to Turnbull's sons. He arrived there on December 28, 1794, the day before Rousseau's flotilla arrived. Ugulayacabé spent several days there with Gayoso to report fully on the trip of Piomingo to Philadelphia to meet with President Washington. As Gayoso said, the chief did not want to talk to Piomingo until he had consulted with Gayoso, with Benjamin Fooy (then, in effect, the Spanish commissioner to the Chickasaws), and with an unnamed "mestizo," perhaps the Turnbull son, who had joined them. Gayoso reported that he stayed with Ugulayacabé most of the time so that he could, "through what would appear to be casual conversation," get him to express himself without reserve. He seemed quite pleased with the meeting for, as he said, "at the end of two or three days I was perfectly informed about the state of affairs in the Chickasaw Nation." Gayoso learned much about the visit of Piomingo and twenty men of his village with the president of the United States. The president received them very well, according to what Ugulayacabé said. In the end, Piomingo apparently accepted the American position. Gifts of "some consideration" were bestowed on Piomingo, particularly the sum of one thousand pesos (later revised down to six hundred), and those who accompanied him.[37]

Ugulayacabé's gesture of loyalty to Spanish interests prompted Gayoso to urge him to oppose concessions to the Americans and remain loyal to the Spanish. He emphasized that the Spanish desired only to maintain peace and unity among the Indian nations and between them and the Spanish. Such unity could not be achieved, Gayoso told Ugulayacabé, if there were people such as Piomingo leading "opposing parties." By being more specific about what he saw as American objectives, Gayoso contrasted their objectives with those of the Spanish. "If one day the Americans establish a Fort at Muscle Shoals, the Iron Mine, [a site farther up the east bank of the Mississippi River from Chickasaw Bluffs], and Chickasaw Bluffs," he said, "they will begin to expand their hunting, depriving the Indians of the only means they have of subsisting." Next, he said, would come an extension of "their cultivation to the very center of the nation," as "they are doing with the Miamis and other Indians."[38]

Gayoso concluded his rather lengthy summary of the conversations with Ugulayacabé by making further observations about the importance of talking with and ultimately securing broad agreement from Indians—very much needed now as the Spanish pressed to gain permission to occupy and fortify the Chickasaw Bluffs. Presents or gifts, he recognized, continued to be an important element in any talk or negotiation, for "no Indian Chief makes journeys for nothing," he said. Furthermore, time and patience must prevail: "The Indians are incapable of being persuaded by reason, and only by tact and over a long period of time; they are alienated by any novelty, and any departure from their accustomed path exasperates them and they cannot be counted on." For these reasons, diplomacy needed to be flexible and everything done to let it be known "that the Chiefs and Individuals of influence be made to know that they can and should come to see us from time to time to discuss with us matters of mutual interest."[39]

Rousseau and his flotilla reached Natchez the day after Ugulayacabé's arrival and remained there for over a week. Now fearing a possible rebellion of French sympathizers in New Orleans and lower Louisiana, Carondelet ordered him to proceed only as far as Nogales and remain there until further orders. He did authorize, however, a small detached force to contest any American designs on Chickasaw Bluffs. By the end of January, after Ugulayacabé's visit to Natchez, conditions had apparently improved enough in New Orleans so that Carondelet could order Rousseau to proceed to New Madrid, stopping at Chickasaw Bluffs only long enough to deliver the Chickasaw's annual gift to Chinubbee, who had become "King" of the Chickasaws after the death sometime in late 1794 of his brother, Taskietoka.[40]

That departure did not occur until March 14, a delay caused in part by bad weather.[41] Shortly thereafter, Gayoso concluded that immediate action was necessary to secure the bluffs. Ugulayacabé had written him a long letter in February to tell him that "my land is at present full of trouble" and then to place the blame fully on the Creeks. "There is no other disturbers here than the Creeks," he said. That established the basis for asking for help and pledging his full support—even his life—to do what might be necessary to eliminate "the trouble."[42] Knowing that he needed the full support of this Chickasaw chief, Gayoso wrote to Benjamin Fooy on March 14, just before Rousseau departed Natchez to continue the trip to New Madrid, and urged him to exploit to the full Ugulayacabé's pledge to help the Spaniards. Do all you can, he told Fooy, "to get him to request that we build a small fort at the bluffs at the place that Mr. Rousseau may indicate." He suggested that Fooy characterize such a fort as a place of refuge "for him and for you in case of a retreat" and the safest place for Turnbull to have his merchandise should that trader wish to locate there. He told Fooy to link the continuation of presents to the granting of a concession to build the fort. "It is impossible," Gayoso wrote, "for him to imagine that we will give them some annual presents without their doing something for us."[43]

Bearing the same date as the letter to Fooy, two other letters of Gayoso went to Carondelet and to Ugulayacabé. Both endeavored to reinforce the support of Ugulayacabé. Gayoso told Carondelet that he had ordered the commandant at Nogales (Beauregard) to hold the five hundred pesos "destined to Ougoulayacabe" until Turnbull could dispose of them, "since the said chief had requested that they be delivered to the said Turnbull." In his letter to Ugulayacabé, he assured the chief that the people who had brought Gayoso his letters had received "a reward for their trouble." More important, Gayoso reaffirmed his friendship and expressed displeasure at the continuation of war between the Creeks and the Chickasaws. He blamed Piomingo for that state of affairs and for disunity rather than unity among the Indians, and he reminded Ugulayacabé of the commitment not to declare war without first consulting about it. On a happier note and to provide support for both Fooy and Rousseau, he reported that the galleys "this very day" had set off for New Madrid with presents to be distributed at the Bluffs.[44]

Because Gayoso had decided that the Bluffs needed to be occupied immediately, he also sent a message to Rousseau to keep the squadron at Chickasaw Bluffs until more detailed instructions came from Carondelet. He also provided guidelines for Rousseau to follow to advance the diplomatic process and secure the site for a fort. Rousseau reported considerable success toward this end in a letter to Gayoso. He wrote that the trader, James Colbert, and his son Billy, a Chickasaw chief, arrived with a number of warriors to receive presents expected from Cumberland. He said that their expectations were disappointed, for the goods had either been destroyed or taken on the Ohio River by "the Creeks, some twenty Chickasaws, and twenty Americans" and that only four Chickasaws had arrived at Chickasaw Bluffs by boat. Rousseau went on to tell Gayoso that he had asked Billy Colbert why two hundred Americans, apparently from Cumberland, were in his nation. Colbert denied that there were that many and went on to say that when he left Illinois (St. Louis), there were ten Americans from Cumberland with him but that they would probably soon leave. He then said that he had received news from Turnbull's store on the Yazoo that Gayoso was en route to the Bluffs with presents and that he would remain there to see him.[45]

Rousseau devoted a substantial portion of his letter to discussion of the arrival of Ugulayacabé and the events that followed. Ugulayacabé talked with Rousseau on board his ship and said that he had expected to find Gayoso there. He then went on to tell Rousseau that he had left his nation "on the verge of being attacked by its enemies" and would not leave until he had seen Gayoso. He asked that before the squadron should leave, he and his people would like to see it under full sail, a request that Rousseau honored by ordering the galleys to put on a show. According to Rousseau, the chief asked often whether the Americans would come by river and take the Bluffs from the Spaniards. Rousseau said that he reassured him that they probably would not but if they did, he had sufficient men and cannon to deter them. Ugulaycabé, according to Rousseau, reaffirmed his loyalty to the Spanish cause by saying that he had told all his nation that the Spanish had sufficient men and cannon as well as money and that they had "a great country nearby" (Cuba) capable of supplying more men and matériel. That statement led Ugulaycabé to question Rousseau about how long it took to go from New Orleans to Havana. Rousseau said he had made the trip in three days and returned in four. After this conversation, Ugulaycabé went ashore to see Fooy.[46]

Rousseau indicated that there was strong support among the Chickasaws present for the establishment of a Spanish post. He said that the distribution of gifts pleased them as did the added attraction of seeing the galleys under full sail accompanied by the firing of cannon—a "charming effect," according to Rousseau, who said that the thunder of the guns brought the Indians to the cliffs to shoot their guns all night.[47] Ugulayacabé viewed the naval and artillery display on board Rousseau's galley. A later conversation between him and Rousseau elicited a warning. Ugulayacabé said that Washington had informed the Chickasaws that he was going to send "all his warriors to make war on the Creeks, and that they would soon be destroyed." Furthermore, according to Ugulayacabé, Washington had said that the Americans intended the fort for which they had asked the Chickasaws permission to build on Chickasaw Bluffs to be for the defense of the Chickasaws. When Rousseau replied by observing that the Americans wanted only the destruction of the "Red Men" and their land, Ugulayacabé said he had tried to tell his people that but they "had hard ears."[48]

Gayoso continued to direct the initiatives to establish the Spanish at Chickasaw Bluffs, with Carondelet's full approval. Gayoso's "prudence and sagacity, and influence among the Indians makes him the proper person to negotiate with the Chickasaws and to take the measures most adapted to the circumstances if the Americans use force to oppose our settlement there," Carondelet told the captain-general in Havana. The Louisiana governor penned those words as Gayoso traveled in his new galiot, *La Vigilante,* to the Bluffs to direct personally the negotiations to secure the site and to begin work on a fort.[49] Accompanied by Elías Beauregard, Gayoso arrived there on May 20, after leaving Natchez on April 16, and remained until August. After arriving and establishing himself across the river, Gayoso reported in a letter of May 23 to Carondelet and in his diary that he sent immediately for Ugulaycabé. Making use of Fooy as interpreter, he informed Ugulayacabé of the object of his commission. The two discussed the Chickasaw-Creek conflict, at which time Ugulayacabé placed the blame for the conflict on the Creeks, in particular the chief known as Efau Hadjo or Mad Dog. On the more immediate matter of the fort, Ugulayacabé assured Gayoso of his support but added that "it was the custom among the Indians when their land was cut up to give them some recompense." On that point, Gayoso told Ugulayacabé that he had not come to buy land but "to propose the construction of a fort for their benefit as well as that of the Spanish nation." He knew, of course, that gifts were expected "in memory of the affection our nation professed," but he also knew that they would be several days late in arriving. This first meeting concluded with Ugulayacabé's joining Gayoso for supper. He lodged with Elías Beauregard.[50]

More talk ensued, much of it described by Gayoso as "inconsequential." Gayoso made it known that some small presents would be given to all the chiefs who assented, and he further pleased Ugulayacabé by accepting his interpretation of the causes of conflict between the Creeks and Chickasaws. During their first meeting, he had suggested that it was probably Piomingo and his party who had provoked the hostilities, knowing they would have the support of Americans or perhaps as a way to involve Americans. Gayoso essentially concluded the matter by accepting the authority of those present, especially Ugulaycabé, to make the concession and assuring them that gifts would be forthcoming. He asked Ugulayacabé's permission to move his camp to the other side of the river and to begin work on the fort. The chief agreed and urged that it be built strong "so that they would not be embarrassed." Gayoso interpreted that to mean that the fort should be strong enough to withstand an attack by the Americans and pointed out that if they were to take it, then they would be hard on Piomingo's opposition. Gayoso wrote that he had convinced Ugulayacabé that it would be so built and fortified with cannons that it could not be taken.[51]

On May 26, Gayoso prepared a letter to Carondelet reporting the successful completion of the discussions with those Chickasaws present to secure a grant of land and to begin work on a fort. He said "tact and patience" were necessary and were rewarded with the acquisition of some three thousand *arpents* of land, including the whole extent of the Bluffs of Margot from the Las Casas River to the Carondelet River. The ceremony by which the Spanish took possession occurred on May 30, the saint's day of the prince of Asturias, Fernando, the future king of Spain. It consisted of raising the royal flag, firing salvos from the many cannons, and naming the post "San Fernando de Las Barrancas" in honor of the prince and future king.[52]

Although Gayoso reported enough success to justify the raising of the Spanish flag and the beginning of work on the post, the formal cession did not occur until almost a month later. Ugulayacabé had made it clear that any final approval was contingent upon his meeting in council with other chiefs and warriors. After agreeing to what Gayoso described, Ugulayacabé returned to his people and met with them to recommend approval of his action. He reported to Gayoso that they had agreed and that the decision would be confirmed by a mission led by the chiefs William Glover (Ulauthapaye) and Payehuma. Piomingo and his faction were not among those giving their assent; indeed, Piomingo, in his response to an invitation from Gayoso delivered to him "by the mouth of Malcolm McGee" to join the others at the Bluffs, told Gayoso quite emphatically that he could not come and that furthermore "it is the voice of the whole Chickasaw Nation in general that you should leave the Chicksaw Bluffs as you found it, and return home to your own land immediately which may prevent the colors from flying over them."[53] Ugulayacabé assured the governor they were very much in the minority.[54] The delegation came to San Fernando to put their signs along with the signatures of the governor and witnesses present on a text to which a map of the site was attached. Dated June 20, both the map and text contained a detailed description of the extent of the cession and its identity as a Spanish post. A stream that had been called "Chickasaw River" became the "Las Casas River," probably in honor of the captain-general in Havana. Two other streams received the appellations "Carondelet River" and "Gayoso Creek." The person who had now become Spain's commissioner to the Chickasaws, Benjamin Fooy, found his name attached to a large island.[55]

The talk went on, however. With work well under way, a large number of Chickasaws arrived at the Bluffs in early August. They included the new king of the Chickasaws and a small number from Piomingo's village to hear more from Gayoso about the reasons for a Spanish fort. They also raised the question of a store and once again asked that it be one operated by Turnbull. Again, what Carondelet characterized to Las Casas as prudence and sagacity on the part of the Natchez governor were put to the test, and, as Gayoso describes the proceedings, he seems to have met and passed it well. He elaborated on the care that he took to embellish the proceedings with appropriate ceremony and protocol and to allow all voices to be heard. The speaker for the king alluded to divisions among the Chickasaws and said that because of them, they often did not hear fully or accurately what others were doing. For that reason, he said, they came to hear Gayoso explain the need for the post. In trying to satisfy that request, Gayoso said he reviewed many of the events, beginning with the designs of O'Fallon and other land speculators on the Nogales site and the decision of the Spanish to occupy it in 1791. He also mentioned the French and their intrigues. Largely in response to a protest from a warrior that the Spanish were usurping land long regarded as inviolably Chickasaw, Gayoso stressed the inappropriateness of the site across the river, including its susceptibility to flooding, and the advantages to the Chickasaws of a Spanish post on their side of the river. As he had done before, he emphasized that, unlike some Americans, the Spanish had no need or desire for land, and to support that point he asked them to note that no houses had been built in the vicinity of the Nogales fort. Gayoso sought to skirt the issue of a Turnbull trading post by saying that the first one would probably be a Panton establishment but that Turnbull would probably be allowed to bring in his goods. In that way, they would not be subject to just one trader.[56]

Just over two months later, however, diplomats on the other side of the Atlantic Ocean undid the diplomatic work of Gayoso and all those who had made possible the agreements reached at Natchez, Boukfouka, Nogales, and San Fernando de las Barrancas between 1791 and 1795. They also laid the basis for a significant reduction in the number of paths that chiefs such as Piomingo could follow. An assessment of the realities of European politics led Spanish diplomats, notably the minister of state Manuel de Godoy, to accept the American contention that the thirty-first parallel should mark the southern boundary between the United States and Spain in North America.[57] In so doing, Godoy rendered hollow Gayoso's words to Franchimastabé and Taboca of four years earlier "that the Spaniards always wished you well & more than any Nation favour the Red People."[58] No Indians took part in that negotiation, which laid the basis for a complete withdrawal of the Spanish from the region, and many reacted by accusing the Spanish of betraying them. Some took stronger action by harassing the commission appointed to survey the boundary. With the gradual retreat of Spain from the region, some of their worst fears soon became very real. Their world changed radically and not for the better. Paths diminished and for many became those of egress rather than access.

Ugulayacabé, who had emerged as the principal friend of the Spanish among the Chickasaws, and other Chickasaws sensed that the world had changed for the worse for them. Expressions of what Louisiana's intendant, Juan Ventura Morales, described as "disgust" at the cession of territory to the Americans occurred by means of visits to the post by many to deliver words on behalf of their people. Such manifestations of displeasure meant to someone like Ventura Morales that the diplomacy of withdrawal would mean no reduction in expenses or care. He cited a letter of Josef Deville de Goutin, who served as a commandant at San Fernando, which described the arrival there in late 1796 of Ugulayacabé, Payehuma, and almost three hundred men and women to deliver a speech for their people. De Goutin reported receiving them with ample provision for food and a military display on the river and that Benjamin Fooy had translated and recorded their words very carefully.[59]

The gist of their message was that the Spanish had abandoned them and put them into the mouth of the wolf. Ugulayacabé elaborated further on that metaphor by likening Americans to tigers, rattlesnakes, and bears and expressing fear that their appetite and power would soon devour them. We, he said, are " 'like the smaller animals to the jaws of the Tiger and the bear' "; " 'We perceive in them the cunning of the Rattle snake who caresses the Squirrel he intends to devour'."[60]

For about a century during which new people arrived from Europe and Africa, a way of talking—a diplomacy—emerged; when supported by trade and gifts, it enabled those European newcomers, some of whom served as agents of empire, to articulate and secure limited interests. It also afforded native elites a way to sustain their traditions while pursuing new opportunities they saw in the advent of Europeans. It was a diplomacy that worked so long as it limited goals and sustained a respect for process or ways of talking that were a significant part of both European and native culture. Sensitive, patient, and intelligent diplomats, like Gayoso, understood such requirements and were rewarded. The withdrawal of Gayoso and other Spaniards and American occupation of what Indians regarded as their land meant there were fewer opportunities for the kind of diplomacy that often worked quite well when power was more widely dispersed and hence limited. The result was more encouragement for the bellicose methods of such people as Andrew Jackson and other Indian fighters so celebrated in much of the popular mythology associated with the expansion of the United States.[61]

Part III

Documents

Translations by Sarah J. Banks and Charles A. Weeks

Most of the documents that follow have been translated from Spanish to English in a three-stage process. Sarah Banks prepared a rough draft translation. I revised it to make it more readable in English. Then the two of us reviewed my revision against the Spanish text to try to make sure the translation represented the original accurately and read reasonably well in English. Interpolated words have been placed in brackets. Each document is prefaced by an identification of the text with which we worked and its archival signature.

1

Diary of Gayoso's Journey to Nogales, March 24–April 23, 1791

Manuel Gayoso de Lemos (signed) to Estevan Miró, Natchez, May 10, 1791. AGI, PC, *leg.* 2352, N.° 84.; transcript copy in MDAH, RG 26, SPT, ledger 3, reel 3, pp. 653–67.

Believing it necessary to inform your lordship about all my operations related to the Nogales post and that the report necessarily ought to be a lengthy one, I will compose it in the form of a diary for greater clarity.

Last March 23, I advised your lordship of the departure of an expedition for Nogales. Having returned here that night I again left the following day to join the convoy. I reached it on the twenty-sixth very early in the morning.

At Bayu Pierre I took proper measures so that as soon as the overland road to Nogales should be opened it would be provided with fresh meat; in like manner, I bought there two hundred barrels of corn for the King's livestock that had already been sent before.

On the first of April, I arrived with the entire convoy at noon at my former camping place of the *Vergel de Duramas.* After eating, we departed for Nogales and, having gone on ahead, I set fire to the cut cane in the clearing that I had made on my first trip.

Having arrived, the convoy was unloaded and made camp at said site. I located the natives of this district at some distance in a campsite that William Smith already had laid out and where there was wood being cut for the stockade for which he had been contracted. This separation seemed to me advantageous in order to avoid the least cause of discord between these people and the troops.

On the second day, [work] began on a road from the bank of the river to the plain where the fort should be placed in order to bring up the artillery which was unloaded that day. Four mounted cannons remained. The clearing continued, and I sent two men accompanied by an Indian who had presented himself in order to open communication with the Black River by a very short path that, according to the same Indian, the Indians were accustomed to using in olden times. This same day, following the old paths that I had tried, I continued my journey, and, although it took much work to penetrate the cane brakes that are very thick, I advanced by different directions much more than in my first trip. Arriving at a range of hills that crosses all this country and passes along there to the Yazu, I found to my astonishment an extraordinary height that dominates all the others in the immediate vicinity. I immediately ordered people to climb up to clear the cane to be able to examine better the place. Quite convincingly there remained no doubt that it exceeded the first height that I had encountered. I estimated the distance from the river at about 200 *toesas*[1] and that it would serve as high ground for the projected fort. I was completely satisfied that this was the greatest height of all those surrounding Nogales. I determined to locate there in place of the small proposed redoubt of the first peak a strong house walled in by a stockade that would secure this post, and I named it *Monte Vigia.*

On Sunday, the third, I received the visit of a chief named Ytilagana of the Choctaw Nation from the village of Boucfuca and six more warriors of the same nation but from different villages. They appeared [to be] in a friendly mood; and, [after] I had told them why I was settling there, they showed [themselves to be] satisfied. I ordered that they be given food. I fed the chief, and in the afternoon I embarked with him in my galiot separating myself from the fort and [going] about a league upstream.[2] On my return, the banner of the King was seen, and they fired the cannons that were mounted, I having arranged [it] from onboard. When I disembarked all the troops and boat's crews saluted the flag with shouts of "Long live the King!". The Natchez company showed equal happiness on this occasion, firing all their carbines. This ceremony was very much admired by the Indians, impressing them and eliciting respect, a circumstance that I wanted to achieve, for it seemed to me fit that they should form a favorable view of our new establishment, all the more because the chief had told me that he was going to return to the nation to inform [them] of our settlement.

On the fourth and fifth the twelve cannons remained mounted prepared to challenge passage of the river; the clearing continued; and John Girault went to explore the direction of a little stream that flows from the Post of Nogales.[3] I continued my inspection of the bluff, and I observed that the bluff follows in the direction of south, southeast to the *Vergel de Duramas* and on the other side seems to continue east, northeast, to the Yazu reaching, as I said in my previous report, to about four leagues above the mouth. All the land to the northwest between this bluff and the Mississippi, excepting a small area next to the Post of Nogales and at the foot of the previously mentioned line of hills, is for the most part flooded land, which includes the cypress swamp I have already explored. This inspection has not only helped convince me that in the area there is no better site for the post, but it has also informed me of the quality of the land and of the various springs that flow from the foot of the bluff hurling themselves at various places over the cliffs and falling alternately from distances of four to ten feet and joining together at the above cited stream. The land is primarily black and light textured and four feet in depth, producing large and thick cane, very tall trees, and many medicinal herbs. On the north side of the stream there is a plain that, although it [has] little frontage, it is sufficient to form a town extending in back bordering the foot of the range to the Yazu according to reports.

From the sixth to the tenth, the clearing continued. The Indian and the two men who had left to open the road to the Black River returned. They had failed to find the trail, having lost and missed it in the range of hills. Because of the uncertainty, I determined for now that only the road that was already known could be used, although it is long. In time it can be improved. On the last day I entered the cypress grove accompanied by the commandant of the post and Don Juan Girault to find the way to the Yazu. Having arrived at a lagoon in the river it was not possible for me to continue in view of the fact that the water was very near the branches of the trees obstructing passage. For that reason and because I had heard the signal of the post indicating boats in view, I returned immediately and found four river boats. In the afternoon of the same day I had a visit from a small-medal chief of the Choctaw nation called Panto Tistabe with a nephew of Franchimastabé and eight more companions, all of whom presented themselves with all the pomp of which they were capable [which included] dancing the calumet. They informed me that they were going to New Orleans to see Your Lordship, but they had no provision and therefore it was necessary to give them [such supplies] to arrive at this town and boat landing so that here they might be sufficiently supplied [to go] to that capital. During the night of this same day, the three yoke of oxen arrived. They had been detained at the Big Black River because the passage in the vicinity of this river was flooded. The driver informed me that from the Black River up to seven miles from Nogales the trail was fairly level through a lightly wooded area but that the last mentioned seven miles was very rough land with very thick cane, but, nevertheless, they made the entire trip in a day and a half, from which I infer that by straight path it would not be much more than seven leagues.

From the eleventh until the seventeenth, the clearing continued; the cane and trees that had been cut were set afire; and they began to make adobe bricks for the oven. During this period on various trips I made, I went up the Mississippi to the vicinity of the Yazu to determine whether there was another cypress swamp, but I did not find one.

On the eighteenth I decided on the location of the buildings, and the store was begun. Finding already cleared the place where the fortification should be placed [and] in spite of the fact that I have already submitted the map, I have considered it wise to alter the design of the curtain between the bulwarks, making it form an angle in the center to accommodate better the contours of the land avoiding thereby the necessity of moving too much earth and increasing at the same time its optimum defense. On the first height that I have called *El Gallo,* I have included within the stockade a small strong house of sixteen feet square; with [a] second height at opposite angles that will serve as both a bulwark and the location of the banner. This change from the original plan is necessary, for it will not add any cost and it conforms better to the lay of the land and takes full advantage of it, as Your Lordship will see by means of the map and explanation that I will send at the first opportunity. In conformity with my wish to be of greatest service to the King, I have been able to be more effective in the use of resources that provided me with a greater number of workers to overcome the many obstacles that otherwise would not have been possible to overcome. I think that this has been better than following blindly my first opinion.

On the nineteenth, the clearing and the collection of materials continued. Construction of the oven began.

On the twentieth I laid out the fortification, marking it with stakes. The former projects continued.

On the twenty-first I left in a *galiot* at four in the morning for the Yazu and, arriving at the cut that the Mississippi made in the floods of that river, I tried to enter through the southern mouth but I found it entirely closed and for that reason entered through the northern mouth. I arrived at the mouth of the Yazu at ten in the morning. At this place and with little difference to where I arrived, it is eighty to one hundred *toesas* wide and is located at latitude thirty two degrees, thirty-three minutes. Since I entered the said river I encountered a current more rapid than that of the Mississippi, but I learned that when the waters from the interior do not join, the current is the reverse because the weight of the water that enters through the mouth is stronger. Going up the river a half league on the northern bank there is a rather significant stream whose current was running from said direction and without doubt it is the one that Thomas Hutchins mentions.[4] He states that this stream communicates with the Mississippi a hundred leagues above the San Francisco River following a course through several lakes. The discovery of this waterway would be of greatest importance, for it might facilitate significantly trade with our posts in the Illinois country. A league above the southern side a branch of the Yazu leaves with a very rapid current and it is where this river joins with the Nogales cypress swamp. In the short time I was there I tried to explore this, for when the waters should be high it will be navigable. About three miles further up and on the same side, there is another stream whose current enters the Yazu. I continued navigating, always against a very strong current, until five in the afternoon, having arrived by my estimate about three leagues following this river without having seen any land that was not covered by water with the exception of a place where I ate and another at the end of my trip, neither one of which had much potential. Nevertheless, I have learned that high ground begins a league farther up on the southern side, [and it is the] place where the French formerly had a fort, a church, and other buildings.[5] It is the spot that should mark the boundary between the King's possessions and those of the Indians. It was now too late to go there, and furthermore it did not seem appropriate for me to present myself without some gift for the Indians who customarily inhabit those territories. For those reasons I returned to Nogales, arriving there at nine that night. I had agreed with the commandant of the post that when I should arrive at different locations along the Yazu I would fire a gun and he would respond in order to determine the distance from which the firing of artillery could be heard. Those in Nogales were able to hear four shots that I fired on the Yazu, but I was able to hear those fired at Nogales only at that side beyond the mouth of that river. I attributed my inability to hear any more to the noise of the current and the thickness of the high trees at that site.

On the twenty-second I made John Girault finish the second line of stakes to mark the thickness of the walls of the fortification and completed taking some notes that still were necessary for the topographic map of the post site at Nogales. I gave instructions that seemed to me necessary to continue the work until I should return there, giving the commandant instructions for his government. That same afternoon I departed for this place, where I arrived on the twenty-third in the afternoon.

When I left Nogales, about seventy *arpanes* in the plain, the entire hill called *El Gallo,* and a large part of *Monte Vigia* had been cleared. About a third of the store was completed, the oven begun, and material collected to continue the work. With respect to all this and with regard to the care of the forces, the commandant, Don Elías Beauregard, demonstrated great zeal, and the workers showed an unusual willingness to work and did so with uncommon energy.

Most of the days I was in Nogales, John Girault and I alternatively would observe the sun by means of an excellent theodolite of modern construction that I have, and with very small difference from one day to another we were able make observations to locate Nogales at thirty-two degrees, eighteen minutes latitude north.

Both during my first trip and my second, I had John Girault, assistant surveyor of the district, with me. Through experience I had formed a good opinion of him. He was of great assistance in surveying the land and marking the places that I had discovered on my explorations. He has carried out his duties with dispatch, providing much support in all my operations. I commend him to Your Lordship for your recognition and the justice that the subject deserves.

God grant you many years. Natchez. May 10, 1791.

2

Franchimastabé and Taboca to Gayoso, Choctaw Nation, May 14, 1791

Three versions of Franchimastabé and Taboca's letter to Gayoso of May 14, 1791, follow: (1) a typescript of N.° 2, enclosed with Estevan Minor to Luis de las Casas, New Orleans, June 28, 1791, N.° 201, AGI, PC, *leg.* 2352; (2) a Spanish translation printed in Manuel Serrano y Sanz, *España y los indios cherokis y chactas en la segunda mitad del siglo XVIII* (Sevilla: Tip. De la 'Guía Oficial,' 1916); and (3) an English translation of the Spanish text (Banks and Weeks). There is another English translation in Samuel Dorris Dickinson, translator and annotator, *Spain and the Cherokee and Choctaw Indians in the Second Half of the Eighteenth Century* (Idabel, Okla.: The Potsherd Press of the Museum of the Red River, 1995), 36–37.

(1)

Sir, I heard that My Father the father of the Cohuus and Chickasaws what is the Reason of your Reason your taking of Our Lands We Red People the King of our Lands never offered to thak the White People Land I thought you was our father and loved us but I find it is not the Case I thought that our talks was as one but I find that you took us for your Children and loved us but I find is not so that it will never be the case white People a like has took of to Eats but that land is where we find game to subsist on what is the reason the you want to take our Lands when I saw the govner of Orleines he sed that he wold love us but it not & that find that you want to starv us if you take Our Land what shall we Eate the Red People that that wants to beg Land but I never grant them yet I am the man that does that If the Govener had Tabocia a sent me would the he that he was going to do so and Sent me word and all the things made it but in Stead of it you have deceived us and take our lands by stydt the man that take this to you will tell you the Chickasaws and us is all to geather and is determined that thar you shant stay here there is Fifteen Towns of our nation that Loves our Land and Begs that you will not stay stay. No more to tell you of at present. . . . Your Friend and Children. Franchumastubia and Tabocuie.

(2)

Estimado Señor: He oído que mi Padre, el Padre de los Chactas y Chicachas, sin saber la razón por qué, toma nuestras tierras. Nosotros los hombres colorados, dueños de nuestras tierras, jamás hemos hecho mal en la de los blancos; juzgué que vosotros erais nuestros amigos, y que nos amabais, pero ahora conozco que no; pensé que vuestras palabras y las mías eran una misma; que nos habiais tomado por vuestros hijos, y que nos queriais; pero ahora veo que no es así, y que jamás lo será; los blancos tienen ganado de que comer, y la tierra en que se quieren poner es donde encontrábamos caza para subsistir; ¿qué razón tienes, pues, para tomar nuestras tierras, cuando veo que el Gobernador de la Nueva Orleáns nos dijo que nos amaría?; pero no es así.

Me parece que quieres quitarnos la subsistencia, pues quieres quitarnos nuestras tierras; ¿qué hemos de comer nosotros los hombres colorados, á quienes pedís tierras?; pero yo jamás las concedo; sin embargo, yo soy el hombre que veo esto.

¡Si el Gobernador que me envió á Taboca me hubiera enviado á decir que iba á hacer esto, y á todos los caciques!; pero en lugar de esto nos habéis engañado, y tomado nuestras tierras por fuerza; él hombre que te lleva esta te dirá que los Chicachas y nosotros estamos todos juntos, determinados á que si os quedáis en estas tierras, hay quince aldeas de nuestra nación que quieren mucho esta tierra, y os suplican que no os quedéis en ella.

No tenemos más que decirte al presente: Somos tus amigos, é hijos, Franchimastabe. Taboca.

(3)

Esteemed Sir: I have heard that my Father, the Father of the Chactas and Chicachas, without knowing why, takes our land. We men red men, masters of our land, never have done anything wrong against the white [men]. I judged that you were our friends and that you loved us, but now I know that not to be so. I thought that your words and mine were the same, that you had taken us as your sons, and that you loved us, but now I see it is not so, and it will never be. The whites have livestock to feed, and the land that they want to put it is where we found hunting to subsist. What reason do you have to take our land, when I see that the Governor of New Orleans told us that you would love us? But it is not so.

It seems to me that you want us to give up our living, for you want to take from us our lands. What do we have to eat, we red men? Whom did you ask [for this] land? I never grant them; nevertheless, I am the man who sees this.

If the Governor who sent me to Taboca would have sent me to say that he was going to do this, and to all the chiefs! But in place of this you have deceived us and taken our lands by force. The man who brings you this will tell you that the Chickasaws and we are all together and determined that if you remain in these lands there are fifteen villages of our nation that love very much this land, and they beg you not to remain in it.

We have nothing more to tell you now. We are your friends and children. Franchimastabé. Taboca.

3

Gayoso's Response to Franchimastabé and Taboca, May 28, 1791

Manuel Gayoso de Lemos to Franchimastabé, Natchez, May 28, 1791, AGI, PC, *leg.* 2352, enclosed as N.° 3, Copy, with Estevan Miró to Luis de las Casas, New Orleans, June 28, 1792, N.° 201, AGI, PC, *leg.* 2352

This letter was written in English and is reproduced here with no changes.

My Dear good friend:

I received a talk signed with your name and that of Tobacaie, dated 14 of this month & brought by the Chief of the great medal Ytelegana.

As I know the affection you have for the Spanish, I believe that whoever wrote the letter did not explain well your meaning.

I send one of my officers, Major Minor, & my own Interpreter that they may explain to you the truth of my talk & when they come back may inform me of yours, and this I send back to the Walnut hills now called Nogales that it may be handed to you by the same Chief Ytelegana.

My good Friend you know that the Spaniards always wished you well & more than any Nation favour the Red People. We never take their Lands. We wish them to be in peace to see their Sons grow up; their fields full of Corn & their hunting ground full of game.

We favour with all our power the house of Panton in Panzacola that he may be able to have great Stores of all sorts of goods there & at Mobile & send traders to the Nation that you may never be in want.

Besides this you know very well that when the Red People come to see their Father at New Orleans he always gives them some thing looking upon them as his Children.

Therefore it is not possible that we should ever do any thing to hurt you.

In your Talk you seem to be apprehensive of the new Fort that we have built at the Nogales near the Yazu.

I am going to explain to you why we do that.

My good Friend you know that formerly the English lived in this Country & were Masters of Panzacola, Mobile, Augustin, Manchack & Natchez; then they bought from you more Land as far as the Yazu. You remember very well that to draw the lines there came some officers from Panzacola who in Company with some of your Chiefs marked the line from Panzacola. As they were nigh your beloved ball ground & that by that line you would lose the said ball ground you would not consent to it.

Then all the Company stoped & some returned to Panzacola. There your Chiefs & the English agreed to carry the line another way, beginning at the Yazu a little below the ball ground to leave it out. In this manner the line was drawn & you all remained contented. The English then began to settle part of that Country & gave Land to some of their People in the Walnut hills, the Big Black & Bayu Pierre as Masters of the Country that you had sold them. After that our Great King of Spain went to war with England & our forces being greater we took from them all their Forts & Lands in this Country & remained in their room as they were before.

By and by our Great King & that of England made peace & agreed that we should ever remain Master of all the Lands he had in this Country.

Directly our Great King gave orders to take care of the good Red People that were nigh this new part of his Dominions that they should never want Traders with plenty of good.

In consequence of that you very well know that a general Congress was held at Mobile where everything was spoke & agreed. You know very well that we have always complied with what we promised then.

Every body finding that there is no Government than ours a great many People have come into this Country to make them selves Spaniards & consequently become true Friends of the Red People, for we always love them. Then our great King ordered to give Lands to all those that should sear to be his Loyal Subjects. A great many have done so & have settled all round the Natchez, Coles Creek, Bayu Pierre, & Big black.

You remember that I have told you & you know it before that we had become Masters of all the Lands the English had in this Country? Well then our Gracious King willing to give protection to all his Subjects & Friends ordered a Fort to be made at the Nogales to prevent bad men from coming there to disturb both his Subjects & the Indians that live in the neighbourhood. You know very well that there was a report some time ago that some Americans against the consent of Congress intended to come there & settle all your Country, which would put you to great distress. You see then that by this Fort we have preserved even your Lands that were close to ours there.

We own the Lands that lay on this side of the line that was drawn between you & the English & by keeping possession of them we keep yours from being taken.

The Principal Chief at New Orleans will tell you the same. In our talk there is no diference; we both love the Red Men & will always give them proofs of our friendship.

If there should be occasion for any great talk the best way is to send some Chiefs to Orleans where by Speaking to the great Chief of the Province every thing will be understood right. Otherwise we all are able to be led into error.

Major Minor the Bearer of this will answer any thing you should wish to know because he has my confidence. Take care of him in the same manner that you take care of you.

I wish that you may write to me by the hand of Major Minor, because with the help of my Interpreter he will write the truth of all you tell them.

I finish by wishing always a bright sky, white road about us, that your fields & woods may produce plenty & that your Children may dance round you full of joy.

From your beloved Father & true Friend.
Manuel Gayoso de Lemos

4

Diary of Stephen Minor's First Mission to the Choctaws May 30 to June 13, 1791

"Diario de Don Esteban Minor. Ayudante de la Plaza de Natchez relativo a la comisión que el Señor Don Manuel Gayoso de Lemos Governador de la Plaza de Natchez la encargó para Franchimastabé principal Gefe de la Nación Chacta," enclosed as N.° 2 with Manuel Gayoso to Estevan Miró, Natchez, July 1, 1791. Miró forwarded the diary to Luis de las Casas, the captain general in Havana: Estevan Miró to Luis de las Casas, New Orleans, July 15, 1791, N.° 206, AGI, SD, *leg.* 2556. Las Casas then sent it along with other documents to Spain: Luis de las Casas to the Conde de Campo Alange, Aug. 3, 1791, #87, Havana, AGI, SD, *leg.* 2556.

May 30, 1791: Having received the sealed letter for Franchimastabé and the necessary instructions for the discharge of my commission, I left this day from the Plaza of Natchez in the company of Ebenezer Fulson, Indian Interpreter, and Don Ricardo King, an inhabitant of this District.[1] We arrived that night at the house of James Truly in Coles Creek.

May 31: We left today at five in the morning and arrived at the home of Mr. Brokeus. Nothing of importance happened except that Don Ricardo King became ill.

June 1: We left at five in the morning leaving the sick Don Ricardo King behind. At about ten o'clock we crossed Bayu Pierre, in front of the house of Mr. Burnel, a distance of about sixty miles from the Plaza of Natchez. At noon I came upon a spring about ten miles from Bayu Pierre where I met two Indians who came from the Nation. I stopped to inform myself of any news. Assured that there was none, I dismissed them and remained there that night.

2: I left from the spring at dawn, and at twelve o'clock I came to a branch of the Big Black, fifty miles from the Bayu Pierre. We crossed said river at this place; and, because all the provisions had become wet, I camped there.

3: I left at dawn from this place, and at ten in the morning I crossed another branch of the Big Black fifty miles from the first [branch]. I camped there without incident.

4: Today I left at daybreak and continued my trip without incident all day until [I came] to a place two miles on this side of the river called the Halfway River, some ninety miles from the second branch of the Big Black.[2]

5: I left early this morning and at six crossed the river on a raft I [had] made. At ten we arrived at an Indian town ten miles from the Halfway River. At four in the afternoon, we passed through another Indian town about fifteen miles from the first. In both, we were well-received by their inhabitants. At seven in the afternoon, we arrived at the town of Sulusmastabé, or "Red Shoes," some fifteen miles from the last place. I went directly to his house where I found only his wife and children. She received me very well and asked me to spend the night there. She told me that she would immediately send [someone] to look for her husband and for her son, a captain who had been wounded in Natchez.[3] The latter, finding himself closer than the father, came immediately, and upon seeing me showed great pleasure, saying that it was very satisfying to him to see a Spanish Chief in his country. He treated me with great hospitality and friendship, offering me his influence and aid in the upcoming discussions. I thanked him and told him that my business was with the head Chief of the Nation, Franchimastabé. I asked him to accompany me to the place of his residence. He willingly agreed to do this. The captain then gave me the best to eat he had, and, as his father had not yet arrived, we went to bed.

6: This morning at eight, said Chief Sulusmastabé arrived at home and showed great pleasure at finding me there in his house. After the customary ceremonies, I told him I was carrying a message from the Chief in Natchez for the Chief of the Choctaw Nation.[4] I asked him to accompany me that same day, and he readily agreed to do so. At ten that morning we set out, accompanied by his son. On our trip we passed through two large Indian towns whose inhabitants showed much pleasure in seeing me, and at almost every house they insisted on my stopping to eat. At four we arrived at Franchimastabé's house, some fifteen miles from the home of Red Shoes. A short time after my arrival he asked me if the Natchez Chief had received his letter. I answered in the affirmative, and, delivering to him the letter with which I was entrusted, I told him that was the reply and that furthermore I wished to speak with him and asked him to grant me an audience the next day. He said that he was very glad to see me in his country, and that with regard to the audience I had requested for the following day that would not be possible, for three days were needed to send to different towns to advise the Chiefs and warriors so that they could be present. Besides, he said that he didn't want to be surprised, and that it was necessary for me to be patient, adding that when he would go to see white people he would have to wait until they wanted to speak and that I should have to do the same in his country where he was as much a Chief as Governor Miró was in New Orleans. I told him that I would gladly wait all the time that should be necessary. He then returned the letter that I had given him, telling me that on the day of the meeting I should return it to him, that then it would be opened in the presence of his Chiefs and warriors. He then excused himself, saying that he was going to dispatch the messages.

Later in the day several white men living in this country visited me, and as a result of our conversations I learned that Turner Brashears, a trader, was the one who had written the letter that Franchimastabé had sent to the governor of Natchez. Through these conversations I tried to find out the basis for the Indian claim to Nogales, and they assured me that the Indians would never cede this country, saying that this was land that truly belonged to them because the English had never paid them for it. In their opinion, the Indians were right in not wanting to give up the land. Nevertheless, they told me that they believed a boundary line had been drawn between the Indian lands and those of the English. A little later I met with Mr. Malcolm McGee, a resident of this nation for many years, and he assured me that the Indians had never been satisfied about the land called the Nogales. Having served as an interpreter for the English at the time the Indians had sold the land, he thought that even though the English had sent the goods for payment from England to the Superintendent of Indians the Indians had not received anything.

From my talks with various traders, I could see that they resent having their trade disrupted and that they want the Indians to refuse to cede Nogales because if that post is established, it could damage their trade, leading me to believe that it is these same traders who encourage the Indians to oppose the cession.

7: This morning at dawn, Franchimastabé came to my lodge and had a long and private conference with Brashears without seeing me. A little later, after the Chief had left, the interpreter Fulson came to me to tell me that he had heard part of the conversation in which Brashears had urged Franchimastabé that he should not under any circumstances cede Nogales nor permit any settlement there, for, if he should, they would all soon become slaves.

At eight Franchimastabé returned to my lodge, and we talked about different things. I told him that I was informed that in his nation there were many stolen horses belonging to the district of Natchez. I asked him if he could assist in their recovery. He answered that he would do all that he could to carry out such a good and legal action. As a consequence, he then sent for Felipe [Philip] Hayes, a trader living in the nation who had according to reports several stolen horses in his possession.[5] Hayes came immediately to my place, and I warned him that, knowing that several stolen horses were found in his possession, I would take him to Natchez with me the same as any other found in similar circumstances if he didn't bring them to me immediately. [I also said] I would tell the Governor in the same destination that traders in this nation were robbing and pillaging the poor residents of his district. I also told him that if such behavior did not stop, those people would be expelled from the land of the Indians.

At three in the afternoon, Franchimastabé and three other Chiefs came to see me, and they informed me that the notices had been sent out for the meeting of Chiefs and warriors for the following day at five in the morning. At this time the above-mentioned Felipe Hayes returned, as a result of my threat, leading three horses, saying that he was sure they had been stolen. He then gave them to me with the understanding that I would return them to the owners.

8: At nine of this morning, Franchimastabé came with six more Chiefs to inform me that at twelve o'clock they would be ready to receive me and hear my word. At the appointed time I presented myself to Franchimastabé in the public space (*Glorieta*) that had been constructed for the purpose with four Spanish flags waving in the wind in its four corners. Franchimastabé gave me a chair in front of him more or less in the middle of his Chiefs and warriors, who numbered about two hundred. He told me that he was ready to hear whatever I had to tell him. As a consequence of this, I presented him the letter with which I had been entrusted. He took it, but, after a few moments of reflection, handed it back to me asking that I have Mr. McGee, who was his interpreter, read it to him. I did so, and Mr. McGee read and explained it to him very carefully. [Franchimsatabé] showed great satisfaction with the contents of the letter and a few minutes later got up and told me to have patience while he spoke with his Chiefs and warriors before he should speak with me. He then addressed his Chiefs and warriors in the following way:

"The day [has] arrived when each one of you can speak for yourself. You have accused me many times of intending to sell your land. You can see now that I am innocent. What you should say, say it. We have with us a Spanish Chief in our territory, and if before him you don't speak I hope you never accuse me or anyone about this matter."

None of the Chiefs or warriors spoke. He turned to me and said that none of his Chiefs or warriors would speak about this unless they were drunk, and that then they would do so in a more insolent manner, and thus (he said) "now I will continue speaking what I have to say" and continued in this way:

"The Chicasas and the Chactas are brothers and one and the same people. Two days ago I had the pleasure of seeing two Chicasa Chiefs, one of them called 'Tesea-ataga' and the other 'Hota-la-apia,' whose final words to me were that if the cane is cut in Nogales, it must be allowed to grow again for they would never consent to these lands being settled by any species of people, that he thought as did these two Chiefs, since the land of Nogales legitimately belonged to the Chicasas, to him and to his people."

I answered him by saying that it was true that the Chiefs of New Orleans and Natchez had ordered the settlement of Nogales, not dreaming that the Chactas had any claim to the land that had long ago been sold to the English.

Said Chief replied by saying that he had agreed to the drawing of a line that would divide English land and his, but regardless of what the line marked, neither he nor any of his people had received payment for the land of Nogales.

I answered him telling him that not only had the great King of Spain and his army conquered all English territory in the country, but when peace was made, the English indicated on a paper all the lines and boundaries of all the land, [and] signed by their own signatures and said to our King, we purchased this land of Nogales from the Chactas, and being in this way ours, we cede it to you.

The Chief answered saying that if the English had done this, it was only because when they left this country, they found themselves defeated. "They were expelled and, consequently, they retired weeping with their hearts full of sadness; and in such situations, anyone is capable of error."

He added, "notwithstanding, however, there is no reason or excuse for me to abandon my lands for which I never received payment. When I go to New Orleans, the great Chief there takes my hand, saying that he loves me and my people. When I go to Natchez, they tell me the same thing. Both tell me that they are our fathers and that we are their sons. With these expressions of friendliness I am satisfied and truly believe that they hold me dear, but now I see that their friendship is feigned because at the same time that they tell me those things they are sending people to take possession of our lands. They are ordering the building of a fort and are cutting the cane and the trees, driving off the game and leaving my people to suffer. This is not the way fathers should treat their children; instead of taking the land they should give it to them."

I replied that our great King had ordered the construction of a fort at Nogales to protect the land of his beloved red people, the Chactas, so that it would not be taken by the Americans. I told him that the Americans were planning to take possession and drive them out, that whenever they took possession of a similar place what inevitably followed was the destruction and expulsion of all the red people that were found in its vicinity, that that had happened in the entire extension of the Ohio region and that surely the same would happen to the Chactas if the Americans were able to set foot in Nogales. The Chiefs of Natchez and New Orleans were informed that the Americans were going to establish themselves at Nogales and build a fort there, and they had decided to stop them. The advantages of the fort would become readily apparent because, once the Americans knew that the Spanish had built a fort there to defend their own land and those [lands] of their beloved red people they would immediately abandon their project. As a result the fort already has done much, and what happens in the future would be of even greater advantage. It seems to me that the greatest proof the Chiefs of New Orleans and Natchez can have of their friendship to you is having constructed that fort to preserve for you the peace.

Said Chief replied that it would be useless for me to make these arguments, for it was clear that should he consent to the establishment of Nogales the results would be that his People would die of hunger for lack of hunting and that as a further consequence the traders would remain ruined.

I answered by saying that a trading store would be established in Nogales to provide for his people, that with respect to his hunting lands they had already lost their value, and none of his people hunt there any longer. I told him they were now crossing the river to do so in the land of our great King, where they kill deer and bear, and afterwards, they carry the product of their hunt by canoes to Nogales when the water is high. Then they have to send for horses from their nation in order to load the skins, meat, and fat to transport them to their villages. As soon as there should be a store at Nogales, this hardship would cease, for the store would buy what the Indians bring and the transport of 300 miles would be saved.

Franchimastabé answered me saying that it was no one else's business as to how his people had to transport their skins. His people had never asked for favors from any nation, and their horses were sufficient for this purpose.

I told him that I was sorry that he was not moved by the interests of his people and that he would not listen to reason, that I was certain that he was trying to please the traders and expressing more their sentiments than his own.

He then asked that I stop talking about Nogales, adding that he would be very pleased to see the Chief of Natchez. I responded by saying that the road to Natchez was open and that that Chief would be very happy to see him and any of his people, in spite of the fact that he had no gifts to give them. My advice to him was that to settle this matter of Nogales it would be better if he went to New Orleans to see the Chief of the entire province since there is where the gifts are to be found for the Indians.

To this he responded that he could not think of going to New Orleans, but that before I left he would speak to me about this matter in private. I noted that said Chief wanted to say something to his people, so I withdrew after telling him that I wanted to speak to him about other matters and that for that purpose I would return to see him within half an hour. I left.

At that time I returned and presented myself to Franchimastabé and told him that what I had to make known to him was for the benefit of the inhabitants of Natchez, and continued as follows: "There are among you a number of whites whose occupation is no other than to steal blacks and horses from the poor citizens of Natchez and bring them to your land and, with the help of the Indians, hide them in the forests. If you continue to protect these men, soon your beloved white friends will become impoverished. They have no other means to provide bread for their women and children, other than employing their blacks and horses. Since arriving in your nation, I have seen many horses that I learned were stolen. If you do not give up the rights to these horses in order that I might return them to their rightful owners, I shall take care to drive the traders that have stolen goods in their power out of the land."

Franchimastabé rose and said that for a long time he wanted to see the day when such vile acts would end. He was sure that in his nation there were over one hundred stolen horses. He said that anyone who found stolen property among his people could claim it, for, not only would he restore it, he would expel the guilty parties from his nation.

I responded by saying that there was a camp of horse thieves on his land near the Big Black, composed of Russell James, Eduardo Lusek, and one named Peake, and that Abraham Castelman and Tory Edwards lived in the towns of his nation. I told him that these people did nothing but steal horses from the Indians and from the people of Natchez and take them back and forth between the two nations. Besides this, the group near the Big Black also robbed and pillaged the travelers that were going to America. Hence, if he wanted to continue to be a friend of the white people, it was necessary that these abuses end.

He responded by saying that he thought I was telling the truth, because he knew that the people I had named were bad men. He was determined that none of them should remain in his nation any longer, that he would immediately send for people to expel them and make sure that they never returned. He said he had also observed that some of his own people were being robbed at the same time those of Natchez were, and he believed that Abraham Castelman was the one who had robbed them and taken the horses to Natchez. He hoped that the Chief of Natchez would do justice to his people as well, when they went there to lay claim to their horses.

I told him that when his people came to Natchez to lay claim to their possessions that the Chief would certainly do them justice, because the Chief of that country loved the red people very much, and nothing would give him more pleasure than to have the opportunity to display to them his friendship and to act as a true father and that I knew that shortly they would have reasons to believe it.

The Chief then asked me to prepare a document for him in order to show those thieves that he and the Chief of Natchez agreed and that they should not remain in his land. I agreed, and the copy is as follows:

"There are a number of white people camped around the Big Black and others from different towns in this nation whose practice it is to rob horses from both the white people and the red people. Being the will of the Governor of Natchez as well as our own that such people do not remain any longer in this land, I present this document with full power authorizing such individuals be expelled from our land. Given in the Choctaw Nation on the eighth of June of the year 1791. Signed Minor and Franchimastabé, Principal Chief of the Choctaw Nation."

Upon giving him this document, I told Franchimastabé that all travelers proceeding from Natchez who did not carry passports with a seal such as the one found on the letter he received from the governor should be considered as fugitives, and what was found on them was stolen. In this way the robberies would stop because every man of good standing would carry a stamp on their passport.

Because it was about five in the afternoon, I excused myself from all of them, and I told them that I hoped they would reflect well on all that I had said, that their dreams would be happy, and as a result they could come to see me in the morning and tell me that I could repeat to my Chief their pleasure in our settlement at Nogales.

Franchimastabé said he would visit me before I left but that he did not expect that he would dream about Nogales.

At eight that night Franchimastabé came to see me and to tell me that four nights later he would send two of his Chiefs to see the governor of Natchez, one named Iteleghana and the other Taboca. He would also send three more men for each to serve as witnesses. He said that sending Chief Iteleghana would be like going himself and that he would trust and approve of whatever he did. He also said that Iteleghana should take precedence over Taboca and should speak before him.

I told him that the Governor of Natchez would be very happy to see them, but I was very sorry to tell them that there would be no gifts for the Indians there as there would be if they went to New Orleans. To this he answered that New Orleans was too unhealthy and that his people would suffer greatly from the mosquitoes, that when some go there, half of them die on the road. He believed that in Natchez the land was as safe and healthy as his. I told him to do as he pleased.

9: This morning at six, Franchimastabé and Taboca came to see me to wish me a good trip. I instructed the interpreter Fulson to determine what each of the Chiefs thought about the matters that had been discussed. The interpreter agreed to my request, and after various conversations came to inform me that Franchimastabé had told him that he loved very much the land of Nogales, but that in the end he would have to cede it to us and allow it to be settled. He insisted, however, that he would not decide until his Chiefs had returned from their visit to see the Governor of Natchez.

At eight, I began my trip to Natchez and left the town of Franchimsatabé. I traveled to the town of Red Shoes, who had offered to house us for the night.

Having arrived at the house of said Chief, I began a conversation with respect to the Nogales affair. He told me that he did not have any objection to a settlement there, and told me to tell that to the Governor of Natchez, for whom he had great love because of the friendship he had shown to him.

10: At five in the morning, I left the house of Red Shoes, who, along with several relatives, accompanied me for two miles. Upon parting, he told me that he had purposely brought his brother with him in order that his brother could accompany me and guide us as far as Nogales. At that time he would say goodbye and bid me farewell. I thanked him very much for his attention and assured him that his brother would be well cared for and well treated while he was with me. I told him that I would bestow upon him some token of appreciation for his work. I continued my trip and camped some forty-five miles from the village of Red Shoes.

11: I left this day at four in the morning, and, although hindered by continuous rain, I covered sixty miles and camped at the spot where the roads of Natchez and Nogales meet.

12: I left this morning at four, and, upon arriving at the Big Black, I made a raft in which I crossed the river. I walked fifty-five miles.

13: I left my camp on the Big Black at five in the morning and struggled through much rain. I arrived at one in the afternoon at Nogales, having traveled some thirty-five miles.

I dined with the commander of the place; and, as the Governor of Natchez was not there, I embarked in a pirogue and traveled as quickly as possible so that I might tell him of the result of my commission and of the coming of the Choctaw Chiefs.

At eight o'clock, I arrived at Natchez, and I delivered this diary to the Governor on June 14, 1791. Minor. This is a copy of the original. Natchez. July 1, 1791. Manuel Gayoso de Lemos to Estevan Miró.

5

Gayoso on Minor's Mission to the Choctaws, July 1, 1791

Manuel Gayoso de Lemos to Estevan Miró, Natchez, July 1, 1791, enclosed as N.° 1 with Estevan Miró to Luis de las Casas, New Orleans, July 15, 1791, N.° 206, AGI, SD, *leg.* 2556.

Gayoso comments on Minor's mission and forwards a translation of his diary to the governor-general in New Orleans.

On last May 28 I informed Your Lordship about the incident, which I then described, relative to the opposition of the Chacta and Chicasa Indians to our settlement in Nogales. On the 30th day of the same [month] Don Estevan Minor left this post with my response for Franchimastabé. [He was] instructed about how much he should discuss not only with that Chief, but with the other [Chiefs] and with traders who were to found there. On the 14th day of the past [month] he returned and handed to me a diary [describing] what he had done, a translated copy of which I send to Your Lordship as N.° 1. By means of it Your Lordship will see the good reception that he encountered among the Chacta Indians and particularly from the same Franchimastabé, Sulemastabé, or Red Shoes, his son, and other Chiefs. The brother of the named Sulemastabé, who guided Don Estevan Minor to Nogales, did it with the greatest care. Instead of returning from [Nogales] from said destination, he preferred to come down to this post where he waited to join with the Chiefs who were supposed to come and to return in their company. I received him very well, and from the day of his arrival I ordered that he be provided a daily ration.

The formality with which they received the Spanish flags with which they [then used] to decorate the space (*Glorieta*) designated for the formal meetings and the expressions of pleasure with which they welcomed a Spanish official in their country confirms their inclination towards our nation. If they have demonstrated dissatisfaction with our settlement at Nogales, it is through the counsel of someone who has particular influence on Franchimastabé in order to avoid damage that might affect his business. This [person] is surely a trader named Turner Brashears, who lives with the mentioned Chief and rewards him with a thousand trinkets that flatter the ambition of his friend and with which he [Brashears] influences his [Franchimastabé's] will. This explains Franchimastabé's opposition to entering into discussion with Don Estevan Minor [and] limiting himself only to [complaining] about not having received any payment from the English for the Nogales lands, [saying that] he ought to keep the land in spite of the fact that in reality he had discussed and agreed afterwards to the cession of said land and even permitted the marking of the dividing lines. To this he added—with other frivolous points—that those lands are the only ones on which they depend for subsistence. He did not want to admit anything that might change his mind; he avoided discussing it and included the Chicasa Nation in the arguments against our occupying Nogales.

The answer that our Interpreter Fulson has heard from Franchimastabé and Brashears proves to be the same as I have just stated. The latter, especially, demands of the Chief that he not allow us [to be] in Nogales. In the future he did not want to be enslaved with all his people. In the end it turns out that because of everything done by Minor, Franchimastabé realizes that finally he would have to agree with what we want and that this good disposition is already to be found in Sulemastabé, who particularly told Minor that he might share it with me. [However], at the time he did not find it best to announce his disposition to the Nation but [rather] decided to do it when it might be most advantageous. [He] is one of the people of major influence among the Chactas. [I know] on the basis of reports I have had up to now, confirmed by Don Estevan Minor.

Because Franchimastabé offered to send me his word through the mouths of the Chiefs Iteleghana and Taboca, he has not written to me. However, by means of the meticulous report that Don Estevan Minor has given to me, I have no doubt concerning the good and exact accomplishment of his charge. I could since then form an opinion as to the reasons for Franchimastabé's opposition and of the results that could be expected, as Your Lordship will be able to judge from the Diary to which I refer.

On the 21st day of the present month most of the Chacta Chiefs arrived and presented themselves to me on that very same day, saying that they only wanted to shake my hand at that time because they were very tired and not able to talk. The Chiefs who came were Iteleghana, Big Medal Chief from the village of Buckufuca, whose residence is some four or five leagues from Nogales on the Yasu, [and] his brother Stonahuma, who, although [a] captain, brought the great medal of Franchimastabé. Taboca did not come because he found the trail very rocky and oppressively hot. Each one of the named [Chiefs] brought three Warriors from different villages to serve as their witnesses whose ranks were inevitably augmented by others during the time that they spent here. To make them content in every possible way I ordered that from that day rations be supplied to them.

The following day at 12 the mentioned Chiefs and Warriors came to present themselves to me to speak, as they had offered, painted in peace with a very happy countenance. Accompanied by the officials of this post I was quick to receive them taking care that no settler might attend, for I thought it best to be wary of any misinterpretation on the part of the Indians that might jeopardize our position on Nogales. Displaying as much ceremony [as possible], I had them enter, having the same two Chiefs taking seats to my left. They remained there, with the Warriors seated in the back of the room.

After a short while Iteleghana stood in front of me, [and] I ordered the Interpreter Fulson to come to his side. In a very agreeable way said Chief revealed to me his pleasure on seeing me again. [He said] he came charged with telling me on behalf of the principal Chief of his nation, Franchimastabé, that he could not view with indifference that we had settled and built a fort at Nogales, that we had cut the trees and cane, [that] the game was fleeing causing his people to perish for lack of this support, and that the Chicasas with whom he had a close brotherhood were of the same opinion. [He said] that he was speaking on their behalf and that he did not expect that we, having always assured them that we would treat them as sons, [that] we would take their lands from them without saying anything to them. This was making them doubt our friendship; nevertheless, he hoped that because of the strength of his presentation we would withdraw people from there. The mentioned Iteleghana seems to place very particular care not only on making moderate expressions but also to refer to them in a pleasing and agreeable way. From the beginning he revealed that he came in peace with a positive order not to exacerbate the matter with explanations that might encourage others to cause discord.

I answered him [by saying] that our building a settlement at Nogales has been because our Great King wanted to protect his Vassals and Friends throughout the extent of his dominions that in this country begin at the mouth of the Yasu. Therefore he ordered the fort to be built at Nogales on territory that had been taken from the English to whom the Chacta Nation had sold and ceded it, proof of which was the line of demarcation that was made in presence of many Chiefs and Warriors of said Nation. [I said] that in the congress at Mobile no Indian nation had presented a claim to any of the land that we took from the English and that we had given proof to the Chactas and the Chicasas of our friendship [by] providing them with whatever advantages are possible, keeping them always in peace [and] providing them with goods in the same way as in the time of the English. [I said] that when they went to see the principal Chief of the province in New Orleans, they [the Spanish] gave them gifts and that above all we never usurped land from the Indians but rather permitted them to go to hunt on our [lands]. Proof of that, [I pointed out], is that the Chactas, not having hunting in abundance in the vicinity of Nogales, go every year to the other side of the Mississippi to hunt on the lands of the great King of Spain without his bothering them. For this reason even when they might have legitimate right to lands that they ceded to the English they should not notice that we might go to settle there. Besides, they well know that at the beginning of this year the Americans most likely will come to occupy said lands, which would cause the entire ruin of the neighboring Indians since undoubtedly wherever they go little by little they destroy and drive away all the Red men as they have done in Ohio and presently are doing in Cumberland, Franklin, and above all Tennessee. Since they found out that we had anticipated them [by] building a fort at Nogales and [that] we were disposed to defend our territory and that of our good friends the Chactas and Chicasas, they stopped their coming and are not thinking any more about it. In this way we not only have stopped the introduction of these people into our lands but we have performed a distinguished service for the neighboring Indians.

He replied to me that he could not enter into more conversation about this matter because Franchimastabé had only charged him thus, that his charge was only to tell me that the Nogales lands were his because the English had never ever paid them. Hence, it was necessary that the canes again grow in that place without which they would have nowhere to hunt and that he could neither hear nor say more about this particular.

In spite of the opposition that he displayed about speaking more about Nogales, I repeated to him in part [and] in his way the same points, adding that matters of this nature require time to consider. [I said] that the way to do it with more formality was to go to New Orleans to present whatever might be offered [and] that Your Lordship could do justice for them if they might merit it.

To this he indicated that it was impossible for him to speak any more about this matter repeating that it was necessary that the canes grow again at Nogales.

I changed my approach, and I told him that as he had a superior Chief to obey I also had another who could [do] more than I [and] to whom I reported whatever I was doing so that now we would cease speaking about Nogales. [I told him] that I would write to Your Lordship whatever he had told me and that you would let them know the answer [by] sending it to them in the Nation with one of my officials. [I said] that it might be possible that Don Estevan Minor would go because they already knew him. With respect to settlements in Nogales, my wish was not to send settlers there, that [I] wanted only to take care that my soldiers might be well housed, and that therefore I no longer planned to cut more cane until further in the future. Then, [I said], our differences would be resolved. With that he could be calm and say the same to Franchimastabé. He remained completely satisfied with these reasons because it seemed to him that with them he would fulfill the charge of his principal Chief.

Pointing to his brother, he said that although seeming of little importance he had something to say. Having referred to this [individual], he sat down, and the mentioned brother came to take his place. He began untying the great medal of Franchimastabé that he was wearing beside his heart. With it in his hand he addressed me saying: "This is the medal of my great Chief who handed it to me to confirm whatever I might say," and he continued. "The Chicasa Nations and the Chacta are the same people, the same interest, and the same will. Recently the other Indian Nations, our neighbors, have sent us words offering to make common cause to support reciprocally each other, for should the white men continue to expel them from their land, and if they do not look out for themselves, in a short time they will not have any place to build a house. They are, therefore, resolved not to permit any nation to settle on their lands. For that reason they could not look with indifference on the fact that we might have cut the trees and cane at Nogales and that we might build a fort there. Franchimastabé said that he had exchanged the medal that the English had given him for that one which he was displaying, [and] that when he received it he told the Great Chief who gave it to him that one [medal] was a symbol of the closest friendship and a sign that the Spanish Nation would always be favorable to him and would help him with all its power. On its authority he hoped that they might not take from him his land at Nogales and that the cane would again grow there. Without this his Warriors would not have a place to hunt and their sons would become thin and grow weak for lack of meat and their wives would die from hunger. [He said he was speaking] for the young people rather than the old, because the latter would be lacking the wherewithal to keep themselves but the former would face the time when surrounded by white people who destroy all the forests they would have nowhere to go to hunt." With this statement he displayed the medal, turning it from one side to the other.

I answered in the same way as I had to Iteleghana. I varied the explanation without altering its meaning, for the purpose of convincing him that his positions were unfounded and pointedly making him see that the lands where they have the most successful hunting are undoubtedly under the dominion of our Great King where we permit them because of the great love we have for them. [I] equally made him see that the lands of Nogales had been ceded to the English.

He again repeated more or less the beginning of his speech, adding expressions that indicated that Franchimastabé's feelings were to renounce the medal that he believed put him under the authority of any whim of ours [and] that from his point of view that was not suitable.

I found that it was necessary to prevent this man from reaching the point of announcing that Franchimastabé was returning the medal. It seemed useful to me to tell him anything that might counter the ideas that he had. Employing this strategy, I told him that because his charge was the same that his brother Iteleghana had just expressed to which I had already responded, it remained to us only to await the reply of Your Lordship.

Being now the dining hour and [seeing] that they must be tired, [I suggested that] we should go and sit down to table and that there, drinking to the health of the Great King of Spain and all of the Chacta Nation, we should have thoughts of other woods than those of Nogales, full of game where the youth of their nation would find abundant reward for their work. He laughed hard at this, and we all rose to our feet. I wanted to take time to sound out the feelings of both and if it might be necessary to win their support. While rising, Iteleghana again repeated to me not to forget to write to Your Lordship concerning the matter we discussed [and] that he was very satisfied about this method. [He said he was] especially satisfied about the assurance that I gave him that at Nogales for now they would not cut any more cane.

I answered him that once I said something I followed through so that on this particular matter we would not speak again until [we] knew Your Lordship's thoughts. On this day as on the others, when they have been here, I gave them lunch and things to eat, and they have observed the greatest sobriety. I have noted that they refused to drink more than what they could moderately support. After eating, they wanted—although without formality—to speak about Nogales. I told them that I would not answer them about any matter of importance, because I did not want at any time that they might think that I was waiting for an occasion when their spirit might be distracted as happens with other Nations. The Spanish never ever tried to take advantage of other men in similar circumstances, [I pointed out]. I was saying this to them not because [I thought] that their judgement was not as clear as before but to remove from them the least suspicion that I might do it on other occasions. They asked me to give them some bottles of wine that they had drunk at table to make merry in their camp, which was about a mile from here, to prepare their senses for pleasant dreams that night. Determined that they might not have the least reason for complaint because of my treatment, I made the firm resolution to give them whatever they asked to improve their disposition. Thus I ordered that a half dozen bottles be given to him, and privately I charged Interpreter Fulson not to abandon them for an instant [so that] he might inform me minutely about whatever he might hear from them in their drunkenness. With this charge he accompanied them to their camp.

The following day Iteleghana, his brother, and the Interpreter came early in the morning at the time I was having breakfast. I had the two Chiefs sit down, and they also ate breakfast. Iteleghana, having been raised with the British, greatly enjoyed the coffee. He asked me if I had slept well and if I had had a pleasant dream, to which I replied of course, for I had dreamed of the answer that I had received from Your Lordship about the matter of which they had spoken to me the previous day. Having informed Franchimastabé, many Chiefs came from the nation to see me; and, while smoking the pipe, all had shown signs of happiness that we were in Nogales so near them. He smiled and told me that he also had dreamed that I had written to Nogales so that they might not cut more cane and to Your Lordship so that you might decide this issue. We repeated the above-described dreams, a method that they have to speak about matters of great importance. Taking Fulson aside, I learned from him that these Chiefs were very satisfied with my manner of receiving them and that he knew that their intention—following the example of Franchimastabé—was to do whatever was necessary to indicate that they were fulfilling their duty to their nation by opposing any establishment at Nogales. In reality, [however], they understood that in the end they would have to tolerate it. He told me more. [He said] that the mentioned Iteleghana, speaking in the camp with his people, spoke to them and reflected upon the good reception that I gave them and that the more he studied my countenance he could see no more than dispositions of true and sincere friendship. He [Iteleghana] [pointed out] that his nation as well as the other neighboring ones were surrounded by white people that, if they wanted, could destroy them without remedy. Therefore, he was of the opinion that they should not oppose our settlement in Nogales.

They said goodbye asking me that they be given a good ration because they were tired and hungry from the trip and needed to restore themselves. I offered it to them, and I particularly ordered that they be made happy. This day they did not come to eat, but during the afternoon they came to see me again and with great cordiality they spoke to me about unimportant matters. When we discussed the English, their old friends, they could not help but display a great affection for that nation. It seemed best to me to tell him that of all the Nations there are in Europe the two that are most similar in character are the Spanish and English. For that reason, [I said,] they will recognize the same propensity in loving them with the difference that we can take advantage of more effective means to protect them and keep them in peace. He answered me that he believes that it is true, for even an English official [had] told him so at the time of saying goodbye to them when they left this country by saying it in the following way: "Fortune wants us to go from here, and we leave you, but other white men will come in our place who will treat you as we [did] so that our absence will become less painful, although it is possible we may see each other again." He also told me that that man looked much like me and that he believed that I might be his relative. I did not disillusion him on this particular, for it seemed to me useful that he retain that illusion. The Interpreter Fulson told me not to be impressed by the repeated visits of these Chiefs because they had confided in him that Franchimastabé charged them to see me at least two times a day to study my mode of thought and to be able to judge if I was constantly of the same opinion and if I was fond of the Indians. This circumstance was a new reason to increase my effort to win their good will and opinion.

They said goodbye as they had the previous day. They asked me for wine to take to camp with two more bottles of rum, which [pleased] them. They withdrew.

On the following day all came here from their camp to have breakfast with me, and Iteleghana, who is the one who always speaks first, told me that he believed what I said because I had never changed my way of thinking and always spoke with the same expression. He said other things of this nature of little importance. The Interpreter told me that the mentioned Iteleghana was so much in our favor that he had charged him to tell me that he would do whatever he could to sway the minds of the rest of the Chiefs of his nation to our interest. In order to be successful, however, he would not display for now any partiality. Only after they received the answer from Your Lordship would he declare his position, but from now on I could count on him. He insisted, nevertheless, that I should not understand that his brother agreed with this. Likewise the Interpreter told me that Franchimastabé had charged those men to ask only for supplies, but if they should be offered more, they should accept. [He said] that Iteleghana, nevertheless, would be happy to receive some token. That point guided me to do it in a way that might please without compromising his duty. I took advantage of the fact that he had asked me to have four guns repaired. His being the worst, I gave him one of those that Your Lordship sent recently, and, recognizing a strong wish on the part of both him and his brother to have saddles, I ordered that one be given to each. [I also gave] indirectly some trifles from my own house that Iteleghana had requested from me, asking him to [accept them] subtly so that the others would not recognize the good rapport that we shared.

This morning he also told me that he had been here as many days as Don Estevan Minor [was] in his country; thus, it was the command of his principal Chief that he leave and that I not request that he stay. He asked me to write to Franchimastabé how he had discharged his commission and briefly tell him what still remained [to be done]. In the same way, he asked me to write another letter to the King of the Chicasas in the same terms. He also asked me to give him a paper signed with my name and with my seal to which he would place his mark as testimony to our friendship. I offered to do whatever he asked so that he could leave on the following day. He stopped and said goodbye, saying that he would return with his brother to eat with me.

At the regular time they returned. Nothing in particular happened except that they adhered to the greatest moderation, and Iteleghana revealed an uncommon knowledge with unusual ideas about the Supreme Divinity. They remained with me the whole afternoon, and from time to time we spoke about suitable means to bring the whole nation around to a way of thinking that I told him would serve the nation best. He offered to do this when it came time to express his position. They said goodbye, taking with them their regular ration of wine and rum. The Interpreter, a man who did not drink much, assured me that the Chief was making good use of the drink that I gave him, for it would make the people in his camp merry, and he could tell them favorable things to make them all supporters. The result would be that with luck they would become indifferent as to whether we were in Nogales or not. I advised Iteleghana to bring his horses the following day, for I wanted to give them an expression of friendship in the name of Our Great King.

The two Chiefs came early the following day with their retinue. They ate breakfast with me, and afterwards I had various conversations privately with Iteleghana, the gist of which was to confirm our good friendship. With this confidence, he asked me for some trifles, and he suggested others, which I offered to give as gifts from me to him. He warned that today he would pretend to become drunk, although in truth he said that he was not going to lose his judgment, for it suited him to be able to say many things that he wanted his Warriors to hear [and] that he could not do in any other way. At 10 I called them all to my reception room, and I read them the letters that I enclose attached to [a] translated copy, n° 2 for Franchimastabé and n° 3 for the King of the Chicasas. That made them very satisfied. They said they wished nothing more but that I might write on the back of my letters [the name of] the white man in the Nation who should open and translate them for Franchimastabé and the King of the Chicasas. I agreed, and I marked the first for Nataniel Fulson and the second for Malcon McGee, because I had been informed that these are honorable men. Privately I handed to Iteleghana the paper of which n° 1 is a copy. I wrote the same to Sulemastabé, letter n° 5, with the purpose of sending him some gifts that he had requested by means of Don Esteban Minor. I did not find it convenient to refuse, because [he] was the Chief of principal influence in his nation and [he] was disposed to embrace our party. In the same way I have written letter n° 6 to Brashears because [he] is the man that I believe to be essential to win over and it seemed to me opportune to open communication with him.

In order to say goodbye to these Indians I ordered that they be given supplies and gifts that our relationship requires, including among them those that Franchimastabé requested and those for Sulemastabé and his family. With that they have all bade farewell greatly pleased. The principal [Chiefs] remained to eat with me. Iteleghana pretended to be drunk and to say a thousand crazy things to his Warriors, but in reality he maintained sober judgment. From time to time he spoke to me apart so that I would be aware of it. Upon saying farewell he asked me for some bottles of wine and rum, which I gave to him from my stock as I had on all other occasions.

On the basis of what these Chiefs have told me and what is in Don Estevan Minor's diary, I understand that the claim of the Chacta and Chicasa Indians to the lands of Nogales derives from the failure of the English to provide the goods by means of which they obtained the cession of that land. Furthermore, they wanted to see if by some means they could get from us [those goods], even though the quantity might be less. I do not know what the agreement was. To this is added the commotion caused among the Indians by news that the Carolina Companies want to come to settle the lands of the Nogales and the Yasu. Sometimes [they are] invited by those interested in the company so that they may agree; on other occasions, [they are] advised by us and by traders already established in the Nation whose interest opposes their being trading posts on the Yasu, whether American or Spanish. They advise the Indians that they not permit either one or the other in the lands of Nogales. The position of the traders is for the present most effective, because they find themselves living in the same Nation mixed and allied with Indian families. At the same time that they try to persuade them, they do it by accompanying their expressions with a bottle of rum in their hand, and afterwards they distribute opportunely some trifles of little value compared to the effect they produce. They influence powerfully the spirit of the Indians. At the moment of enthusiasm and gratitude, they [the traders] make them say whatever they wish, leading them entirely with their advice. This is exactly the case with Turner Brashears, who lives in the same house as Franchimastabé and who provides him whatever trifles that can flatter the will of this old man. He plays, therefore, with his emotions and makes him do whatever he wishes, even to the extent of refusing to enter discussions that might cause a change of mind.

On the other hand, it is clear to me that not only the same Franchimastabé but all the Chiefs of his Nation who have influence can be won to the party of reason, which is ours, through some brief sacrifice that may let them recognize that more compelling arguments are accompanied by more positive benefits than the promise of the English when they bought the lands of Nogales for which they certainly received nothing because of the bad faith of agents who should have given them the gifts. According to what I have understood, it has been principally Frazer, who agreed to provide appropriately the goods designated to that end. I believe that it is essential not only skillfully to please the principal Chacta and Chicasa Chiefs but also to attract to our Party not all the traders but certainly Turner Brashears, who has at his disposition the ear and mouth of Franchimastabé. However his support may be obtained I am sure that no one else will say a word.

I don't say by this that this is the only recourse that remains, but I dare to say that having means to maintain some of the principal Indians I can do whatever I want with them, for, in addition to the argument that the King has an indisputable right to that land, it will be easy to direct them and make them see clearly [that it is] reasonable and in true interest. This could be carried out by indirect means, but my view is that it should be with solemnity, for only in this way can this matter be resolved along with others of political economy that now have become indispensable to resolve again with these people. Such a deed will serve to cement more and more the foundations of friendship, removing in this way the bad impressions that my competitors—whoever they may be—try to implant. [I hope] it might be possible to celebrate—I don't mean a congress—but a meeting attended by only the principal Chiefs with some Warriors in the vicinity of this district. I am humanly persuaded that in it all our differences would be resolved.. However, an abuse might arise from a private meeting. A congress of these Nations might turn out to be much more costly. If Your Lordship does not wish to commit yourself to it one can tentatively try to see if [by] winning only the Chiefs of greatest importance one can peacefully achieve our establishment in Nogales. Or, rather, the great experience that Your Lordship has in these matters may suggest that the arguments are not sufficiently compelling to persuade the Indians. It is necessary to accompany them with the prudent distribution [of] some gifts.

The Court is not unaware of this, for it not only realizes it through long experience in similar cases with the Indians but also with the Nations of the Berber Coast. One continually sees the pressure of some of these same means. Therefore, if Your Lordship feels that the decisions of the Treasury Board of Havana might essentially endanger the King's interest, [he should take appropriate measures]. That Board, full of good will, is accustomed to scrutinize minutely the distribution of the [funds] of the Royal Treasury in a way that almost never permits any adjustment. It is ignorant of the means that are needed to deal with the Indians. Thus I urge Your Lordship to decide in the present case what your knowledge dictates and give [an] explanation to the Court about your resolution. I myself offer right now to make the sacrifice of my salary to cover any extraordinary expense that may have been incurred at my request, if the King doesn't approve it. In view of all I have said, Your Lordship, informed by all the documents that I include, will need to make the judgment that you decide. You should follow up the proceedings [by] advising me not only the answer that I should give to Franchimastabé but also what my conduct should be in the circumstances that may result, whether they may be favorable or not, on the intelligence that the necessity of this answer is not so urgent that you may not take all the time that Your Lordship needs to deliberate, for, finding ourselves in the heat of the summer, [it] is the period in which the Indians wish to be at home to avoid the discomfort of this season. With Your Lordship's decision I will send Don Esteban Minor again to the Chacta Nation and, if necessary, to the Chicasa, for [he] is a subject who works well with the Indians and truly knows the way to carry out any commission with them. [I] can do no less than commend the zeal which has been lately demonstrated along with the loyalty and determination which the Interpreter Fulson has employed in matters of Royal Service. I have seen him as indispensable in the precision of my discharging this office, explaining the most minimal. Since Your Lordship is the one to decide this matter, it would be a serious flaw in my obligation if my report is not detailed with all trifling nicety. May God grant Your Lordship many years. Natchez. July 1, 1791. Manuel Gayoso de Lemos = Señor Don Estevan Miró = Miró.

6

Gayoso to Franchimastabé, March 12, 1792

Manuel Gayoso de Lemos to Franchimastabé, Natchez, March 12, 1792, N.° 1, copy enclosed with Manuel Gayoso de Lemos to the Conde de Floridablanca, Natchez, April 13, 1792, AHN, *Estado*, leg. 3885 bis, *exp.* 7. A printed text is in [Serrano y Sanz], *Documentos históricos de la Florida y la Luisiana*, 406–7.

Gayoso prepared this letter for Minor to deliver to Franchimastabé on his second mission to the Choctaws. He enclosed a copy, in Spanish, as the first of several enclosures related to Minor's mission, with a letter he sent directly to the Spanish Minister of State, the Count of Floridablanca. His letter to Taskietoka (document 9) is one of the other documents enclosed with this letter.

My dear friend and brother Franchimastabé: I would now be perfectly satisfied if you had found me in this [place] when you came to see me, but you know that busy men who find themselves in charge of many people as you and I cannot always manage time at our pleasure.

I had gone to New Orleans to receive the new Governor General and to speak with him [about] matters of great importance. One of them was about you and your nation, for whom I have the greatest esteem, not only because I love your nation, but even more because our Great King has charged me in particular [with] it. But contrary winds detained the new Governor at sea longer than he or I should have wished, and for this reason I was not able to return here when you came.

I spoke with him about everything that you had sent Itelaghana to tell me. Your pretensions are such, however, that neither he nor I can decide without consulting His Majesty, because even though we find that your major complaint is that the English did not fulfill their arrangement for the lands the truth is that they were in possession of them when our Great King took them [the lands] from them with all this territory. Although we willingly made you a regular gift on behalf of the affection that we have for you, it is such an extraordinary matter [that] the new Governor has determined not to do it on his own authority for you without asking permission from the King.

Although I could give you something from what I have, I am certain that it would be more worthwhile for you and your chiefs to await what the Great King might send; thus, I advise you to be patient a little while longer with the expectation of gaining more. Nevertheless, if you have enough confidence in me to believe that I will satisfy you, tell it to me, for I am certain I will satisfy you.

Major Minor is a man of my confidence, and in proof of it, I return to you by his hand the white beads that you had sent me. Believe, therefore, everything that he should tell you on my behalf, for I entrust to him very especially various matters, some of which interest me personally.

He will tell you also that on all occasions it will please me greatly to see you, but advise me [of] it so that you find me at home. He will also tell you many other things. Treat him well and in the same way as the other two subjects who go with him.

I sincerely love you and I wish you good health and prosperity to your nation, and until I have the pleasure of seeing you, I remain your most devoted brother and friend, Manuel Gayoso de Lemos. Natchez, 12 March 1792.

7

Diary of Minor's Second Mission to the Choctaws, March 13–April 3, 1792

"Diario del Don Estevan Minor Ayudante Mayor de la Plaza de Natchez, Comisionado por su Governador el Coronel Don Manuel Gayoso de Lemos, para ir a la Nación Chacta con un Carta Credencial para Franchimastabé, con el fin de tratar con él, sobre el territorio de los Nogales, según las Instrucciones para dicho efecto le he dado," enclosed with Manuel Gayoso de Lemos to the Baron de Carondelet, Natchez, April 30, 1792. Gayoso's letter, the diary, a Spanish translation of Franchimastabé's March 28 letter to Gayoso, and a copy of Gayoso's letter of April 10 to Elías Beauregard instructing him to suspend all traffic with the Indians were enclosed with The Baron de Carondelet to the Conde de Floridablanca, New Orleans, May 4, 1792, N.° 26, AHN, *Estado, leg.* 3898, *exp.* 5.[1]

Diary of Lt. Estevan Minor, Adjutant Major of the town of Natchez, charged by its Governor Col. Don Manuel Gayoso de Lemos, to go to the Chacta Nation with an official letter for Franchimastabé, with the purpose of discussing with him the territory of Nogales, according to instructions for which effect I have given him.

March 13: I left the Plaza of Natchez and I went to sleep at Coles Creek, 25 miles from this town.

14: I left for Bayu Pierre and on the road the Interpreter Ebenecer Fulson joined me. I went to sleep there, having gone 25 miles; and Don Ricardo King, a resident of this district joined me.

15: The excessive rain had swollen the streams to such an extent that it was not possible for me to leave.

16: The water in the streams having receded somewhat, I took to the road; nevertheless, within the distance of 7 miles, it was necessary to cross Bayu Pierre and two of its branches by swimming and to make rafts to transport supplies and baggage, which was accomplished with great difficulty. The pack horse wore out and having found an opportunity to exchange it I did so giving 15 pesos in return. I continued my journey, and I went to camp 25 miles from where I left close to a spring of water that they call Stony Spring or Fuente de Pedregal. By this same spot the dividing line passes, marked on the trees, between this district and the Chacta nation.

17: I took to the road; I passed three streams that carried much water and after 35 miles, I camped without incident.

18: I traveled 5 miles without incident.

19: I took to the road; this day I met some Indians who received me with friendship, and at 50 miles I camped again.

20: I left my camp and at two in the afternoon, I met an Indian Chief called Sulushmastabé, or Red Shoes, who was going to Natchez. I informed him of my charge, and I asked him to return with me because I supposed that nothing could be done in that Nation without his being there. He told me that for himself he did not have an objection but that the condition of his horse was such that it could not carry him. To this I replied that I would give him a horse to ride, which made up his mind and [he] came with me. We camped on the bank of the River of Pearls where we found another camp of Indians, among whom there was a Chief called Yagahnahuma, or Red Earth, with whom I, having undertaken conversation, found to be a man of judgment and [one] who had great influence on his nation. I pleaded with him that he might also return with me because I had matters of great consequence to discuss in his country. After many convincing arguments and offering him, as [I had] Red Shoes, something extraordinary if they might accompany me and might assist me with their influence to the good outcome of the business that I had to discuss with their Nation, he agreed, as [had] the other, offering me his aid [and] assuring me at the same time it was his desire that we possess the lands from west of the line that the English had marked for which we might give them some gift, since the English had never paid anything for them. To this I responded to him that I would speak about this matter the day that I would deliver my word in his country. This day we traveled 55 miles, and my horse was found to be very tired.

21: This day [at] about seven in the morning we crossed the River of Pearls on a raft; about ten miles from there we reached an Indian village, where we bought potatoes. The residents showed themselves to be very friendly. About 3 miles from there we passed through another town, and we continued on to the house of Red Shoes, where we stopped to spend the night. We journeyed today about 30 miles.

22: We left this house; we took to the road, and we reached Franchimastabé's [house] in the town they call Yazu. Not finding him at home, I went to stop at Mr. Davenport's, leaving a message that in the morning I would return to see him.

23: I returned to Franchimastabé's house, who was found to be there, and I informed him that I was bringing to him a letter from the governor of Natchez and a word for his Nation. He told me that he was very happy about this news and that five days from now he would receive me with all formality since he needed all this time to summon his Chiefs and warriors and that he was asking me that I might keep the letter until then, since on that occasion his people would witness what it said, because he didn't want them to think that he had dealings [that he was] hiding from his Nation. I answered him that I would wait with pleasure the five days.

24: Various Traders came to my house, and after some conversations I understood that they were very upset with the commerce and the trading house that there was in Nogales. I then charged Richard King to take advantage of all occasions to speak with them and to ascertain their opinion with respect to the business that I had with the Indians. He did so, and he informed me later that several Traders had assured him that the Indians would never consent to our establishment at Nogales while there was trade there. I repeated my visit to Franchimastabé and [after] having had with him a long conference he got up and he spoke to me in these terms: "I suppose that you come here in order to get from me my lands." I answered him that it was true, since that was my only object and that I trusted that he would not let me go without them because I had so many things to tell him to his own benefit and of all his people. [I told him] that beforehand he was persuaded that His Majesty Our Great King would preserve the peaceful possession of a land that he had already conquered with the sword. He told me that he had many objections to raise and that one of them was that in his country he had a number of white people who after many years in this place had provided his warriors and he himself with merchandise and that they were good men and that he loved them. He added that "these subjects are married to women of my country and they have children with them and seeing them ruined by the Nogales trade is a thing with which I can never agree. When I may see them satisfied, it can be then I may respond favorably with respect to the establishment of Nogales." I told him that he might call all the white Traders that I might confer with them and that afterwards he might inform me what was his opinion and what [was] theirs with respect to the trade which he was talking about. He said that he would do so, because the greater part were to be found in that town. They were called to the house of Mr. Brashears the next day where I also met to hear their positions. Since I am aware of the influence that Mr. Benjamin James has with the Indians and Whites, because [he is] a man of great talent, wealth and [has] lived in that country 20 years, I sent to search for him so that he also might help. I have also held it to be advantageous that he might be present because for many years to this area he is named by the government as a kind of deputy, and I wished to have him present to consult with him.

25: About twelve, Mr. Benjamin James arrived and [after I had] communicated to him what had happened to me with the principal Chief and with the Traders with respect to the Nogales trade, together with the charge that I was bringing to that country, he responded to me that he had heard Franchimastabé say many times that he considered the Traders close to ruin because of the Nogales trade and that if it were not stopped [the situation] would never be calm. He had heard the Traders say the same. It was his opinion that the Indians would never consent to our Establishment of Nogales while the Traders were not happy. It seemed to him that they would never consent to it so long as that trade is not stopped, because, in reality, he said, it is obvious that otherwise they will be ruined, which perhaps would be the cause that might provoke the Indians to do us some damage [by] stealing from us horses, Blacks, and other things. He was not speaking on his own behalf, because of the fact that his residence was in the southern part of the Nation. It [the trade] was not damaging his business, since the Indians of that area did not go hunting on the other side of the Mississippi. [All of] what he told me was a sincere and confident expression of what he thought. We went to the house of Brashears where we found all the traders gathered with Franchimastabé. Upon my arrival they told me that they had discussed with the Chief their situation and that the latter had offered to protect them while they lived in his lands; and, as far as he was able, he would not allow anything which might injure them. [They said] if I wished they might help me with their influence to obtain from the Indians the peaceful possession of Nogales, [but] I had, of course, to promise that the trade there would be stopped and that the commandant would give orders so that they might not take more furs from the Indians than they [the traders] had provided. I responded that I would consider their offers and propositions and would give my answer the day of the meeting. Depending on how they might behave, [I said] it would be such that they would become believers. Thus I hoped that they would consider their own good and the interest of His Majesty, who was protecting them and that in this way they would not put me in the situation of refusing their claim. With this I left them to continue their meeting.

26: At ten, I went with Don Ricardo King and the Interpreter to a nearby town where an old Chief that the English called Snaggle lived, but his Indian name is Tabuca or Paoyanatagha, [a] man of much influence and [a] great speaker. After [our] arrival there and some conversation about the object of my commission, he gave me his word that if on the day of meeting nothing was done on my behalf, he at least would be quiet. He gave us a good meal, while a Spanish flag was waving over us. After eating he took out a small box in which he had his papers, and he told me that I might read them all. I examined them, and I found an English patent and another Spanish one, a letter from an English official and another from the Americans to their account from Philadelphia. Both contained nothing more than mere expressions of friendship. He also had portraits of General Washington, of his wife, of Governor Penn and various others. At three in the afternoon, I said goodbye and returned to my house, where I found news that Franchimastabé had been to see me to tell me that on the following day at twelve he would be ready to receive the word from the Governor of Natchez. I spent the rest of the day and part of the night pondering the different opinions of the white men and the Indians relative to my charge.

27: I communicated the reflections that I had made the previous day to Don Ricardo King and to Mr. Benjamin James, who agreed with me that if I did not offer to stop the trade in Nogales, the results would be the entire ruin of the inhabitants of Natchez along the frontier not by means of open war but with thefts committed by the Indians at the instigation of the traders to compensate the loss that they might have suffered with the Nogales trade..

At twelve Franchimastabé came to tell me that he was nearly ready to hear my word, that all his Chiefs were together, and that if I were ready he would be happy that I might go to introduce myself because he had much to say that consequently he would need much time. I responded to him that I was ready. I went to the site where the gathering was held, and I took the seat that was designated for me in front of Franchimastabé and on each side of me were seated Don Ricardo King and Mr. Benjamin James.

The Chief called Iteleghana in a loud voice summoned the white men and Indians to the gathering to hear the word from the Governor of Natchez and [admonished] them to pay the greatest attention. The venerable old man Franchimastabé, principal Chief of all, rose to his feet and spoke to his people in this way: "I have just arrived from the Chicasa Nation. My oldest brothers, the Talapuches and the Cherokees, had been there before to deal with that Nation. They had charged the King of the Chicasas with a word for me, being the wish of these nations to be at peace and to form a union. In proof of their friendship they left me a package of white beads, charging me to show to my nation their disposition toward a permanent peace." He distributed the beads among the principal Chiefs, and, turning toward me, he said to me, "I have just spoken with my people; I will now hear what you have to say."

I stood up, and I handed him the letter that I was carrying from the Governor of Natchez to him, telling him that in it he would see part of what I had to relate. At the same time I handed to him the white beads that I was carrying on behalf of my Governor. Franchimastabé stood again and asked Mr. Benjamin James to open the letter and inform him of the contents. [After] Mr. James did this and with the audience informed, they all displayed great satisfaction with expressions of approbation. Franchimastabé personally said: "The word seems very good to me, but having been many times deceived by another governor, I do not know whom to believe." To this I responded that governors that no longer existed should not have power over him, that his whole Nation was familiar with the one from Natchez and knew that he was a man incapable of breaking his word, that to New Orleans had arrived a new Governor General chosen by our Great King who was very good and a very close friend of the Indians, that what I had to say to him on behalf of the Natchez governor would show him that I was coming on behalf of a good man and friend of his children the red men. To this he answered that time and not explanations would convince him.

I replied to him: "It is futile that we should spend time speaking about things that do nothing to advance the business on which I come." He agreed to it with pleasure.

I began my speech, saying: "Our Great King of Spain conquered through strength of arms in the last war with the English all the lands that they had in this country and when the English had to deliver them on a piece of paper they showed the lines that demarcated their limits, saying to the King of Spain: 'This is our land and we deliver it to you.'"

Addressing the word to Franchimastabé directly, I told him: "You and all your people had taken the King of Spain by the hand. You received from him in proof of reciprocal friendship flags, medals, and patents in replacement of those which you discarded from the English." [I continued by telling him] that their opposition to the establishment by their Father and protector of a fort at Nogales, whose principal object was not only to protect his own land but also that of the Indian, was contradictory. [It was, I said, to be] carried out in a territory that was won with the sword.

I said this with a tone of firmness and appearance of anger. Franchimastabé answered saying that it was true what I was referring [to] except the matter of the land because he could not believe that the English had paid, and besides he said that the Indians who had sold them [the lands] did not have the right to do it because those lands belonged solely to those of the Upper Villages and the ones who sold them were from the Lower Villages.

I replied to him that it was far from friendship what they were now doing with us, because they had allowed the English the peaceful possession of that land, permitting them to distribute it among the inhabitants, [proof of which is that] at the present time [there were] in Natchez individuals from that time who were still able to show papers that support the same. Those lands of Nogales were surveyed by the English. The Indians of the Upper Villages did not oppose the drawing of the lines or the distribution of the lands. Now, without having told us that they have the least claim to them, they object to our remaining there. "This then is proof that you still esteem more a people whom you have rejected and who abandoned you than those who today you have by the hand and who protect you." I added, "I beg you to consider your misery and your small number and that you reflect on how large and how numerous the Spanish nation is. If you don't tell me that you do not love that land, then I will tell you that the King does not value his gifts."

Franchimastabé responded to me that in his last talk with the Chicasas, his oldest brothers, they recommended that [the Indians] never sell their lands because for them they never received another thing than ornaments for their women, that these would be used and that the lands never. He said: "I have always loved the white man and I would like to be on good terms with them, but I cannot bring about the sale of my lands and allow red men to laugh at me saying that I am a King who sells the lands of my women and children for goods to dress them. No, this is something that I will never do; nevertheless, here there are many Chiefs and warriors who may speak, since they have the right to do so and I wish to know their feeling: 'Speak that this Spanish official who is here may listen to you.'"

Only two spoke, saying that they would not be happy to see their lands occupied by white men.

To this I replied that I would regret having to say to our children, the red men, that they were no longer to go to hunt on the other side of the Mississippi and on their return to ask that we should help them transport their pelts, that we should give them houses to keep them while they should return to their country to look for horses to transport them. "We are happy to see them when they go to visit us; if they ask us for a blanket, a bandage, powder, shot, or any other thing they never are left unhappy. Why then [do] the red men have to love a piece of land that is of no value to them and that already on another occasion they have ceded? Are not the Spanish the best neighbors that you have ever had? When is it that your nation has been as rich as now? When is it that you have been so much time without war, as since you have given your hand to the Spanish? Consider all this, my friends, and you will see that you are mistaken in saying only a single word against our settlement at Nogales." I turned my gaze all around me, watching the different Chiefs, telling them that it seemed to me that I knew those faces because of having seen them in Natchez taking the Governor by the hand and telling him that he would peacefully possess all the lands within the limits drawn between the English and the Chactas. That [was] the will of their principal Chief, the one who spoke, that also was mine, because as they were men who obtained patents if they did not say there the same that I had heard them in Natchez that I would consider them as women and men of two words.

At this Franchimastabé stood up and said to his people: "what the Spanish official speaks is just; why don't you speak?" The old Chief called Red Earth stood and said some words in favor of our settlement at Nogales. Iteleghana also said something in the manner of Franchimastabé, but none of the other Chiefs spoke. Then I told them: "I have come from very far away and with much effort to see you for the second time. Will it be possible that I may return ashamed like a man who has stolen something, and they have caught him in the crime? No, it is not possible that this may happen. If the red people, children of our sovereign, wish to have his protection, it is necessary that you give me a positive answer. Thus, again, I beg you to speak. This is the last time that I will propose it to you."

To this Franchimastabé again stood and addressing me said: "Have I not responded to you various times that your word was good? In order that I say more on the matter it is necessary that you assure me that the trade of Nogales will be stopped because on the contrary my white men will be ruined. That is what I cannot consent to, because in my country there are many old men and women who cannot go to Nogales to look for a needle, a little vermilion or similar trifles when they need them. How will they live if our white men see themselves ruined and unable to help us? By stopping that trade it will cause two good effects: the one will be that my traders will charge the hunters what they owe them; the other [is] that they won't deceive the traders of Nogales. My red people will take whatever they can get; and, if they can, will not pay anyone. When they have so much credit, they think only of drinking. If the trade was not stopped appropriately, the traders of the Nation would have to follow the hunters to the other side of the river with much inconvenience to them.

Then I told him: "If you want the trade stopped, it is necessary that you do not speak more words about reclaiming those lands." He repeated to me: "Your word is good." "And yours also," I said to him. He asked that I stop speaking while he consulted the will of his people. I agreed to it, it being four in the afternoon.

At about five he turned to me and said to me: "I always thought that the debate concerning the matter of the land had to be long and that I would leave a liar if I might cede it before next year. You have told me that if I did not love my land, the great King would not love his gifts." I asked him whether he had considered carefully what he had said, adding at the same time that we white men, when we were discussing matters of such importance, we did not want the least doubt to remain. "So I beg you to explain what it is that you want to say and what I should understand from the expression 'my word is good.'" He responded to me that I was able to understand that it was agreeable to him and that he would have no difficulty complying with it if he saw that His Majesty scorned their merchandise. "You can be certain that for my part I will do whatever may be possible in favor of the interest of the great King of Spain. Tomorrow we will talk more at length concerning this matter because the rest of the afternoon I want to use in conferences with my Chiefs and warriors."

Shortly after this, those in attendance began to withdraw, and they left us alone. I took advantage [of this] in order to tell him that I wanted to have with him a private conference. He assured me that he would also value it, and he asked me to go to his house the following day at twilight, that then he would be alone, adding that I still had two days to be with him, to which I answered that it would at his pleasure. I withdrew at about seven in the afternoon.

28: At eight in the morning he [Franchimastabé] came to my house to see me and, embracing the chance of finding ourselves alone, I decided to tell him that what I had to communicate to him at night. I continued in this way: "You know my friend that the success of my business depends entirely on you. You are the man on whom all your nation places its trust and from whom they expect counsel. So you now have an opportunity to show the great King of Spain how much you strongly support his interest; and at the same time you can take advantage of many opportunities, as it is right so to do. The Governor of Natchez observes very justly that you are at the head of a great nation and that your expenses and labors in holding gatherings and having speeches certainly are very considerable and that now you can be compensated for all of it [by] appropriating the greater part of the gifts that are destined for the Chiefs and that [if] this suited, it would remain a best-kept secret."

He answered me: "I always thought that at the end you would find the true path to my heart." He added that he might not have shown until now such repugnance against the establishment of Nogales, were it not for the suspicion he had of his young warriors, who often had already threatened him with his life, but now they were beginning to accept the matter. It was almost ten o'clock, other Chiefs came, and we stopped the conversation. He told me afterward in private that everything was on course, that at twilight I could go to his house as we had arranged and that there he would tell me the rest. That suited me.

This afternoon at seven I went to the house of Franchimastabé, and this old Chief opened the conversation telling me that he would write a letter to the Governor of Natchez relative to the matter of the lands and that I could inform him that he could freely continue in Nogales, that while he might have vital breaths, a drop of blood would not be shed by his peoples in that land nor in any other of the dominion of the great King of Spain nor would he consent to the passage through his lands of our enemy with his permission. I answered him that now I saw that he had just given proof to the Governor of Natchez of the regard that he had for the white men who were protecting him. I was sure that he would never lack anything that he might wish, and I asked him at the same time that he might send a horse with me to the Governor, to be loaded with those things that at the present time might be most necessary. He told me he would do it, but the things that he might send him ought to go under the name of Mr. Turner Brashears, who was the subject that he planned to send with his letter, who merited all his confidence. He [said] he would come in my company in order to be a witness that the trade in Nogales was stopped because everything that we had said and done would the same as nothing if the trade were not ended for the reasons that he had described. I assured him that it would be done in the most expeditious way and [in conformance with] the interest of the traders and his wishes. He also told me that since Mr. Brashears was the man who had his entire confidence, I could assure the Governor to speak with him freely knowing thereby it would be accurately and fully communicated. I assured him [that] with the greatest precision I would tell the Governor what he was charging me, adding that he had for a long time wanted to see him. I asked him if he planned to pay him a visit soon. He answered me that he would be very happy to do so as soon as the Governor should write him and indicate a time. Immediately he would prepare to go to shake his hand, because all the white people had assured him that he was a good man. I confirmed him in this opinion, and I told him that if he wanted something more than what was customarily given to the Indians, he might communicate it to me since I believed that the Governor would send it to him. Then he asked me for the following: a saddle with its bridle and spurs, four kegs of brandy, one ax, some sugar and coffee, some tweezers to pluck the beard, and two dozen combs for his children and grandchildren.

I told him that it seemed to me that we had spoken about all our essential matters, that now, with the knowledge that I had that he was a man of talent and information, I would be very pleased to hear him speak, out of pure curiosity, about other matters of which he wanted to inform me. He told me with great pleasure he would answer as many questions I might ask him. I told him then that I was a man who spoke Spanish, English, and French and that I was able to read those languages when they were put on paper, that I was his and his nation's particular friend. I wanted to tell him that some Americans had informed me that they wanted to have treaties with him and to buy a piece of his lands. He answered me that it is true that they should want to be on friendly terms with his nation, to which he did not have objection since he wanted to be in peace with the whole world, but that he would never sell them lands nor would he negotiate treaties with them for such purpose. I told him that his way of thinking caused great pleasure because I knew that what the Americans wanted was to take possession of a small part of his land so that shortly afterwards they could expel them from the rest, [thereby] destroying his people, as they had already done and were doing with all the Indians of the north. "Surely they would promise you many and great presents of goods and advantages of trade and many other good things. I am certain that they would never ever fulfill [these promises] since you know as well as I that the Great King of Spain is the master of all the waters that surround the land and that those who here may want to have trade with you, bringing you goods in exchange for your skins, must come and go by water. You know that the Americans cannot do that. Thus it is true that however much they may tell you with respect to trade, it is only to deceive you. Remember that I am your friend and that I have told you what will happen to you or your nation if you listen to the Americans." He answered me that he had reasons to believe that what I had told him was true. He was determined to live forewarned, since he was not ignoring the desire of Americans to take lands from the Indians and impoverish them whenever they could do so.

I remarked that yesterday in the Assembly he had told me that only the Indians of the Upper Villages had claim to the lands of Nogales and that I had forgotten to ask him how many villages were the ones that they called Upper. He answered me that fifteen were the ones who had rights to those lands. I asked him if he would be able to tell me how many Indians there were in each village. He answered me that he was not able to say it but that if I asked some white man, it could be that he might know. To this I replied that I was not planning to speak with any white man about this matter, that when I definitely might need to know it would be that then he might be able to give me this information.

It did not seem advisable to me to speak about the lands that are between the Pearl River and the Natchez district while the matter of Nogales was pending. Therefore, I thought it best only to speak indirectly about the matter, saying to Franchimastabé that on the road to his nation I had passed through some lands that were very pleasing to me, that I had thought that it would be best for me to build there a settlement for the many herds that I had in the Natchez district. He flattered me [by saying] that he would sell me six square miles. Smiling he [further] responded [by saying] that the lands between the line and the Pearl River were the best that his nation possessed, that the time of hunting and of men's living by means of the gun were, according to his opinion, near its end, that when this period might arrive his people would have to live from their labor like the white men and that those lands were the only ones that they had for the purpose. Then I replied to him that if some day might arrive in which they might wish to dispose of them in part or entirely, I was begging him that he might give preference to me and to the Spanish nation. He answered that it was true that all the days had not ended and that it would happen that the case of selling those lands might arrive. If it should happen, he would give preference to me and the Spanish nation. I told him that I trusted him in this because of [my] believing [him to be] a man of [his] word.

With this our conversation ended, and I said goodbye to him, [it] being two in the morning. He squeezed my hand very tightly reiterating that all the business was concluded and [extended to me] other expressions of friendship and offering me that in the morning at nine he had to see me to wish me good journey to Natchez.

29: I will make mention here that during my residence in this nation, my two companions, Don Ricardo King and the Interpreter Ebenecer Fulson, have helped me with the greatest diligence and effectiveness in whatever I have charged them, conducting themselves in a way that confirms their fidelity to the King and the interest that they take in the good of their service, circumstances that oblige me to mention them in this diary, citing their merit.

Of all the white Traders of this nation the one that I have found the most inclined to our interests is Mr. Turner Brashears with whom I have consulted from time to time [on] matters relative to my charge, and I have always found him [a] man of truth and of influence in this nation. He is also the intimate friend of Franchimastabé and [one] in whom he places his greatest confidence, [and the] reason why he sends him to Natchez to meet with that Governor. I should also say that the rest of the traders treated me with all kind of consideration and politeness.

I have tried to discover the person who will succeed Franchimastabé after his death. The opinion of the people is divided on this matter. Some say that it might be Red Shoes and others Iteleghana, but Brashears has positively assured me that it would be given to a son of the old Chief Taboca, who is at present captain. So the same Franchimastabé has entrusted it to him, who, according to their laws, has the discretion to leave his position to the Indian of his choice. Because this news was communicated by a subject who has good reason for knowing it, I believe that it is the most probable.

I have also been informed that the Chacta Nation consists of a few more or less of twelve thousand individuals of both sexes, among whom there would be three or four thousand men at arms; in the Chicasas, about two thousand individuals and some six hundred men at arms.

At ten Franchimastabé came to my house to say good bye and after having drunk with him, I took the road in [the] company of Brashears and my other two companions. We went to sleep in a town fifteen miles distant. This day, when I was preparing to leave, one of the horses could not be found, which forced me to buy another for 30 pesos from Mr. Davenport; and I had to exchange my horse, finding it not able to make the journey, for another, and give sixty pesos in return.

30: At six in the morning, I took to the road, and I went . . . miles, having swum three streams and moved our luggage on a raft.[2]

31: This day we traveled 60 miles without incident.

April 1: This day at two in the afternoon I met Mr. Hayward, who handed me an envelope from the Governor of Natchez, whose contents were about matters that did not necessitate my return to the Nation. We traveled 55 miles.

2: This day we traveled 70 miles and we arrived at the house of Mr. Brokas at eight at night, having swum two streams.

3: I left for Natchez, where I arrived at ten at night, having traveled 60 miles, with which I conclude my diary, which I hand to the Governor and by word I will inform him about whatever he may ask me.

Natchez, 3 April 1792.

8

Franchimastabé to Gayoso, March 28, 1792

Probably written by Turner Brashears, the particular text of this letter forms part of a file entitled "Cartas de Don Juan de la Villebeuvre Comisario en la Nación Chacta. Año 1793" (Letters of Don Juan de la Villebeuvre Commissioner in the Choctaw Nation Year of 1793), AGI, PC, *leg.* 2353. It is reproduced here in the original English.

Dear Father,

My friend and Brother. You are at the Natchez and sends talks to me and I believe them as you put trust in the man that you sent to talk with me and I have had a great deal of talk with him and I believe you and I hope you will believe me. And if I was to say that there was but seven or eight I should tell you a lye. I don't want to beg anything of you I leave it all to yourself a man that sells goods can trade as they please. But I still leave it to your own generosity. I want to see you myself. I shall come but I intend to wait your own time for it. When I hear from you and everything is straight then I shall know better what to do. I send you this writing to let you know that I intend to let the Chickasaws hear of this. There is but two towns of them that I have any concern with. This I send you. I expect you will send to New Orleans. All tho I am a red man and make use of coffee & sugar but I have nothing to buy it

I am not a man of two talks and I hope that you are so likewise and I hope that you will not let any settlers be at that place but the fort and to sit still till all matters is settled. I hope that you will be still untill we meet. I am an old man and am the head of all the white men hear and loves them and don't want to make them ashamed, the goods being there makes great confusion in the nation and I beg that it will be stopt and during your reign there will be more goods kept there. I received Major Minor with friendship and I hope you will do the same with the man that I have sent to hear and to receive your talks and to tell me the straight talks on his return from there and to see that you stop the traid with the Indians in that District of the Natchez. Major Minor has promised me that it shall be stopt, and you in your letter to me tells me that whatever he says shall be so and I expect that you are a man of your word. I remain your friend and loving son.

Franchimastabé

9

Gayoso to Tascahetuca [Taskietoka], March 28, 1792

Manuel Gayoso de Lemos to Tascahetuca, Natchez, March 21, 1792, N.° 3, *Copia,* with Manuel Gayoso de Lemos to the Conde de Floridablanca, Natchez, April 13, 1792, N.° 5, *Reservado,* AHN, *Estado, leg.* 3885bis, *exp.* 7. Serrano y Sanz includes the letter in *España y los indios cherokis y chactas,* 44n.2, and *Documentos históricos de la Florida y la Luisiana,* 414–15. Another translation is that of Samuel Dorris Dickinson in *Spain and the Cherokee and Choctaw Indians by Manuel Serrano y Sanz,* 50n.3.

In the context of Minor's second mission to the Choctaws, Gayoso wrote this letter to the "King of the Chickasaws." He sent a copy of it, along with his letter to Franchimastabé, his instructions to Minor, and other documents directly to the minister of state, the count of Floridablanca, in Spain.

To the King of the Chicacha Nation

Although I have never had the pleasure of seeing you, I profess to you and to your nation the most sincere affection who my great King loves and wishes all well. It is true that we are good friends and allies, and for this consideration I always make and will do all that might be in my power to serve you in what can be personally satisfactory, as in helping your nation in case that it should need it.

If we were looking at each other and our hands enclosing themselves, my heart should tell you many good things for your nation, and they would assure you that I am [a] true friend of all the Indians, but as we are so distant, I only advise you that you constantly maintain unity among the Chactas, Talapuches, Cherokees and the rest of the Indian nations that should be in your vicinity. Then you will have nothing to fear; your nations will find themselves protected, your young sons will grow up, the adults will reach old age; your country will produce abundance; the Heaven over your head will always be benign, and your land will not see itself stained with a single drop of human blood. All this time the great Spanish nation will look at you smiling; she will give you whatever she has to serve you and help you in your hands how much it has to serve you and help you. Its arms will always be open and ready to embrace and welcome in her heart her friends the Indians.

If on some occasion you should like to come to see me, let me know before so that I am at home to receive you. It seems to me that it would be best that we should speak and as your nation and the Choctaw are brothers, it would be good that Franchimastabé should come with you. Until then I tell you no more except that right now I am imagining that my arm extends to where you are and that my hand grasps yours and I cannot loosen it, and my heart tells me that I keep it [there] always. In this situation I remain your most devoted friend and brother. Manuel Gayoso de Lemos. To my friend and brother Tascahetuca.

10

Gayoso's Account of the Natchez Congress, May 1792

Manuel Gayoso de Lemos to Baron de Carondelet. Natchez. May 29, 1792, N.° 86, *Copia,* enclosed with Baron de Carondelet to Conde de Aranda, New Orleans, June 11, 1792, N.° 3, *Reservado,* AHN, *Estado, leg.* 3898, *exp.* 5.

On the tenth of the current month [May] I received information from Franchimastabé that he was to be found in this district accompanied by the King of the Chicachas and more than two hundred Indians, including Chiefs and warriors, and that the following day he was waiting for me at Coles Creek. He asked me for various things to eat and drink and for eight shirts.

I arranged that everything be sent to him at Coles Creek on the following day; but, before [the supplies] might leave, I received other information that they would come straight away to see me. I immediately sent my assistant Don Estevan Minor, to go to meet them on the road, and I gathered at my house the officials of this garrison and all the distinguished residents of the area in order to receive the visit of these Indians. At the same time I ordered twenty men-at-arms to come to increase the watch and to give a greater air of ceremony to the event.

They arrived at ten in the morning of the agreed-upon eleventh day [of May]. As soon as they were seen, the flags were raised on my house and on the fort. I received them on the stairs of my gallery, accompanied by all the officials, and I led them to the place that I had prepared in my garden under a very large tent surrounded by trees and placed near my own house.

In the place of honor at this site [there] was an armchair for me, and on the sides, forming a semi-circle, others for my companions. In front of my chair, there was a table with paper and an inkwell; in front of this table at a very short distance [there] were two armchairs for the King of the Chicachas and for Franchimastabé, and on each side forming a circle with mine [were other chairs] for their Chiefs. Behind there were benches for the warriors.

In this same arrangement, everyone was placed giving preference to the King of the Chicachas, followed by Franchimastabé, Ytelaghana, Stonahuma, Tapenahuma, Necjahumaachó, Comfield, Abahuly, Cafatabe and Sulouchemastabé all Chactas, and many captains and warriors of both nations. The women and children with some warriors had remained at a campsite about half a league away.

The interpreter Fulson stood close to the side of the table. I made Turner Brashears, who had returned with them [the Indians] from the road, sit among those who accompanied me, determined that this subject should not miss any of the public ceremonies that they might have with the Indians. Being held in the greatest of confidence by Fran-

Figure 6. The Spanish governor's house, "Concord," in Natchez, ca. 1900. This picture is probably of the palatial house Gayoso built for himself. It may not be the house he refers to as his residence in the account of the Natchez assembly and in other documents. When he arrived as governor, he lived in a house rented from Juan Vauchet. He began construction of a house, but before completion it was destroyed by a tornado. He began construction of a new house, which may not have been completed at the time of these meetings. Between 1790 and 1797, Stephen Minor's house on the bluff was rented for use as Government House. "Concord" was destroyed by fire in 1900. Jack D. Elliott, Jr., "City and Empire: The Spanish Origins of Natchez," *Journal of Mississippi History* 59 (Winter 1997), 288. Courtesy of the Mississippi Department of Archives and History, Accession No.: PI/HH/C66.3/Box 12 folder 32#1.

chimastabé, [it was best for him] to serve as a witness [to prevent] that at any time [the Indians] might allege lack of information about what was being discussed. Before anyone might speak or greet the Chiefs formally, I told them through my interpreter that Turner Brashears was there [and that] he understood English perfectly, [which was] the language in which I would speak to them, and it [everything] would be explained in Chicacha and Chacta which he [Brashears] equally understood. From now on I charged him [Brashears] to pay close attention so that he might correct or warn about any error or omission. He agreed to do it in this way.

It is the normal custom that when the Indians come to see the white Chiefs they speak first, but because on this occasion they came at my request, I decided to open the discussion. So, addressing the King of the Chicachas, I told him that I had great satisfaction upon seeing him in my country in the company of Franchimastabé and the other Chiefs [who were] present. I thanked him for the promptness with which he had come to discuss and resolve a matter that was disturbing the sincere harmony that always had existed between our nations.

In a matter of a minute afterwards, the previously mentioned King of the Chicachas answered me that as he was about to leave for Mobile he received my letter from the hand of Mr. Estevan Hayward and that at that moment changed his journey and came to the Chacta nation to join with Franchimastabé, as I requested. They planned to have come with a very small group, but when the people found out their destination on the road, they joined [the group] so they arrived here with many [people]. He was very happy to see me, and, although he had come from very far away, he considered meeting me worth the effort. Because they had just arrived, [he regarded] that visit as purely ceremonial; later we would name a day to discuss business. He got up and shook my hand, and, sitting down again, he said it was very hot and that he wanted to drink wine with water and smoke. Immediately I ordered brought what was necessary for both. Meanwhile I addressed Franchimastabé, complimenting him and explaining to him that I had regretted very much his not finding me here on the other two occasions when he came to see me, but that finally we had been able to meet personally. We shook hands, following Ytelaghana and the rest of the Chiefs already my acquaintances.

At this point the wine and water arrived, with glasses for all those who were in the circle. At the time I was going to fill the glasses, Franchimastabé said that he wanted to speak some words before. I gave him my attention, and he referred [to the fact] that, although he came to see me before receiving my last letter that Brashears was to bring him, as the King of the Chicachas arrived in his country on the journey here, it seemed best to him [Franchimastabé] not to delay the trip. He hoped it would not turn out badly.

I answered him, referring to our agreement, that he almost did not find me at home; but since my desire to see him was so great, as a precaution I had delayed a trip that I had planned to Nogales, without which he might not have found me, but since everything has turned out well I was eagerly looking forward to the forthcoming meeting.

He [Franchimastabé] began again and continued: "the King of the Chicachas is present; all the Indian nations look to him as our older brother; he will speak for himself and for us; whatever he may do, we will approve; our heart and our breath are all one; thus you will discuss with him whatever you may have to tell us, assured that he is the one who has all the power. [Neither] I nor my Chiefs will speak other than to approve whatever he may do or say."

I responded that it was very agreeable to me to see their feelings gathered together in the breast of only one, and that it might be in that of the King of the Chicachas in whom they had so much confidence, merited by his superior talent and by being the one who governed not only his nation but also the Chacta, who were the only ones with whom I wished to discuss the present matter. I filled the glasses. I gave the first to the aforementioned King, the second to Franchimastabé. I continued with the rest of the Chiefs, and afterwards I took one myself, and I distributed others to those who were accompanying me. We all drank to the health of our August Sovereign at the request of the King of the Chicachas who asked me afterwards that I might order to be distributed a refreshment of brandy and water to the rest who had come with them. I gave him that pleasure, and I also had tobacco and fire brought, and we all smoked with the greatest cordiality and proof of friendship.

Since it was not a day to talk about business, matters of little importance were discussed, all contributing, however, to securing the good faith of the Indians. Among other things, I told the King of the Chicachas and Franchimastabé that since I considered them [to be] tired and that the weather was threatening rain, I was hoping that they might give me the pleasure of remaining to lodge with me while they remained here, that the other Chiefs would take care of the campsite and that we would all eat and we would always be together all the days. They thanked me for the offer, answering me that they had all come together so that for now they did not plan to sleep away from camp. I didn't insist too much, since it was best for me to be able to be alone at home in order to have private conferences as they might be needed. Besides, already, from my sources the day before, I was informed about the nature of the King of the Chicachas and that everything depended on him, so I rather wanted to be alone in order to be able to win him, persuading him to reason in private conferences.

We continued drinking and smoking with great moderation until almost one, when we got up.

I had food for everyone, and at the usual hour we sat down to table, the same ones who had been [seated] in the circle.

Everyone, and particularly the King of the Chicachas, toasted the good treatment, the last [the King] said that he already regretted having decided to go to the camp at night, but that he would now pay me visits. This was with the purpose of deceiving the rest so that with the pretext that he was proposing, [he] could come to see me at all hours.

For my part, since the success of this negotiation was to depend on what might be the disposition of the spirits of the individual Indians on the day of the Congress, I wanted to have time to win them. Besides, informed that they brought many spare horses, I thought that [even] if the matter of Nogales was not concluded now, I would nevertheless have to make them happy with gifts [now] and [allow] others of more consideration remain pending for the future. Thus, I proposed to devote all my efforts to conclude everything, since in the letter that I wrote for Don Estevan Minor to Franchimastabé I told him that if he trusted me, I would respond by making him happy when he came to see me. For this it was necessary for me to take some days, so, indirectly I hinted to the principal Chiefs that the following day was very busy for me, because it was Saturday, on which [day] I gave audience to all the white people in my district; that the next [day] was Sunday, devoted to public worship; that on Monday we could hold the Congress. Brashears, a subject whom I favored, and whose inclination to serve me I had already obtained, spoke privately with the King of the Chicachas and with Franchimastabé and afterwards they themselves proposed to me that on the next two days they would not come to see me because of the reasons given by me, but which they gave as theirs, and that on Monday we would discuss our business.

I welcomed their decision, and I offered to be ready at the time they indicated to me.

During the meal different toasts were drunk to our August Sovereign, the Captain General, to Your Lordship, and to all the officials present. I, for my part, taking turns [offering toasts] to each one of them, recognized these people to be of good faith, [and] welcomed hearing from them many sentences that revealed it.

At five in the afternoon, they all said goodbye and [went off] to the campsite, requesting various quantities of brandy and wine, which I ordered that [they be] given, part from the royal warehouses and part from my house, determined that they might not have the least cause for complaint.

Beginning the night of the eleventh, I ordered that the guards be strengthened, that a party of twenty-two men should leave the fort, and that the rest of the garrison should sleep with their clothes on while the Indians were here, but without noise so that it should not become known in the neighborhood. I also had brought to the fort a supply of gunpowder, prepared cartridges, and one-hundred rifles from the supply, ready to be able to be fired under the pretext that on Monday a triple salute would be fired should the matter be concluded. I ordered all the artillery loaded, but secretly I warned Lieutenant Don Antonio Soler that he have it [the artillery] aimed well on all the streets.

The crew of my galiot reinforced my guard at night. With these precautions I was sure that nothing could surprise me.

The following day, the twelfth, it seemed to me normal to go to the campsite to visit the King of the Chicachas, Franchimastabé, and the rest of the Chiefs. I advised them of my intention; and at nine in the morning, accompanied by some officials and with the two interpreters, I went with all possible ceremony to see them. On my approach, the King of the Chicachas and Franchimastabé advanced and came to meet me at the entrance to the campsite, where I dismounted, and together we reached a place that they had prepared under a great tree, the ground covered with deer skins, where they offered me a seat beside the mentioned King. We all sat on the deer skins in the following order: the King of the Chicachas, Franchimastabé on his right, and Ytelaghana and the rest of the Chiefs following, forming a circle; I was on the left, Lt. Col. don Carlos de Grand-Pré followed, my adjutant Don Estevan Minor and the rest who accompanied me, closing the circle, and the interpreters in the middle.[1] In front of this place, there was an Indian playing a tambourine and around him all the Indian women dancing and singing; within a short distance, close to us, there was one who played a kind of flute. The young Indians continuously brought branches with which they decorated that site, and all the warriors surrounded us.

The King thanked me for the visit, and Franchimastabé the same; and the rest gave many demonstrations of contentment. The former asked me how his campsite appeared to me, [together] with other questions that showed his satisfaction.

I told him what truly struck me: that whatever I saw was extremely pleasant, and most particularly his manner and the fine discipline that I observed in the camp. They brought tobacco, and we smoked casually as a sign of close friendship. I studiously refused to speak about any business and only about unimportant and pleasant things. The King told me that at twilight he would come alone to see me, which I welcomed greatly, indicating to him that we had an infinite [number of matters] to discuss. He showed satisfaction in this, gripping my hand.

Franchimastabé repeated to me that he and all the Chacta Nation were under the orders of the King of the Chicachas, that the latter was the big brother of all the Indian nations, and that thus they considered him, that lately the Cherokees, the Talapuches, the Chactas, and the Chicachas made an alliance in which they now form a single Nation for their defense, and that they chose for the head, the King of the Chicachas, for which reason it was to him [King of the Chicachas] that the Cherokees sent the strings of beads so that he might distribute them among the rest of the nations. He [Franchimastabé] added that Don Estevan Minor had observed this in part, since when he [Minor] went to see him [Franchimastabé] on my behalf, the white beads sent by the King of the Chicachas arrived. Minor had spoken to me concerning the mentioned treaty, but he was unaware of the preeminence that it gave to that King. All the Chiefs present confirmed what Franchimastabé said, and in truth, it was well-recognized by the veneration that they were paying to him. I responded, with some variation, the same as on the previous day, having them believe that I was aware of the esteem that the King of the Chicachas had among them.

I said goodbye about eleven, telling the principal Chiefs that since they were not coming to eat with me, I would send them something from my table and my wine cellar, which I did.

They accompanied me until I mounted my horse, and I came home.

Fulson came to tell me that he had discovered that the King of the Chicachas was determined to conclude the matter of Nogales, but he was counting on being thanked for it. He [Fulson] heard him [the King] say to Franchimastabé: "What more do you want from this man?" (speaking about me). "You see how he receives us and how he has treated all those who have come to see him; they all say he is good and so he seems to me; thus, if he has sufficient goods to present gifts to your Chiefs and warriors, I am going to deal now with him." He added some other reflections favorable to us and in everything he showed good attitudes.

I immediately made an inspection of the Indian goods that existed in these royal warehouses to see if with them it would be possible for me to please these people, although I might have to add something more [by] purchase from the settlers. On the enclosed report, number 1, you will see what existed; the remnant of which attachment number 2 shows, which a year ago, at my request, Señor Don Estevan Miró sent me for the purpose of ingratiating myself with the Indians, which with the greatest economy I have been distributing in the referred period. Those left to me are recorded in the mentioned enclosure number 1.

About three in the afternoon, the King of the Chicachas arrived at my house with Ytelaghana and Stonahuma, and in spite of [the fact] that I had sent food to the camp, they again ate with me.

At five the King moved away from the others, asking me for wine and brandy in order to say good-bye to them. I gave it to him.

Remaining alone, he entered my room with the interpreter, and we began our private conference.

I opened the discussion telling him that [for] men like us, charged with public affairs, it was best that we might see each other privately in order to communicate our secrets freely without being forced to restrain ourselves, by not revealing them to everyone.

He answered that he greatly approved this procedure, and that he had an infinite number of things to communicate to me.

I began making him an individual report about the project of the Carolina Companies and about the O'Fallon operations in Kentucky, with the fixed purpose of coming to establish themselves in Nogales, although without the authority of the Congress.[2] I explained to him how the United States was at peace with us and that it was a nation that we looked upon as friends, but that among them there were many people who, disregarding their country's laws, were gathering together in groups and usurping Indian lands and that the mentioned companies, through O'Fallon, were also intending to come and occupy our [lands]; that with this news I immediately went up to Nogales with many warriors and heavy artillery to build there. [I said] that at that time, shortly after I had been here, Ytelaghana came to see me, and he told me that those lands belonged to the Indians, that he was going to the [Chacta] Nation to alert Franchimastabé about what he had seen, who would come to an understanding with me. In fact I received and sent various messages about this matter until the present time, referring to him [the King] the substance of them [the messages]. I showed him then the indispensable right that our august Sovereign has over the described lands, having conquered them from the English, adding whatever I could to convince him. Finally I referred to him whatever I had communicated about this matter to that general Government, making it clear to him the ingratitude of the Chacta Nation and how little I was advancing in this negotiation with them, which forced me to write to him, knowing the influence that he has had on all the Indian nations, begging him to come with Franchimastabé to see me.[3]

He answered that from the beginning he was informed about everything because Franchimastabé had communicated it to him while events were happening, that lastly when he received my letter, although he was about to leave for Mobile, he decided to agree to my urgings; that he came to the Chacta Nation and obliged Franchimastabé to follow him, and being already convinced that right was on my side, he [the King] told him [Franchimastabé] that it was madness to fight with us over the Nogales territory; that if they persisted, we had the means to deprive them of all trade. Besides he [the King] told him [Franchimastabé]: "You are already very old, you can live [only a] little [longer]; you are the only one opposed to the Spanish living peacefully at Nogales; in the four days that I have been in your Nation, I have recognized that all your people are disposed to cede [the territory]; they all have abandoned you; only one is committed to your way of thinking" (making reference to Brashears, whose advice Franchimastabé follows); "so, take advantage during your life of what the Governor of Natchez might give you, since he tells you that he has in his power sufficient goods to make you happy;" that on the road he [the King] repeated these same ideas to him.

[The King] then told me himself how he was the one who during the time of the English had arranged to give a great medal to the predecessor of Franchimastabé; that when that one died the English consulted with him [the King] about to whom they should give it; and because of his advice they gave it to Franchimastabé; that when much later the Spanish took over this country. he [the King] received a message from Mr. Estevan Miró, by means of Don Juan de la Villebeuvre, that he might persuade the mentioned Franchimastabé that he exchange his English medal for a Spanish one; that because of his [the King's] advice he [Franchimastabé] agreed to it, and [the King] even accompanied him [Franchimastabé] to New Orleans where he returned his English medal and because the Spanish hadn't struck one yet, they sent it on to him in his nation afterwards. On that occasion [the trip to New Orleans] they only gave him a flag, in recognition of which he [the King] considers Franchimastabé as his creation, and that he [Franchimastabé] is obliged not only for this reason but also because of the preference that he [the King] has over him in the Chacta Nation to obey him and in truth, Franchimastabé recognizes it [to be] so and is disposed to agree with whatever he [the King] may direct as he [Franchimastabé) told me on his arrival and a second time in the camp.

I made various observations concerning the common interest of the Indian nations, which is always to live united and allied as if they were only one Nation for the defense of all; that if they were to do so, they could surely count on the powerful aid of Spain, who in the event of seeing them attacked, would assist them vigorously, providing them with arms and ammunition and whatever else might be possible, but that in return the Spanish nation expected them to be faithful allies, and that they will not form alliances with anyone else, because it would not be right that while we were favoring them so much, they [the Indians] might have direct contact with anyone else.

He [the King] responded to me that he recognized that his interest was none other than that of remaining subject to Spain; that in Pensacola and Mobile, he found whatever he needed, so that he did not wish another connection. Nevertheless, it was necessary [he said] that I not become angry with him because of what he was going to tell me, and [the fact] was that he wanted to be at peace with everyone, he received in a friendly fashion a message from the Americans with a gift of powder and shot that he accepted purely so as not to anger them and that afterwards he received another [message] several months ago, in which they sent him a white shirt with the expression that it was to be worn next to his skin as a sign of intimacy and alliance that they wanted to form with him. Suspecting that the intention of the Americans would be to want to take his lands, he didn't accept the shirt, responding that he did not need shirts, that he was having good hunting and that with the skins he was going to Pensacola and Mobile [to get] what he needed.

I answered him that we were not opposed to his being at peace with the Americans, but what was not fair would be the intimacy that they were displaying. Besides that, what had not been realized by the Indians [was the fact that] the King of Spain, being master of all the waters over which goods can be carried to his country, it would be easy for him [the King of Spain] to cut this communication if he saw that they [the Indians] were also trading with the Americans. To which he [the King of the Chicachas] answered me that [even though] it was true that the Americans, in order to bring them anything, had to cross great mountains and very difficult roads, he could [do] no less than deal with them sometimes because he found himself bordering on their lands, and to live in peace it was necessary to sometimes listen to them, but he would never form any alliance at all with them, because he knew them too well.

As I was satisfied by his very declaration that he had not done anything that might damage us, I immediately found it best not to make this matter a subject of dispute, and I devoted myself only to the principal point of ending the Nogales matter. We concluded, then, that if the goods I had in my power were sufficient, we would be from then on in accord and in absolute possession of that territory.

I did not want to lose a moment, and we agreed that dissembling we would leave my house, and by different routes we would meet at the Royal Warehouses, so that he might examine what there was in them, so that afterwards he could return to the camp in full knowledge of what he could propose to the rest.

We met in the warehouse; he [the King] saw what there was in it, and he decided [that] with some more goods and a sufficient quantity of brandy, powder, and shot, the distribution might include everyone, [and] he would be able to convince them to follow his opinion and that everything might be finished by next Monday when the Congress ought to take place. I offered to add whatever I could, and that if the on day of the Congress they might tell me that the lands of Nogales were indisputably of the King [of Spain], and that neither they nor their descendants would speak again about this matter, I would hand over to him and Franchimastabé the keys to those warehouses in return for his compliance. He agreed to this and returned to the camp.

The next day, which was Sunday, they sent me in the morning to ask for drink, which I forwarded to them, [for it was] clear to me that when the Indians discuss any issue, they are more favorably disposed towards the one who gives them drink.

The King of the Chicachas, Franchimastabé, and four more Chiefs came to eat with me. The first one [the King] told me that it had not been possible for him to resolve [anything] the preceding night, but that he had already said something to Franchimastabé, and that during the discussion of that afternoon and evening, everything would be arranged. [He further said] that in order to do it with more freedom, they were all coming to my house to sleep. I greatly approved this suggestion. Since it was necessary to be on one's guard with Turner Brashears, confidante of Franchimastabé, in order that he might not give bad advice to this Chief, I arranged that he [Brashears] might spend the night away from my house on the pretext of a diversion that there was a certain distance away. That was accomplished. Then, while he [Brashears] was absent, the Indian Chiefs began their meetings alone; and at about nine at night they told me I could enter. Having done that I sat in a circle with them, and with an unbelievable formality for Indians, the King of the Chicachas began to speak. He told me that he had conferred with those principal Chiefs who were present, and they agreed unanimously that the territory of Nogales might belong indisputably to the King of Spain, so he might do with it whatever he might wish; that this was a concluded matter that would be ratified the following day, very early, in the Congress, but convinced as they were, they would all go to the campsite the following morning at dawn to speak with the other Chiefs and with the warriors who were there, to explain to them and persuade them to their position.

Such agreeable news produced in me expressions that revealed to them my satisfaction and pleasure seeing them won over to reason. Now, if they gave proof of being true friends of the Spanish, in the same way they could depend on what we had offered to them. We said to each other whatever the most perfect harmony would suggest.

The mentioned King [of the Chicachas] told me then that besides what he had seen in the warehouses, he found necessary an increase of about nine kegs of powder and much brandy to satisfy the warriors; that he might order all who were present to be content with what I might be able [to provide] for now: that in addition, he needed eight guns to distribute among the Chiefs, five saddles, and some other trifles, all of which are to be found in the attached document number 3 that I am sending.[4] He also told me that Stonahuma, who was present, was the subject of much distinction in both the Chicacha and Chacta nations for being a trustworthy man whom they always chose to send messages. Because he had never had a medal, he was now asking that he be given a commission and a large medal as Chief of this class. As this seemed to be true, I offered it to him, and agreeing to [what] they were asking of me, I would make it a provisional appointment since Your Lordship was not sending anyone who could truly bestow honors on him, the same with two others, whom they also recommended to me. They are all described in the attached document number 4.[5] Besides the gift that they actually deserved, they also demanded another particular one, which is described in the attached document number 5, and that I would ask Your Lordship and to have here at their disposition, all of which I also offered him [the King of the Chicachas].[6]

I left them about eleven at night, after having eaten; and they all lodged in my living room, where I provided them with the necessary conveniences.

I spent the rest of the night arranging the strings of beads for each one of the Chiefs, and two longer ones that signified the paths to peace between this country and the Chicacha and Chacta nations, with an equal number of pieces of tobacco, a sign of friendship, for each one of the Chiefs.

In like manner I spent that night in formulating the articles of the treaty that would be signed the following day so that nothing might be missing during the course of the Congress, taking advantage in this way of the good atmosphere in which it was being held, providing a happy conclusion to a matter of such importance. I found myself with the difficulty of not having a permanent secretary, and so that no essential requirement might be missing, I right then made the appointment of Don Joseph Vidal, announcing it in the following morning in the orders of the garrison.[7]

It was raining very hard at dawn, and it was absolutely impossible to hold the Congress where I first received these Indians or within my house, because of lack of sufficient space to contain them. Only a new barracks within the Fort would serve, but it did not seem advisable to admit them inside. I had no other recourse than to meet with Don Gregorio White, who was carrying out the duties of priest in the absence of the regular one, who was to be found in Nogales for the building of a church.[8] Hence, by making a separation in the parish church of this settlement, the Congress might be held there. The separation was done effectively, from the steps on down, with a divider covered with the royal flag of this fort, and on the two curtains on the sides were placed two smaller ones [flags].

At the upper end of this space, I made a placement of chairs and a table, in the same manner as when I received them the first time.

I ordered that a guard be sent to the door of the mentioned church [and] to reinforce all the posts of the town. [I also directed] that all the rest of the troop be kept within the fort and the artillery loaded and ready to do the triple salute when I should give the sign from the church to begin it in celebration of having completed the treaty.

I invited all the officials who were not on duty, the employees of this settlement, and the distinguished residents of the surrounding area.

The hour of eleven was agreed upon for the arrival of the Indians. In anticipation I went to the church with the retinue which I have just described, and we placed ourselves in each one's assigned seats. On the table [were placed] paper, an inkwell, and a tray on which were the beads, tobacco and pipe, everything covered with a white cloth. Finding myself in this arrangement, the King of the Chicachas and Franchimastabé arrived, accompanied by all the rest of the Chiefs and warriors who were in the camp, where only the women remained.

I went out to receive them; and I placed them as the first time in my house.

After a small pause, I told Turner Brashears, who was paying close attention to what I said and to what Ebenecer Fulson, the interpreter of this garrison, was translating, that he should notice any mistake or omission that might occur, since my intention was that we might understand each other with the greatest clarity. He agreed to do it; and, addressing the Chiefs, I began in this way:

"You have told me on the first day that I saw you that you had given all your confidence to the King of the Chicachas, who is present, that I should discuss with him the pending matter of Nogales, that whatever he [the King of the Chicachas] might decide you would approve, because [he was] the man who governs you, regarding him as the eldest brother of all the Indian nations."

They agreed that this was their will, and turning directly to the mentioned king, I began the speech, explaining in part the cause that motivated the establishment of a fort in Nogales, the first visit that I had there from Ytelaghana, Franchimastabe's opposition to that establishment, basing [it on the fact] that those lands belonged to his nation and to the Chicachas, and that although they had sold them [the lands] to the English, they had never ever paid for them, although they possessed them. I detailed all the negotiations that there have been concerning this matter; that, tired of sending and receiving messages that did not advance the conclusion of this matter, I had determined to discuss it personally with Franchimastabé, and that since I was aware of the confidence that the entire Chacta nation had in the King of the Chicachas, I also wrote to him so that he might be here when Franchimastabé came. [I said] although I was not expecting them so soon, I was happy to see them now, because it was proof that they were coming in good will to discuss this matter. I added as many reasons as I could to establish the unquestionable right of His Majesty to all the lands which the English possessed in this country, and the few reasons to support the Chacta nation in opposing it, although it may be in the smallest part, when it [the Chacta nation] has received and constantly receives many benefits from us. [I pointed out] that not only every year [do] we give numerous presents to their individuals, but their principal existence also depends on the hunting that they do on the river lands on the other side of the Mississippi, without which they would be unhappy and would perish. I ended my speech by saying that I was happy that the Chacta nation had chosen him [the King] to resolve this matter, which I considered very wise, because as long as the opinions of various men were not united into one single will, it is not possible to form a common interest. [I said] that thus I looked upon this day as the happiest for all of us, since I anticipated that we would not separate without resolving our differences, eliminating in this way whatever might alter our reciprocal good harmony.

The mentioned King responded to me that he was perfectly informed about what had occurred concerning the establishment of Nogales. [He said] that he also knew that the Chacta nation should not have opposed it with such ill-will, since truly we were their best friends. [He continued by saying] that from the results of the conferences that he had had with me, he had conferred with Franchimastabé and with the rest of the Chiefs and warriors whose feelings, as [those] of all the nation, [are] now found to be disposed to reasonable terms. In view of that he told me I could from now on do whatever I might wish in the lands of Nogales [and] view them as His Catholic Majesty's from the line. [He said] that they would no longer come from far away to talk, that they were already many when they entered this district, whose number daily was increasing with others who came afterwards, and that they all expected to be compensated. Therefore, [he concluded] he was leaving it to my generosity the award to them of a suitable gift, that they being content, he would say nothing more about the matter.

I responded to him that I was happy to hear him speak with such reason [and] that only he was capable of concluding with so much judgment a matter of this kind. [I told him] that if to him it seemed that I had behaved with generosity, I was going to give him proof that the Spanish nation loves the Indians and favors them with the greatest liberality.

I then called the quartermaster of this garrison, Don Francisco Candel, and I ordered him to give me the keys of the Royal Warehouses which housed the Indian goods.[9] He did so, and I, giving them [the keys] to the King of the Chicachas, told him: "There are the keys to the warehouses where the goods belonging to His Majesty are to be found, take them, and whatever is in them [the warehouses] divide among your Chiefs and warriors until they are satisfied. In this way, putting at your disposition whatever I have, you will not be able to say that I have treated you with stinginess, and this matter finally is concluded in a way that neither the Chicacha nor Chacta nations will have the least wish to demand from Spain another thing for the [disputed] lands. So that no doubts will remain concerning which ones they are, we will agree that the line that separates us begins at the Mississippi at the mouth of the Yazu river and goes up in the center of the river until near the ball game [court], to the same place where the English, in agreement with the Chacta nation, marked a line on the trees. That [line] continues to the boundary line of the Alibamones and Talapuches. You will recognize the lands that are on the south and west of the stated lines of the Alibamones and Talapuches as indisputably under the dominion of His Catholic Majesty our great King; and [the lands] on the other side are yours."

Not only the King of the Chicachas, but also Franchimastabé, the rest of the Chiefs and warriors all replied, yes, they agreed to the stated [terms]; and the mentioned King showed himself greatly pleased with having the keys to the storehouses in his hands, saying a thousand things in a good humor about the matter.

I continued always addressing the mentioned King. Uncovering the tray, I picked up the string of beads chosen for him, speaking to him in this way: "I give you this string of white beads as a sign of purest friendship." Showing him another even longer, which was tied to the first, representing the peaceful journey of this nation to the Chicacha nation, I told him similar things to these two objects. I handed him likewise a piece of tobacco so that smoking it, he should remember the purest friendship between us.

I did the same with Franchimastabé, and afterwards I placed in front of ten single strings with as many pieces of tobacco so that they could distribute [them] among the rest of the Chiefs, which they did with much ceremony.

This done, I ordered fire brought, and I lit a pipe, and I was with said Chiefs ratifying our agreement during which they said to each other various things one to another, produced from good humor and from the satisfaction that each one was experiencing.

I said to them that since we had concluded a matter that interested all of us, I was going to announce [it] to the whole district with the thunder of great cannons, for which I was going to give a signal for them to begin. [The signal] was to tie the white cloth that was on the table to my cane and order it pushed through a window causing no little admiration from the Indians on hearing the shooting of the artillery immediately. During this we repeated speeches appropriate to what had been discussed.

Seeing them favorably disposed to the point that I was hoping, I told them that all men had superiors until reaching the person of the King, that, consequently, I also had them, and that I needed them to tell them how it operated. Since it was necessary that they might know what I had just done, I wanted that a great paper explaining everything might reach the hands of the King and that all of us who were present should sign as proof of its being true, that two identical ones would be made, one which would remain with them, and the other to send to our August Sovereign. This pleased them greatly, and they agreed it might be done.

The Secretary, Don Joseph Vidal, took out the mentioned two papers, that are the Treaty in duplicate that I had already drawn up, as I previously said, relying on the private pact that the previous night I had agreed to with the already referred to Chiefs.

Ceremoniously I handed one to Lieutenant Colonel Don Carlos de Grand-Pré so that he might compare it with the other that I was reading and the interpreter repeating.

At the end of each article the Indians made a sign of approval in the presence of a numerous crowd that was present. The reading concluded, I told them that I was going to attach the coat of arms of the King, which I executed on the table in the presence of everyone. I signed the two [documents], and successively the King of the Chicachas, Franchimastabé and the rest of the Chiefs [each] making his signs to which I put the name of each one; afterwards followed employed officials, residents from here and various American travelers who were present, and they applauded the legality of this act. The signature of Turner Brashears is one of the most important, because of his having been the subject who until then [had] suggested to Franchimastabé the idea of opposition that he displayed. Equally important was that of the American travelers because as rivals they will not be able in the future to say anything against the legality of [our claim].

Concluding the signatures with that of the Secretary, I handed a copy to the King of the Chicachas, and the other is the one that I attach, without number, so that your

Lordship may either keep it in that Archive or you may return it to me for deposit in this one [Archive], doing everything that you may consider [to be] more suitable.

Although many ideas have occurred to me that at first view seemed suitable, I finally concluded that it was more important to omit [them] rather than expose our Court to a compromise with that of Great Britain, or with the United States. [I] contented myself and [it] seemed to me greatly advantageous to clarify the boundaries between ourselves and those nations in the way that is expressed in the stated treaty by which the indisputable dominion of His Majesty over the lands of Nogales remains perfectly clarified.

It was two o'clock, and I proposed we withdraw and that everyone come to eat at my house.

Franchimastabé said then that he was very happy about it, since up to then he had been quiet. [He said] that he proposed to speak about many things after he had eaten well, and that then, since Fulson had been my interpreter he chose Brashears for his. I answered him that [should be so] with great pleasure. All the party of white men and Indians came to my house.

Dinner concluded, Franchimastabé told me he had eaten well, so he was going to fulfill what he offered, speaking to me with frankness whatever occurred to him. I answered him that I had taken particular care in serving him what was on the table, since he had told me in the Congress that when he had his appetite satisfied he spoke with more frankness, and I asked him if he still wanted to take something more before beginning to speak. He responded no, that he had never eaten better, so he was going to speak.

He called Turner Brashears to his side and he asked that Don Estevan Minor might come to stand by mine.

He began by making a description of my first settlement in Nogales, of the different messages that we had sent to each other and what finally Don Estevan Minor agreed with him in his nation, and even what I told him in the letter that I sent to him by the armed official. It was that our August Sovereign was to have ordered a considerable gift given to them if they agreed not to speak any more about Nogales so that he considered that by next fall they would be here, and that then he would come with many more people to receive them, because now the ones who were present, although they seemed to be many, they were nothing in comparison to the ones who remained in his country. [He said] he would not believe it until he saw it; that they had offered him many things that they had never delivered to him so that, punished in this way he didn't trust what I had proposed to him until [he] saw it delivered.

He continued with some other reasons similar to these, revealing an unwarranted suspicious nature. I being perfectly persuaded that without more motive than the one he had at the present, he let Don Estevan Minor understand in the nation, that the Lord Don Estevan Miró had not honored his word. He finished by saying that Don Estevan Minor and Turner Brashears had told him that I did not have goods here, and that therefore it was necessary to wait for His Majesty to send them. As is customary among the Indians, he made a thousand repetitions, and, finally, said that he had finished.

Although the injustice and superficiality of this Chief could anger anyone, I welcomed having had the occasion of telling him some truths with clarity and firmness to teach him how he ought to treat us and to make him see in the presence of everyone that the complaints that he had of Lord Don Estevan Miró were no better grounded than in reality to reveal a person dominated by distrust that governed his way of thinking.

I assumed a dry and firm air and focusing on him, I said to him: "I remember what we agreed in the Congress: you have told me that only after having eaten well would you be able to speak; that since Fulson was my interpreter, you wanted Brashears to be yours. I agreed that it would be so. I have given you [good things] to eat; when you have wished, you spoke, and you have said whatever has seemed to you; well now I am going to respond to you."

The Indian Chiefs as well as the rest in attendance were awaiting with impatience and caution the results of my speech. I noticed that [they] generally, particularly the King of the Chicachas, [were] irritated with Franchimastabé.

I continued calling Fulson to my side, telling him: "Take care that your grace is to refer, word for word, whatever I might speak, giving in the Chacta language the most energetic meaning to my expressions. Turning to Brashears, I charged him to pay close attention to what Fulson was interpreting in the event that he [Fulson] omitted or disguised the least expression. I informed Franchimastabé of that particular recommendation.

I reminded him that at our first visit he had informed me that, as a result of my letter, he had come to see me, accompanied by the King of the Chicachas, in order to conclude the matter of Nogales and that he would not say anything in those negotiations; and would, along with all his nation, only agree with whatever the stated King would decide since he [Franchimastabé] looked to him [the King] as an older brother, and the one who governed all the Indian nations. "With this assumption I have dealt with him, but I have not stopped negotiating with you during our conferences, neither now, nor from the first negotiation about Nogales. I have infallibly kept my word in whatever I have offered you. All these days you have given proof of being satisfied, and lastly, this morning, in the Congress, you have agreed with the rest in that not a single word was to be spoken again concerning Nogales. Ytelaghana himself, in the most interesting act of our final meeting, has remembered as principal messenger that you have used in this negotiation, that he had never noticed the least lack of good faith in me, that whatever I had offered, I have fulfilled punctually. You have challenged this with nothing. Now, in the most unexpected way, you are the one who fails [to honor] your word, and you prove with this and with your unfounded reasons that you have never had a reason to complain about the previous governor of this province nor of any Chief of it.

"As to what you have referred, you have contradicted the knowledge of everyone. Where is that confidence that you said [you] had in the King of the Chicachas? Look me in the face (grasping him by the hand), look at me, I again tell you, tell me if you see something in it that may indicate falsehood to you; tell me right now, in presence of everyone, in what have either I or the previous governor of this province failed you; if you have any just reason, it will convince me, and I will give you the satisfaction that may suit you."

At this point Franchimastabé now found himself humiliated, and it was all to tell me: "This is finished; I have nothing more to say; I only referred to those reasons because I had offered to speak after eating, and it was necessary to say something."

I replied to him: "No; one never says [anything] without reasons, and much less when they are in front of a Chief like me; so I want you to stop shaming [yourself] in front of all your companions and in presence of all those who are here, so the least doubt may remain to them that you have a suspicious nature and that you speak without motive, and you can believe it when there is no one who may make clear the truth."

I continued telling him: "It is true that I informed you in my letter that our great

King of Spain should send me goods to make a fine present for the Yazu lands, but that this would take some time; nevertheless, that if you wanted to come now to negotiate with me, I would look for goods to make you happy. You have come even before I expected you. Thus you have agreed to what I proposed to you. What does Don Estevan Minor or Turner Brashears know if I had or didn't [have] sufficient goods, or if I have received them after they spoke to you? Look at the King of the Chicachas, the man who has done so much good for you, and tell me if you are not ashamed of having failed him, as your speech shows."

Turning to the King of the Chicachas: "What do you think of Franchimastabé's conduct?" He answered giving me to understand that what he had spoken was foolishness and that what remained to be done was to reject it and drink a glass of wine to the health of the great King of Spain. All the other Chiefs applauded this, and Franchimastabé, repentant of his rashness, made me a thousand apologies. The one who was most embarrassed was Brashears, who surely had advised his Chief to speak in those terms, since it was known that it did not proceed from the heart of Franchimastabé.

Afterwards everything was happiness and contentment, the Indians proposing to celebrate the treaty that they had concluded with two consecutive days of ball game, which I greatly approved, and we fixed the first [game] for the next day.

We got up from the table. Taking advantage of the first occasion to talk to me alone, Franchimastabé told me that he regretted having given me reason to become angry with him, that this was a political step he had taken so that his nation might not ever accuse him that he had not looked out for their interest. [He continued telling me] that he was old, but still wanted to show his people that he had energy and that he watched out for them; but that in his heart there was not any other thing more than what we had agreed; so that everything was concluded. Brashears, who served as an interpreter then, repeated the same to me about what concerned him, one to the other, giving me the greatest assurance of friendship.

We returned where the others were, and the rest of the afternoon was spent in great harmony all speaking about the sincere friendship that would prevail among the three nations.

Some withdrew to the camp; but the King of the Chicachas, Franchimastabé, Ytelaghana and two more of the principal Chiefs remained in my house, where they have stayed until they began their journey back to their country.

The two following days they used the mornings to pass out the gifts, the distribution of which the same King of the Chicachas did by his hand. During the afternoons the ball game took place, which has been one of the most splendid that has been seen; all of which shows how satisfied they were, with the fortune that there has not been the slightest mishap, something that astonishes all who know the character of these people.

To satisfy myself completely about the sincerity of these Indians, I provided much drink for them in their camp, keeping Ebenecer Fulson there every night so that he might inform me about all their conversations, since when these people enjoy their drink they speak their feeling without disguise.

A word of discontent has never been heard from them; on the contrary they are very satisfied with what has been given to them, repeating that Nogales would never be spoken about again.

The King of the Chicachas, although with much moderation, now brought up his personal interest. He told me that he wanted to keep something for himself that the rest didn't know about; so would I present him with a quantity of pesos in a bag that he would return to me so, with them [the pesos], make the rest believe that it was his money with which he planned to buy goods. I ordered 200 pesos be placed in a bag, and I handed them to him. He carried out the pretence that he planned, and he returned them to me; but at the time of returning them [the pesos] he asked me to give him some money from that [bag] in order effectively to buy something on the journey and in his country. I was about to give him the same 200 pesos, but I thought he would be content with half, as it so happened.

At different times he [the King] asked me for a quantity of trifles, that it did not seem to me prudent to refuse him. I thus supplied him with whatever he wanted without limit, and the same with Franchimastabé and some other Chiefs with influence, but to these [Chiefs] with more restriction, all of which is recorded in the reports which I forward attached [to this document].[10] [I do not] mention many valuable things which I have given from my own house.

Among other things of consideration that it was necessary to buy to complete the gift was the brandy, which is now very expensive and scarce.

Ebenecer Fulson has displayed on this occasion a very special zeal, informing me minute by minute of whatever was going on among the Indians and scattering among them whatever ideas I charged him with, which has contributed significantly to the great success of my negotiation and to the good discipline that they have observed. For those useful services I made a gift of 100 *pesos fuertes.*

It was not possible to allow Brashears to go without some gift, since he is going to get it in whatever way is possible, and this is the most effective way with a man like him. Consequently, I have given him 50 pesos in cash, and I offered to propose him as our commissioner in the Chacta nation with some monthly salary, which has greatly satisfied him and flattered Franchimastabé. Although the matter of Nogales is concluded, I consider [it] necessary always to preserve good intelligence with subjects of similar influence and have them dependent on some gift that comes only while they are behaving well.

During the Indians' stay here they lost some horses. Whether they were stolen or escaped back to the Nation, it was not advantageous that such a loss should be the cause of unhappiness for them. Therefore, the one [horse] was replaced [to its owner] and the others [Indians who lost horses] were satisfied with 60 pesos divided among them. It was also inevitable to distribute some more pesos to various Chiefs in the quantity of 70 pesos, provided in small quantities.

I did my best with particular care in treating all the Indians well after the treaty [was] signed, the reason why sometimes I had cattle slaughtered in their camp, which has pleased them greatly.

Since during their stay here, many others attended. Their number was considerable, exceeding 300, without counting women and children. Possessing as much drink as they were carrying, they were in the position to be a problem to the district at the time of withdrawing. [With] the day of their departure then fixed for Saturday, the 19th of the current [month], I ordered Don Estevan Minor, a constable, and two more people in his confidence to accompany them to Bayu Pierre to provide them with supplies on the journey and take care of proper order. That same day the stated official notified me that he was very hard put to take care of all the Indians, because the majority were drunk and divided into groups, some were going forward and others were remaining behind. I immediately sent Don Ricardo King, a resident of this district, that he might help the Lieutenant of the Royal Artillery, Don Antonio Soler; another constable and two more residents, who will need to have some reward, which I have not arranged because they have not returned.

A few days ago Don Estevan Minor and Don Antonio Soler returned notifying me having left the Indians very satisfied and content. [They} left from Bayou Pierre in the hands of Turner Brashears. [I have just received from him] a letter with yesterday's date [stating] that they were now beyond the wilderness and that he had found it necessary to take 15 more barrels of corn, the cost of which was passed on to me in order to avoid problems with so many people. He conveys to me a thousand expressions of gratitude and friendship on behalf of the King of the Chicachas, Franchimastabé and the rest of the Chiefs, assuring me that they all are withdrawing perfectly satisfied.

From this town to Bayu Pierre, Don Estevan Minor provided them with the supplies that are listed on the attached report number 6, to which you will have to add what Brashears took when I find out its value and something more, of very short listing.

Free already from these people, it is now that I consider perfectly concluded this important matter of Nogales, having delayed giving this detailed account to Your Lordship just in case some incident would occur while they were in the District.

Notwithstanding that it is a finished matter and that there is no obligation to give more gifts, many months will pass in which time Indians will come here with the hope of obtaining some gift. It is not my wish to propose to Your Lordship more presents than those I have detailed; however, of course, for an extraordinary case, I am of the opinion that there ought to be something here to please some Chief or Messenger that the King of the Chicachas or Franchimastabé might send to this place. In like manner, Your Lordship may authorize me to send from time to time some slight gift of coffee, sugar or similar things for the two mentioned principal Chiefs with whom it will be necessary to preserve an intimate and friendly correspondence.

I have taken special care to go beyond the usual in providing you with detail about the smallest occurrence that the matter of Nogales has produced. In this way Your Lordship may not be ignorant of the slightest thing that has happened. Because it is a matter of such importance, it remains to me for another occasion to inform Your Lordship of some points relative to preserving the good harmony between this province and the Indian nation neighbors.

As Lieutenant Don Estevan Minor, Major Adjutant of this garrison, has played a great role in this matter, it has seemed fair to me to provide him the satisfaction of delivering to Your Lordship the original described treaty and to avoid exposing this precious document to the contingencies of sending it by less secure means.

I remind Your Lordship the merit what this official has achieved so that it may be appropriate to recommend him as I have proposed for the rank and salary of captain.[11]

I have placed all my vigilance in the performance of this matter and although not the least remorse to me of having omitted anything that might suit the best service of the King, the satisfaction of knowing if what I have done deserves Your Lordship's approbation is lacking to me.

It is not possible for me to overlook the patriotism of Don Juan Smith, resident of the community of Coles Creek who, when the Indians passed within three leagues of his house, learned that the King needed corn to provide supplies to these people. [He] sent there with his cart [loaded with] eleven measures of this grain, for which he refused any payment at all at a time when there was a great shortage and [the grain] was very expensive. May God keep Your Lordship for many years. Natchez, May 29, 1792. Manuel Gayoso de Lemos. Sr. Baron de Carondelet.

El Baron de Carondelet

11

Treaty of Natchez, May 14, 1792

The text for this translation is the copy enclosed with the Baron de Carondelet to the Conde de Floridablanca, New Orleans, May 22, 1792, N.° 28, AHN, *Estado, leg.* 3898, *exp.* 5. A published Spanish text of the treaty is included in [Serrano y Sanz], *Documentos históricos de la Florida y la Luisiana,* 436–39.

Treaty of Friendship between His Catholic Majesty, Great King of the Spains and of the Indies, on the one part, represented by Don Manuel Gayoso de Lemos, Colonel of his Royal Armies, Governor of the Plaza and district of Natchez; and, on the other, Taskaotuca, King of the Chicachas, and of Franchimastabé, Principal Chief of the Chacta Nation, accompanied by Yteleghana, Stonahuma and Tapenahuma and Nocjaumaachó, all Chiefs, and the presence of numerous captains and warriors of both nations who came to the referred to Plaza voluntarily and gathered before the expressed Governor and all the officials, employees, and many notable residents [and] offered reciprocally perpetual friendship among the peoples of the three nations, Spanish, Chicacha, and Chacta; and, so that nothing in the future disturb nor alter this good harmony, they agreed unanimously on the following articles:

1° That all the individuals of the Spanish, Chicacha, and Chacta nations will love one another reciprocally and give prompt advice each to the others about whatever may be favorable or adverse to each other in particular and to all in general.

2° That in order to remove any motive of discord that in future times might occur concerning borders the Chicacha and Chacta Nations acknowledge that the boundaries of the dominions of His Majesty in the vicinity of their territories begin in the west on the Mississippi River [and extend] to the mouth of the Yazú River and go up the middle of this river until near the place called [the] Ball Field (*Juego de Pelota*) where the English Nation, in agreement with the Chacta Nation, marked a dividing line that continued [south] until entering west Florida and following the same line from the mentioned Ball Field until encountering the ones that separate the rest of the dominions of His Catholic Majesty with Alibamone and Talapuche Nations.

3° The cited Chicacha and Chacta Nations declare that all the lands that are found to the south and to the west of the expressed line belong indisputably to His Catholic Majesty, Great King of the Spains and of the Indies, and that they and their descendants renounce all rights to them or any claim to them under any pretext or reason and in addition they offer to support the Spanish Nation in possession of the mentioned lands, in which especially are found the Government and territory of Natchez to the waters of the Yazú.

4° The Spanish Nation declares and recognizes that all the lands to the east of the expressed dividing line in Article 2 belong legitimately [and] indisputably to the Chicacha and Chacta Nations, offering to sustain them with all its power.

5° The Chicacha and Chacta Nations will maintain harmony with the Governor General of Louisiana, of both Floridas, with the particular one of Natchez, and with the Commandants of the other Plazas and Posts of the Dominions of His Catholic Majesty, in this part of the world to resolve among themselves matters of trade and law and order that may be for the reciprocal benefit and utility of the three mentioned Nations.

6° The referred two nations leave to the judgment of the Governor of Natchez the award to them of a generous acknowledgement of the good will with which they have ceded all their rights to the territory of Nogales (in English, Wallnut Hills) beside the Yazú and within the dividing line outlined in Article 2.

7° The Governor of Natchez offers to make a gift in the name of His Catholic Majesty to the Chiefs present; and so that they may divide with the other individuals who may consider deserving so as to give them this one additional proof of the generosity of the Spanish Nation and the good harmony that it wishes to conserve with the Indian Nations, their neighbors. So that this act may not be delayed, he [the governor] hands over at the present time to the mentioned Chiefs the keys to these royal warehouses in which the goods are [stored] so that they may take from them whatever they wish to satisfy themselves.

8° The said Chiefs already named are satisfied with the goods that they have in their power with the keys of the named warehouses in hand, having already seen what is in them.

9° Finally, the Chicacha and Chacta Nations ratify among themselves and promise to be constant friends of the Spanish Nation and to keep with it whatever was agreed upon in the Mobile Congress and whatever afterwards they may have agreed upon with the Governors of Louisiana and both Floridas and with the particular one of the District of Natchez. The Spanish Nation offers them equal perpetual friendship and guarantee of all the agreed upon conditions in the cited Mobile Congress and whatever the above-mentioned Governors may have concluded afterwards. In proof of what we promise to uphold expressed in the present treaty, we all sign it, the mentioned Indian Chiefs, Tascaotuca, Franchimastabé, Yteleghana, Stonahuma, Tapenahuma, and Nocjahumaachó, putting our signs with [the mentioned] Don Manuel Gayoso de Lemos, Colonel of the Royal Armies, Military and Political Governor of the Post of Natchez and its district, and the witnesses present, who also sign it. Sealed with the royal seal and countersigned by the undersigned secretary Don José Vidal, being gathered in the Parochial Church entitled "Savior of the World" of the mentioned post of Natchez on the fourteenth day of the month of May, 1792. Place of the Seal. Manuel Gayoso de Lemos, King of the Chicachas, Franchimastabé, Yteleghana, Stonahuma, Tapenahuma, Nocjauhumaachó, Carlos de Grand-Pré, Blas de Bouchet, Estevan Minor, Turner Brashears, Bryan Bruin, Gregorio White, Ygancio Soyes, Agustín Macarty, Jorge Cochran, Francisco Candel, Luis Friere, Juan Girault, Carlos Fold, Ebenecer Fulson, Antonio Soler, Jorge Tompson, Guillermo Wasthoff, Jayme McFarland, Elias Smith, Kenneth Thomson. By order of Your Lordship Joseph Vidal.

The Baron de Carondelet.

12

Gayoso's Account of the Visit to Natchez of Cherokee Chiefs, December 1792–January 1793

Manuel Gayoso de Lemos to the Barón de Carondelet. Natchez, January 8, 1793, N.° 235, AGI, PC, *leg.* 42.

The first of this year the Cherokee Indian Chiefs, whose arrival to this Plaza I had already described to Your Lordship, left from here. Now I will make a report of the way in which I have treated them and the result of our conferences.

Considering the importance of making these chiefs happy for the purpose of favorably impressing them with respect to the Spanish nation, I lodged them in a decent room in the Hospital, and I told them that they might come every day to have breakfast and eat with me. They have done so all the time of their stay at this post. [I also provided] rations for good dinners and that additional rations be supplied if they needed them.

When they arrived here on December 18, there were many people in my house, and they behaved with the greatest discretion without speaking a word about their business until after eating. Taylor told me on behalf of Bloody Fellow that the following day in the morning when no one might see them they would come to my room to discuss the subject of our charge. [He] reminded me that it has been awhile since they had sent two men from their nation to this province to determine if the Spanish would give them assistance if they place[d] themselves under the protection of His Majesty. [He said] that the two individuals on their return informed their Nation that the Spanish would receive them well and that the Commandant of Panzacola had advised them to attack the Americans vigorously as a way to obtain our protection. [This report] along with other circumstances made them doubt the accuracy of the two subjects that they had sent [and] convinced Bloody Fellow to come personally, bringing with him Chucumogo Charles as a witness to whatever might happen to them in this Province. So that they not lack an interpreter, they brought Juan Taylor, and another who from that capital returned to his nation. They praised the fine reception that they received from Your Lordship. After several conferences, Your Lordship offered them our aid, presenting to Your Majesty the situation of the Cherokee Nation so that he might deign to take them under his Royal Protection, interposing his mediation with the United States so they might return to them the lands that they had usurped from them and might establish their borders in a permanent fashion.

They have agreed with Your Lordship that if it might be possible, a congress should be established in the Chacta nation, not in the village [of] Yazu but rather at the place called Hicory Ground below the falls on the Mobile River. [They agree] that it [should be] composed of some chiefs of all the nations of neighboring Indians presided over by a Commissioner of the King and that in said congress general matters of all the nations should be discussed.

He [Bloody Fellow] spoke of a fort on the Barrancas de Margó but [believed] that this depends on the Chicachas. He also revealed a strong desire that on the great bend of the Tennessee at the place they call Muscle Shoals there should be a Spanish fort to protect his nation until the Americans have ceased to bother them. Then it would no longer be necessary for it to exist, and it could be abandoned.

Bloody Fellow also told me that he is always the one who has the last word. [He said] that in that Capital he had seen the King of the Chicachas and Franchimastabé and the other chiefs of the Chacta Nation and had spoken with them. However, [he said] that he could not rely much upon what they said because they were always drunk. [Furthermore, he found] that they were not truly determined to join the league because the danger was still at a distance and the Cherokees were between them and the Americans. Because of this lack of interest, he hopes that Your Lordship will exercise his influence to make sure these Nations will do what is best for everyone. [He said] that they were going to travel through the Chacta and Chicacha nations to see about ratifying there what they had agreed with Your Lordship in that Capital and to see if they can attract Payomingo to the party of the King. Finally, they asked me for my advice.

I learned through what I had observed in their conversations that it was his custom and [that] of his companions to discuss separately with different chiefs of this Province to see if they all said the same. I took very particular care to confirm with them the many ideas you had stressed with them, giving them arguments to convince them that it was the only party that was best for them in their present circumstance. I achieved my objective in the way I wanted, while telling them the truth. I managed to get them to show great satisfaction upon seeing that at such a great distance Your Lordship and I were telling them the same thing.

They advised me as to the manner of addressing the Chacta and Chicacha nations, leading [me] to understand that since they had seen Franchimastabé in that Capital it was unnecessary to return to speak with him. [However], I made them aware that it was best that they should go there because the Chacta Nation greatly enjoyed hearing words and were accustomed to forget them if they were not repeated often. They should go through the Chacta Nation with my letters, [I said], for the King's Commissioners there and for Franchimastabé and that with the support of our Commissioner [they should] reaffirm there in the presence of many chiefs what they had discussed in New Orleans. [I said] they should travel to the Chicacha Nation with my letters for officials of that Nation, for Payomingo [Piomingo] and Ugulayacabé, and for Hardy Perry [and] include in the one for Payomingo a word from Your Lordship that would greatly facilitate their mission. I tried to show them and to persuade them that there might be a division in the Chicacha Nation [and] that it would be difficult to convene the league which might discuss the well-being of all the Indian Nations. [Therefore, I said] it was necessary that he meet separately with Payomingo to win him to the side of reason and to re-establish the King of that Nation in all his power. Bringing together the [various] dispositions in this way, [they] could then discuss the general well being. They agreed.

Your Lordship will see the contents of my previously mentioned letters by the copies which I attach together under the numbers 1, 2, 3, 4, and 5.

[At] different times we spoke of matters of his country, among them the establishment of borders with the United States of America and his Nation. He complained bitterly about the usurpations that the Americans have carried out on his lands and even more of the deception which they were dealt in the Hopewell Treaty. Then they began to discuss the mentioned demarcation at the mouth of the Duck River on the Tennessee, whose name in the Cherokee language is confused with that of the Green River that flows into the Ohio to the north of the Cumberland River. That deception they discovered when they went to mark the borders. He showed me a map made in his hand with which he explained to me what [was] related to the Hopewell Treaty, but he was astonished to see that I had another exactly like that one, done by an Indian that I have had in my possession for four years. The ideas of Bloody Fellow agreed with the ones that I had acquired at that time.

The United States or its representatives not only have deceived the Cherokee Nation in the Hopewell [Treaty] and the demarcation of borders but on the very same day they exceeded what the same Congress has published in an edict of September 1, 1788, a copy of which I attach under number 6 just in case Your Lordship has not seen it. I am not sending a copy of the map on account of being told that another was left in Your Lordship's hands.

I missed [no] opportunity to cultivate the friendship of these Cherokee Chiefs and particularly that of Bloody Fellow. Because Bloody Fellow had with him a son of a good age to be educated, I asked him why he didn't leave the boy with us so that he might receive this advantage. He replied to me that that was his wish, but he had not dared to tell me so because of fear that, without means to pay for the expenses that this would require, his requesting it would be imprudent. However, since I was proposing it, he asked me if I were truly in earnest. Because I believe it very important that those young men who some day should govern our friends the Indian Nations have a Spanish education and heart, in the present case [I concluded it would be] a good guarantee for the conduct of Bloody Fellow [that he should] leave a son in our power. Therefore, I answered him with sincerity by telling him that I would take care of the education of his son. He replied to me that that being so, he was handing him over to me on condition that I would treat him in the same way that we are accustomed to treat the sons of noblemen. [He asked me] to dress him like ourselves and not permit him to go among the common people. [He asked] that he might send him to that Capital to learn to speak, to read, and to write but that afterwards he wanted him to be sent to Spain to complete his education there, although seven or eight years might be needed for this. Because I was not ignorant of the fact that it was impossible to acquire much knowledge in less than this time and that much might happen to his son—whether from illness or other risks to which youths are exposed—[I told him] that if he might hear of his death he would regret it and that he should find unusual my treatment of him and disciplining him as the white people [do]. [In addition] he asked me if in the course of this year he could bring another son with the same purpose and carried out according to the same reasons given for the first. I responded "yes," and right then I gave him a passport just in case he wanted to send him before the same [passport] might come. This greatly pleased him, and right then he handed the mentioned son over to me agreeing to his taking a Christian name, that it would be Charles [along] with that of his family, which is Bloody Fellow Swan. He asked me that on the day of his departure I might send him to the camp to lessen the feeling of his separation, and he also asked that whenever I might need to write to him in the Cherokee Nation about any matters I might include news of his son.

The mentioned Cherokee chiefs have told me that Your Lordship had arranged for them to come by this post because it was easier to take their passage from here and that I would provide whatever was necessary. They called that to [my] attention to advise me about it and that they had a very long journey in the harshness of winter. Since they traveled burdened with matters that did not permit delay they could not be held up on the trail with hunting for provisions, they asked me to provide supplies for the entire trip, including horses and some clothing [to serve] as coats. According to the terms that Your Lordship recommended these Chiefs to me and [knowing] how important it is that nothing make them unhappy, without delay I told them they would have whatever they needed, and, although I displayed generosity in what I have given to them, Your Lordship will see from the attached report Number 7 it is of very little consideration with respect to the proposed objective.

While they remained at this post Sulemastabe, or Red Shoes, came here. They all became friends, and at my request he provided the Cherokees two of his warriors to show them the road, rejoicing greatly to be able to provide this courtesy to some men who were working for the good of all the Indian nations. Separately I will inform Your Lordship of the conversations that I have had with Red Shoes.

The son of Bloody Fellow named Charles Bloody Fellow Swan, of eleven years of age, comes to that Capital in the care of Josef Vidal. I ask Your Lordship to see to it to order that he be admitted to the Public School, entrusting his education to the Director of it. As to yourself, you may arrange that from my salary his support may be provided until His Majesty determines however it might be served with respect to the education of this boy, if Your Lordship does not decide to resolve the point yourself.

God keep Your Lordship many years. Natchez. January 8, 1793.

13

Treaty of Boukfouka, May 1793

The text for this translation is the copy enclosed with the Baron de Carondelet to the Duque de Alcudia, New Orleans, June 11, 1793, *Reservado,* N.° 10, AHN, *Estado, leg.* 3898, *exp.* 6.

Treaty of Friendship between His Catholic Majesty great King the Spains and the Indies for one part represented by Lieutenant Colonel Don Juan de la Villebeuvre, Grenadier Captain of the Louisiana Regiment and Commissioner of His Catholic Majesty in the Chacta and Chicacha Nations and for the other by Nanhoulo mastabé, Pathia Opaye, totehouma, Panchi mantla, Tapina akio, Taska patapo, Taska huna Opaye, Tanimingui mastabé, Poncha houma, Alpatak houma, Estonaka Opaye, Atougoulabé opaye houma, Tanap houma, Payemastabé, Tichou mastabé, Taskienia, Tatala houman Emalabé, Poncha houma, Pancha houma, Estatche Tiaka, Tanapi mastabé, Pancha Bahnole, Tasca patapo macheanche, all Large and Small Medal Chiefs and Captains of the small party of the Chacta Nation, and together voluntarily in the Village of Boucfouca. They offered and consented unanimously to the following Articles.

1.° That for better provision of what the small party, and all the Choctaw Nation, needs from their brothers the Spanish, [it concedes] to them full ownership of thirty square *arpanes,* more or less that which the French formerly possessed, to erect on it a Store or warehouse for Gifts and provisions. To provide security against the Nations with which the Chacta Nation might in the future have war, its brothers the Spanish will construct a Fort with Cannon and in which they will maintain their Warriors. For their part and for their descendants [they, the Choctaws, promise] they will never reclaim the ceded Land. Rather, on the contrary, they promise to assist their brothers the Spanish to hold the requested Store, fort, and Land against all those that might intend to disturb them in their possessions.

2.° The Spanish Nation declares, and offers reciprocally to protect, defend, and to shelter all the Chacta Nation, its faithful ally, in the possession of its land, [and] not allow some Nation to disturb it in said possession.

3.° The referred to Chiefs ratify and promise to be steadfast friends of all the Spanish Nation and to preserve with it all that was agreed to in the Mobile Congress with the Governors general of Louisiana and West Florida, and the Spanish Nation equally offers them perpetual friendship, and preservation of the conditions agreed to in said Mobile Congress, and what said Governors might have offered them afterwards; in proof of which they we promise to hold and to preserve all that is expressed in the present Treaty. All of us, [we] the mentioned Indian Chiefs, large, small Medal, and Captains of the small party of the Chacta Nation, before all the Warriors, sign it, [by] placing our signs, with [the signatures] of the mentioned Don Juan de la Villebeuvrę, Lieutenant Colonel, Captain of the Grenadiers of the Regiment of Louisiana, and Commissioner of His Catholic Majesty in the Chacta and Chicacha Nations, and the Witnesses present that also sign it in Bouckfouka, the tenth [day] of the month of May, one thousand seven hundred ninety-three. Juan de la Villebeuvre, Nanoulimastabé, Atougoulabec, Panchi mantla, Tapena atchio, Pochaouman, Etolouman, Estiaoupayé, Lasconaoupayé, Pancha baule, Alpalacouman, Estonacaoupaye, Oupayeounan imalabé, Mastiohe, Tanapouman, Payemastabé, Tichoumastabé, Lascaema, Talala ouman, Panchaouman, Tanequemastabé, Esfalieliaya, Pochaouman, Simon Favre, Thomas Price, Chastang son, Enrique Feis.

El Baron de Carondelet

14

Gayoso's Account of the Nogales Assembly, October 1793

The text for this translation is Manuel Gayoso de Lemos to Baron de Carondelet. Natchez. December 6, 1793, AGI, PC, *leg.* 42, N.° 13). A copy was enclosed with The Baron de Carondelet to the Duque de Alcudia, New Orleans, Jan. 24, 1794, N.° 26, *Reservado,* AHN, *Estado, leg.* 3899, *exp.* 1.

"Latest of the Assembly"

After you charged me to describe part of what happened in the assembly up to the conclusion of the treaty, I received orders from Your Lordship to send assistance from this jurisdiction to our capital and then to the upper reaches of the river. I therefore postponed until now informing Your Lordship about said assembly, sending in advance a copy of the treaty to be followed by the original with reference to your directive by means of Lt. Colonel Don Juan de la Villebeuvre.

Now I will give you the same, considering this detailed report to be more suitable.

In my official letter [to] Your Lordship, concerning the assembly convened in Nogales on the 18th of [October], I informed Your Lordship of what [had] happened until [that] time when there were already more than a thousand Indians [present]. Subsequently, others from the Six Villages arrived, and on the 24th Franchimastavé presented himself without advising me in advance of his arrival, quite contrary to custom. He brought with him Taboca, Soulushemastavé, Itelagana from his nation and various other chiefs, with many captains and [an] infinite number of warriors. The Indians are accustomed to appear in order of precedence, and, since this body of Indians was represented by the Large Part of the Chacta nation, I noted that Taboca had stepped in front of Franchimastave. I took advantage of this occasion to make known the displeasure the first had deserved from me and to reestablish the second in the esteem of his nation, which he had lost. I ignored Taboca; I gave my hand to Franchimastabé and accordingly afterwards to the rest, leaving Taboca and Itelagana as the last of the chiefs. I made [it] known to Franchimastavé [his] error in coming to see me without advising me of his visit according to custom. To lift his spirit I quickly praised him for his good conduct from which, nevertheless, he had apparently [for] some time strayed. [I said] that I was totally convinced that it was not his fault, that [he may have been] compelled by some evil chiefs in his nation who were not only advising him badly but who also by means of violence were forcing him to do what he did not plan. One of the problems [I said] was [his] having brought so many Indians, which was not only against my orders but also prejudicial to the rest because it would not be possible for me to give presents to all [of them]. [In addition], I [said I] would be very hard pressed to provide them with food because I had never counted on such a much larger number of Indians. The Chactas alone exceeded 1,500 at that time. In addition, that in order to bring so many Indians, he had delayed the arrival with serious damage to the Chicachás and Creeks who had waited for a long time [and] consumed many supplies. I added other expressions that clearly amounted to scolding on my part [that also] fell upon Taboca and Itelagana. After I had alternately scolded and praised them, I made them sit down under my tent and I served them refreshment with which they showed themselves to be very pleased.

It was necessary to leave Franchimastavé and his party to rest [until] the next day. I chose the day following, the 26th, for the opening of the assembly. I sent word to the other nations to attend at ten in the morning.

They had advised me that in the Chacta camps there have been many meetings [and that] there were some determined to speak against the treaty and the cession of the Old Tombegbe. I warned Lt. Col. Don Juan de la Villebeuvre that I will inform him about this situation and that I will try to avoid such discord, [for] it was damaging principally to a negotiation that he had carried out.

Ugulayacabe also came to inform me that many Chactas had been to his camp to speak to him about this same matter and to ask him that in the assembly he might be the one to speak for the Chacta nation. [He said] that he had excused himself, telling them that they themselves ought to present their views. The Chactas specifically wanted him to speak against the cession of the Old Tombegbe. I then charged said Ugulayacabe that he might shame the Chactas with their instability, since having discussed and voluntarily ceded the said Tombegbe [they] were now regretting [the cession] to their discredit. Besides, in reality, nothing could suit them better than having us for neighbors. They could be helped more quickly than [from] the plazas and posts of a province. He agreed to do so.

Don Juan de la Villebeuvre did not take long to inform me that the same chiefs who had caused these difficulties had been to see him and [had] withdrawn their unjust demands. At the same time a Chicachá mestizo called Tompson, a very passionate member, came to inform me that he had been to the Chacta camps and that all were determined not to disagree with whatever might be proposed or what had been proposed, especially with respect to the old Tombegbe fort.

I had determined not to give a single gift until the assembly [was] finished. However, some chiefs noticed that I had given Mingo Puscus the rich outfit that Your Lordship [had] sent separately to him and insisted on attending the assembly in the clothes that they knew I had prepared for them. Being assured at this time of the good disposition of all, I yielded to their pleas and ordered that they [the clothes] be distributed among them, which was accomplished.

On the 26th day in the morning, the great tent was ready to receive those in attendance. At the end of the tent [there] was an armchair for me and at the sides others [armchairs] for those who accompanied me. In front there was a large table covered with a scarlet cloth with a silver writing set and other necessary [things], with a rich pipe of black stone that the northern Indians had given me [and] an urn of tobacco mixed with wine (*zumague*) ready to smoke. It [the table] also had a large number of strings of white beads to distribute in sign of friendship. In front of the table at a certain distance were six chairs designated for Ugulayacabe, who should speak for the Chicachá nation and be seated in the center; to his right the chiefs Tasquenilia [and] Sulushemastavé, who should represent the Creek, Talapuche, Alibamon, and the Cherokee nations; to the left of Ugulayacabe should follow Franchimastavé for the Large Part of the Chacta nation, Mingo Puscus for the Small, and Mistichó for the Six Villages of the same. Behind these six chairs there were three divisions of seats where three hundred men would be placed: the ones in the center for the Chicachá nation, the ones on the right for the Creeks, and the ones on the left for the Chactas, who because of their greater number also should occupy the vacant places that remained in the other [sections]. I arranged that behind me were twenty-four well-dressed sailors; at the entrance to the tent a guard of a sergeant and twelve soldiers.

The hour of the meeting arrived, and with my entourage I went to the tent to occupy my seat. [I placed] to my right Lieutenant Colonel Don Juan de la Villebeuvre as the King's Commissioner to the Chacta and Chicachá nations [and] Don José Vidal as Secretary of the assembly. Following him on that side [I then placed] Don Juan Girault as Commissioner charged with subjects that might arise if it might be necessary to do some translation in the English and French languages, since it is against protocol among the Indians that such operations [be] done [by] the President, even though he may understand them. Then followed Don Antonio Marmillión as Minister entrusted with the Royal Treasury. To my left was Captain Don Elías Beauregard, Commandant of the Post of Nogales; [and] following him [was] Don Juan Turnbull, seeming best to me to give him this place [for he was] a man of great importance to the Chicachá nation, Don Juan Barnó y Ferrusola, Quartermaster of the Nogales post, followed [them]. Don Benjamin Fooy, Interpreter for His Majesty in the Chicachá nation; Don Simon Favre, His Majesty's Interpreter to the Chacta nation; and Juan Bautista Trenier, my interpreter in this town, had seats [that] they were accustomed to leave whenever one [of them] might be called upon to translate.

Finding all the flags displayed, the Indians of the mentioned nations entered the tent in order, the chiefs coming in the rich clothing that I had distributed among them. They placed themselves in the order already explained, putting thus the Talapuche chiefs [and] the Chacta interpreter whom they had brought, since this language was to be the one spoken in the assembly. The Chicachás didn't have one because they all understood the Chacta. Around the seats there were more than two hundred Indians under the same tent. We held in this way five hundred participants [who were] standing, and [there] were many others around the edges listening to what was being discussed, since the sides [of the tent] were raised.

I advised Favre that he stand at one corner of the table to interpret the speeches that might occur during the present assembly, and to do it [the translation] if the Indians asked because of the perfection with which he speaks Chacta and the confidence that they have in him and that I might speak to the representatives of the nations [to tell them] that the very hoped for moment had arrived in which we will gather together. As proof of the satisfaction that it caused me and of the consideration that his Majesty had for them, [I said] that I was going to greet them. The greeting began by the strong house of *Mt. Vigía* and continued by *El Gallo,* Abamada, and *Pan de Azúcar,* firing the artillery and mortars with great regularity, which greatly flattered the Indians. I ordered Favre to fill the pipe, which I lit myself; and, having smoked it a short while, I sent it by Favre to the chiefs who represented the nations in the order that they were named. I told them that the greatest sign of friendship among the red men was to smoke the same pipe and that because I now wished to express myself in the terms that might persuade them more about how the Spanish nation was receiving them on that day I was adopting the custom, presenting to them a pipe, [a] gift from the Indians of the north, who, although they were not present, should not be forgotten by us. Afterwards I had it passed to my retinue.

Directing myself to Ugulayacave, I picked up a string [of beads]. Touching one end to my heart, I extended the other, telling him: "this white necklace represents the smooth path without difficulty or danger between your nation and mine, and I hand it to you so that you may have it present on this day in which we are going to renew and tighten the bonds of our friendship." Ugulayacabe stood up, received the string of beads with [the] greatest respect and satisfaction, and hung it around his neck. I said to him afterwards that for the same reason I [would] choose from the necklaces that I had before [me] the number that [he might] wish to take to his nation to distribute in my name to the chiefs, accompanied by a piece of tobacco for each one so that when they might smoke it, the memory of our friendship might rise to the clouds as the smoke might rise from their pipes.

Then, changing the expressions, I repeated the same [thing] to each one of those who were representing the other nations, and [after I had] concluded my preamble a profound silence was observed for a short space of time, because this is also the custom of the Indians.

When I realized that they were prepared to pay attention, I opened the discussion in the following way:

"A long time has passed since this assembly was planned. Although called for an earlier date, its meeting has been changed several times. The first [postponement] [occurred] because of the unexpected war between the Chicachás and the Creeks. It was not possible that they might have attended then, because, given their change of spirit, such a meeting might have exposed them to some accident rather than provide them with the good [results] that we wanted. I sent at the same time notices to postpone our meeting until the two nations might be at peace, an achievement that the Lord Governor of this province and I have worked [to achieve] and [have] happily accomplished, with the help of our good friends the Chactas in whose nation the referred to peace was discussed between Ugulayacave, who is present [to represent] his Chicachá nation and the Creek delegates who were there disposed to the same purpose. When I had news of this happy event I again sent announcements about holding this assembly, but Ugulayacave, on one hand, advised me that it would be best to postpone our meeting for three moons when the weather would be less warm and less prone to cause sickness. On the other hand, the commissioner of the King in the Creek nation warned at the same time that it was not possible for that nation to leave their country until after the feast of the corn and new fire. For these reasons I felt obliged to postpone this meeting, leaving it for the full moon in this month. Nevertheless, [because of] the care and attention with which I always treated this matter so that there might not be mistakes and that everyone might attend at the same time, I was surprised by the news during this interval that many chiefs and warriors of the Chicachá and Chacta nations had arrived at the Yazú, believing that it was the right time for the celebration of the assembly and that they were waiting for me there for that purpose and that many other Indians would follow them. That fact forced me to move up my arrival at this post, bringing with me everything necessary [in the way of] supplies and gifts. This sudden change caused much expense and work. On my arrival here I received other news from the Chacta nation by which they notified me that in accord with my wish the principal chiefs of that nation and the Chicachá would come only for the month of October. This made me aware that it had been a mistake on the part of those who were at the Yazú. [They had] not received the announcements that the others [had]. Thus I provided them abundantly with supplies during their stay and for their journey [while] I, without having accomplished anything, returned to Natchez with my numerous retinue. A month before the time set I received news that the Creeks had been to this post to inform me that they were bringing authority from the Cherokee nation to represent it in this assembly and that the other nations would arrive within a few days, because on the journey through the Chacta nation they had arranged it thus and sent word to the Chicachás. I then came here where I expected to find the rest of the nations together, with no more than a delay of a few days. [Instead,] I have been waiting here a month. The Chacta nation [has caused] this delay with no other purpose than that of gathering many people with the hope that they all would be given presents. My announcements expressly said that only chiefs with very few warriors might come, because I was not inviting them in order to distribute gifts but only to discuss with them matters that were very important to them. The result is that finding more than two thousand men together, the gifts that I had for five hundred would not satisfy them all, hence you will not have anything to complain about except having failed at what I had advised. Now that we are all present, I am going to tell you the purpose of this conference."

"Last year the Cherokee nation described to the Lord Governor General the critical situation in which they found themselves without the protection of any nation of white men. Since they were not able to go to where the great King of Spain was, they were coming to him as his [the King's] representative to plead with him that he accept them under the protection of His Majesty in the same way that the Chicachá, Creek, and Chacta nations were, and that he call all [the nations] to an assembly for the purpose of taking appropriate means for their protection and to agree that our August Sovereign mediate with the American States for the purpose of establishing boundaries and putting an end to [the] present differences. [The assembly] at the same time [should] establish a permanent assembly of three representative chiefs from each nation who [would be] changed every year. [This assembly] would return for that time at any site that they might select to discuss together the issues of their nations."

"The Lord Governor General, as the representative in this province of our great King and who bears the title of Protector of All the Red Men, agreed to the plea of the Cherokees. For the purpose of carrying out this great assembly he ordered it [to] be called. Because other matters occupied him, he has charged me to preside over it [the assembly]; thus, whatever I may say to you is what he [the Governor General] has charged me. I am, [therefore] going to relate it to you:

The well-being of all the red men is to live in peace with one another, and your greatest happiness is to be under the protection of a sovereign such as the Great King of Spain, who only wishes to see them [the red men] prosper. To this end he charges all his governors to care for and reward the Indians. It is then my duty to explain to you now what is best for you. I have already told you what the Cherokee Indians want; what they propose [is] not only what is best for them in the present situation (of which none of you is ignorant) but which is also useful to each one of you. The lack of unity in a family causes great disorder: if the family of a nation is not unified, the disorder is general, and the remedy is more difficult however more time the stated disorder lasts. If all the nations of red men are to be found in this state, their destruction is assured. The Chicachá nation offers an example of the very same thing that I am telling you. For a long time in this region, there [has been] disunity caused by a single chief who strays from the way of thinking of the rest. It was the group that he controls and its opposition to the interest of the Creeks [that] was the cause of the last war between these two nations, in spite of the fact that the greatest number of Creeks and Chicachás were friends. If it were not that these two nations are under the protection of the Great King of Spain and that his governors have tried to make peace, the ravages of war would still be occurring. When the two nations might be destroyed, it is possible that some other enemy, taking advantage of such an occasion, might seize control of their lands, becoming in this way lost forever. It is best then that you think in time about preventing future evils [and] from now on build an alliance [through which you will] promise each other not to harm the other and, in case some one inadvertently may do it, to provide the corresponding satisfaction to help one another whenever anyone may need it; to consider themselves, the four nations, as only one, and to insist that [they] not declare war or make peace without each other's consent and the approval of the Governor General of this Province as the representative of His Majesty, your Protector. Prompted by the example that others [dangers] present as a consequence of carelessness, it is necessary to keep in mind the dangers that might occur in the future, although they may not be present now, persuaded by the example that others offer through carelessness. Perhaps the Chacta nation has been until now in the knowledge that it has nothing to fear since no danger threatens it. Although it apparently seems to be so, this in reality is not so, because [if] it [the Chacta nation] fails to unite with the other nations for the purpose of supporting them, the same thing would happen as [might] when four houses are close together fire [will] threaten the one farthest away, if the residents of the others do not help to put it out. Not only will [the fire] destroy that one, but continuing on to the others it will burn them equally. So now is the time to unite that this may be the period of our alliance forever.

It would be best to form a council of three chiefs from each nation so that each nation may be quickly informed of what is happening in the others, and your words may be communicated with regularity. [It would meet] on the site that best suited everyone. These chiefs would change every year. Said council [should] be presided over by one of those chiefs so that all matters important to the nations would be discussed there. The King's commissioner should only advise said council without having authority over it. Said commissioner will communicate to the council everything that the Governor General of this Province recommends and will receive there all the words that the nations might want to send us. Because the red men live by hunting, it would not be possible for the chiefs who form that council to stay always in the same place for their means of subsistence [would not always be] in the same place. In order to provide for these named chiefs they will be supplied by his Majesty's commissioner at the place where the council meets, and at the end of the year they will receive a gift as compensation for their work.

Many of the evils that happen to the red men proceed from the bad advice of some white men who they [the red men] see in the nations. [These white men], for the most part, are fugitives from this Province or from the United States [and are] accustomed to live by stealing, and, not knowing where to take refuge, they go to the Indian nations with the attitude of doing the same there. Because they are wicked people who do not know how to hunt, work the land or how to do any other thing to survive, they try to deceive the red men with lies in order to obtain protection from them. At meal time someone may give them a bite to eat, and when they see the Indian trusting their apparent friendship they steal their horses and go off to another village having caused much damage with their bad advice and lastly with their stealing. It is necessary to distrust these people. Because you cannot recognize them as well as the King's commissioner, all of you should not permit any white man in the nation unless he [the commissioner] approves him, acknowledging him for this purpose chief of all the white men who live among you. With respect to those white men who live in your nations with families and who try to do good by you and live honorably, these we will consider to be your very own people.

[I am concerned about] not only the evil white men about whom I have spoken to you but also some Indians [who are] accustomed to stealing horses and some other things in this country and taking them to yours. Other times they steal them in your country and bring them to sell in this Province. It is necessary that we agree that such people will be detained where they may be found and [compelled to] return the stolen goods to their owners.

[These disorders] are the result of the lack of respect that the warriors have for the chiefs and [the fact that] these do not come from their villages as they used to. In large part the disorder is also the consequence of their being too large a number of [chiefs] who believe that they no longer should obey or even that they are subjects of the principal chief of each group. From this, confusion arises in the nation, with danger for all of you. It is necessary then to respect the principal chief [and] to listen to his words, and it is also necessary that each chief consult with the others, searching always for the good of all the people. What I say with respect to each group should also be observed in each village. Following this policy, I declare to you that from now on we will listen to only the words of the principal chief of each group, whether from their own mouths or through the mediator of the King's commissioner. In the same way we will discuss business only with the principal chiefs.

Since this problem has been most obviously observed in the Chacta nation, I now declare that the principal chiefs that I recognize in it are Franchimastabé for the whole nation and particularly for the Large Party, Mingo Puscus for the Small Party, and Mistichicó for the Six Villages. The rest of the chiefs, therefore, should unite with them in their respective divisions to contribute to the general good of the entire nation.

Because I have been in the Province a long time, I recognize everything that is best for the red men, given their life style. The most prosperous nation is the one that most dedicates itself to the hunt, since with this product they can buy whatever is necessary for them and their families. Although they sometimes use the gifts that we give them in this [way], they mainly rely on the hunt. Now the red men do not collect as many skins as in the past. This [fact] does not mean, as many believe, that the hunt has gone far away. Although this [circumstance] is frightening, it is true. It would also mean the difference of one day more of traveling a little farther where those Indians go who enjoy hunting for their livelihood. Of course, the true reason for the scarcity of skins originates from [the fact] that there are many lazy Indians who believe they can acquire what they need without going hunting [and] by coming to our posts with false words to see if in this way they may obtain a gift. They go from post to post all year leaving their miserably suffering families in the nation. Although they have received many gifts, it does not help them at all because, before returning to their country, they change them for drink, [and] they reach their homes without anything. To stop this we have planned to give you those customary presents once a year in your very own nations or near them in the village that you will now indicate so that you will not waste time. Then you will also see the great quantity of gifts that our Great King gives you, and you will know to appreciate them more. [Following] this method it will also be easier to provide you with corn, if some year you suffer the same scarcity as during the present one, and, even more, it will be possible to give with preference those goods that you are lacking most.

[You must advise, however,] on time the King's commissioner in your nations. In order [to do] this it will be necessary to register the number of people that there are in each settlement so that gifts may be distributed, [as much as possible, equally]. This [being arranged] in this fashion, you will soon recognize the advantages that come to you, but you do not have to think that gifts will be given to you at any other spot, not even in New Orleans, since only an Indian who may come carrying letters from the King's commissioner in your nations will be paid whatever said commissioners may have offered him. Hence, the Indians will not have to inconvenience themselves in going to see the principal chiefs in your nation to ask for something that they need since they will have everything without difficulty. I repeat again that if some Indians might have to go on their business passing through our settlements they will receive no kind of present, and only two or three days of supplies will be given to them.

At the beginning, when I called this assembly one of its principal objectives was to prevent war between the Chicachá nation and the Creek. But, hostilities having begun before [we could] meet, war could not be prevented. Everyone, however, has again become friends, and I have only to recommend to you that you do not again have conflicts. Surely, in view of what we are discussing here, they will not happen.

I know that many [of you] have believed that I called this assembly to advise you to take up arms and to kill all the Americans that you will find, but my intention is not this, as you will now see. The Americans are our friends and brothers; thus we do not wish them any evil nor do we want anyone to do [harm] to them. When you see an American, shake his hand, and if he is in need, help him. This I say for those good Americans who likewise do not wish to harm anyone. I make this distinction because it happens in the American states, as in all the great countries where it is not easy to prevent damages done by some people in remote areas. Often neither the President nor the Congress can prevent the evils of some Americans who live in the forest areas. These are not good Americans about whom I speak to you, since the same United States looks at them as enemies. Such people are accustomed to traveling together in great numbers and carrying arms. There are men who lose judgment and become like mad dogs doing evil to whomever they meet. This is happening today in the French nation, and many of them are found in the United States. I do not doubt that their rage or illness brought them to your country or to this province. It is possible also that their evil may have contaminated some Americans and that they, together some with others, may be going through the world doing all the evil that they can. If they should come to your villages, you can be sure to see your women, children, and everything that cannot escape perish. Thus, [be] careful with them and don't shake their hand or permit them to pass. I also will do the same so that they do not reach your [country crossing] through my country. These people, although they may come from the direction of the American states and speak like them, are not Americans, since they are coming armed to do evil. I can assure you that the President cannot remedy it and that because they disobey his orders he looks at them as enemies.

I have given you all the good advice for which I have called you. You will go to your camps, and, reflecting on what I have said, tomorrow each one will tell me in the name of his nation what it may find advisable. Whatever we determine and agree we will have to put it in writing so that each one may carry a paper in which everything is explained and [is] in agreement for the future. The paper that I will keep I have to send to New Orleans so that the Lord Governor General of this Province may know what we have done here. Hence we have to put in writing what we agree we have done in all the treaties before now. In the same way we will explain again [what we have done]. Because the

Great King of Spain offers to help and protect the Indians, they also [must] offer to help to defend these Provinces and to inform about whatever they may know that can endanger them [the provinces]."

After I had finished this speech, Ugulayacabe got up and, showing great courage, approached the table and, extending his hand, grasped mine with a great expression of friendship. [He proceeded to tell me the following:] "Although I have always had a good opinion of the words of the Spanish, this day has eliminated entirely my misgivings that I secretly had. In this great assembly matters might be proposed that might immediately force us to take up arms, and, instead of ending, our evils might now begin again. But, what I have heard calms my heart, filling it with joy with the hope that [when] ratified what you propose we will live in security. Hence, even though you have told us that tomorrow you will await our answer, giving us this time to deliberate, from this moment I declare that I receive your word and promise to observe it. Because I have followed the advice that you have always given me without alteration, I have a long time pondered what is best for my nation. Since now you have not said anything that may have changed my first opinion, I do not need more time to state my point of view.

The analogy that you have drawn of the four houses in which help is needed from all of the dwellings to save the one that is on fire reminds me of another thing that I have never forgotten. It is that the four nations that we represent here appear as the four fingers of a hand that, when working together, can lift a great weight, but if to the four fingers are added the help of a thumb, in this case the Spanish nation, then the power of all is increased significantly. Therefore, nothing is better for us all then as keeping ourselves united." Turning his face to the Indians whom he had at his back, he concluded by saying "this is my way of thinking," and he returned to his seat.

Immediately, the Alibamon chiefs got up, and, shaking my hand, in a few words, but spoken with fervor, told me: "We in the name of the nations that we represent confirm the same that we just have heard from Ugulayacabe." Grasping my hand one after the other they withdrew to their places. Franchimastabé, Mingo Puscus, and Mistichicó [did] the same for the whole Chacta nation.

Addressing myself to [them] all, [I said] that I greatly rejoiced seeing their good disposition, but that, since what we [would] discuss in the assembly had to be carefully explained, reflected upon, and resolved, I could not change my plan that they should go to their campgrounds and there deliberate among themselves [on] what I had explained, [and] the following day meet together again in the same way we found ourselves. [Then] they would give me their answer to each one of the items that I had explained to them [by] confirming them or making some change. Because we were all together for the good purpose of arranging the surest method of keeping the red men in peace, each one had the freedom to say with frankness what he thought. Because it was already late all the chiefs would remain to eat with me [and] afterwards go to rest until the next day.

We all got up. The warriors returned to their campgrounds, [and] the eighty chiefs ate in the same tent at tables that I had provided for that purpose. All were in a very good mood, and in the dinner conversation on their own accord they offered the following toasts: To the health of the Great King of Spain, to [the health] of the Lord Governor of this Province, following to my [health] and to the [health] of the officials present. Near nightfall they withdrew to their campgrounds.

I sent various unofficial individuals to reconnoiter the campground, and they informed me of what was happening.

I found out with great satisfaction that everyone had been very merry, spending the greater part of the night in dances [with] the Indians of some nations going to the camps of the others.

The following day at 10 in the morning the Indians came again to meet, and they placed themselves under the canopy in the same order as the previous day.

In place of the pipe that we had smoked the previous day I presented them on this [day] a very large one of two pounds in weight, a very rare antique. It is of very strong stone similar to the [kind] that there is in the mountains of the Escorial, and [was] carved by the hands of Indians. The ancient Indians of Natchez were accustomed to smoke [the pipe] at the Temple of the Sun when they used to gather together to discuss serious matters. It was discovered in the district of Bufalo some twelve leagues from this village in one of the mounds [on which] they used to place their temples.

Since it is the custom among the Indians to smoke before beginning anything, I had Favre pack the pipe, and, lighting it, smoked it myself. Afterwards I had it passed to the representatives of the nations, telling them that since the ancient Indians of Natchez were the most renown among those of their color and were consulted by all their neighbors on matters of great significance, they all used to smoke the same pipe on [such] occasions. Fortunately I had inherited [the very same pipe, and it was appropriate that we] put it to the same use to confirm our friendship. Said chiefs smoked and afterwards passed it to all who constituted the Assembly who rejoiced in seeing it.

[After] this ceremony [was] concluded, Ugulayacabe, who came without the suit that he had been given before, arose and, dressed in the clothing that he is accustomed to wear in his nation and giving me his hand said to me: "As soon as I went to my camp I removed the suit that you had given me and put on this garment that is the one that I am accustomed to wear in my nation so that the white men's clothing would not disturb my understanding. However much I have pondered remembering everything that yesterday you told me I do not find another answer to give you than the same one that you heard from me yesterday that everything seems good to me and that I approve it all in the name of my nation." Again grasping my hand, he withdrew to his seat. The other representatives of the other nations did the same with very little difference. Because they have great respect for Ugulayacave, they try to imitate him in whatever he does. Before entering in the tent Ugulayacave had sent to tell me that he needed three more strings of beads. I had them prepared on the table. He approached to take them and, putting them around his neck, he addressed the Alibamon chiefs. Taking Soulushemastabé by the hand he made him stand and delivered the following speech.

"Your nation has been at war with mine but thanks to our protectors, the Spanish, peace again reigns between us. I was one of those most offended by your nation, since you killed my nephew whom I greatly loved; but, being concerned about the welfare of my people, I have forgotten my own injury, and I worked harder than anyone else to achieve the peace. In this [peace] your representatives and I happily meet in the Chacta nation. Now that I see you all here I can do no less than renew here the same act giving you this string of white beads as proof of my friendship. Finding all the roads and trails free of dangerous difficulties, and without stain, I, for my part, will always keep [them] in this same way, [I will] deliver this string to the great chief of the Cuitas and tell him the same, giving him at the same time this piece of tobacco so that he may smoke. This other white string [of beads] is for the Talapuche, and this for the Alibamones, with these two pieces of tobacco." Soulushemastavé for his part answered appropriately, ratifying the peace established in the Chacta nation between the Chicachás and the Creeks.

Ugulayacabe in this speech directed his remarks especially to Soulushemastabé, because he is his uncle and a man of great wisdom and [one who] has greater facility in speaking than Tasquemiha. Grasping hands, they sat down. Uguluyacabe again rose and, turning to the chiefs whom he had at each side [and who were] representatives of the other nations, took them by the hands as if to make a chain, giving his right hand to the one who was at his left and the left [hand] to the one who was to his right, which was copied by the rest, who formed a kind of chain whose links were their arms. During this Ugulayacabe, approaching the table, directed a word to me. "Here you see before you all the nations united so intimately in agreement and as friends that nothing will ever separate us. We will consider each other as brothers, and we will help each other to keep the peace and our lands, having foremost the good advice you have given to us."

It seemed that this was the conclusion of his speech; therefore, before they could withdraw, I rose and, giving my hands to the two who were at the ends [of the chain], I said to them: "In the same way I join with all of you in the name of the Great King of Spain, Emperor of the Indies, to ratify in this act all the treaties and conventions that we have made from the year 1784 to now, whether in this Province, in Florida, or in your own nations, promising each other to observe them exactly and in the same way even though we here do not mention each item. From now on we will look upon each other as brothers, reciprocally helping and advising each other [in] whatever may reach our notice that may interest us." On hearing this expression everyone demonstrated happiness and approval, confirming what I had said and, freeing their hands, each one withdrew to his seat. Taking mine, I said to them that it was very agreeable to me to see that they so unanimously approved my speech. [However, I added] that on this occasion I needed a clearer answer [that would respond] to each one of the other points I had expressed the previous day, for the act just concluded treated only the offensive and defensive alliance between His Catholic Majesty and the Indian nations represented there. To facilitate their telling me what they thought, [I said] I was going to repeat the rest that I had told them the previous day, and at the end of each statement they would tell me what they thought.

I did it in that way, and at the end of each article they unanimously made demonstrations of approval. When we reached the place that [stipulated where] each nation should receive its yearly gift, Ugulayacabe said that his nation wanted to receive it on the banks of the Mississippi because [it] was the place most convenient to all their villages and that the most suitable time was the spring. [He said] that as soon as they knew that our boats were waiting for them at the mentioned place they would go there to receive whatever might be given them, that they would return to their villages, and that our ships would leave. This approach of Ugulayacabe was to facilitate our going to the Bluffs of Margó and leave for the future the projected establishment of a post there, a point we had agreed to in our private conferences. The Alibamon chiefs stated that with respect to the Creeks and the Talapuches it suited them to receive their gifts in Panzacola at the same time in the spring and that the Alibamones might receive them in Movila. The representatives of the Cherokees asked that their gifts also might be given to them in Panzacola.

Franchimastavé got up and, turning to the people of his nation, delivered a long harangue to them greatly changing everything, telling them: "Speak now if you have something to say, since you are never satisfied with what I do for you. I know that many [of you] want to receive your gifts on this old Tombegbe. I, for my part, am accustomed to going to Movila, and I do not want to go to another place." He continued this speech, speaking with very little basis, and he sat down without giving a complete answer. [Because] I knew at that moment that some plot was devised to oppose the establishment at the old Tombegbe, I told Franchimastavé that since he was speaking for only the Large party I would hear the rest before responding to him. Mingo Puscus stood and with great determination said that in spite of what he had heard from Franchimastabé he knew that the wish of all the Chacta nation would be to receive their gifts on the old Tombegbe on the same spot that they had lately ceded to Spain in order to build a fort there, that, of course, for the Small party that he represented he asked that their gifts might be given to them on the old Tombegbe. His explanation was short but very clear and well conceived, revealing that Franchimastavé was not behaving well. He sat down, and immediately Mistichicó rose and said [that] it was certainly necessary to choose a place in which the whole nation might receive their gifts. Although he was as close to Movila as to Tombegbe [and] that the first would better accommodate [them], he preferred the second to avoid the problems that some Indians caused when they are in the lands of the white men. He sat down.

I then addressed Franchimastavé to remind him that he should be the first to set a good example for his nation and to support the easiest means of receiving gifts without going far away. He had stated, solely on a whim and without reason, that Movila was the most convenient spot. [I said] that the receiving of gifts in their nation was more to their advantage but that for us it did not matter where we gave the gifts. [Furthermore I said], because it was a general rule that the Chacta nation unanimously agree, they should discuss the matter among themselves and then afterwards give me the answer. As a consequence of the knowledge of what I knew the other nations asked, [I said] that during the next spring the gifts would be given where they had chosen. However, [I said] that the gifts would be stopped to the entire Chacta nation until they decided where they wanted to receive them and [that this decision should be made so that we had] sufficient time to be able to send them. Franchimastavé was left in a state of confusion, and I continued with the rest of the items that I still had to repeat. They all agreed [to them]. I omit referring to them here, for they are the same ones with which I opened the assembly and are found in the treaty. I will only make mention, of course, that all the chiefs unanimously told me that it would be impossible to implement the permanent congress, not because it might not be good, but because no red man, even though he might be chief, could be persuaded to live a year without going to his villages. Hence, even though they might agree to it, it would not be achieved.

Because I already realized this [fact], I didn't insist and satisfied myself with advising them that because the Assembly would not be able to institute a permanent assembly the chiefs, from now on, should not delay in meeting together whenever they may be called from their nations to hear words sent to them or for any other reason [for which] the king's commissioner might call them. They agreed.

Addressing myself to the Chacta nation, I told them that I had a major reason to be angry with some of their chiefs, who, motivated by their own whims, wanted to make their words stand against the [well-being] of their nation, contradicting the [words] of the principal chiefs and giving bad information to the king's commissioner, who was present, leading the nation's community to believe that the named commissioner often was not speaking the truth. Since the commissioner has always told them whatever the governors of this province have charged him and because he was an honest man, our Great king sent him to that nation with a patent that gave him great authority. Hence, from now on they should respect him and never doubt whatever he may tell them and that they should take whatever advice he might give them, because they should know that he was raised in their Nation and that he looks at them with great affection.

Speaking to all [of them], I told them that since we had agreed to all the items that I had presented to that Assembly I was going to inform them that I was going to put everything in written form, making five identical copies. [I said] that we would all sign each one and one would be sent to the Great King of Spain, another for the Cherokee Nation, another for the Creek, Talapuche, and Alibamon, one for the Chicachá, and another for the Chacta, so that we will always remember what we had agreed in order to carry it out. [I said] that the following day we would meet at the same time as the other days and that we would read the papers referred to and sign them. [I also said] that If at that very same time they had some other thing to present to me and might want to add, I would do it. My intention in this was to provide the Chacta nation an opportunity to declare before signing the treaty the place decided upon to receive their gifts while providing additional time to work at persuading them to it.

The previous day some Chacta chiefs had come to inform me that the nation proposed to give me an Indian name. They asked me whether I would permit it. I told them that I had no hesitation about receiving this proof of their esteem, especially if from this it might result that they might be more punctual in carrying out what I advised them for the well being of their nation. With that they withdrew satisfied.

When the conferences of this day were completed, Taboca rose and, approaching Franchimastavé, received from him a collar that he put around his neck, becoming in this way authorized to carry out the ceremony of giving me a name. He turned toward all the Indians and told them that I, being acknowledged as a friend of the red men, it was best that I have a name as one of them so that they might easily use my name that was recognized by all. He then took a pipe that the northern Indians had sent as a gift to Franchimastavé, and he put it on my table. Addressing me, he said: "In order to give you proof of the consideration we have for you we are going to give you an Indian name so that all the red men may know you by it." He added other similar reasons. He made another speech to his people, and, after raising his voice and lifting his arm, he shouted three times "CHACTIMATAHA." The rest of the Indians responded and confirmed each time with the word "good." He took my hand and the lighted pipe. After having smoked, he passed [it] to all the chiefs and warriors, and lastly he handed it to me in memory of the name they had given me. The word "Chactimataha" means "King of the Chactas." I made a speech to them in a comic tone, with allusions to the nature of the Chacta, which made them laugh a lot. Satisfied, they all rose. Ninety chiefs and captains of all the nations stayed to eat with me.

I continued to send trusted individuals to find out what was happening in the different camps. In this way I found out that the Chactas were planning to raise some difficulties to delay the ending of the Assembly in order to have provisions and to see if their pleading [would provide] some more gifts than those that were allotted to them. The Indians seem never to lack resourcefulness to look for goods whenever we want [them to come together].

The following day, the 28th, at 10 in the morning I went to my tent and in passing met Franchimastavé, who happily gave me his hand, showing me that he was satisfied.

I placed on the table the five copies of the Treaty and the pipe that they had given me the day before.

A little while after I [had] been in the tent, the Indians entered, Franchimastavé one of the first, but before they had all finished entering Franchimastavé left the tent with the intention of returning promptly. A half hour passed, however, without his returning. I asked those of his nation if they had news of him and to go look for him. It greatly surprised me when Soulushemastavé of Castasha told me that it was unnecessary to send to search for him, for he had left with the intention of not returning unless he might be certain to have what he wanted with respect to gifts. I noted the irregularity of Franchimastabé's conduct [by saying] than since the others and I were there he should not behave as a child, that the Chacta nation was the reason that the Assembly had taken so long, with grave injury to the rest. [I said] that I [would] agree to his whim regarding gifts, even though [this] was more irregular that what I should do. Since he [Soulushemastavé] was informed of the intentions of Franchimastavé and since I also supposed that he knew where he [Franchimastavé] was, [I said] that he should go to look for him. Recognizing malice and little inclination in Soulushemastavé, I sent an interpreter to tell Franchimastavé that I was hoping he might return to the Assembly instantly. In a little while Franchimastavé returned with the interpreter, exhibiting great contentment and saying: "I had withdrawn to see if it was worth your sending to look for me and since you have done it I am very pleased to return." Although I was quite angry on seeing the irregularity of his behavior, I decided that it was best to dismiss it in order not to offend even more the spirits of the Creeks and Talapuches who I realized were already angry. I tried to put them all in a good humor and, after having smoked, I picked up the five copies and said to the Indians "these are the five papers that I spoke to you about yesterday [and] that now, as I told you, I am going to read so that you can see if there is something different from what we have discussed." I had the five papers in my hand and, addressing Ugulayacave, I told him that he could choose which ever one he wished, since all were the same and that by reading one we could save a lot of time. He approached the table and choosing the first he put it in my hand. I myself took another, and I handed it to Lieutenant Colonel D. Juan de la Villebeuvre in order to give more ceremony to this act. That greatly pleased the Indians.

I cautioned everyone that I was going to read what those papers contained, according to what we had discussed. At the end of each sentence, [I said], everyone should give a sign of approval or raise the objection that they might wish to offer. They promised to do so. Thus I began to read the treaty in the way that conformed to Indian practice. At the end of each article, which was carefully and exactly explained, they shouted "good." Having finished Article 11, I particularly addressed the Chacta nation, and I explained to them the contents of 12, adding that I had no pledge that they should now fix the most convenient spot to receive their yearly gifts. [I told them] I could do no less than declare to them that until they might follow the example of the other nations they would not receive a single gift. Those that represented the Small Party and the Six Villages told me that they agreed, as they had said the previous day, to receive their gifts at the old Tombegbe Fort. However, Franchimastavé had not decided or answered anything that could give hope to resolving the matter on this day. I knew that they had informed me that there was an agreement among the chiefs of the Large Party not to decide but [rather] stop the Assembly with the hope that I would see myself persuaded to offer them some extraordinary gift. I destroyed their plot by declaring that for a bagatelle of this kind I would not wait an hour longer; the other nations were in agreement, and I myself was determined to leave the following day. This surprised them very much and threw them into confusion. I continued reading the other articles of the Treaty up to 17, always with the same applause.

In this interval the Chicachá mestizo named Tompson, of whom I have spoken, let me know that I had done well by saying that I was leaving the following day [and] that this would convince the Chactas, because it was told to him that the Large Party was now agreeable to receiving their gifts at the old Tombegbe [Fort] and that they were only bringing up difficulties to detain me.

I spoke to all the nations, announcing to them that [they had] ratified and concluded the treaty in this way. I only needed to add the last article so that we all could sign it to conclude that congress and return each one to our homes. [I said], however, that I wanted to know with respect to the Chacta nation [whether] the small difficulty remaining between us could be decided afterwards. [I said] that I had left article 16 open to take care of that matter and other things.

The Chicachás and Creeks showed great pleasure with what I had just said; and Mingo Puscus, principal chief of the Small Party, got up and told Franchimastavé that he only knew how to create difficulties, and with the fear that was coming to his people he never did anything worthwhile, adding some other reasons to the argument. His self-esteem stung, Franchimastavé, rising to his feet, turned to his people, telling them: "Now see what you expose me to. I am the one who pays for all your plots. Why do you all not speak if you have something to say?" No one responding, he turned to me, saying that since I was leaving the next day he didn't want to leave for another occasion the selection of a spot to receive the annual gifts; therefore, he agreed with the choice of the Small Party and the Six Villages, which was the old Tombegbe Fort in the spring. I praised him and excused his conduct, attributing it to the bad advice of those who wanted to influence him. I explained article 18, and I concluded with the 19th, so that then the treaty was concluded.

All the Assembly displayed great happiness, and I continued speaking with all [of them]. So that the treaty would be completed and no doubt remain, [I said that] I was going to put on the copies the seal of the Great King of Spain that would have the same effect as if His Majesty had signed.

I had placed on the table a large embosser and the seal of the Royal Arms, so that it might be affixed to each one of the copies. [I enacted] this ceremony with the greatest solemnity that was possible for me. I signed afterwards, the representatives of each nation following, and, as witnesses, the persons who accompanied me. [After] it [was] finished, I announced to them that in celebration of the alliance and the rest we had discussed, I was going to have a salute by my heavy artillery. I gave the signal, and the cannons of the fort's battery fired. That had a great effect on the Indians, since I had arranged [that] the twelve-inch cannons be placed on the face of the northern bulwark that was twenty *toesas* from the tent. We smoked and withdrew to eat.

I have described in detail what has happened in the Assembly in view of everyone. Now I will describe the essential [part] of the private meetings that I have had, and particularly [those] with Ugulayacave.

Since the Creeks came from Nogales to see me at this Plaza, I have not neglected anything that could contribute to making them understand the importance of the union to be proposed by me in the Assembly and the rest of the items that your Lordship had advised me about. That seemed very good to them, [and they] displayed [their pleasure] with demonstrations of the most sincere gratitude.

Because the influence of these chiefs could do much for the cause of the success of the assembly and because the Creeks were a very sensitive nation, it seemed best to me to treat them with extraordinary attention. Therefore, I sent them from here to Nogales in the galley *Felipa.* I followed two days later. I caught up with them in the small Gulf, and I gave them supplies to continue the trip. However, [I was] informed by D. Benjamin Fooy, who was accompanying them, that these people were not satisfied with normal treatment. Also agreeing that the trip was probably going to be longer than usual, because the northern winds [were] beginning to blow, I decided to advance to Bayou Pierre, where I ordered a cow slaughtered. I took on board the galley enough for both the Indians and the daily rations of the crew. Hoping to meet the Chicachás and Chactas in Nogales, I continued my journey but on my arrival the first day of October found only Talapuches and about 190 Chactas with no chief of importance. Lieutenant Colonel D. Juan de la Villebuevre had also arrived, [and he] informed me that the Chacta nation was probably [going to] follow him within six days and that the ones coming would be infinite [in number], in spite of his request and Soulushemastavé's of Castasha agreement that only the chiefs should come with very few warriors. Taboca and Itelagana were gathering people saying publicly that because I had many gifts to give them it was necessary that all come to clean out my warehouses.

I cannot help but mention here the state in which I found Don Juan de la Villebeuvre. For many months he had suffered hunger in the Chacta Nation, and he suffered more on the trip because lack of supplies that at no price could be acquired. [He had been] reduced to a deplorable state. I make mention of this to commend the zeal and constancy with which he has carried out his assignment in the Chacta nation, in spite of similar hardships that he suffered for more than six months.

On day 6, I had news that Ugulayacave with his nation's people were to be found at the Ball Field and that on the journey they had suffered great hunger. In recognition of this I sent a supply of meat, bread, and three necklaces of white beads as an expression of pleasure that he had arrived. I sent him this gift by a mestizo named Fretcher, who from then on I employed in the Treasury. Ugulayacave brought with him 320 individuals on foot, and, as I observed that the Chactas were delayed and that the Indians were not reliable in terms of estimating how many would attend the assembly, I ordered Ebenecer Dayton to send for a larger number of cattle so that we would not be caught short with supplies in view of the number of people that I expected for an assembly of this kind. It was customary on such occasions not to follow the regular ration, for it is impossible otherwise to count on the Indians. I also arranged that the supplies might be distributed with the greatest formality, with the assistance of Lieutenant Colonel D. Juan de la Villebuevre as Commissioner of the Chicachás and Chactas in charge of the interpreters.

On the morning of the ninth, the galley [La] Felipa was spied at a distance. At that moment I sent my galley to transport the Creek chiefs before time to eat. From this day forward I opened my table so that all the chiefs who might want to [could] come to eat.

Daily I sent supplies to Ugulayacave, who arrived with his people on day 12. He established his camp two leagues [from the] fort from where he sent his big medal chief to announce their arrival and [to say] that he would come two days from then to see me. That proved to be the 14th day, when I had my first meeting with him. It turned out that [I] found him well-disposed and quite decidedly inclined to our interest. He informed me that Payemingo had gone to see the Americans and that from now on it was necessary not to count on him nor think that he might have influence in the affairs of his nation since, in view of his persistence in favor of the Americans, it had entirely abandoned him. The two principal ones attracted to his party and favor Payemingo are called Colberts, one of whom is also called Payemingo. [He] is a man of great influence, more so than the chief of this name. These two subjects, [according to Ugulayacave], had gone to the Creek nation, and they had assured him, that if it were agreeable, they would come to the Assembly. It was necessary for me to count on them to reward them with presents. He assured me that I need not have the least suspicion that the Americans might establish themselves on the Bluffs of Margó because the Chicachá nation was determined not to permit any nation there and that the Americans could remember a similar case and what happened, namely [at] the site called Iron Bluffs. The Chicachás didn't stop until they drove them from there. I supported this way of thinking, keeping to myself for another occasion the proposal to them for an establishment of our own on the mentioned Bluffs of Margó. Now, with the object of preparing [for that moment], I told him that I greatly regretted that Turnbull might not continue his activity on the Yazú, explaining to him all the inconveniences and adding that for me it was a matter totally indifferent because I had no interest in his activity and that the King did not receive from it any benefit except that of facilitating the supply of goods that were needed by the Indians as well as a route to their trading post (for furs). It [would be] the same whether it were Panton or Turnbull, who owned it, but since Panton had made a contract we could do no less than comply with it, even though I was a particular friend of Turnbull and knew that the Chicachá nation greatly respected him. I wanted to provide him with an arrangement with their nation, but it was impossible to accomplish this in the jurisdiction that was assigned to Panton. Hence, I left it up to him so that afterwards he might tell me if on the same Mississippi River he [could] find some spot where Turnbull might set up shop. He agreed to do so, and, having given him a sizeable gift for his wife, he withdrew to his camp where I visited him the following day. I carried two small boxes with sugar and coffee and some trifles that I distributed to his family.

Every day Chacta Indians arrived from the Small Party and the Six Villages but none from the Large Party.

On the 17th the interpreters Favre and Trenier arrived, and they told me that those of the Large Party would not arrive for six more days. [That news] greatly annoyed the Creeks and Ugulayacave, the first ones saying that the Chactas should not treat them so, for they themselves [had] been in their nation and arranged with them that they [the Chactas] would follow them [the Creeks] at that moment. Also, this delay was a great danger to the Royal Treasury because of the large consumption of supplies that were being used by the more than one thousand Indians who had gathered together. Nevertheless, [we] could not begin the assembly because there was no one from the Large Party.

During the repeated visits that Ugulayacave was paying me, I always found confirmation of the good opinion that I had formed of him. However, with respect to Turnbull's chicanery on the Bluffs of Margó I knew that he [Ugulayacave] did not want to decide anything without the opinion of Turnbull, since this individual has an increasingly extraordinary [influence] on the minds of all the Indians and particularly on the Chicachás. Since already at this time Your Lordship had advised me that Turnbull was about to arrive, I rejoiced seeing this attitude in Ugulayacave; and, finding him entirely favorable to what I wanted from him, I suggested to him that it was Your Lordship's wish that he be the only person with whom we [would] discuss the concerns of his nation and to provide him with the means of retaining his influence in it [and] that he would be given annually a sufficient sum to compensate him for his work and to enable him to acquire new friends. I recognized that it was not displeasing to him. I decided to suspend all private conferences with him until Turnbull arrived.

They had assured me that, although chiefs and Indians from the Six Villages would come, Mistichicó was planning to go straight to New Orleans to make amends to Your Lordship for the death and disorders that some of his Indians had caused in Movila. Seeing him arrive in Nogales surprised me. I told him that it was not possible for me to see him in the Assembly until he had made the amends that Your Lordship had requested for the disorders committed by his Indians. He emphasized to me that the disorders that were committed were not by his dependent peoples but by those of a village that was in his area. As an independent people they were, nevertheless, determined to make sufficient amends. This seemed satisfactory to me, and, in order not to disturb the principal object of the assembly, I sent to tell him that, given what he assured me, he could come to see me.

On day 24, I found out that Franchimastavé was a mile away, and during the afternoon without advising me he presented himself, as is described at the beginning of this report.

All the time that passed between my arrival until the opening of the Assembly I devoted to conferences with the chiefs of each nation as they arrived, discussing all those issues that Your Lordship stressed in your instructions.

I was able to persuade them to everything except the permanent congress. It is not possible to subject them [to this congress] because all the Indian groups who inhabit the lands between the Mississippi and the Atlantic Ocean have different customs than those who live in lands under the dominion of His Majesty and, because they are of an unstable nature they live only from the hunt. [Even though] they like to wander, they return to their homes from time to time. Although great rewards may be offered to them, they are not capable of staying a long time in a spot knowing that they are tied there.

It has also seemed best to me to change the section of Your Lordship's instruction in which you asked me that the allied nations might send the names of all deputies to the United States to propose the arrangement of borders or to threaten war should their just proposals be rejected. The present circumstances allow us to adapt to the American States since they also on their part, even if it is not a reality, pretend a good relationship. I thought they could achieve the same objective if they, placed under the protection of His Majesty, might request that their differences with the American States be discussed by one of his ministers. The treaty, therefore, contains such provision. It seemed to me the same to establish and arrange that the Chacta gifts be given at the Old Tombegbe, since [it] is the most convenient spot and in this way [would] eliminate some obstacles to the cession of said post, which is of the greatest importance to occupy, as Your Lordship foresaw by insisting that its acquisition be discussed. It seemed the surest way also to convince the Chicachás that some day they may permit our settling on the Bluffs of Margó. Persuading Ugulayacave to ask for gifts at the Bluffs of Margó, to which he agreed and ratified during the assembly, [seemed], to my way of thinking, worthy of admiration. It gives no one cause for jealousy and seems a simple request of an Indian as well as consideration on my part for the greatest convenience to his nation.

This same day, the 24th, Don Juan Turnbull arrived. I discussed with him everything that mattered to us in order to destroy completely all of the influence of Payemingo in the Chicachá nation and to promote our settlement on the Bluffs of Margó with the pretext of his activity. This individual agreed with everything and assured me that he would do whatever he could to promote my ideas. Although he was ill, he went off immediately to the Chicachá camp. He returned the next day and warned me that Ugulayacave would come that night to meet with me and that he [Turnbull] would come as interpreter. We agreed then that the proposed plan would rest in the assembly, that in his nation he [Ugulayacave] would try to increase contempt for Payemingo and to make an effort for Turnbull to have a trading post on the Bluffs. I considered that it would matter a lot to him to counteract the reputation of Payemingo, who had gone to the American States, and that he should assure his supporters that I would return in the spring with many presents for them. [I stressed] that if Ugulayacave did not see the same ways to promote our interests it would greatly damage our designs. I told him that during the spring he also would receive the annual gifts, which would be sufficient to make his nation see the preference that they ought to give us. I also arranged that his annual reward would be five hundred pesos in silver delivered by Turnbull each spring. In this way I considered him [to have] sufficient resources to carry our project forward. He was very satisfied, and he promised me his most efficient efforts. He made me aware that the people he brought were necessary, that I [should] treat them the best that I could, because many of them had been of Payemingo's party, and if now they did not experience the effects of our generosity they would hesitate concerning the party that they should support. He also asked me for a special present for the two Colbert brothers and some clothing for him to distribute at his discretion. I agreed to all of this.

Franchimastavé also came twice to meet with me at night, but he confined himself to things of little worth and primarily to ask for secret presents [thereby] revealing in all of his actions a panicky fear of his own people. I tried to discuss this [matter] and to advise him to insist on respect and that if he wanted to achieve success that he consult with the King's commissioner about everything.

I can do no less than make plain to Your Lordship that if there is much delay in beginning the construction of the Tombegbe Fort we run a great risk that the Indians, forgetting the very same thing that they want [today], may place obstacles that in the future may make it difficult. This post is of the greatest importance not only to control the Indians but to assure that at a future time the Americans do not threaten us on that side. This is the critical moment to take advantage of a favorable opportunity that is presented. I will stop adding other arguments in support of what I already have said because it is clear to me that Your Lordship is aware of them.

I have informed Your Lordship up to this point of everything that I myself have observed essential relative to the treaty. All that remains is the distribution of gifts. I marked the larger part that was to be given now to each nation. [I have] tried to reserve some of them to return to Your Lordship in case some day the Cherokees appear with claims to some [gifts] related to this treaty.

Since the season was already very cold I could not resist giving some blankets, although very few, to some individuals who deserved them. [Because] I found a way of buying Indian shirts at a reasonable price, I have saved [the] greater number of shirts of the finer kind that Your Lordship had sent me.

Since all the Indians who had come were hungry, it was indispensable to provide them with supplies in abundance, not only for their present subsistence but also that they might smoke meat and make *sacamite* [for] their return. Besides, it is the custom at all congresses not to skimp on supplies, since otherwise one cannot count on the Indians. With this knowledge the consumption of supplies in this assembly has been greater than corresponds to normal rations but infinitely less than what is practiced among the Americans. The reason so many people came is that in that capital the interpreter, D. Luis Forneret, perhaps with the good purpose of avoiding providing some gifts, told several Indians there that the gifts would be given in the assembly. For that purpose Your Lordship had sent to me many boats loaded with goods. The Indians who easily believe what is most favorable disregarded all my advice that only a few should come and allowed themselves to be swayed by the unfounded beliefs of Forneret. Combined with the malice of Taboca and Itelagana, four times greater number came than was usual. However, because the treaty established sites for the distribution of gifts, the Royal Treasury might experience a great benefit and all of the expense that was caused can be justified as very well invested. In addition, political advantages resulted from it.

On these terms I decided to withdraw the day after having signed the treaty, leaving the distribution of gifts to D. Juan de la Villebeuvre and to D. Antonio Marmillión, as charged to the Royal Treasury for the distribution of the gifts and provisions allotted for this Assembly.

All the people who accompanied me on this expedition took great pains in the execution of their duties. Each one displayed great zeal in his respective job.

I can no less than single out the conduct of Lieutenant Colonel D. Juan de la Villebeuvre, D. Benjamin Fooy, and Don Simon Favre. Don Juan de la Villebeuvre has great knowledge of the Indians and consequently knows how to manage them with great value to the Royal Service. For that reason I have taken particular care in the Assembly to make clear to the Indians the esteem with which we hold him. I trust that will have good results.

It is possible that D. Simon Favre is the most eloquent man that there is in [the use of] the limited Chacta language. The Indians [rely on him to use it], and they listen to speeches made by him with more pleasure than [those] from the mouth of any other. I consider him attentive and faithful to his obligation. His manner of conducting himself is very commendable.

Don Benjamin Fooy knows particularly the Chicachá Indians and has the esteem of Ugulayacave and other individuals of rank. His honor, intelligence, and zeal for our interest make him very valuable. Added to this, being Dutch, he is the most appropriate for being employed in the service of His Majesty than any other non-Spaniard. Because of his intelligence and the absolute necessity to have a King's man in the Chicachá nation, I very particularly recommend to Your Lordship the appointment of said D. Benjamin Fooy as commissioner so that with the title of commissioner of our nation there and with the salary of sixty pesos monthly he can carry out said charge. Without an individual of this kind, I believe our affairs may not go well in the Chicachá nation.

On the 29th in the morning I received the order of Your Lordship to come down to that capital with three hundred volunteers from this jurisdiction. I left [with them] from that post [after] saying goodbye from the galley to all the chiefs that were in the assembly.

I have already sent to Your Lordship the original Treaty under a separate number. If Your Lordship approves it, it seems to me that it would be best to archive it with this report, for it will be valuable to understand it, [and it informs] Your Lordship of everything [that I did] as your agent.

I hope to have fulfilled the intentions of Your Lordship. I assure you that I have not omitted anything that I might think best for the service of the King. [I have tried] to adjust myself according to the present circumstances assured that Your Lordship would have done the same thing.

God keep Your Lordship many years. Natchez. December 6, 1793.

Manuel Gayoso de Lemos
S. Baron de Carondelet

15

Treaty of Nogales, October 28, 1793

The text for this translation is a copy, written by José Vidal and signed by him, of the original. It can be found in AGI, PC, *leg.* 42. Another translation is in *SMV,* IV, pt. 3, *223–27*. The original can be found in AGI, *Documentos Reales y Solemnes,* 7.

Treaty of Friendship and Guarantee between His Catholic Majesty King of Spain and Emperor of the Indies on the one hand and on the other the Chickasaw, Creek, Talapuche, Alibamon, Cherokee, and Choctaw Nations, represented in name of His Majesty by Don Manuel Gayoso de Lemos, Colonel of the Royal Armies, Military and Political Governor of the City and District of Natchez, commissioned to this effect by the Baron de Carondelet, Knight of the Order of St.John, Colonel of the Royal Armies, Governor, Intendant, Vice Patron of the Provinces of Louisiana and western Florida, and inspector of the Veteran Troops and Militias of them, and in name of the Chickasaw Nation: Ugulayacabé Mingo, Atakabeholacta, Mongoulachamingo, Chicacha Olactaopaye, Stanapayahacho, Ufehuma, and Enchuiantha, Chiefs of large and small medals, and honored men of the said Nation: in name of the Creek, Talapuche, and Alibamon [nations], Tasquesuha, Sulusmastabe, Chiefs of Great Medal; Tashaopaye, Opaye Ataque Chiefs of the small [medal] and their interpreter Payemingo deputies and representatives of their Nation named for this purpose in a general council. The said chiefs are commissioned by the Cherokee nation to represent them in this treaty because of the inability of any of their own chiefs to attend because such chiefs found themselves involved in a war against the American states; and in name of the Choctaw Nation, Franchimastabé principal chief of it, Mingo Puscus, Mistichico, Sulushemastabe, Taboca, Ytelaghana, Naulomastabe, Eachaopaye, Opahulo, Tapenahuma, Totehuma, Puchimataha, Taskaouinaopaye, Taskapataho, Yaganehuma, Nocjahumaacho, Taskaoupa, chiefs of the large Medal of the said nation, and of the small, Hayupahouma, Stonahuma, Puchimastabe, Stonahacho, Pouchantiabe, Taskaamedo, Olactaopaye, Panchabaonele, Payehouma, Ockhanahouman; and in the presence of various other chiefs and a great number of captains and warriors of the mentioned nations that were present and together in congress called at the request of the Cherokee Nation [and] held in the vicinity of the Fort of Nogales. The said representatives unanimously agreed to the following articles:

1. That the Spanish, Chickasaw, Creek, Talapuche and Alibamon and Choctaw nations ratified in the present act all the treaties and conventions that they have reciprocally made since the year 1784 until the present time, whether in this province, in those of the Floridas, or in any of the said Nations, promising to keep and obey whatever is contained in them in the same manner as if expressed in this [treaty].

2. The Cherokee Nation begs Your Catholic Majesty to admit it under your immediate protection as are the previous nations.

3. Your Catholic Majesty grants to the Cherokees the protection that it requests and will consider it from now on in the same way as those Nations mentioned in Article 1 of this Treaty.

4. The Chickasaw, Creek, Talapuche and Alibamon, Cherokee and Choctaw Nations agree to an offensive and defensive Alliance so that all in general and each one in particular promise to consider each other as part of their own nations and reciprocally to help each other and not to decide [any] essential point that may influence the security and preservation of the others without consulting them.

5. The nations mentioned in the previous article, being under the protection of His Catholic Majesty, promise not to decide matters of the type that are stated in the same article without consulting the Governor of this Province, as Representative of His Catholic Majesty in it.

6. The mentioned nations, in exchange for the protection that they enjoy, provided them by His Catholic Majesty, guarantee and oblige themselves to contribute their part to the preservation of his Dominion throughout all of the Provinces of Louisiana and both Floridas.

7. The mentioned Nations, being under the protection of His Catholic Majesty, ask that his ministers establish and agree with the American States the limits of each one, fixing them in a permanent way in order to avoid any reason for discord and to end the differences that there are over them between the mentioned American States and the Creek and Cherokee Nations.

8. His Catholic Majesty, [as] immediate Protector of said Nations, will mediate with the American States for the establishment of borders mentioned in the previous article for the object of preserving each one peaceful possession of their lands.

9. The Chickasaw Nation wants to receive the annual gifts that the generosity of His Catholic Majesty provides in their very own nation on the shore of the Mississippi where they will go to look for them each year in the spring.

10. The Creek, Talapuche, and Cherokee Nations want to receive said gifts in Pensacola at the same time.

11. The Alibamon Nation wants to receive theirs in the same way in Mobile.

12. The Choctaw Nation postpones to another occasion the selection of a place for the distribution of its gifts.

13. The gifts that His Catholic Majesty provide annually to the mentioned Nations will be delivered at the time and place that they have designated, with the exception of the Choctaw [nation], which will be suspended until, in conformity with the rest, a site is determined, approved by the Governor of this Province, for the distribution of such gifts.

14. Because the annual gifts to the Nations will be distributed at the sites mentioned in articles 9, 10, and 11, they [the nations] will stop receiving them in any other part of these provinces. The same will be observed with regard to the Choctaw Nation.

15. The other points that have been discussed in the present Congress but require greater reflection will be decided from here on in the same Indian Nations by His Majesty's Commissioners with the approval of the Governor of this Province and, so approved, these same resolutions will have the same force as if they were expressed in this Treaty.

16. All of the Indian Nations mentioned in this Treaty will admit into their Nations

the Commissioners that His Catholic Majesty may send to them, and they will receive all of the messages that may be sent to them by the governors of these provinces, and to the respective Commissioners they will deliver those that they have to send to the mentioned Governors. They will respect the said Commissioner, and they will accept from him all the advice and warnings that he might give them, and they will inform him of whatever happens concerning the general interests of their Nations and whatever may affect the tranquility and security of these provinces. They will also consider him as the exclusive judge (*Juez Privativo*) of the white residents of these same Nations.

17. The White men settled with families or business in said Nations will be considered as belonging to them, but those not involved in any kind of activity will be expelled from them.

18. The Choctaw Nation at this moment decides and states that it wishes to receive the annual gifts that His Catholic Majesty bestows on them at the Old Tombegbe that they have recently ceded to His Catholic Majesty and that they also want them distributed to them at the same time as to the other Nations.

19. Finally the Spanish Nation and all the Indian Nations named in this Treaty approve and ratify everything that it contains, and they reciprocally promise and swear to be guarantors each to the other and to consider said Indian Nations to be only one [nation] under the protection of His Catholic Majesty, King of Spain and Emperor of the Indies, and His Catholic Majesty assures them of his protection in every case whenever they may need it. In proof of this all the Representatives of the Nations who make this Treaty and are mentioned at the beginning sign it, and the mentioned Indians make their customary mark. In witness whereof: Captain D. Elías Beauregard, Commandant of this Post, Lieutenant Colonel D. Juan de la Villebeuvre, Commissioner for His Majesty in the Choctaw and Chickasaw Nations, the Interpreters for the same D. Benjamin Fooy and D. Simon Favre, D. Juan Turnbull, D. Juan Girault, D. Antonio Marmillión and D. Juan Barnó y Ferrusola. Sealed with the Royal Seal, and countersigned by the Secretary of His Majesty of the Government of Natchez, named by the said governor, Don Manuel Gayoso de Lemos to assist in this Treaty in capacity as secretary, which is concluded on the third day of meetings at this Post of Nogales, October 28, 1793. Manuel Gayoso de Lemos; Chickasaw Nation Ugulaycacabé for his Nation; Suluchemastabe for the Creek, Talapoosa, and Alibamon Nations; Suluchemastabe for the Cherokee Nation; Franchimastabé for the Large Party, Mingo Puscus for the Small Party, Mistichico for the Six Villages, of the Choctaw Nation. Witness: Juan de la Villebeuvre, Elías Beauregard, Juan Turnbull, Benjamin Fooy, Simon Favre, Antonio Marmillión, Juan Girault, Juan Barnó y Ferrusola. By Command of His Lordship Josef Vidal.

16

Cession of the Barrancas de Margó or Chickasaw Bluffs to the Spanish Nation, June 20, 1795

Archivo General de Simancas, Mapas y Planos. M. P. y D. XIX-45; G. M. leg. 7244, copy.

This document takes the form of a map followed by a verbal "representation." The reproduction, which is included here, is a copy from the Archivo General de Simancas of a copy submitted by Manuel Gayoso de Lemos to the Baron de Carondelet, which he signed and then forwarded to Spain (see Figure 7). We have translated the text portion of the document.

Representation of the Margo Bluffs or Chickasaw Bluffs on the Mississippi which Cliffs the Chickasaw Nation cedes to the Spanish Nation so that they should be able to occupy them in the way they choose forever without any future claim by the Chickasaw Nation to said Cliffs or the territory enclosed by the following boundaries: on the North by the Las Casas River or Chickasaw River and Fooy Island, from the mouth of Gayoso Creek to the Mississippi; on the West the Mississippi running two leagues from the mouth of the Las Casas River to the mouth of the Carondelet River; on the South the Carondelet River from its mouth to the first branch on the north side; and on the east, Gayoso Creek from its mouth in the Las Casas River to its source at where it is approached most closely by the first branch of the Carondelet River whose middle part will be marked with a straight line in the narrowest spot. Said boundaries will be marked on the Map by a gold line. The referred to cession was negotiated in the name of his Catholic Majesty by Colonel Don Manuel Gayoso de Lemos, Governor of the District of Natchez with Ugulayacabé Mingo one of the first Chiefs of the Chickasaw Nation who withdrew afterwards to his Nation [and] took part in a general Council with [its] King, Chiefs, and Warriors who approved it and as a consequence named as envoys William Glover or Ulathaupayé and Payehuma to treat definitively with the referred to Governor of Natchez about the expressed cession and its boundaries. Having finally agreed to the same boundaries already established and marked on the Map to be on record perpetually the referred to Chiefs made their mark and the named Governor signed it with witnesses present under the seal of the Royal Arms in the partially laid-out Field of San Fernando de las Barrancas where the Royal Flag is found flying and at the sound of small arms and thunder of artillery on twentieth of June 1795. Signature place: Manuel Gayoso de Lemos, William Glover (his sign), Sign of Payehuma, Elías Beauregard, Pedro Rousseau, Domingo Bontoux de la Blache, Manuel García y Muñiz,

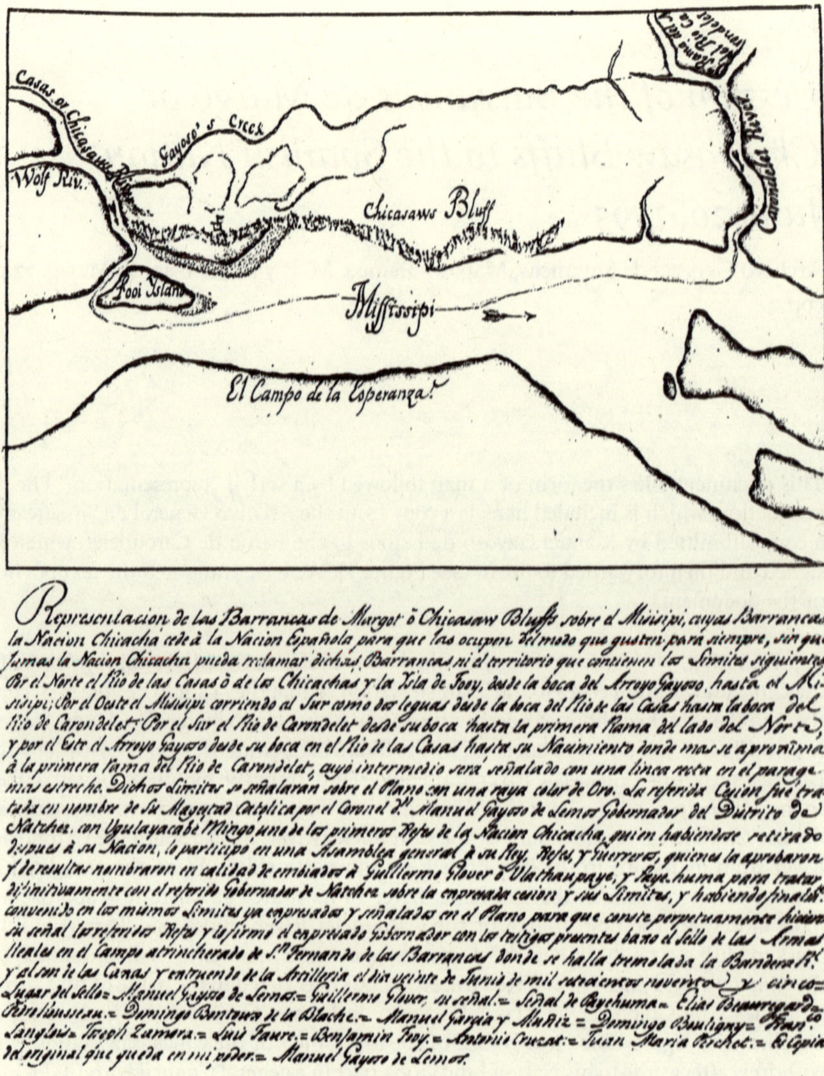

Representacion de las Barrancas de Margot ô Chicasaw Bluffs sobre el Misisipi, cuyas Barrancas la Nacion Chicacha cede à la Nacion Española para que las ocupen del modo que gusten para siempre, sin que jamas la Nacion Chicacha pueda reclamar dichas Barrancas, ni el territorio que contienen los Limites siguientes. Por el Norte el Rio de las Casas ô de los Chicachas y la Ysla de Fooy, desde la boca del Arroyo Gayoso hasta el Misisipi; Por el Oeste el Misisipi corriendo al Sur como dos leguas desde la boca del Rio de las Casas hasta la boca del Rio de Carondelet; Por el Sur el Rio de Carondelet desde su boca hasta la primera Rama del lado del Norte, y por el Este el Arroyo Gayoso desde su boca en el Rio de las Casas hasta su Nacimiento donde mas se aproxima à la primera rama del Rio de Carondelet, cuyo intermedio será señalado con una linea recta en el parage mas estrecho. Dichos Limites se señalaran sobre el Plano con una raya color de Oro. La referida Cesion fue tratada en nombre de Su Magestad Catolica por el Coronel D.n Manuel Gayoso de Lemos Gobernador del Distrito de Natchez con Ugulayacabe Mingo, uno de los primeros Xefes de la Nacion Chicacha, quien habiendose retirado despues à su Nacion, lo participó en una Asamblea general à su Rey, Xefes, y Guerreros, quienes la aprobaron y de resultas nombraron en calidad de enbiados à Guillermo Glover ô Ulathanpaye, y Payehuma para tratar difinitivamente con el referido Gobernador de Natchez sobre la expresada cesion y sus Limites, y habiendo finalm.te convenido en los mismos Limites ya expresados y señalados en el Plano para que conste perpetuamente hicieron su señal los referidos Xefes y lo firmó el expresado Gobernador con los testigos presentes baxo el Sello de las Armas Reales en el Campo atrincherado de S.n Fernando de las Barrancas donde se halla tremolada la Bandera R.l y al son de las Cajas y estruendo de la Artilleria el dia veinte de Junio de mil setecientos noventa y cinco= Lugar del Sello= Manuel Gayoso de Lemos.= Guillermo Glover, su señal.= Señal de Payehuma.= Elias Beauregard= Pedro Rousseau.= Domingo Bonbouer de la Blache.= Manuel Garcia y Muñiz = Domingo Bouligny= Fran.co Langlois= Joseph Zamora.= Luis Faure.= Benjamin Fooy.= Antonio Cruzat.= Juan Maria Perchet.= Es Copia del original que queda en mi poder.= Manuel Gayoso de Lemos.

El B.n Baron de Carondelet

Figure 7. Representation of the Barrancas de Margot or Chickasaw Bluffs ceded by the Chickasaw Nation to the Spanish Nation (1795). Carondelet forwarded a copy of this document along with others relating to the cession of the Barrancas de Margot to Spain. Baron de Carondelet to the Duque de Alcudia, New Orleans, July 12, 1795, AHN, *Estado, leg.* 3899, *Reservada,* N.° 56. Courtesy of the Ministerio de Educación, Cultura y Deporte de España, Archivo General de Simancas, Simancas, MPD, XIX-45. Also in MDAH, RG 26, SPT, ledger 5, reel 5, following p. 886.

Domingo Bouligny, Francisco Langlois, Joseph Zamora, Luis Favre, Benjamin Fooy, Antonio Cruzat, Juan María Perchet. A copy of the original that remains in my power, Manuel Gayoso de Lemos.

El Baron de Carondelet

17

Gayoso's Account of a Meeting with the Chickasaw King at San Fernando de las Barrancas, August 1795

Manuel Gayoso de Lemos to the Baron de Carondelet, San Fernando de las Barrancas, August 12, 1795, *reservado* n.° 15, enclosed with de Carondelet to Duque de la Alcudia, New Orleans, Sept. 15, 1795, n.° 60, AHN, *Estado, leg.* 3899, *exp.* 2. The text used for this translation is the transcript of the Gayoso letter in MDAH, RG 26, SPT, ledger 6, 46–73.

When Ugulayacabé recently left this post, he informed me that he knew that a great number of people from the Large Village planned to have followed him here but that he was not sure if that had happened. [He said] that in case he met them on the road he would make them return home, since it was clear to him I had no gifts to give them.

Two days later I received a messenger sent by Guillermo Glover with a letter for me.[1] I pass a copy to Your Lordship's hands [as an attachment] under the number one, keeping the original since [it was] written with water and powder [and] is not very legible.

Because of the content of said letter, I remain completely convinced of the good faith of said Glover and that he has had the fortune of earning it completely when he requests that I treat well those who come to see me, even when I might leave him without anything. That, according to the nature of the Indian, is the greatest proof that can be given of his allegiance. With the above-mentioned messenger [there] also came a small party from Payemingo's village led by his nephew, which seems strange, given the opposition that he (Payemingo) revealed to me in his letter. The above-mentioned nephew told him, however, that, although he believed I had nothing to give him, he should come nevertheless to see me, [and] that he was sure that even though I might have only some *aguardiente* I could arrange to send [it] to him one day.

Despite the fact that Ugulayacabé believed that I had already distributed all the presents I had, I still found a reserve I had kept to deal with any difficulty that might appear. That precaution benefited me greatly in this case because I could immediately offer presents not only to the messenger but also to those [of the party] of Payemingo, whom I sent back the following day with an answer for Glover. Your Lordship will see [my reply] by the copy of my letter that I include under the number two.

Among those who accompanied the said messenger, one [individual] came who was wearing the great medal that was presented to the deceased King of the Chicachas.[2] He showed it to me saying that it belonged to the son that he left, and it was to announce his arrival in company of the King, who was determined to make the journey, finding himself much improved from the malady he suffered in his feet. The same [journey] that he spoke about [was] made easier by a very gentle horse.

The following day some others arrived from Payemingo's village, but although they reside in his jurisdiction a great part are loyal to Ugulayacabé and follow his opinion. I have not wanted to write to him because otherwise they would use up too many resources that would be needed for the gift that I had to give to the King and his retinue.

During the evening of that day, the fourth of the present month, I was notified of the arrival of the King about two miles from this fort and that very early the following morning he planned to come to see me. Through the reports that Don Benjamin Fooy received, I realized that he was bringing many people with him, but it was not possible to determine exactly their number.

That same night, after the-end-of-day ceremonies, repeated shots were heard in the different Indian camps, which was an extraordinary thing because among them it indicates great surprise. I immediately ordered reinforcement of the guard with other precautions that seemed opportune, and I immediately ordered Juan Fraser to investigate that reaction of those same Indians. He returned at the end of two hours informing me that the Indians at the first encampment were at ease. They believed, however, that there might not be [calm] in the other camps, but not being able to determine the cause they had replied, nevertheless, with some shots to those that they heard from those (camps) farther away. I continued, however, with due caution all night. The following morning Fooy came to tell me that the shots of the previous evening had been a political gesture of the Indians believing that the military ceremonies had been a salute from the Fort to them [executed] as soon as we learned of their arrival. In the morning I ordered that it be thanked, and I took measures to receive them under a great canopy that I ordered to be raised in front of my tent.

Everything being prepared, they arrived in view of the Fort at 9:30 in the morning of the fifth day, and they all discharged a general volley to salute the Fort. I immediately raised the flag, and at the moment the King appeared at the gate the salute that I had ordered for him by the strong house farthest away from him began. As soon as he reached the front of my tent, the other strong house, through which he had made his entrance, continued it; and as soon as he gave me his hand and sat down, the battery that was to our front fired. During the whole time a march was played. Everything flattered him as well as his people greatly.

Under the same canopy there was room to accommodate the warriors. They did so, forming a circle that surrounded everyone, an operation that they carried out with great skill and silence. About one hundred twenty warriors accompanied the King, more or less well armed with excellent rifles.

Recognizing that surely the Indians would come armed, I had taken my precautions to avoid the most remote surprise. I knew to distribute fifty men in the two Strong Houses and another fifty in separate groups secretly in the Fort, in addition to the laborers that I employed that day in the Fort's surroundings. The rest of the squadron had orders to respond at the first signal. [I was assured] in this way no disaster would occur.

All the officials accompanied me except for Don Pedro Rousseau, who was indisposed. After the customary ceremony, I noticed that the King, although with a pleasant air, was determined not to speak. At that instant that [observation] let me know it was a matter agreed upon among them that another [person] would speak for him. I continued telling him general things but all intended to elicit information until the conversation again coming to an end, one of the chiefs, giving me his hand with a pleasant air, began to speak. [He] told me that they had come from their villages to see me in a place where it had never been believed that any white man would dare to settle. [He said] that their ancestors had always been opposed to it with all their power and that they had done the same, imitating that example. [However], upon arriving here they saw the face of the earth so altered that it seemed a marvel that they could attribute only to the determined will of the Great Spirit, which they would not dare oppose. Therefore, they congratulated me on my being there; and he repeated the action of gripping my hand, doing his best to display a pleasant countenance.

Since it is the custom not to interrupt the Indians until they have concluded their speech, I said only two words of thanks.

He stood again and gave me his hand and he began to describe the great esteem that they had for their King and that one of their greatest pleasures was to see me together with him on that day. [He said] that long ago all of the events that occurred and all the words that were sent to their nation were directed to their ancestors but that from some time to now it seemed that Payemingo's party had gone to one side and that of Ugulayacabé to another. They continued to be impartial and detached from their intrigues; as a consequence, [they] found that they, who should have been the first, were often the last to be informed, even of that which most closely interested them. In part that was the principal reason that obliged them to come then to hear from my very own lips the reasons that I had to take over this place.

I answered him that his demand was very just, and, although I knew that Ugulayacabé had expressed all of my reasons in the great assembly of the nation, the occasion demanded that I should repeat to them with great specificity before the King, Chiefs, Captains, and Warriors of the Large Village. [I said] I was convinced that not only would they be satisfied with my conduct but they would begin to feel from that very same moment the advantages that would come from having us so near.

Since this cession was so very important and since it promised me advantages of great importance that would end once and for all the difficulties and dangers that I have successively encountered in this operation, I determined to keep far away from the details regarding our military operations, trusting that their total effect would favorably influence the spirit of the Indians. So I began my speech with the project of the companies of both Carolinas and the preparations of O'Fallon to take over the Nogales territory that belongs to my King and many other Indian lands along the Yazoo, which forced me to occupy the mentioned Nogales territory with a great fortification. News [of it] was sufficient [to cause] O'Fallon to stop his invasion. In this way I then saved the lands of my King but also those of the Indians, our friends [and] neighbors. [I continued by saying] that at that time the Choctaw Nation and even theirs were opposed to the mentioned Nogales establishment, for reasons that I explained to them at length, but after some time they agreed and confirmed my King's possession of that territory. [I said that] even the King of the Chicachas, brother of the one who was present, had been the one who concluded that important matter with me. As for proof that my King has a very great number of lands and does not need the Indians' [land] to give to his subjects is that after four years since our taking possession of Nogales, there are still no houses in its surroundings.

I continued afterwards with the French war and their premeditated attack against this province from both Baliza and the upper reaches of this river. I explained the French method and goals in their present war in such a way that I horrified them. I continued telling them [that] in order to defend the King's lands and that of the Indians, our friends, the squadron of galleys (*galeras*) was sent for the first time to Nuevo Madrid, an operation [which along with] other preparations discouraged our common enemy so much that they didn't dare to attack us. I informed the Great King of Spain how exposed his vassals were along the Mississippi River. [Having] seen the previous items that I have just described, he ordered another fort built between Nogales and Nuevo Madrid on his very own lands, but it happened that there were no lands on that river bank that didn't flood. They asked the Chicachas to cede a piece of high land along this river, assured that it would not be denied once they saw they would also be protected in this way.

[I told them that] just as the King's view had reached New Orleans, the news also arrived that the state of Georgia, needing money, had sold to some very rich men, all the lands of the Chicacha Nation, those of the Chactas, Cherokees, and a very large part of those [belonging] to the Creeks and even part of those of the government in my charge.[3] So informed by Your Lordship and not having time to send this news to the Chicacha Nation and before proceeding to any other decision, Your Excellency had ordered me to come to build a fort on one of these places to prevent those who bought the land from coming to occupy them to our detriment and to that of our friends the Indian nations.

I made a very particular digression about what they were to understand about Americans [namely] that the President was a friend of our Great King and that both he and the Congress disapproved what some white men were doing against other nations but that they could not often prevent the enterprises of such people who were found in the forest without being subject to any law [and] who truly should not be considered Americans but rather people of bad faith.

I continued telling them that I immediately sent a *piragua* from Natchez and ordered that the squadron wait for me here and [that] I myself followed with other boats loaded with cannon and many other things and the troops that you see.

[That] when I arrived the squadron was on the opposite side where a considerable clearing had already been made, I immediately recognized that one could not build anything permanent because it flooded when the river swells to its greatest height; that at the time specified for my arrival Ugulayacabé was there with some chiefs and warriors on this side on the same spot that we are at the present time; that I sent to call him and carefully informed him of all the reasons to which I have referred, adding that during the war with the Creeks they had their trade interrupted because they did not dare to go to Mobile or even to [the] Yazoo to Turnbull's house, so that it was best to build the fort here as much to protect our lands as to promote trade. I carefully explained everything about this matter I had discussed with Ugulayacabé, who, persuaded by the truth of my arguments, agreed that he could no longer oppose a white settlement here with what happened then. That it was with the consent of Ugulayacabé and all his people I began to cut down the first trees and even now his being present and with his express knowledge I also moved my camp here from the other side of the river. That Ugulayacabé, withdrawing to his nation, charged by me to inform them about the events just described and my intentions, informed me that he had done so in a full assembly, which the King himself and all the other Chiefs, Captains, and Warriors attended. He also informed me that, approving what he had discussed with me, they sent here Guillermo Glover and Payehuma to discuss and finish this matter with me; and I explained to them how, as a consequence of our agreement to consider it [the matter] completely finished, the news had been included with all that would soon be relayed to our Great King. [I said] that a short time later I received a letter from Payemingo in which the King and others wrote to me things that I did not expect, asking me to leave the trees here as they were before, but since I had already informed my Great King about having taken possession of this territory I could not abandon it without his express order. Moreover, [I said] that I believed it would be a mistaken interpretation of the one who wrote his letter, and I added other explanations. Shortly afterward [I continued] Ugulayacabé arrived. What he told me eliminated the doubts that I had and assured me that it was no more than gossip of a small party. [He said] that it did not alter at all what [had] been previously agreed upon with me. I, agreeing that [neither] the King nor the people of his village would come to see me, had given to the large party that came with Ugulayacabé the rest of the presents that I still had. Even then I had assured him that I planned to withdraw to my house within a few days, which would have happened if [I] had not wanted to wait a few days to see if the King had something to send me. The delay worked out well because it provided me the opportunity of seeing him with all his Chiefs, Captains, and Warriors and to explain to them myself all the important news which I had just given to them. Then I discovered that he was on his way with a great number of his people and, finding myself with empty hands, I began to search here and there [for] whatever I could find. I even purchased from a small boat headed towards Nuevo Madrid whatever goods it carried in order to have [something] to give them. Seeing that I did not have *aguardiente,* I even had kept the ration for my soldiers in order to be able to give them [some] for their journey and to celebrate in their country when they returned. I ended my narration.

The one who was speaking for the King said that until that moment they had not heard matters of which I was speaking so well explained. He repeated to me that for some years the other two parties had paid little attention to them in this area. As a result, the negotiations in which they were involved were such that the King was the one who was to decide it all. Since the matters were as I was telling them and the Great Spirit was doing what he had wanted, he was no longer opposed to our remaining here. Standing, he gave me his hand with signs of happiness that I was the one to occupy this post. Realizing that things had reached this state and that we were owners of this land, he continued by asking me to charge my soldiers not to drive away their hunt or permit others to do it, suggesting [thereby] to me that this would easily happen, that when the Chactas found out that there was a trading post here they would trade with it and would establish their hunt in these parts with grave danger to them [to the extent of leading to] the destruction of the nation.

I assured them that the trading post that would be built here would be only for their nation; and, furthermore, I would give express orders to the manager of said post not to deal at all with the Chacta Indians here, since they had other sites designated for it [their trade].

He asked if Turnbull would be the one who will have the post, but, recognizing that this would create some difficulty, I decided to cut it short (the subject of Turnbull's store), telling him that the first who would have people here would be the Panton house, but that I also believed Turnbull would be permitted to bring goods, which, if it happened, would be a great advantage to the nation since they would not be subject to only one trader. [By that means] with other things I tried to divert them, leaving them satisfied.

The same person again gave me his hand, telling me that surely we had among us people of small consideration and that they did not always agree with what the chiefs decided, so that I should not be surprised if among them there were some that might disagree and might even say extraordinary things. I gave a general response, but I understood very clearly that the intention was that the warriors were going to be opposed to our establishment, since I noticed that the King with effect had made an important warrior painted for war sit next to him although not in the same line. For that purpose the said warrior, a man of much boldness and verbosity, began to speak in a harsh manner and as if angry. [He said] that since it was necessary to build a fort we should have done it on the other side on land belonging to the Spanish and not come to cut the trees on theirs, which was a favorite hunting land that ancient Paye-mataha and his successors had determined never to permit white men to settle, [a policy] they had sustained even at the cost of blood. [He said] that the present warriors were also of the same way of thinking, that it is not that they determined to oppose what their chiefs had done but that the loss of the most precious part of their lands cost them great pain.

I answered this complaint in the most persuasive way that occurred to me, repeating to him that already, upon seeing a clearing of trees on the other side of the river and before experiencing the flooding of those lands, they by themselves were crumbling away. [I pointed out] they could see it (the site) would not be able to support [neither] the weight of the cannons nor of the great houses seen here, such as this fort as useful for them as for us. For this reason I proposed it (the San Fernando site) to Ugulaycabé, [recognizing] that certainly without his consent and that of his warriors one would not have planned to cut even one single tree here, let alone build such great works as they now see constructed.

He continued producing a thousand complaints in harsh terms very similar to the previous ones that he expressed. I had spoken quietly, and I was answering tactfully, so that at the end of a long time he finished by giving me his hand and agreeing with what the chiefs had done in deference to the respect that they felt for the King and repeating that they were the true owners of this place but since I was already here they were glad to see me and that he would not speak again about this matter. [He continued by saying] that they came to see me not because of a desire to receive gifts but only to accompany their King and have the pleasure of seeing him seated at my side in the way we were. Hence, in spite of the fact that Ugulayacabé met them on the journey and wanted to dissuade them from continuing [by] assuring them that I had nothing to give them, they persisted in their intention of having the pleasure of seeing me and speaking with me so that, although I might give them only a tiny piece of iron, they would be content.

To this I gave a proper response to answer the warriors and to convince them of the honor we paid to them in such a way that they all applauded, concluding [by urging] that I take care that the Chactas do not come to kill their game. The King then told me that he was happy that his people had expressed themselves to me and that this matter might then be viewed as closed, and he gave me his hand. He asked me for tobacco for his chiefs, which I immediately had brought, and they all smoked, concluding in this way a very interesting and decisive scene after which it is no longer possible that more objections remain than those that Payemingo may individually produce but not in the name of the Nation.

We arose to eat, I having invited the King and the two that spoke and another two of rank, an invitation I repeated all the time that they were here.

The following day I distributed to them the gifts that I had been provided by the Commandant of the post and Don Benjamin Fooy. [That procedure] satisfied everyone because they prefer the equity with which the white men make the distribution, which does not happen when it is given altogether. It was not possible, however, for me to fill all the little kegs that they brought with *aguardiente*, because there were more than three hundred. I filled the bottoms of only a hundred.[4] For that I had to buy four casks in addition to the one and a half that was left to me from what the *Cerez* brought.

In a separate letter to the one I offered previously to Your Lordship, I will send on this occasion an accounting of the gift that the *Cerez* brought and what I have purchased here, all of which I hope will meet with your approbation and will serve you as satisfaction [to] a favorable conclusion so definitive after the raising of so many difficulties and opposition that have been offered in this delicate and critical undertaking that resulted in the greatest advantages for the security and prosperity of this Province.

All of the officials who are serving in this expedition have displayed the sincerest desire for its success and even would have been willing to sacrifice themselves if it might have been necessary to achieve success through force of arms. I must commend as a person of rank in this expedition Don Benjamin Fooy, whose zeal, determination, and activity merit my particular attention.

When I may have the honor of sending to Your Excellency the original document of the cession of this land that will be carried when the *galeras* travel south for complete safety, I will name all the officials and employees so that Your Excellency may be able to recommend them to Your Majesty's attention. God grant you a long life. San Fernando de las Barrancas, August 15, 1795.

Abbreviations

AGI, PC	Archivo General de Indias: Cuba
AGI, SD	Archivo General de Indias: Santo Domingo
AHN	Archivo Histórico Nacional
ASP: IA	*American State Papers: Indian Affairs* (Washington: Galesburg Publishing Company, 1832). Vol. 1 of 2.
CO 5	Great Britain Public Record Office: Colonial Papers, Class 5, America and the West Indies
exp.	*Expediente*
leg.	*Legajo*
LC	Library of Congress
MDAH	Mississippi Department of Archives and History
MPA	Mississippi Provincial Archives
MPA: ED	*Mississippi Provincial Archives: English Dominion, 1763–66*, ed. by Dunbar Rowland (Nashville: Press of Brandon Printing Co., 1905).
MPA: FD	*Mississippi Provincial Archives: French Dominion, 1701–1763*. 5 vols. Volumes 1–3 edited and translated by Dunbar Rowland and A. G. Sanders (Jackson: Press of the Mississippi Department of Archives and History, 1927–33); Volumes 4–5, collected, edited, and translated by Dunbar Rowland and A. G. Sanders; revised and edited by Patricia Kay Galloway (Baton Rouge and London: Louisiana State University Press, 1984).
PETHS	*Publications of the East Tennessee Historical Society/East Tennessee Historical Society Publications*
PL	Panton, Leslie Papers, microfilm copies
RG	Record Group
SMV	Lawrence Kinnaird, ed., *Spain in the Mississippi Valley, 1765–1794*, Annual Report of the American Historical Association for the Year 1945 (Washington, D.C.: U.S. Government Printing Office, 1945–46). Vols. 2–4: pt. 1, *The Revolutionary Period, 1765–1781;* pt. 2, *The Post-War Decade, 1782–1791;* pt. 3, *Problems of Frontier Defense, 1792–1794*.
SPT	Spanish Provincial Transcripts
trans.	Translation

Notes to Chapters

INTRODUCTION: AN ARGUMENT

1. "Indian Speeches Made at Long Town," June 1, 1793, *SMV*, 4, pt. 3, 167. The speeches apparently were recorded by the trader Benjamin James. Two copies with his signature can be found as N.°2 in AGI, PC, *leg.* 2353. Piomingo, or "Mountain Leader," receives considerable attention in James R. Atkinson's *Splendid Land, Splendid People: The Chickasaw Indians to Removal* (Tuscaloosa: The University of Alabama Press, 2004), and in Atkinson, trans. and ed., "A Narrative Based on an Interview with Malcolm McGee by Lyman C. Draper," *Journal of Mississippi History* 66 (Spring 2004), 48–50.

2. The particular reference is to the Iroquois and their diplomacy; Francis J. Jennings, ed., *The History and Culture of Iroquois Diplomacy* (Syracuse: Syracuse University Press, 1995), 121. For an extensive discussion of elements of diplomatic discourse employed by Indians and Europeans, see Robert A. Williams, Jr., *Linking Arms Together: American Indian Treaty Visions of Law and Peace, 1600–1800* (New York: Oxford University Press, 1997). Morris S. Arnold discusses the metaphoric dimension of Indian-European discourse in *The Rumble of a Distant Drum: The Quapaws and Old New World Newcomers, 1763–1804* (Fayetteville: University of Arkansas Press, 2000), esp. 108–10.

3. James H. Merrell, *The Indians' New World: Catawbas and Their Neighbors from European Contact through the Era of Removal* (Chapel Hill: University of North Carolina Press, 1989; New York: W. H. Norton and Company), 148; David Murray, *Forked Tongues: Speech, Writing and Representation in North American Indian Texts* (Bloomington: Indiana University Press, 1991), esp. 42–44.

4. See Garrett Mattingly, *Renaissance Diplomacy* (New York: Houghton Mifflin, 1955; Dover Publications, Inc., 1988), esp. 23–38; Williams, *Linking Arms Together*, 30–31.

5. Williams, *Linking Arms Together*, 11.

6. Manuel Gayoso de Lemos to Estevan Miró, Natchez, Feb. 1, 1791, N.° 8, AGI, PC, *leg.* 41.

7. Thomas P. Abernethy, *The South in the New Nation, 1789–1819* (Louisiana State University Press and The Littlefield Fund of the University of Texas, 1961), 78–85; Manuel Gayoso de Lemos, "Instrucciones que deverá observar el comandante del Puesto de los Nogales," Nogales, Apr. 1, 1791, AGI, PC, *leg.* 2352, transcript in MDAH, SPT, ledger 3, 503–20. For a discussion of the transformation of Natchez from a military post to a city, see Jack D. Elliott, Jr., "City and Empire: The Spanish Origins of Natchez," *Journal of Mississippi History* 59 (Winter 1997), 271–321.

8. There is reference to a village of Natchez Indians called "The Walnut-trees" in "Minutes of the Council of War," Jan. 7, 1724, in *MPA, FD,* 3: 385–87. The British created the Natchez District within the province of West Florida as part of the reorganization of their North American empire after the French and Indian War of 1754–63. See Cecil Johnson, *British West Florida, 1763–1783* (New Haven: Yale University Press, 1943), 108; Robin F. Fabel, *The Economy of British West Florida, 1763–1783* (Tuscaloosa: University of Alabama Press, 1988), 1–2, 157–58. See also Robert V. Haynes, *The Natchez District and the American Revolution* (Jackson: University Press of Mississippi, 1976), 3–26; H. B. Cushman, *History of the Choctaw, Chickasaw and Natchez Indians* (1899), abridged and ed. by Angie Debo, intro. by Clara Sue Kidwell (Norman: University of Oklahoma Press, 1999), 41.

9. "Instrucciones," 503–20. Manuel Gayoso de Lemos to Estevan Miró, Natchez, Mar. 19, 1791, AGI, PC, *leg.* 41; Estevan Miró to Elías Beauregard, New Orleans, Feb. 12, 1791, AGI, PC, *leg.* 17; "Appointment of Pedro Foucher as Commandant of New Madrid 1789," in Louis Houck, ed., *The Spanish Regime in Missouri,* 2 vols. (Chicago: R. R. Donnelley and Sons, 1909), 2: 309.

10. Document 1.

11. Franchimastabé and Taboca to Manuel Gayoso de Lemos, Choctaw Nation, May 14, 1791, AGI, PC, *leg.* 2352, trans. and copy enclosed with Manuel Gayoso de Lemos to Estevan Miró, Natchez, May 28, 1791, AGI, PC, *leg.* 41, quoted in Manuel Serrano y Sanz, *España y los indios Cherokis y Chactas en la segunda mitad del siglo XVIII* (Sevilla: Tip. de la "Guía Oficial," 1916), 44.

12. Frank Paul De Fina, "Rivalidades y contactos entre España, Norte América y las Naciones Indias Chactas, Chicasaws, Cherokis y Criks en la segunda mitad del Siglo XVIII" (Ph.D. thesis, Universidad de Madrid, 1962), 2 vols., 1: ii;. Arthur Preston Whitaker, *The Spanish-American Frontier, 1783–1795: The Westward Movement and the Spanish Retreat in the Mississippi Valley* (1927 by Arthur Preston Whitaker, repr., Lincoln: University of Nebraska Press), 32. On the incompatibility of Indian ways with American, see Anthony F. C. Wallace, *Jefferson and the Indians: The Tragic Fate of the First Americans* (Cambridge, Mass.: Belknap Press of Harvard University Press, 1999), esp. 276–317; Jacqueline DuVal, "'Faithful Nations' and 'Ruthless Savages': The Rise and Fall of Indian Diplomacy in the Arkansas River Valley, 1673–1828" (Ph.D. diss., University of California–Davis, 2001), 6, 171–265.

13. The Choctaw chief, "Tunnahthoomah, or Red Enemy," used the phrase *middle ground*—at least in the words of the translator and recorder—in his speech before Governor Blount and Americans during a major congress in Nashville in August 1792 in which he said, "I want to have peace and good talks at this middle ground": *ASP: IA,* 285. Richard White uses the phrase as the central metaphor in his *The Middle Ground: Indians, empires, and republics in the Great Lakes region, 1650–1815* (Cambridge: Cambridge University Press, 1991). See also Colin Calloway, *One Vast Winter Count: The Native American West Before Lewis and Clark* (Lincoln: University of Nebraska Press, 2003), 236. Anthropologist Marshall Sahlins also emphasizes the flexibility of native peoples to accommodate new people in *Islands of History* (Chicago: University of Chicago Press, 1985), esp. xiv, 32–72. That view informs much of Daniel H. Usner, Jr., *Indians, Settlers, & Slaves in a Frontier Exchange Economy: The Lower Mississippi Valley Before 1783* (Chapel Hill: University of North Carolina Press, 1992).

14. John Richard Alden, *John Stuart and the Southern Colonial Frontier: A Study of Indian Relations, War, Trade, and Land Problems in the Southern Wilderness, 1754–1775* (Ann Arbor: University of Michigan Press, 1944), 14; Richard White, *The Roots of Dependency: Subsis-*

tence, Environment, and Social Change among the Choctaws, Pawnees, and Navahos (Lincoln: University of Nebraska Press, 1983), esp. 81–82.

15. Greg O'Brien, *Choctaws in a Revolutionary Age, 1750–1830* (Lincoln: University of Nebraska Press, 2002).

16. Claudio Saunt, *A New Order of Things: Property, Power, and the Transformation of the Creek Indians, 1733–1816* (copyright 1999 by Claudio Saunt, Cambridge University Press, 1999), esp. 39, 67–89, 96, 190–91, 198–99.

17. Ibid., 139–63; Theda Perdue, *Cherokee Women: Gender and Culture Change, 1700–1835* (Lincoln: University of Nebraska Press, 1998), esp. 13, 28, 48, 62, 91; Kathryn E. Holland Braund, *Deerskins & Duffels: The Creek Indian Trade with Anglo-America, 1685–1815* (Lincoln: University of Nebraska Press, 1993), 22–23.

18. Williams, *Linking Arms Together*, 20.

19. With reference to New England, historian Jill Lepore observes that "under the lens of Enlightenment theories about language and civilization, Indian speech came to be seen not as especially awful but as especially eloquent—more so than the speech of civilized peoples who, having learned to write well, had lost the power to speak forcefully": Lepore, "Wigwam Words," *The American Scholar* 70 (Winter 2001), 98. See also Williams, *Linking Arms Together*, 36.

20. "Indian Speeches Made at Long Town, June, 1793," in *SMV*, 4, pt. 3, 166; Colin G. Calloway, *The American Revolution in Indian Country: Crisis and diversity in Native American communities* (Cambridge: Cambridge University Press, 1995), 228; see also his essay "The Continuing Revolution in Indian Country" in Frederick E. Hoxie, Ronald Hoffman, and Peter J. Albert, eds., *Native Americans and the New Republic* (Charlottesville: University Press of Virginia, 1999), 3–33. Louis Houck notes that Piomingo could read and write English and had a secretary: Houck, *The Spanish Regime in Missouri*, 2: 27n.5.

21. "A Talk of Payemingo [Piomingo], Chief of the Chickasaws, Addressed to the Governor of North Carolina, 28 September 1789," ms. 722, Ayer Collection, The Newberry Library, Chicago. "Cumberland," when used, usually means the Cumberland settlements, an area into which Americans moved in the 1780s around the present city of Nashville. It can refer to just the specific settlement that became Nashville, the capital of Tennessee after it became a state in 1796.

22. "Liberty" for Jefferson, argues Wallace, applied only to those who met his standards of civilization and culture: Wallace, *Jefferson and the Indians*, esp. 13–20. See also Reginald Horsman, "The Indian Policy of an 'Empire for Liberty,'" in Hoxie et al., *Native Americans and the New Republic*, 37–61, esp. 48. See also Horsman's earlier study, of which this essay is a summary: *Expansion and American Indian Policy, 1783–1812* (Michigan State University Press, 1967, repr., University of Oklahoma Press, 1992), esp. 104–15. See also Robert F. Berkhofer, Jr., *The White Man's Indian: Images of the American Indian from Columbus to the Present* (Robert F. Berkhofer, Jr., 1978; New York: Vintage Books, 1979), 139. Eric Hinderaker argues that "by the end of the Revolutionary era, Ohio Indians discovered that the terms of their relations with Euro-Americans had shifted fundamentally as they were progressively denied recognition as independent sovereign peoples": Hinderaker, *Elusive Empires: Constructing Colonialism in the Ohio Valley, 1673–1800* (Cambridge and New York: Cambridge University Press, 1997), xiii.

23. William S. Coker and Thomas D. Watson, *Indian Traders of the Southeastern Spanish Borderlands: Panton, Leslie & Company and Thomas Forbes & Company, 1783–1847* (Pensacola: University of West Florida Press, 1986), 158.

24. An emphatic point of De Fina's University of Madrid thesis, "Rivalidades y contactos," 1: vi. A depiction of Chickasaws as "pawns" can be found in Joseph C. Clift's thesis, "'Pawns of the Game': The Role of the Chickasaws in U.S.-Spanish Relations, 1783-1803" (Master's thesis, University of Memphis, May 1972).

25. James Taylor Carson, *Searching for the Bright Path: The Mississippi Choctaws from Prehistory to Removal* (Lincoln: University of Nebraska Press, 1999), 40–41; O'Brien, *Choctaws in a Revolutionary Age, 1750–1830*, 55; *MPA, ED*, 239; Greg O'Brien, "The Conqueror Meets the Unconquered: Negotiating Cultural Boundaries on the Post-Revolutionary Southern Frontier," *Journal of Southern History*, 67 (Feb. 2001), 39–72; Henry Knox to the President of the United States, War Office, July 7, 1789, in Thomas C. Cochran, gen'l ed., *The New American State Papers—Indian Affairs*, 13 vols. (Wilmington, Del.: Scholarly Resources, Inc., 1972), 6: 59–60.

26. Carson, *Searching for the Bright Path*, 38–39; F. de Borja Medina Rojas, *José de Ezpeleta Gobernador de la Mobila, 1780–1781* (Sevilla: Escuela de Estudios Hispano-Americanos, 1980), 651, 758, 761n.12. After Pensacola, Franchimastabé protested lack of sufficient British support and inadequate presents: "Talk by Franchimastabé Great Medal Chief of the Choctaw Nation. To Alexander Cameron, Esq. His Majesty's Superintendent At Six Mile Creek the 1st of April 1781," CO 5: 82, 377–78.

27. Manuel Gayoso de Lemos to Baron de Carondelet, Walnut Hills, July 21, 1793, AGI, PC, *leg.* 178, trans. in *PETHS* 34: 94–97.

28. Patricia Galloway, *Choctaw Genesis* (Lincoln: University of Nebraska Press, 1995), 1; Williams, *Linking Arms Together*, 21.

29. Tuskeatokamingo to [Dela]villebeuvre, Chickasaws, Apr. 2, 1793, AGI, PC, *leg.* 208, in *PETHS* 30 (1958), 102.

30. O'Brien, *Choctaws in a Revolutionary Age*, 55–69. See also Williams, *Linking Arms Together*, esp. 36–79.

31. Whitaker, *The Spanish American Frontier*, 26.

32. Ibid., 120–21; Manuel de Lanzos to Baron de Carondelet, Mobile, Apr. 25, 1793, in *SPT*, 4, pt. 3, 152–53; White, *Roots of Dependency*, 73.

33. O'Brien, *Choctaws in a Revolutionary Age*, 70–97; White, *Roots of Dependency*, 79–80.

CHAPTER 1. INITIAL AND SUSTAINED CONTACTS IN THE GULF SOUTH

1. Galloway, *Choctaw Genesis*, 181; Jack D. L. Holmes, "Andrés de Pez and Spanish Reaction to French Expansion into the Gulf of Mexico," in Patricia K. Galloway, ed., *La Salle and His Legacy: Frenchmen and Indians in the Lower Mississippi Valley* (Jackson: University Press of Mississippi, 1982), 106–28; William S. Coker, "The English Reaction to La Salle," in Galloway, ibid., 129–35. On encounters between Indians and Europeans with particular emphasis on Florida, see David Hurst Thomas, ed., *Columbian Consequences*, vol. 2, *Archaeological and Historical Perspectives on the Spanish Borderlands East* (Washington: Smithsonian Institution Press, 1990). On English expansion in the Carolinas and other parts of the South, see Verner W. Crane, *The Southern Frontier 1670–1732* (Ann Arbor: University of Michigan Press, 1929), 22–46, and Allan Gallay, *The Indian Slave Trade: The Rise of the English Empire in the American South, 1670–1717* (New Haven: Yale University Press, 2002). See also Williams, *Linking Arms Together*, 20–21.

2. Gallay, *The Indian Slave Trade*, 26, 34–35.

3. Patricia Galloway, "The Emergence of Historic Indian Tribes in the Southeast," in

Barbara Carpenter, ed., *Ethnic Heritage in Mississippi* (Jackson: University Press of Mississippi, 1992), 39.

4. James Axtell, *The Indians' New South: Cultural Change in the Colonial Southeast* (Baton Rouge: Louisiana State University Press, 1997), 5–24.

5. David Ewing Duncan, *Hernando de Soto: A Savage Quest in the Americas* (Norman: University of Oklahoma Press, 1996), xxxiv; Lewis Hanke, ed., *History of Latin American Civilization: Sources and Interpretations,* 2 vols., vol. 2, *The Colonial Experience* (Boston: Little, Brown and Company, 1967), 119–54.

6. Duncan, *Hernando de Soto,* 423–24; Robert Weddle, "European Interest in the Gulf Coast," in Carpenter, *Ethnic Heritage in Mississippi,* 106.

7. Cited in Calloway, *One Vast Winter Count,* 245.

8. Wilson, *Linking Arms Together,* 20. White uses the phrase *play-off* to describe the ways that Europeans and Indians dealt with one another; see *Roots of Dependency,* 90.

9. Williams, *Linking Arms Together,* 22.

10. William J. Eccles, *Essays on New France* (Toronto: Oxford University Press, 1987), 98, 164–65; Calloway, *One Vast Winter Count,* 245. Two important narratives of French expeditions along the Gulf coast and up the Mississippi River are Pierre Le Moyne d'Iberville, *Iberville's Gulf Journals,* trans. and ed. by Richebourg Gaillard McWilliams (Tuscaloosa: The University of Alabama Press, 1981), and [Jean Pénicault], *Fleur de Lys and Calumet: Being the Pénicault Narrative of French Adventure in Louisiana,* trans. and ed. by Richebourg Gaillard McWilliams (Tuscaloosa: The University of Alabama Press, 1953).

11. Jay Higginbotham, *Fort Maurepas: The Birth of Louisiana* (n.p., 1968), and Higginbotham, *Old Mobile: Fort Louis de la Louisiane, 1702–1711* (University: University of Alabama Press, 1977), 47–51; *Iberville's Gulf Journals,* 7–8, 11, 92–94, 157–60; Nellie M. Crouse, *Lemoyne d'Iberville: Soldier of New France* (Ithaca, N.Y.: Cornell University Press, 1954), 193; Jack D. Elliott, Jr., "The Fort at Natchez and the Colonial Origins of Mississippi," *Journal of Mississippi History* 52 (August 1990), 159–97

12. Galloway, *La Salle and His Legacy,* xiii; Glen Conrad, "Reluctant Imperialists: France in North America," in Galloway, ibid., 93–105.

13. White, *Roots of Dependency,* 53–68; Mary Ann Wells, *Native Land: Mississippi 1540–1798* (Jackson: University Press of Mississippi, 1994), 132–52.

14. Cayetano Alcazar Molina, *Lo virreinato en el siglo XVIII* (Barcelona, 1945), 140.

15. De Fina, "Rivalidades y contactos," 160–63; John Walton Caughey, *The American West: Frontier & Region* (Los Angeles: Ward Ritchie Press, 1969), 42–72, esp. 46.

16. "Parole des Iroquoix, Loups, et Chamaneux," Fort Bill (Fort Pitt), Oct. 2, 1763, in AHN, *leg.* 3882, *exp.* 9, copy in French signed by D'Abbadie, trans. by Robert L. Smith.

17. Alden, *John Stuart,* 224–29, 315.

18. John Walton Caughey, *Bernardo de Gálvez in Louisiana, 1776–1783* (Regents of the University of California, 1934; repr., Gretna, La.: Pelican Publishing Company, Inc., 1972), 135–214.

19. Bernardo de Gálvez to José de Gálvez, New Orleans, Jan. 28, 1777, N.° 3, AGI, SD, *leg.* 2566; Caughey, *Bernardo de Gálvez,* 85–101.

20. Elena Sánchez-Fabrés Mirat, *Situación histórica de las Floridas en la segunda mitad del siglo XVIII: Los problemas de una región de frontera* (Madrid: Ministerio de Asuntos Exteriores. Dirección General de Relaciones Culturales, 1977), 87.

21. Texts of several of these treaties in Vine Deloria, Jr., and Raymond J. DeMallie, *Documents of American Indian Diplomacy: Treaties, Agreements, and Conventions, 1775–1979,* 2 vols. (Norman: University of Oklahoma Press, 1999).

22. *The Federalist. A Commentary on the Constitution of the United States. Being a Collection of Essays written in Support of the Constitution agreed upon September 17, 1787, by the Federal Convention. From the original text of Alexander Hamilton, John Jay, and James Madison* (New York: The Modern Library, n.d.), 38–39.

23. Wallace, *Jefferson and the Indians,* 162–70, 177–80; Whitaker, *The Spanish-American Frontier,* 26–32, 47–62; Randolph Downes, "Indian Affairs in the Southwest Territory, 1790–1796," Tennessee Historical Magazine 3 (January 1937), 240–68; Sánchez-Fabrés Mirat, *Situación histórica de las Floridas,* esp. 67–76; Robert A. Williams, Jr., *The American Indian in Western Legal Thought: The Discourses of Conquest* (New York: Oxford University Press, 1990), 288.

24. *New American State Papers—Indian Affairs,* 6: 15.

25. Estevan Miró to Bernardo de Gálvez, New Orleans, Mar. 12, 1784, AGI, PC, *leg.* 3, trans. in *PETHS* 9 (1937), 115–16.

26. Whitaker, *Spanish-American Frontier,* 253.

27. The diplomacy of this treaty is the subject of Sanuel Flagg Bemis, *Pinckney's Treaty: America's Advantage from Europe's Distress, 1783–1800,* rev. ed. (New Haven: Yale University Press, 1960).

28. De Fina, "Rivalidades y contactos," ii; Manuel Gayoso de Lemos to the Príncipe de Paz [Godoy], New Orleans, June 6, 1798, MDAH, RG 26, SPT, vol. 5, reel 5, 571–74; Durouzeaux to Vicente Folch, Coweittaw [Coweta?], May 27, 1798, AGI, PC, *leg.* 208-A; Manuel Gayoso de Lemos to the Príncipe de Paz, New Orleans, June 6, 1798, N.° 22, AHN, *Estado, leg.* 3900, *exp.* 4.; Andrew Ellicott, *The Journal of Andrew Ellicott* (Chicago: Quadrangle Books, 1962, repr. of 1803 first edition); James Wilkinson, Benjamin Hawkins, Andrew Pickens to Henry Dearborn, Loftus Heights, Fort Adams, Dec. 18, 1800, in *ASP: IA,* 658–59.

29. Axtell, *The Indians' New South,* 46; Anthony F. C. Wallace, *The Death and Rebirth of the Seneca* (Anthony F. C. Wallace, 1969; New York: Vintage Books, 1972), 111–14.

CHAPTER 2. FORGING DIPLOMATIC PATHS

1. Timothy Silver describes ecological changes accompanying the advent of Europeans in *A New Country Face on the Countryside: Indians, colonists, and slaves in South Atlantic forests, 1500–1800* (Cambridge University Press, 1990). Usner characterizes the eighteenth-century region as a "frontier exchange economy" in *Indians, Settlers, & Slaves in a Frontier Exchange Economy,* 1–9.

2. Calloway, *One Vast Winter Count,* 313. On the education of Americans at Hopewell, see O'Brien, "The Conqueror Meets the Unconquered," 49. For Henry Knox and the formulation of American Indian policy, see Horsman, "The Indian Policy of an 'Empire for Liberty,'" 37–61, and Wallace, *Jefferson and the Indians,* 165–70.

3. Arturo O'Neill to the Marqués de Sonora, Pensacola, July 11, 1787, AHN, Estado, *leg.* 3888, *exp.* 1.

4. John R. Swanton, *The Indians of the Southeastern United States* (Washington: Smithsonian Institution Press, 1946, repr. 1979), 641–70; Robbie Ethridge, *Creek Country: The Creek Indians and Their World* (Chapel Hill: University of North Carolina Press, 2003), 25.

5. Ethridge, *Creek Country,* 23.

6. White, *The Middle Ground,* 413; José Antonio Armillas Vicente, "La Gran Confederación India: Interacción Hispano-Angloamericana con las naciones indias del Sudeste norteamericano a fines del S. XVIII," in *Estudios sobre política indigenista española en América,* II, *Evangelizacióm. Régimen de vida y ecología, servicios personales, encomiendas y tributos* (Val-

ladolid, 1976), 225–66. In contrast to White, Perdue argues for a much more cohesive unity and distinctiveness among native groups; see *Cherokee Women*, 7, 41–59. On the formation of "confederacies" or "coalescent societies" in response to French and English penetration, see Colin G. Calloway, *New Worlds for All: Indians, Europeans, and the Remaking of Early America* (Baltimore: Johns Hopkins University Press, 1997), 185, and Ethridge, *Creek Country*, 22–31.

7. Calloway, *The American Revolution in Indian Country*, 9; Perdue, *Cherokee Women*, 56.

8. Williams, *Linking Arms Together*, 36.

9. Perdue, *Cherokee Women*, 7, 41–59; Ethridge, *Creek Country*, 109–11.

10. Calloway, *New Worlds for All*, 120; Swanton, *The Indians of the Southeastern United States*, 121–23. See also Charles Hudson, *The Southeastern Indians* (copyright by Charles Hudson, 1976; University of Tennessee Press), 427–43. On Choctaw social and ceremonial life, see John R. Swanton, *Source Material for the Social and Ceremonial Life of the Choctaw Indians*, foreword by Kenneth H. Carleton (Tuscaloosa: The University of Alabama Press, 2001); O'Brien, *Choctaws in a Revolutionary Age*, 12–26.

11. Bernard Romans, *A Concise Natural History of East and West Florida* (New York, 1775; repr. Gretna, La.: Pelican Publishing Company, 1998, with introduction by Louise Richardson), 49. Delavillebeuvre counted sixty-seven in 1787; see "Noms des Villages de la grande Partie Petite Partie et Ceux [?] des Six Villages," J[ua]n. Delavillebeuvre, Grands Yasous, Nov. 2, 1787, AGI, PC, *leg.* 200. The Jesuit missionary Father Beaudouin reported in 1732 "forty-two villages of people who speak exclusively the same language": Beaudouin (Baudouin) to Maurepas, Chickasaway, Nov. 23, 1732, in *MPA, FD*, I, 155–63. Earlier, Henri de Tonti suggested well over forty: Patricia Galloway, "Henri de Tonti du village des Chacta, 1702: The Beginning of the French Alliance, in Galloway, ed. *La Salle and His Legacy*, 151. See also Galloway, *Choctaw Genesis*, 205–63.

12. At the turn of the eighteenth century the so-called Six Towns and Chickasawhay peoples may not have yet been part of the Choctaw group; see Galloway, *Choctaw Genesis*, 204, and "Henri de Tonti du village des Chacta, 1702," 146–75. Henry Knox located the Choctaws at the headwaters of the Pascagoula and Pearl rivers: General Knox, Secretary of War, to the President of the United States, War Office, July 7, 1789, *ASP: IA*, 59. O'Brien emphasizes a tripartite division of the Choctaws (western, eastern, and Sixtowns); see *Choctaws in a Revolutionary Age*, 13–14.

13. Galloway, *Choctaw Genesis*, 2; Carson, *Searching for the Bright Path*, 26–28.

14. Vaudreuil to Maurepas, New Orleans, Feb. 12, 1744, in *MPA: FD*, 4: 216.

15. Swanton, *The Indians of the Southeastern United States*, 116–19; Atkinson, *Splendid Land, Splendid People*, 1–24; Ethridge, *Creek Country*, 26.

16. Gen. Knox, Secretary of War, to the President of the United States, War Office, July 7, 1789, *ASP:IA*, 59.

17. Calloway, *American Revolution in Indian Country*, 213–21 (quote on 221); Swanton, *Indians of the Southeastern United States*, 116–19; Atkinson, *Splendid Land, Splendid People*, 97–98.

18. While noting divisions among the Chickasaws in the wars and diplomacy of the eighteenth century, Calloway finds that they remained essentially united; see *American Revolution in Indian Country*, 220. See also Atkinson, *Splendid Land, Splendid People*, esp. 100–19, and Atkinson, trans. and ed., "A Narrative of Malcolm McGee," 44–72.

19. Armillas Vicente, "La Gran Confederación India"; Gregory Evans Dowd, *A Spirited Resistance: The North American Indian Struggle for Unity, 1745–1815* (Baltimore: Johns Hopkins University Press, 1992), 90.

20. Swanton, *The Indians of the Southeastern United States,* 128, 153–54; Ethridge, *Creek Country,* 26–31, 92–119.

21. *The Collected Works of Benjamin Hawkins, 1796–1810,* ed. Thomas Foster (Tuscaloosa: The University of Alabama Press, 2003), 13s–85s. See also Crane, *The Southern Frontier, 1670–1732,* 36, 254; Braund, *Deerskins and Duffels,* 8–9. The Spanish commissioner to the Creeks, Pedro Olivier, reported the population of what he categorized as Upper Creek and Lower Creek towns at just over fifteen thousand: Pedro Olivier to Baron de Carondelet, Wetonka, December 1, 1793, in *SMV,* 4, pt. 3, 230–33. On seventeenth-century roots of a common Creek identity, see Joseph Hall, "Confederacy Formation on the Fringes of Spanish Florida," *Mediterranean Studies* 9 (2000), 123–41; Joseph Hall, personal communication, February 12, 2002.

22. *Collected Works of Benjamin Hawkins,* 24s; Braund, *Deerskins & Duffels,* 3–5; Ethridge, *Creek Country,* 26–31.

23. *Collected Works of Benjamin Hawkins,* 12s–15s; Mark Van Doren, ed., *Travels of William Bartram* (Macy-Masius, Publishers, 1928; repr. New York: Dover Publications, Inc., 1955), 366 67; Braund, *Deerskins & Duffels,* 3–5.

24. Braund, *Deerskins & Duffels,* 5; *Collected Works of Benjamin Hawkins,* 27s–31s; Ethridge, *Creek Country,* 27, 68.

25. Pedro Olivier to Baron de Carondelet, Mongulacha, June 11, 1793, in *SMV,* 4, pt. 3, 167–73; R. S. Cotterill, *The Southern Indians: The Story of the Civilized Tribes* (Norman: University of Oklahoma Press, 1954), 97; "*Message of Carondelet to Choctaws and Chickasaws,*" [1793], in *SMV,* 4, pt. 3, 140–41.

26. Michael D. Green, "The Creek Confederacy in the American Revolution," in William S. Coker and Robert R. Rea, eds., *Anglo-American Confrontation on the Gulf Coast During the American Revolution* (Pensacola, Fla.: Gulf Coast History and Humanities Conference, 1982), 57.

27. Braund, *Deerskins & Duffels,* 6.

28. Carolinians used the word Creek as a translation of "Muscogee," meaning land that is prone to flooding; ibid., 3; Saunt, *A New Order of Things,* 13; Gallay, *Indian Slave Trade,* 33.

29. The phrase often appearing in documents is "Talapuche o Crik."

30. Saunt, *New Order of Things,* 13; Henry Knox, Secretary of War, to the President of the United States, War Office, July 6, 1789, *New American State Papers, Indian Affairs,* 6: 17; Braund, *Deerskins & Duffels,* 7.

31. Document 15.

32. A. P. Whitaker, "Spain and the Cherokee Indians, 1783–98," *North Carolina Historical Review* 4 (July 1926), 253. Swanton describes the Cherokees as the "largest tribe in the Southeast, and belonging to the Iroquois family" in his *The Indians of the Southeastern United States,* 110–15.

33. Dowd, *A Spirited Resistance,* 90.

34. Duane H. King, ed., *The Cherokee Indian Nation: A Troubled History* (Knoxville: University of Tennessee Press, 1979), ix.

35. The first count comes from Stanley W. Hoig, *The Cherokees and Their Chiefs* (Fayettville: University of Arkansas Press, 1998), 4, the second from Betty Anderson Smith, "Distribution of Eighteenth-Century Cherokee Settlements," in King, *The Cherokee Nation,* 47.

36. Hudson, *Southeastern Indians,* 237–38.

37. Swanton, *Indians of the Southeastern United States,* 112; William G. McLoughlin, "Cherokee Anomie, 1794–1810: New Roles for Red Men, Red Women, and Black Slaves," in Peter C. Mancall and James H. Merrell, eds., *American Encounters: Natives and Newcomers from European Contact to Indian Removal, 1500–1850* (New York: Routledge, 2000), 453–54.

38. General Knox, the Secretary of War, to the President of the United States, War Office, July 7, 1789, *ASP, IA*, 38.

39. Cherokee names or titles for Bloody Fellow were Eskaqua or Clear Sky, the one used by the American land speculator and governor of the territory south of the Ohio, William Blount, and Nenetuyah. See Hoig, *Cherokees and Their Chiefs*, 63–64, 325; Coker and Watson, *Indian Traders*, 160. I will honor the Spanish use of Bloody Fellow or El hombre sangriente in their documents even though the name hardly seems to fit his peaceful diplomatic role in the 1790s.

40. A full report of the formalities associated with the visit to Philadelphia is in *ASP, IA*, 203–6. See also Horsman, *Expansion and American Indian Policy*, 73–75.

41. Discussed more fully in chapter 6.

CHAPTER 3. FORGING DIPLOMATIC PATHS

1. Calloway, *New Worlds for All*, esp. 115–33.

2. William N. Fenton, "Structure, Continuity, and Change in the Process of Iroquois Treaty Making," in Jennings, ed., *The History and Culture of Iroquois Diplomacy*, 3–36; Williams, *The American Indian in Western Legal Thought;* José Joaquín Real Díaz, *Estudio Diplomático del Documento Indiano* (Madrid: Dirección de Archivos Estatales, 1970); Mary A. Druke, "Iroquois Treaties: Common Forms, Varying Interpretations," in Jennings, *The History and Culture of Iroquois Diplomacy*, 85–90.

3. Mattingly, *Renaissance Diplomacy*, esp. 47–70.

4. DuVal, "'Faithful Nations' and 'Ruthless Savages,'" 57.

5. Alexis de Tocqueville's *Democracy in America* (various editions) and other observations about America in the late eighteenth and early nineteenth century support this point.

6. Pierre Clastres, *Society Against the State: The Leader as Servant and the Humane Uses of Power Among the Indians of the Americas*, trans. by Robert Hurley (New York: Mole Editions, Urizen Books, 1977), 1–20.

7. Galloway, "Henri de Tonti," in *La Salle and His Legacy*, 146–47.

8. DuVal, "'Faithful Nations' and 'Ruthless Savages,'" esp. 2; Williams, *Linking Arms Together*.

9. "Sobre la asamblea proyectada," no. 4, Manuel Gayoso de Lemos to Baron de Carondelet, Natchez, June 20, 1793, AGI, PC, *leg.* 2353.

10. John C. Ewers, "Symbols of Chiefly Authority in Spanish Louisiana," in John Francis McDermott, ed., *The Spanish in the Mississippi Valley, 1762–1804* (Urbana: University of Illinois Press, 1974), 272–84.

11. Alejandro O'Reilly to the Marqués de Grimaldi, New Orleans, Oct. 17, 1769, AGI, SD, *leg.* 2585; *SMV*, 3, pt 2, 98–103; Bibiano Torres Ramírez, *Alejandro O'Reilly en las Indias* (Sevilla: Escuela de Estudios Hispano-Americanos, 1969), 148–49; Vicente Rodríguez Casado, "O'Reilly en la Luisiana," *Revista de Indias* 2 (1941), 134; Alcazar Molina, *Lo virreinato en el siglo XVIII*, 145.

12. De Fina, "Rivalidades y contactos," 162–63.

13. Talks of Piomingo and Mingatushka, Hopewell, Jan. 9, 1786, *New American State Papers: Indian Affairs*, 6: 62 (the modern spelling of the name of the chief identified as Mingatushka is Minko' Tashka', a war chief title [personal communication, John Dyson, Dec. 9, 2004]; Wilbur R. Jacobs, "Wampum, the Protocol of Indian Diplomacy," *William and Mary Quarterly* 6 (Oct. 1949), 596–98 and his book, *Dispossessing the American Indian: Indians and Whites on the Colonial Frontier* (Norman: University of Oklahoma Press, 1972, 1985), 41–49.

See also Michael K. Foster, "Another Look at the Function of Wampum in Iroquois-White Councils," in Jennings, *The History and Culture of Iroquois Diplomacy,* 99–114.

14. Daniel K. Richter, *The Ordeal of the Longhouse: The Peoples of the Iroquois League in the Era of European Colonization* (Chapel Hill: University of North Carolina Press for the Omohundro Institute of Early American History and Culture, 1992), 47. See also Andrew R. L. Clayton, "'Noble Actors' upon 'The Theatre of Honor': Power and Civility in the Treaty of Greenville," in Andrew R. L. Clayton and Fredrika J. Teute, eds., *Contact Points: American Frontiers from the Mohawk Valley to the Mississippi, 1750–1830* (Chapel Hill: University of North Carolina Press for the Omohundro Institute of Early American History and Culture, The Newberry Library, Chicago, and The Historic New Orleans Collection, 1998), 254; O'Brien, "The Conqueror Meets the Unconquered," 39–72.

15. Ewers, "Symbols of Chiefly Authority in Spanish Louisiana," 272–84.

16. Juan Delavillebeuvre to Manuel Gayoso de Lemos, Boukfouka, Feb. 5, 1793, AGI, PC, *leg.* 208, trans. in *PETHS* 29 (1959), 149–50.

17. Fred Eggan, "Historical Changes in the Choctaw Kinship System," *American Anthropologist* 39 (1939), 35; Hudson, *Southeastern Indians,* 185.

18. Galloway, *Choctaw Genesis,* 2.

19. Cruzat to Miró, Aug. 23, 1784, *SMV,* 3, pt. 2, 117.

20. Manuel de Zéspedes to Juan de Prado, Pensacola, Oct. 1, 1761, AGI, SD, *leg.* 2585.

21. On the importance of kinship terms in Catawba discourse, see Merrell, *The Indians' New World,* 148; on the term *father* in Quapaw-European discourse, see Arnold, *Rumble of a Distant Drum,* 108–11. See also Williams, *Linking Arms Together,* 71–74; Gallay, *The Indian Slave Trade,* 108–10; Patricia Galloway, "'The Chief Who Is Your Father': Choctaw and French Views of the Diplomatic Relation," in Peter Wood, Gregory A. Waselkov, and M. Thomas Hatley, eds., *Powhatan's Mantle: Indians in the Colonial Southeast* (Lincoln: University of Nebraska Press, 1989), 254–78.

22. Michael P. Morris, *The Bringing of Wonder: Trade and the Indians of the Southeast, 1700–1783* (Westport: Greenwood Press, 1999), 2.

23. See, for example, Beaudouin, J. to Maurepas, Chickasawhay, Nov. 23, 1731, in *MPA: FD,* 1: 156–58. Merrell, *The Indians' New World,* 149–55.

24. Goods as gifts and goods as commodities and the values related to both are the subject of Lewis Hyde's *The Gift: Imagination and the Erotic Gift of Property* (New York: Vintage, 1969), esp. 56.

25. *Iberville's Gulf Journals,* 43.

26. Calloway, *One Vast Winter Count,* 349.

27. Antonio de Ulloa to the Marqués de Grimaldi, New Orleans, Mar. 31, 1766, N° 13, AGI, SD, *leg.* 2585. In addition to the Chickasaw delegation, more than fifteen hundred Choctaws attended the Mobile congress of 1771–72 and required provisions from the British. See Alden, *John Stuart and the Southern Colonial Frontier,* 322–23. Almost two thousand Choctaws and Chickasaws attended the 1784 meeting with the Spanish and required sustenance and gifts. AGI, PC, *leg.* 271.

28. "Governmental Expenses. 1767. Colony of Louisiana" in *SMV,* 2, pt. 1, 1, 18.

29. Carondelet to Gayoso, New Orleans, Mar. 5, 1793, AGI, PC, *leg.* 2353, in *PETHS* 31 (1959), 65.

30. Usner, *Indians, Settlers, & Slaves in a Frontier Exchange Economy,* 27.

31. Document 2; CO 5: 78.

32. James H. O'Donnell III, "Hamstrung by Penury: Alexander Cameron's Failure at Pensacola," in Coker and Rea, eds., *Anglo-American Confrontation,* 82.

33. CO 5: 81, 210. O'Donnell, "Hamstrung By Penury," 87; James A. Padgett, ed., "Bernardo

de Gálvez's Siege of Pensacola in 1781 (as related in Robert Farmar's Journal)," *Louisiana Historical Quarterly* 26 (Apr. 1943), 311–29; F. de Borja Medina Rojas, *José de Ezpeleta*, esp. 99–135, 301–93.

34. Williams, *Linking Arms Together*, 5.

35. Hyde, *The Gift*, 5.

36. Ethridge, *Creek Country*, 9–11; Saunt, *New Order of Things*, 32–63.

37. Charles A. Weeks, "Politics and Trade: Delavillebeuvre's 1787 Mission to the Choctaws and Journal," *Journal of Mississippi History* 65 (Spring 2003), 33–72, esp. 69–71.

38. Perdue, *Cherokee Women*, 81–82; Merrell, *The Indians' New World*, 63–65, 86–87; O'Brien, *Choctaws in a Revolutionary Age*, 88–89; Weeks, "Politics and Trade," 50–51.

39. Estevan Miró and Martín Navarro to the Marqués de Sonora, New Orleans, Mar. 24, 1787, AGI, PC, *leg.* 86-6-16, trans. in *PETHS* 11 (1939), 69.

40. Carondelet to Gayoso, New Orleans, Mar. 5, 1793, AGI, PC, *leg.* 2353, trans. in *PETHS* 31 (1959), 65.

41. James H. Merrell, *Into the Woods: Negotiators on the Pennsylvania Frontier* (New York: W. W. Norton and Company, 1999), esp. 19–41; Daniel H. Usner, Jr., "The Frontier Exchange Economy of the Lower Mississippi Valley in the Eighteenth Century," in Mancall and Merrell, ed., *American Encounters*, 217–39, esp. 224–26; Calloway, *American Revolution in Indian Country*, 16.

42. *Fleur de Lys and Calumet*; Patricia Galloway, "Talking with Indians: Interpreters and Diplomacy in French Louisiana," in Winthrop D. Jordan and Sheila L. Kemp, eds., *Race and Family in the Colonial South* (Jackson: University Press of Mississippi, 1987), 109–29.

43. Jack D. L. Holmes, "Juan de la Villebeuvre and Spanish Indian Policy in West Florida, 1784–1797," *Florida Historical Quarterly* 58 (April 1980), 387–99, esp. 392–99; Holmes, "Juan de la Villebeuvre: Spain's Commandant of Natchez During the American Revolution," *Journal of Mississippi History* 37 (1975), 97–129; Holmes, "Up the Tombigbee with the Spaniards: Juan de la Villebeuvre and the Treaty of Boucfouca (1793)," *Alabama Historical Quarterly* 40 (Spring and Summer 1978), 51–61.

44. Abraham P. Nasatir, *Spanish War Vessels on the Mississippi 1792–1796* (New Haven: Yale University Press, 1968), 254n.36; Atkinson, *Splendid Land, Splendid People*, 160.

45. Williams, *Linking Arms Together*, 31–67.

46. Estevan Miró to the Marqués de Sonora, New Orleans, June 1, 1787, AGI, PC, *leg.* 200, no. 12, trans. in *PETHS* 11 (1939), 79.

47. *Relaciones* in AGI, PC, *leg.* 271.

48. Galloway, "Talking with Indians," 117–18; O'Brien, *Choctaws in a Revolutionary Age*, 50–63; Kerlérec to Rouillé, August 29, 1753, in *MPA: FD*, 5: 130; Document 14.

49. Alden, *John Stuart and the Southern Colonial Frontier*, 201; Morris, *The Bringing of Wonder*, 137; Patricia Galloway, "'So Many Little Republics': British Negotiations with the Choctaw Confederacy, 1765," *Ethnohistory* 41 (Fall 1994), 513–37; O'Brien, *Choctaws in a Revolutionary Age*, 50–51.

50. Alden, *John Stuart and the Southern Colonial Frontier*, 321–23.

51. CO 5: 73.

52. Ibid.; Arnold, *Rumble of a Distant Drum*, 87–88.

53. O'Donnell, "Hamstrung by Penury," 76–80.

54. De Fina, "Rivalidades y contactos," 185–86.

55. CO 5: 78.

56. Pousuhama, "A Talk from the Six Towns in the Choctaw Nation to Capt. Cabert, Acting Commissary," Pousuhama, English Town, Nov. 19, 1779, CO 5: 78.

57. Arnold, *Rumble of a Distant Drum*, 100; DuVal, "'Faithful Nations,' and 'Ruthless

Savages,'" 75–107, quote from 88. To the north of the Quapaws the Osage proved intractable: DuVal, ibid., 107–16; Gilbert C. Din and A. P. Nasatir, *The Imperial Osages: Spanish-Indian Diplomacy in the Mississippi Valley* (Norman: University of Oklahoma Press, 1983).

58. Alden, *John Stuart and the Southern Colonial Frontier*, 240–41.

59. Vicente Armillas, "La Gran Confederación india," 248.

60. Alexander McGillivray to Arturo O' Neill, Little Talassie, Jan. 1, 1784, trans. and copy, AGI, SD, *leg.* 2611, *Relación* 216. See Michael D. Green, "Alexander McGillivray," in R. David Edmunds, ed., *American Indian Leaders: Studies in Diversity* (Lincoln: University of Nebraska Press, 1980), 41–63; Thomas D. Watson, "Strivings for Sovereignty: Alexander McGillivray, Creek Warfare and Diplomacy, 1783–1790," *Florida Historical Quarterly* 58 (Apr. 1980), 401; Saunt, *A New Order of Things*, 67–69; Caroline Maude Burson, *The Stewardship of Don Esteban Miró 1782–1792: A Study of Louisiana Based Largely on the Documents in New Orleans* (New Orleans: American Printing Company, Ltd., 1940), 48.

61. De Fina, "Rivalidades y contactos," 217–23; Horsman, *Expansion and American Indian Policy*, 24; Coker and Watson, *Indian Traders*, 55–56; Watson, "Strivings for Sovereignty," 403; Williams, *American Indian in Western Legal Thought*, 306.

62. Horsman, *Expansion and American Indian Policy*, 27–28; Cotterill, *The Southern Indians: The Story of the Civilized Tribes*, 57; Abernethy, *The South in the New Nation*, 60, 75; J. Leitch Wright, Jr., "Creek-American Treaty of 1790: Alexander McGillivray and the Diplomacy of the Old Southwest," *Georgia Historical Quarterly* 51 (1967), 383; Justin Winsor, *The Westward Movement: The Colonies and the Republic West of the Alleghenies, 1763–1799* (Boston and New York: Houghton Mifflin and Company, 1897), 327; Ethridge, *Creek Country*, 197.

63. Gilbert C. Din, *Francisco Bouligny: A Bourbon Soldier in Spanish Louisiana* (Baton Rouge: Louisiana State University Press, 1993), 141.

64. Sánchez-Fabrés Mirat, *Situación histórica de las Floridas*, 50. The letter is Bernardo del Campo to the Conde de Floridablanca, London, Nov. 16, 1783, N.° 28, AHN, Estado, *leg.* 3885, *exp.* 1.

65. Cruzat to Miró, Aug. 23, 1784, *SMV*, 3, pt. 2, 117.

66. Favre to Tugean [Turnbull?], Mobile, Dec. 4, 1783, *SMV*, 3, pt. 2, 92; Coker and Watson, *Indian Traders*, 8–14; Gilbert C. Din and John E. Harkins, *The New Orleans Cabildo: Colonial Louisiana's First City Government, 1769–1803* (Baton Rouge: Louisiana State University Press, 1996), 90; Caughey, *Bernardo de Gálvez*, 14, 17, 18.

67. DeFina, "Rivalidades y contactos," 277.

68. Sánchez-Fabrés Mirat, *Situación histórica de las Floridas*, 52–54; Instrucción sobre los límites de las Floridas y Luisiana y sobre la navegación del Mississippi por Floridablanca, San Ildefonso, June 29, 1784, AHN, *Estado, leg.* 3384; Estevan Miró to Bernardo de Gálvez, New Orleans, Mar. 12, 1784, AGI, PC, *leg.* 3, trans.in *PETHS* 9 (1937), 115–16.

69. De Fina, "Rivalidades y contactos," 256–74. Miró served as acting governor of Louisiana from 1782 to 1785, then as proprietary governor in 1785, serving in that capacity until 1791, when he was succeeded by the Baron de Carondelet. Navarro was intendant, chief treasury officer of the province, from 1780 to 1788; Din and Harkins, *New Orleans Cabildo*, 84n.2, 93–95.

70. Estevan Miró to Martín Navarro, New Orleans, Apr. 15, 1784, AGI, SD, *leg.* 2611; Sánchez Fabrés-Mirat, *Situación histórica de las Floridas*, 112.

71. Martín Navarro to José de Gálvez, New Orleans, Apr. 16, 1784, N.° 216, AGI, SD, *leg.* 2611.

72. Ibid.; McGillivray to Miró, Little Tallassie, May 1, 1784, in *SMV*, 3, pt. 2, 101; Burson, *The Stewardship of Don Esteban Miró*, 51–52.

73. Martín Navarro to José de Gálvez, New Orleans, July 27, 1784, N.° 239, AGI, SD, *leg.* 2611; Burson, *The Stewardship of Don Esteban Miró,* 51–53.

74. "Instrucciones a que deberá conformarse Don Alexandro McGillivray Comisario por la Nación Española en la Nación Talapuche," New Orleans, July 20, 1784, AGI, PC, *leg.* 2360, *copia,* typescript in LC.

75. *PETHS* 9 (1937), 121n.16; Coker and Watson, *Indian Traders,* 59–71, 126; Burson, *The Stewardship of Don Esteban Miró,* 59; Saunt, *New Order of Things,* 76.

76. Navarro to Gálvez, New Orleans, July 27, 1784, N.° 239,AGI, SD, *leg.* 2611; Congreso, Mobila, Relaciones, AGI, PC, *leg.* 271; De Fina, "Rivalidades y contactos," 194; Burson, *The Stewardship of Don Esteban Miró,* 53.

77. Burson, *The Stewardship of Don Esteban Miró,* 55, 58.

78. Coker and Watson, *Indian Traders,* 71; Estevan Miró and Martín Navarro to Antonio Valdés, New Orleans, Apr. 1, 1788, AGI, PC, leg. 86-6-8, trans. in *PETHS* 14 (1942), 97.

79. [William] Panton to [Baron de] Carondelet, Pensacola, November 6, 1792, AGI, PC, *leg.* 177, in *PETHS* 28 (1955), 132–33.

80. Carson, *Searching for the Bright Path,* 40; O'Brien, "The Conqueror Meets the Unconquered"; Atkinson, *Splendid Land Splendid People,* 128–29.

81. The Georgia treaties were Augusta (1783), Shoulder Bone (1785), and Galphinton (1786). See Sánchez-Fabrés Mirat, *Situación histórica de las Floridas,* 69; Coker and Watson, *Indian Traders,* 79.

82. Alexander McGillivray to Estevan Miró Little Tallassie, May 1, 1786, AGI, PC, *leg.* 2352, trans. in *PETHS* 10 (1938), 131–35; Ben James to Vicente Folch, Nación Chactá, Apr. 22, 1789, *traducción;* Alexander McGillivray to Vicente Folch, Pequeño Talassie, Apr. 22, 1789, *traducción;* both included with Estevan Miró to Antonio Valdés, New Orleans, May 20, 1789, AGI, SD, *leg.* 2553.

83. Wright, "Creek-American Treaty of 1790"; Sánchez-Fabrés Mirat, *Situación histórica de las Florídas,* 72–73; Horsman, *Expansion and American Indian Policy,* 72.

84. Herman Melville, *The Confidence Man,* many editions.

85. On Bowles see J. Leitch Wright, *William Augustus Bowles: Director General of the Creek Nation* (Athens: University of Georgia Press, 1967), and William C. Sturtevant, "The Cherokee Frontiers: The French Revolution, and William Augustus Bowles," in King, *Cherokee Indian Nation,* 61–91.

CHAPTER 4. THE NOGALES DISPUTE

1. Armillas Vicente, "La gran confederación india," 225–26; Elliott, "City and Empire: The Spanish Origins of Natchez," 271–77.

2. Estevan Miró to Antonio Valdés, New Orleans, May 20, 1789, N.° 38, Reserved, AHN, *Estado, leg.* 3887, *exp.* 1; Jack D. L. Holmes, "Notes on the Spanish Fort San Estevan de Tombecbé," *The Alabama Review* (October 1965), 281–82.

3. O'Brien, *Choctaws in a Revolutionary Age,* 1–3, 28–30, 40–41, 55–56, 72–73.

4. Georgia designated thirteen justices of the peace to organize the county's government. Four of them were present in 1785 to receive their commissions: Thomas Green, William Davenport, Nicholas Long, and Nathaniel Christmas. See Coker and Watson, *Indian Traders,* 77.

5. Quoted in Gilbert C. Din, "War Clouds on the Mississippi: Spain's 1785 Crisis in West Florida," *Florida Historical Quarterly* 60 (July 1981), 51.

6. Ibid., 51–76; Din, *Francisco Bouligny,* 143–53.

7. Estevan Miró to Francisco Bouligny, New Orleans, Dec. 21, 1785, AGI, PC, *leg.* 3, trans. in *PETHS* 9 (1937), 141; Estevan Miró to Alexander McGillivray, New Orleans, Apr. 26, 1786, AGI, PC, *leg.* 4, trans. in *PETHS* 10 (1938), 130–31; Estevan Miró to Carlos de Grand-Pré, New Orleans, May 11, 1786, AGI, PC, *leg.* 4, trans. in ibid., 141.

8. O'Brien, "The Conqueror Meets the Unconquered," 45.

9. "An Act Creating Bourbon County," Feb. 7, 1785, in *SMV,* 3, pt. 2, 120–22; Edward C. Burnett, "Papers relating to Bourbon County, Georgia, 1785–1786," *American Historical Review* 15 (Oct. 1909–July 1910), 66–111, 297–353; Sánchez-Fabrés Mirat, *Situación histórica de las Floridas,* 96, 133; Din, "War Clouds on the Mississippi," 52–53; Whitaker, *The Spanish-American Frontier,* 126–29; Abernethy, *The South in the New Nation,* 74–101; Horsman, "Indian Policy of an 'Empire for Liberty,'" 47; Wallace, *Jefferson and the Indians,* 165–70; Estevan Miró to Antonio Valdés, New Orleans, Aug. 10, 1790, transcript copy in MDAH, RG 26, SPT, ledger 3, reel 3, 458–76.

10. Richard Slotkin examines the emergence of a myth of the frontier in political rhetoric, literature, and film in three books: *Regeneration through Violence: The Mythology of the American Frontier, 1600–1860* (Norman: University of Oklahoma Press, 1973); *The Fatal Environment: The Myth of the Frontier in an Age of Industrialization* (Norman: University of Oklahoma Press, 1985); and *Gunfighter Nation: The Myth of the Frontier in Twentieth-Century America* (New York: Harper Perennial, 1993).

11. Wallace, *Jefferson and the Indians,* 164.

12. Horsman, *Expansion and American Indian Policy,* 49.

13. Francis S. Philbrick, *The Rise of the West, 1754–1830* (New York: Harper and Row, 1965), 166; "An Ordinance for the regulation of Indian Affairs," Aug. 7, 1786, in *ASP: IA,* 15. On the same date as the ordinance, a public notice appeared stating that only citizens of the United States "will be permitted in the future to reside among or trade with any Indian nation whatever southward of the River Ohio." See broadside in The Draper Manuscript Collection, Series U, Georgia, Alabama, and South Carolina Papers; Sánchez-Fabrés Mirat, *Situación histórica de las Floridas,* 66–67; McGillivray to O'Neill, Little Talassie, Apr. 11, 1787, AGI, PC, *leg.* 202, in *PETHS* 11 (1939), 71n.20; Randolph C. Downes, "Creek-American Relations, 1782–1790," *Georgia Historical Quarterly* 21 (June 1937), 165.

14. Estevan Miró to the Marqués de Sonora, New Orelans, June 1, 1787, AGI, SD, *leg.* 2352; James O'Fallon to Estevan Miró, Crabb-Orchard (Kentucky), Feb. 18, 1791, in *SMV,* 3, pt. 2, 401–3.

15. Diego de Gardoqui was born into a family of important Bilbao merchants. See María Jesús Cava y Begoña Cava, *Diego María de Gardoqui: Un bilbaino en la diplomacia del siglo XVIII* (Bilbao: BBK-Bilbao Bizkaia Kutxa, n.d.), 17, 32–42; Whitaker, *Spanish-American Frontier,* 63–77.

16. James Wilkinson to the Baron de Carondelet, Fort Jefferson, Feb. 26, 1794, AGI, PC, *leg.* 2374, repr. in *PETHS* 38 (1966), 73. Wilkinson had reported the rumors to Carondelet in [James] Wilkinson to [Manuel] Gayoso[de Lemos], Fort Washington, Dec. 17, 1792, AGI, PC, *leg.* 2374, in *PETHS* 28 (1955), 142–43. José Navarro Latorre and Fernando Solano Costa argue that what Americans later often saw as a Spanish conspiracy was in fact an American one: *¿Conspiración española? 1787–1789. Contribución al estudio de las primeras realciones históricas entre España y los Estados Unidos de Norteamérica* (Zaragoza: Institución Fernando el Católico, 1949).

17. Estevan Miró to Arturo O'Neill, New Orleans, May 4, 1787, AGI, PC, *leg.* 4, trans. in *PETHS* 11 (1939), 73–74.

18. De Fina, "Rivalidades y contactos," 299; Braund, *Deerskins & Duffels,* esp. 178.

19. Downes, "Creek-American Relations, 1782–1790," 156–60; "A Copy of the talk given in the Choctaw Nation by William Davenport," enclosed with Vicente Folch to Estevan Miró, Mobile, Aug. 21, 1787, N.° 12, AGI, PC, *leg.* 52.

20. "Palabra dicha en el Yazu el 19 de marzo de 1787," n.° 2, enclosed with Estevan Miró to the Marqués de Sonora, New Orleans, June 1, 1787, AGI, SD, *leg.* 2552, no. 10; also in AHN, *leg.* 3887, *exp.* 1, trans. in *PETHS* 11 (1939), 76–77. Most of what Juzan recorded is reproduced in Serrano y Sanz, *España y los indios cherokis y chactas,* 32–34.

21. James tried to explain his position in a long letter to Mather and Strother to whom the Spanish had given the task of supplying the Choctaw and Chickasaw trade. James was one of their traders and, with John Joyce, was for a time in charge of the store in Mobile. He admitted that both he and Davenport had been appointed by the State of Georgia to act for it but that he had done so in large part as a kind of ruse to recover some "Negroes" taken from him by an American from whom the Spanish had seized property at Natchez. The American regarded James as a Spanish commissioner. James told Mather and Strother that he should be regarded as a "Spanish subject and pay no regard to Davenport, for he was only a Bankrupt and to that Purpose upon which I desired him to take the Comitons and Papers and return from whence he came." Ben'n James to Mess'rs Mather & Strother, Choctaw Nation, July 23, 1787, AGI, PC, *leg.* 200, in *PETHS* 11 (1939), 86. Downes writes that James was appointed to replace John Wood as Georgia's agent in the Choctaw nation in "Creek-American Relations, 1782–1790," 155. As late as 1792, being identified as "an American" rankled James. In a letter to William Blount, governor of the southern territory, James said that "every white man in this nation must be dependent to the Spanish government. If you are not sensible of it, you must have heard that the Spaniards are a jealous people, and I have always been pointed out as an American. But I have been true to the power that protected me; but the whole is, I am protected at my own expense. My reason of speaking to you in this manner is that I have received several insults from the Creeks, and obliged to put up with it. For what reason? Because I am not able to help myself"; Ben James to Governor Blount, Choctaw Nation, June 30, 1792, *ASP: IA,* 284.

22. Samuel Dorris Dickinson, trans., *Spain and the Cherokee and Choctaw Indians in the Second Half of the Eighteenth Century by Manuel Serrano y Sanz* (Idabel, Okla.: Potsherd Press, Museum of the Red River, 1995), 25–26.

23. Estevan Miró to Pedro Favrot, New Orleans, May 15, 1787, AGI, PC., *leg.* 4, trans. in *PETHS* 11 (1939), 75; Pedro Juzan, "Palabra dicha en el Yazu el 19 de marzo de 1787," enclosure no. 2 in Estevan Miró to the Marqués de Sonora, New Orleans, June 1, 1787, *reservada* #10, AHN, Estado, *leg.* 3887, *exp.* 1; Serrano y Sanz, *España y los indios cherokis y chactas,* 32–34. The English translation of the Serrano y Sanz text omits Franchimastabé's speech. See Dickinson, *Spain and the Cherokee and Choctaw Indians,* 25–26.

24. Alexander McGillivray to Estevan Miró, Little Tallassie, July 25, 1787, AGI, PC, *leg.* 200, trans. in *PETHS* 11 (1939), 88–89; Benjamin James to John Joyce, Choctaw Nation, July 23, 1787, AGI, PC, *leg.* 52, trans. in ibid., 87. John Joyce and John Turrnbull were in charge of Mather and Strother's store in Mobile. See also Ben'n James to Mess'rs Mather and Strother, Choctaw Nation, July 23, 1787, AGI, PC, *leg.* 200, trans. in ibid., 86. A trader, Andrew Frazer, reported that Americans had finally persuaded "Headmen of the Chie Nation" to make them a cession of land on the Chickasaw Bluffs along the Mississippi River, "where a number of Battoes with Indian Goods are arrived." Alexander Frazer to Gov'r O'Neill, Yazoo, June 12, 1787, enclosed with Arturo O'Neill to Estevan Miró, Pensacola, July 18, 1787, AGI, PC, *leg.* 37, trans. in ibid., 84–85; Atkinson, *Splendid Land, Splendid People,* 134; Downes, "Creek-American Relations, 1782–1790," 160.

25. De Fina, "Rivalidades y contactos," 337; Whitaker, *Spanish-American Frontier,* 63–77.

26. Coker and Watson, *Indian Traders,* 99–101.

27. De Fina, "Rivalidades y contactos," 194; Holmes, "Juan de la Villebeuvre and Spanish Indian Policy in West Florida," 392.

28. Estevan Miró to the Marqués de Sonora, New Orleans, June 1, 1787, *Reservado,* N.° 10 AGI, PC, *leg.* 2552; Juan Delavillebeuvre to His Christian Majesty, New Orleans, February 24, 1792, attached to Luis de las Casas to the Conde de Campo Alange, Havana, Mar. 1, 1792, AGI, SD, *leg.* 2560; Burson, *The Stewardship of Don Esteban Miró,* 60.

29. "Instrucción que debe observar Don Juan de La Villebeuvre, Capitán del Regimiento fijo de esta plaza que pasa comisionado a la Nación Chacta para responder a la representación que hace hecho sus Jefes y los de Chicachas solicitando se remedie el que en la Movila no le rechasen tantos pieles y que se observe la tarifa," transcript in MDAH, RG 26, SPT, reel 5, doc. 6, ledger 3, 163–70.

30. "Journal of Jean [Juan] Delavillebeuvre," trans. by Robert L. Smith in Weeks, "Politics and Trade," 63–72.

31. Ibid.

32. Ibid.; Estevan Miró to Antonio Valdés, New Orleans, May 20, 1789, N.° 38, *Reservado,* AGI, SD, *leg.* 2553. Romans reports being housed by a Ben James in Chickasawhay in the early 1770s in Romans, *A Concise Natural History of East and West Florida,* 207.

33. Coker and Watson, *Indian Traders,* 168. James also raised cattle. James to Gayoso, Chactaw Nation, Sept. 4, 1792, AGI, PC, *leg.* 41, in *PETHS* 28 (1955), 127.

34. "Respuesta de Franchimastabé a la Harenga que el Capitán Don Juan de la Villebeuvre hizo en la Aldea del Yazu el día 1.° de noviembre del año de 1787," copia n.° 1, AGI, PC, *leg.* 177-B.

35. "Respuesta de Mingo-huma de la aldea de Okelusas in nombre de toda la pequeña partida," ibid.

36. "Respuesta hecha por Chetonaque Gefe de Gran Medalla en nombre de los Gefes de las Seis Aldeas," ibid.

37. "Harenga de Taskietoka Rey de los Chicachas en presencia del refirido Sr. Governador, el 3 de enero de 1788," copia, AGI, SD, *leg.* 2554; "Harenga de Yagane huma Jefe de Gran Medalla de la Gran Partida 2.° de Franchimastabé principal de ella en presencia del Sr. Gob. Don Estevan Miró el 3 de enero de 1788. Interpretada por Luis Forneret, copia N.° 2, ibid., also in AGI, PC, *leg.* 177-B.

38. Delavillebeuvre, "Journal," in Weeks, "Politics and Trade," 67.

39. Jack D. L. Holmes, *Gayoso: The Life of a Spanish Governor in the Mississippi Valley, 1789–1799* (Baton Rouge: Louisiana State University Press, 1965, repr. Gloucester, Mass.: Peter Smith, 1968), 4, 9–10; Jack D. Elliott, Jr., "The Spanish Origins of Natchez," *Journal of Mississippi History* 59 (Winter 1997), 271–321.

40. Estevan Miró to Domingo Cabello, New Orleans, Jan. 18, 1790, AGI, PC, *leg.* 86, 6–17, trans. in *PETHS* 22 (1950), 132n.13, and Domingo Cabello to Antonio Valdés, Havana, Feb. 26, 1790, trans. in ibid., 142.

41. Clayton, "'Noble Actors' upon 'the Theatre of Honor': Power and Civility in the Treaty of Greenville," in Clayton and Teute, eds., *Contact Points,* 249; Abernethy, *The South in the New Nation,* 78.

42. Armillas Vicente, "La gran confederación india," 253; James Wilkinson to Alexander Moultier [*sic*], Isaac Huger, Major William Snipes, and T. Washington, Lexington, Jan. 4, 1790, *PETHS* 20 (1948), 128–30; Wilkinson to Miró, Lexington, January 26, 1790, AHN, *Estado, leg.* 3898, *exp.* 4, also in *PETHS* 22 (1950), 133–39; Abernethy, *The South in the New*

Nation, 64, 78–85; Estevan Miró to Antonio Valdés, New Orleans, Aug. 10, 1790, transcript of letter and enclosures in MDAH, MPA, SPT, ledger 3, reel 3, 458–76.

43. Estevan Miró to Domingo Cabello, New Orleans, May 19, 1790, AHN, *Estado, leg.* 3898, *exp.* 4.

44. Luis de Las Casas to Estevan Miró, Havana, Nov. 20, 1790, AGI, PC, *leg.* 1446.

45. John Williams to Manuel Gayoso de Lemos, Jan. 16, 1791, enclosed in Manuel Gayoso de Lemos to Estevan Miró, Natchez, Jan. 17, 1791, AGI, PC, *leg.* 41.

46. See the "Fuerte de los Nogales, proyectado y delineado por el coronel don Manuel Gayoso de Lemos, gobernador de la plaza y distrito de Natchez," AGI, PC, *leg.* 1439; Julio González, *Catálogo de mapas y planos de la Florida y de la Luisiana* (Madrid: Dirección general del patrimonio artístico, archivos y museos, 1979), #140, 53.

47. Estevan Miró to Elías Beauregard, New Orleans, Feb. 12, 1791, AGI, PC, *leg.* 17.

48. Manuel Gayoso de Lemos to Estevan Miró, Natchez, Feb. 13, 1791, AGI, PC, *leg.* 41, no. 12, and Mar. 12, 1791, ibid., no. 41.

49. Manuel Gayoso de Lemos, "Instrucciones y orden de marcha que deberá observar el Comboy que sale de este Puesto para los Nogales," Natchez, Mar. 22, 1791, AGI, PC, *leg.* 41.

50. Manuel Gayoso de Lemos to Estevan Miró, Bayu Pierre, abordo de la flecha, Mar. 27, 1791, N.° 51, ibid.; Manuel Gayoso de Lemos to Estevan Miró, Natchez, May 12, 1791, N.° 89, ibid.

51. John Girault was born in London. He was with George Rogers Clark on his 1778 western expedition during the American Revolution and settled in the Natchez district in the 1780s, where he became a major landowner. He knew both French and Spanish and served as "the King's translator" until 1794. See *Biographical and Historical Memoirs of Mississippi* (Chicago: Goodspeed Publishing Co., 1891), 2 vols., 1: 672.

52. Manuel Gayoso de Lemos to Estevan Miró, Natchez, May 10, 1791, N.° 84, AGI, PC, *leg.* 2352; Document 1.

53. "Fuerte de los Nogales, proyectado y delineado por el coronel don Manuel Gayoso de Lemos, goberandor de la plaza y distrito de Natchez," AGI, PC, *leg.* 1439.

54. For a discussion of the *galiot* and other vessels used by the Spanish on the Mississippi River, see Nasatir, *Spanish War Vessels on the Mississippi,* esp. 30n.

55. Document 1.

CHAPTER 5. DIPLOMACY OF THE NOGALES DISPUTE

1. Document 2.

2. Document 3. See also Jack D. L. Holmes, "Stephen Minor: Natchez Pioneer," *Journal of Mississippi History* 42 (Feb. 1980), 17–26; Holmes, *Gayoso,* 41, 50–51, 146–47, 147n. Ebenezer Fulson was the brother of Nathaniel Fulson, both of whom worked as traders and married Choctaw women. Ebenezer worked for the Panton, Leslie firm of Pensacola; see Carson, *Searching for the Bright Path,* 44–45

3. Document 3.

4. Eighteenth-century documents record many chiefs with this title, spelled variously, as with all names or titles Europeans recorded. The French transcribed the Choctaw as "Soulouche Oumastabé," which was part of a war chief title. A French translation was "Soulier Rouge." See *MPA, FD,* 4, 16–17n; Cyrus A. Byington, *A Dictionary of the Choctaw Language* (Washington, D.C.: Smithsonian Institution, Bureau of American Ethnology, 1931), Bulletin 46.

5. Document 4.

6. Document 3; O'Brien, *Choctaws in a Revolutionary Age*, 89; Panton to Carondelet, Pensacola, Nov. 6, 1792, AGI, PC, *leg.* 41, in *PETHS* 28 (1955), 132; Coker and Watson, *Indian Traders*, 94–95, 102–9.

7. Document 3.

8. Ibid.

9. Manuel Gayoso de Lemos to Estevan Miró, Natchez, July 1, 1791, copy, AGI, SD, *leg.* 2556.

10. Document 3.

11. Ibid.

12. Document 5.

13. Ibid.; Manuel Gayoso de Lemos to Baron de Carondelet, Natchez, Mar. 24, 1792, N.° 14, AGI, PC, *leg.* 41.

14. Stephen Minor to Manuel Gayoso de Lemos, Natchez, Oct. 27, 28, 1791, AGI, PC, *leg.* 46.

15. Manuel Gayoso de Lemos to Baron de Carondelet, Natchez, Apr. 2, 1792, N.° 27, AGI, PC, *leg.* 2353.

16. Manuel Gayoso de Lemos to Elías Beauregard, Natchez, July 7, 1791, AGI, PC, *leg.* 41; Manuel Gayoso de Lemos to the Baron de Carondelet, New Orleans, Jan. 31, 1792, AGI, PC, *leg.* 2353.

17. Manuel Gayoso de Lemos to Baron de Carondelet, New Orleans, Jan. 17, 1792, AGI, PC, *leg.* 2353.

18. Document 6; Manuel Gayoso de Lemos to Baron de Carondelet, Natchez, March 24, 1792, N.° 12, ibid., printed in [Manuel Serrano y Sanz, ed.], *Documentos históricos de la Florida y la Luisiana. Siglos XVI al XVIII* (Madrid: Librería General de Victoriano Suárez, 1912), 406–7.

19. Manuel Gayoso de Lemos to Taskietoka, Natchez, Mar. 21, 1792, enclosure #3 with Manuel Gayoso de Lemos to Baron de Carondelet, Natchez, Mar. 24, 1792, N.°12, AHN, *Estado, leg.* 3885 *bis, exp.* 7; Estevan Minor to Manuel Gayoso de Lemos, Natchez, Dec. 12, 1791, AGI, PC, *leg.* 204, trans. in *PETHS* 26 (1954), 66.

20. Manuel Gayoso de Lemos to Estevan Minor, Natchez, Mar. 13, 1792, AHN, *Estado, leg.* 3883, printed in [Serrano y Sanz], *Documentos históricos de la Florida y la Luisiana*, 407–14, also enclosed with Manuel Gayoso de Lemos to Baron de Carondelet, Natchez, Mar. 24, 1792, AGI, PC, *leg.* 2353.

21. Estevan Minor to Manuel Gayoso de Lemos, Bayu Pierre, March 17, 1792, also enclosed with Manuel Gayoso de Lemos to the Baron de Carondelet, Natchez, Mar. 24, 1792, AGI, PC, *leg.* 2353.

22. Manuel Gayoso de Lemos to Estevan Minor, Natchez, Mar. 24, 1792, N.° 24, AHN, *Estado, leg.* 3885 bis, exp. 7, reprinted as "Carta en que D. Manuel Gayoso de Lemos da nuevas instrucciones a D. Esteban Minor," Natchez, Mar. 24, 1792, in [Serrano y Sanz], *Documentos históricos de la Florida y la Luisiana*, 416–18.

23. Baron de Carondelet to Juan Delavillebeuvre, New Orleans, Mar. 28, 1792, AGI, PC, *leg.* 18.

24. Baron de Carondelet to Franchimastabé, New Orleans, Mar. 23, 1792, copy enclosed with Baron de Carondelet to the Conde de Floridablanca, New Orleans, Mar. 29, 1792, N.° 17, AHN, *Estado, leg.* 3898, *exp.* 5.

25. Baron de Carondelet to Manuel Gayoso de Lemos, New Orleans, Mar. 29, 1792, AGI, PC, *leg.* 18.

26. Document 7.

27. Ibid.

28. Ibid. Coker and Watson describe Franchimastabé as "a master extortionist of gifts": *Indian Traders,* 78.

29. Document 7.

30. Ibid.

31. Manuel Gayoso de Lemos to Baron de Carondelet, Natchez, Apr. 20, 1792, and enclosed with Baron de Carondelet to Conde de Floridablanca, New Orleans, May 4, 1792, N.° 26, *Reservado,* AHN, *Estado, leg.* 3898, *exp.* 5.

32. Manuel Gayoso de Lemos to the Chickasaw King, Natchez, AGI, PC, *leg.* 2353.

33. Manuel Gayoso de Lemos to Baron de Carondelet, Natchez, April 3, 1792, copy, N.° 33, enclosed with Baron de Carondelet to Conde de Floridablanca, New Orleans, Apr. 7, 1792, *Reservado,* AHN, *leg.* 3898, *exp.* 5.

34. Manuel Gayoso de Lemos to Baron de Carondelet, Natchez, Apr. 14, 1792, N.° 2, *Reservado, copia,* enclosed with Baron de Carondelet to Conde de Floridablanca, New Orleans, Apr. 21, 1792, N.° 24, *Reservado,* AHN *Estado, leg.* 3893, *exp.* 5.

35. Ibid.

36. Ibid.

37. Ibid.

38. Ibid.; Wright, *William August Bowles,* vii, 13; Saunt, *New Order of Things,* 86–87.

39. Manuel Gayoso de Lemos to Carondelet, Natchez, Apr. 14, 1792, N.°2, *Reservado,* copy, enclosed with Baron de Carondelet to Conde de Floridablanca, New Orleans, Apr. 21, 1792, N.° 24, *Reservado,* AHN, *Estado, leg.* 3898, *exp.* 5.

40. Ibid.

41. Henry Knox to the Chiefs and Warriors of the Choctaw Nation, Philadelphia, Feb. 17, 1792; William Blount to the chiefs and warriors of the Choctaw Nation, Apr. 21, 1792; Payemingo to the King of the Choctaw Nation Franchimastabé and English Will of the Choctaws, in *SMV,* 4, pt. 3, 4–8.

42. Swanton, *The Indians of the Southeastern United States,* 674–86; Document 10.

43. Document 10.

44. Ibid.; Minor to Gayoso, Natchez, Dec. 12, 1791, trans. in *PETHS* 26 (1954), 66.

45. Document 10.

46. Delavillebeuvre to the Chickasaw Nation, Boukfouka, Mar. 22, 1793, AGI, PC, *leg.* 208, trans. in *PETHS* 30 (1958), 99.

47. Document 10.

48. Ibid.

49. Ibid.

50. Anthony Forster to Governor Blount, July 29, 1792, enclosed with Governor Blount to the Secretary of War, Knoxville, Sept. 20, 1792, in *ASP: IA,* 282–84.

51. Ben James to Governor Blount, Choctaw Nation, June 30, 1792, in ibid., 284.

CHAPTER 6. PATHS TO BOUKFOUKA AND THE TOMBIGBEE

1. Manuel Gayoso de Lemos to the Conde de Aranda, Natchez, July 5, 1792, N.° 1, AHN, *Estado, leg.* 3885 *bis, exp.* 7. and "Estado político de la Provincia de la Luisiana expuesto por Coronel Don Manuel Gayoso de Lemos Governador de la Plaza y Districto de Natchez," AGI, PC, *leg.* 2353. Gayoso's essay exists in English translation as "The Political Condition of the Province of Louisiana Described by Colonel Don Manuel Gayoso [de Lemos] Governor of the Place and Districts of Natchez," in James Alexander Robertson, ed., *Louisiana Under the*

Rule of Spain, France, and the United States 1785–1807: Social, Economic, and Political Conditions of the Territory represented in the Louisiana Purchase, 2 vols. (pub. 1910–11; repr. in 2 vols., Freeport, N.Y.: Books for Libraries Press, 1969), 1: 271–89. See also Abernethy, *The South in the New Nation,* 59–73, 136–68.

2. Philbrick, *The Rise of the West, 1754–1830,* 148–49; Dowd, *A Spirited Resistance,* 104–7.

3. Horsman, "The Indian Policy of Empire for Liberty", in Hoxie et al., *Native Americans and the New Republic,* 45–47.

4. *ASP, IA,* 245–48; Coker and Watson, *Indian Traders,* 160.

5. Anthony Foster to Governor Blount, July 29, 1792; "Governor Blount to the Headmen and Chiefs of the Chickasaws and Choctaws," Nashville, Aug. 7, 1792, in *ASP: IA,* 282–85.

6. Gayoso, "Estado político de la Provincia de la Luisiana."

7. Ibid.; Arturo O'Neill to the Conde de Gálvez, Pensacola, Oct. 11, 1786, AGI, PC, *leg.* 2357, trans. in *PETHS* 10 (1938), 150; Weeks, "Politics and Trade," 33–72.

8. Downes, "Creek-American Relations, 1782–1790," 182–84; Saunt, *A New Order of Things,* 80.

9. Gayoso, "Estado político." "Providence" was New Providence in the Bahamas on which the town of Nassau was located. For more on Wilkinson, see Bemis, *Pinkney's Treaty,* 109–25.

10. Gayoso, "Estado politico"; Document 10; Manuel Gayoso de Lemos to Baron de Carondelet, Natchez, July 21, 1792, N.° 11, Archivo Nacional de Cuba, *leg.* 2, trans. in *PETHS* 27 (1955), 87–90.

11. Ibid.; Willliam Panton to Arturo O'Neill, Hickory Ground, May 28, 1792, AGI, PC, *leg.* 39; Coker and Watson, *Indian Traders,* 158–59, 161–62.

12. Manuel Gayoso de Lemos to Baron de Carondelet, Natchez, July 21, 1792, n.° 11, Archivo Nacional de Cuba, *leg.* 2, trans. in *PETHS* 27 (1955), 87–90.

13. Ibid.

14. See, for example, "Instructions to Leonard Shaw, temporary agent to the Cherokee nation of Indians," Feb. 17, 1792, in *ASP: IA,* 247–48.

15. The Secretary of War to Governor Blount, Apr. 22, 1792, *ASP: IA,* 252–53.

16. Quotes from Wallace, *Jefferson and the Indians,* 166, and "Conference Ground, near Nashville, Thursday, Aug. 9, 1792," *ASP: IA,* 287.

17. Dowd, *A Spirited Resistance,* 75–89.

18. Ibid., 90; White, *Middle Ground,* 413–68.

19. Dowd, *A Spirited Resistance,* 90–109.

20. Document 7; Dowd, *A Spirited Resistance,* 90–115; *ASP: IA,* 203–6, 288–95; Hoig, *The Cherokees and Their Chiefs,* 74–75.

21. Whitaker, "Spain and the Cherokee Indians," 255.

22. "Report of David Craig to William Blount, Superintendent of Indian Affairs for the Southern District, made at Knoxville, March 15, 1792," *ASP:IA,* 264.

23. *SMV,* 4, pt. 3, xiii; Coker and Watson, *Indian Traders,* 162–63; Cherokees to the Spanish Governor in Mobile, Cherokee Nation, June 29, 1792, AGI, PC, *leg.* 38, trans. in *PETHS* 27 (1955), 91–92.

24. *ASP: IA,* 269–94; Hoig, *The Cherokees and Their Chiefs,* 76–80.

25. *ASP: IA,* 267–69.

26. William Panton to Arturo O'Neill, Hickory Ground, May 28, 1792, AGI, PC, *leg.* 39; John McDonald to William Panton, Cherokees, Oct. 6, 1792, AGI, PC, *leg.* 39; Coker and Watson, *Indian Traders,* 162–63; Whitaker, "Spain and the Cherokee Indians," 257.

27. Juan de la Villebeuvre to Señor Baron de Carondelet, Bouctouca, Oct. 12, 1792, in Serrano y Sanz, *Spain and the Cherokee and Choctaw Nations,* Dickinson trans., 59–61.

28. Baron de Carondelet to Conde de Aranda, New Orleans, Nov. 13, 1792, n.° 22, *reservado,* AGI, PC, *leg.* 177; Luis de las Casas to Señor Gobernador de la Luisiana, Havana, Jan. 5, 1793, AGI, PC, *leg.* 152A.

29. Armillas Vicente, "La gran confederación india"; Baron de Carondelet to Luis de las Casas, New Orleans, Nov. 20, 1792, AGI, SD, *leg.* 9, trans. in *SMV,* 4, pt. 3, 96–98; Cotterill, *Southern Indians,* 97.

30. "A los Jefes, Guerreros, y demás de la Nación Cheraquí," New Orleans, Nov. 24, 1792, AGI, PC, *leg.* 18, trans. in *PETHS* 28 (1955), 137–38.

31. Baron de Carondelet to Conde de Aranda, New Orleans, Nov. 13, 20, 28, 1792, *Reservados* 22, 23, 24, AHN, *Estado, leg.* 3898, esp. 5; "A los Jefes, Guerreros, y demás de la Nación Cherakee," Baron de Carondelet, New Orleans, Nov. 24, 1792, AGI, PC, *leg.* 18, also in AHN, *Estado, leg.* 3893, *exp.* 5, no. 2; and AGI, PC, *leg.* 177, trans. in *PETHS* 28 (1955), 137–38.

32. [William] Panton to Carondelet, Pensacola, Nov. 6, 1792, AGI, PC, leg. 203 in *PETHS* 28 (1955), 134.

33. "Message of Carondelet to Choctaws and Chickasaws [1793]," and Baron de Carondelet, "Proposals for an Indian Congress," New Orleans, Feb. 26, 1793, in *SMV,* 4, pt. 3, 140–43.

34. Baron de Carondelet, "Proposals for an Indian Congress," ibid.; "A los Jefes, Guerreros, y demás de la Nación Cheraqui," AGI, PC, *leg.* 18; trans. "Carondelet to the Cherokee Nation, New Orleans, November 24, 1792," in *PETHS* 28 (1955), 137–38.

35. Carondelet, "Proposals for an Indian Congress, New Orleans, Feb. 26, 1793 in *SMV,* 4, pt. 3, 140–43.

36. Villebeuvre to Carondelet, Boukfouka, Jan. 16, 1793, AGI, PC, *leg.* 208, and Villebeuvre to Gayoso, Boukfouka, Feb. 5, 1793, AGI, PC, *leg.* 208, trans. in *PETHS* 29 (1957), 142, 149.

37. Manuel Gayoso de Lemos to Turner Brashears, Natchez, Aug. 1, 1792, *copia,* N.° 2, AGI, PC, *leg.* 2353; Manuel Gayoso de Lemos to Baron de Carondelet, Natchez, July 21, 1792, N.° 11, Archivo Nacional de Cuba, *leg.* 2, trans. in *PETHS* 27 (1955), 87–90. Brashears's wife was probably also a niece of Taboca, according to O'Brien, *Choctaws in a Revolutionary Age,* 88. See the three essays of Holmes on Delavillebeuvre: "Juan de la Villebeuvre and Spanish Indian Policy in West Florida, 1784–1797," 387–99; "Juan de la Villebeuvre: Spain's Commandant of Natchez During the American Revolution," 97–129; "Up the Tombigbee with the Spaniards: Juan de la Villebeuvre and the Treaty of Boucfouca (1793)," 51–61.

38. Manuel Gayoso de Lemos to Juan Delavillebeuvre, Natchez, July 31, 1792, AGI, PC, *leg.* 2353. The instructions were probably prepared by Carondelet.

39. Manuel Gayoso de Lemos to Baron de Carondelet, Natchez, Aug. 5, 1792, ibid.

40. Manuel Gayoso de Lemos to Baron de Carondelet, Natchez, Aug. 26, 1792, N.° 184, ibid.; Juan Delavillebeuvre to Baron de Carondelet, At the Choctaws, Sept. 5, 1792, trans. in *SMV,* 4, pt. 3, 76.

41. [Juan] Delavillebeuvre to [Baron de] Carondelet, At the Choctaws, Sept. 5, 1792, trans. from the French in *SMV,* 4, pt. 3, 74–77. A letter of Gayoso to Delavillebuevre dated September 4 asked Delavillebeuvre to tell Franchimastabé that he was grateful to have the two medals and the letters brought by Iteleghana and that he would send them to Carondelet as proof of his friendship: [Manuel] Gayoso [de Lemos] to [Juan] Delavillebeuvre, Natchez, Sept. 4, 1792, AGI, PC, *leg.* 2353; Jack D. L. Holmes, "The Ebb Tide of Spanish Military Power on the Mississippi: Fort San Fernando de las Barrancas," *PETHS* 34 (1962), 31.

42. Minutes of this congress for August 7–11 can be found in *ASP: IA,* 284–88; William Blount to the Secretary of War, Knoxville, Sept. 20, 1792, ibid., 283; Juan Delavillebeuvre to

Baron de Carondelet, At the Choctaws, Sept. 5, 1792, trans. in *SMV,* 4, pt. 3, 74–77; Juan Delavillebeuvre to Baron de Carondelet (?), Yazoo, Aug. 22, 1792, AGI, PC, *leg.* 2353, trans. from the French by Robert L. Smith; [Juan] Delavillebeuvre to [Manuel] Gayoso [de Lemos], Boukfouka, Sept. 10, 1792, trans. from the French in *SMV,* 4, pt. 3, 79–80; [Juan] Delavillebeuvre to [Baron de] Carondelet, Boucfouca, Sept. 12, 1792, trans. from the French in ibid., 80–83; [Juan} Delavillebeuvre to Baron de Carondelet, Boukfouka, Jan. 16, 1793, AGI, PC, *leg.* 208, trans. in *PETHS* 29 (1957), 146; Atkinson, *Splendid Land, Splendid People,* 151–55.

43. [Juan] Delavillebeuvre to [Baron de Carondelet], Boukfouka, Sept. 12, 1792, trans. from the French in *SMV,* 4, pt. 3, 83. Bear Creek, according to General Pickens, was the place agreed upon at Hopewell. See "Minutes of a Conference Held at Nashville, 7, 8, and 10 August, 1792," *ASI: IA,* 1: 287; Carson, *Searching for the Bright Path,* 46. The bracketed Ilepooenantla is the name listed in the American minutes: "Minutes," *ASP: IA,* 285.

44. Manuel Gayoso de Lemos to Baron de Carondelet, Natchez, Sept. 27, 1792, N.° 176, AGI, PC, *leg.* 2353.

45. Delavillebeuvre to Carondelet, At the Choctaws, Sept. 5, 1792, in *SMV,* 4, pt. 3, 74–75. This meeting may have been the same one described by Juan de la Villebeuvre to Baron de Carondelet, Bouctoca [*sic*], Oct. 12, 1792, in Serrano y Sanz, *Spain and the Cherokee and Choctaw Indians,* Dickinson trans., 59–61.

46. "Harangue delivered to the Small Party in the village of Atchontchouba this third day of September 1792 in the name of the Governor General of the Province of Louisiana, Baron de Carondelet," Jn. Delavillebuevre, Boukfouka, Sept. 10, 1792, AGI, PC, *leg.* 2353, trans. from the French by Robert L. Smith; Juan Delavillebeuvre to Manuel Gayoso de Lemos, Boukfouka, Apr. 4, 1793, ibid., trans. in *PETHS* 31 (1959), 69.

47. "Lanzos to Indians, St. Stephen, September 21, 1792", *SMV,* 4, pt. 3, 87–88.

48. [Juan] Delavillebeuvre to [Manuel] Gayoso [de Lemos], Boucfouka, Sept. 10, 1792, and Juan Delavillebeuvre to [Carondelet], Boucfouka, Sept. 12, 1792, *SMV,* 4, pt. 3, 79–83.

49. Jn. Delavillebeuvre [to Gayoso], Yazoo, Aug. 22, 1792, AGI, PC, *leg.* 2353, Smith trans.; [Minutes] Conference Ground Near Nashville, Aug. 7, 1792, *ASP: IA,* 285–87.

50. Jn. Delavillebeuvre to the Baron de Carondelet, At the Choctaws, Sept. 5, 1792, *SMV,* 4, pt. 3, 76.

51. Jn. Delavillebeuvre to Manuel Gayoso de Lemos, Boukfouka, Sept. 10, 1792, and Juan Delavillebeuvre to [Carondelet], Boukfouka, Sept. 12, 1792, *SMV,* 4, pt. 3, 79–83.

52. Manuel Gayoso de Lemos to Juan Delavillebeuvre, Natchez, Sept. 28, 1792, N.° 3, *copia,* AGI, PC, *leg.* 2353.

53. Manuel Gayoso de Lemos to Baron de Carondelet, Natchez, Sept. 13, 1792, N.° 161, *copia,* ibid.

54. Manuel Gayoso de Lemos to Baron de Carondelet, Natchez, Oct. 26, 1792, N.° 184, *copia,* ibid.

55. Panton to Carondelet, Pensacola, Nov. 9, 1792, AGI, PC, 177, in *PETHS* 28 (1955), 132. The traders Hardy Perry and Alexander Fraser reported to the Spanish commandant in Mobile, Vicente Folch, that "Turnbull" was the particular object of Creek raids on American settlements in the Tombigbee River valley in early 1789: Hardy Perry and Alexander Fraser to Vicente Folch, Choctaw Nation(?), Apr. 27, 1789, *traducción,* enclosed with Estevan Miró to Antonio Valdés, New Orleans, May 20, 1789, *Reservado* N.° 38, AGI, SD, *leg.* 2553.

56. [Baron de] Carondelet to [Manuel] Gayoso [de Lemos], New Orleans, Dec. 18, 1792, trans. in *SMV,* 4, pt. 3, 103–6. Carondelet tried to persuade Panton to accept a Turnbull store: Baron de Carondelet to William Panton, New Orleans, Dec. 13, 1792, AGI, PC, *leg.* 2362.

57. Coker and Watson, *Indian Traders,* 258–59.

58. Baron de Carondelet to Luis de las Casas, New Orleans, May 22, 1793, *Reservado*, AGI, PC, *leg.* 15-B.

59. Document 12; Whitaker, "Spain and the Cherokee Indians," 260.

60. Manuel Gayoso to Payemingo and Ubulayacabé, Great Chiefs of the Chickasaw Nation, Natchez, Dec. 29, 1792, *copia*, AGI, PC, leg. 42; Manuel Gayoso de Lemos to Hardy Perry, Natchez, Dec. 29, 1792, *copia*, ibid.

61. [Juan] Delavillebeuvre to [Baron de] Carondelet, Boukfouka, Jan. 16, Feb. 4, 5, 7, 1793, AGI, PC, *leg.* 208, trans. in *PETHS* 29 (1957), 142–44, 147–50, 153.

62. Juan de la Villebeuvre to Baron de Carondelet, Boukfouka, Feb. 4, 1793, AGI, PC, *leg.* 208, trans. in *PETHS*, 29 (1957), 147–48.

63. Bloody Fellow to [Baron de] Carondelet, Boukfouka, Feb. (?), 1793, Tchoukafala, Feb. 11, 1793, AGI, PC *leg.* 208, repr. in *PETHS* 29 (1957), 155–56; Piomingo and Others to Carondelet, Chickasaws, Feb. 11, 1793, AGI, PC, *leg.* 208, repr. in *PETHS* 29 (1957), 154–55.

64. Juan de la Villebeuvre to Baron de Carondelet, Boukfouka, Jan. 16 (two letters), 21, Feb. 4, 7, 9, 27, [Boukfouka ?] Feb. [28?], 1793, Juan de la Villebeuvre to Manuel Gayoso de Lemos, Boukfouka, Feb. 5, 1793; all in AGI, PC, *leg.* 208, trans. in *PETHS* 29 (1957), 142–60.

65. Juan Delavillebeuvre to Manuel Gayoso de Lemos, Boukfouka, May 12, 1793, AGI, PC, leg. 2353, trans. from French by Robert L. Smith; James P. Pate, "The Fort of the Confederation: The Spanish on the Upper Tombigbee," *Alabama Historical Quarterly* 44 (Fall and Winter 1982), 173; Sánchez-Fabrés, *Situación histórica de las Floridas*, 31, 79; Document 13.

66. Carson, *Searching for the Bright Path*, 133.

67. [Carondelet] to Luis de las Casas, New Orleans, June 11, 1793, AGI, PC, *leg.* 2363; Pate, "The Fort of the Confederation," 174.

68. Pate describes in detail the plan and construction of the fort in ibid., 174–86; Juan Delavillebeuvre to Manuel Gayoso de Lemos, Boukfouka, Aug. 30, 1793, AGI, PC, *leg.* 2353, trans. from the French by Robert L. Smith, another trans. in *PETHS* 35 (1963), 87.

CHAPTER 7. TANGLED AND TWISTED PATHS TO NOGALES

1. Gregory Evans Dowd, *War Under Heaven: Pontiac, the Indian Nations, and the British Empire* (Baltimore: Johns Hopkins University Press, 2002), 43–44.

2. Pate, "The Fort of the Confederation," 170–86.

3. Manuel Gayoso de Lemos to Carlos de Grand-Pré, Cuartel General del Molino de Bayu Pierre, Oct. 31, 1792, copy; Manuel Gayoso de Lemos to Baron de Carondelet, Natchez, Nov. 1, 1792, N.° 186; Manuel Gayoso de Lemos to Juan Delavillebeuvre, Natchez, Nov. 16, 1792, N.° 2, copy; all in AGI, PC, *leg.* 2353.

4. Din and Nasatir, *The Imperial Osage*, esp. 217–54; Arnold, *Rumble of a Distant Drum*, 100–115; DuVal, "'Faithful Nations,' and 'Ruthless Savages'," 138–49. The northern Indians were Loups, Miamis, Ottawas, Potawatamis, Shawnees, and Peorias. See "Northern Indians to Trudeau," *SMV*, 4, pt. 3, 110–11.

5. Luis de Blanc to Baron de Carondelet, Natchitoches, December 1, 1792, *SMV*, 4, pt. 3, 99–100.

6. Baron de Carondelet to Luis Carlos de Blanc, New Orleans, Oct. 18, 1792, ibid., 92–93.

7. Manuel Gayoso de Lemos to Baron de Carondelet, Natchez, Nov. 27, 1792, N.° 200, and Natchez, May 1, 1793, both in AGI, PC, *leg.* 2353.

8. Baron de Carondelet, "Proposals for Indian Congress," New Orleans, Feb. 26, 1793, in *SMV*, 4, pt. 3, 141–43.

9. Manuel Gayoso de Lemos to John Turnbull, Natchez, Apr. 7, 1793, N.° 1, copy, AGI, PC, *leg.* 2353; also in *PETHS* 31 (1959), 72–74; Document 3.

10. Manuel Gayoso de Lemos to John Turnbull, Natchez, Apr. 7, 1793 N.° 1, AGI, PC, *leg.* 2353, copy, *PETHS* 31 (1959), 73–75.

11. "Indian Speeches Made at Long Town," in *SMV,* 4, pt. 3, 164–67.

12. Ibid.

13. "Haujo" is another variant. Saunt identifies the name as a war chief title and notes, "A Muskogee-English dictionary from the late nineteenth century glosses the Creek term hache as 'drunk, crazy, resolute, daring,' a word related etymologically to hadjo, as in the warrior titles Efau Hadjo, meaning 'mad dog' or 'drunken dog'." Saunt suggests that Creeks appeared in the eighteenth century to associate drunkenness with madness and conducive to bravery: *A New Order of Things,* 146.

14. Ibid., 99–100.

15. Pedro Olivier to Baron de Carondelet, Mongulacha, June 11, 1793, in *SMV,* 4, pt. 3, 167–73. With regard to the "fiesta of the maize," the reference is probably to the green corn ceremony, the most important seasonal ceremony for all southeastern Indians because of the importance of corn to them and, indeed, to other Native Americans. See Hudson, *Southeastern Indians,* 366; Calloway, *One Vast Winter Count,* 67–115.

16. Calloway, *One Vast Winter Count,* 168–71. Carondelet identified the "Chief of the Cusitas, Kiskilisaki" as one of those important for the success of confederation. See Baron de Carondelet to William Panton, New Orleans, Dec. 13, 1792, AGI, PC, *leg.* 2362.

17. Piomingo to [James] Seagrove, Chickasaw Nation, Longtown, Sept. 1, 1793, in AGI, PC, *leg.* 203, also in *PETHS* 35 (1963), 90–91.

18. Baron de Carondelet to Manuel Gayoso de Lemos, New Orleans, Mar. 5, 1793, AGI, PC, *leg.* 2353, trans. in *PETHS* 31 (1959), 65.

19. On warfare among southeastern Indians, see Hudson, *Southeastern Indians,* 239–57, and as practiced by Cherokees, see John Philip Reid, *A Law of Blood: The Primitive Law of the Cherokee Nation* (New York: New York University Press, 1970).

20. Manuel Gayoso de Lemos to Baron de Carondelet, Natchez, June 8, 1793, AGI, PC, leg. 2353, trans. in *PETHS* 33 (1961), 67–71.

21. Ibid.; Abernethy, *The South in the New Nation,* 49, 59.

22. Manuel Gayoso de Lemos to Baron de Carondelet, June 8, 1793, AGI, PC, leg. 2353, trans. in *PETHS* 33 (1961), 67–71.

23. Ibid., 68–69.

24. Ibid.; Juan de la Villebeuvre to Baron de Carondelet, Boukfouka, Mar. 8, 1793, AGI, PC, *leg.* 208, trans. in *PETHS* 30 (1958), 97; Manuel Gayoso de Lemos to Baron de Carondelet, Walnut Hills, July 19, 1793, AGI, PC, *leg.* 42, trans. in *PETHS* 34 (1962), 90.

25. Manuel Gayoso de Lemos to Baron de Carondelet, Natchez, June 8, 1793, AGI, PC, *leg.* 2353, trans. in *PETHS* 33 (1961), 67–71.

26. Ibid.

27. Ibid.

28. De Milfort to Baron de Carondelet, Tuquet Bachet, May 26, 1793, trans. from French, in *SMV,* 4, pt. 3, 160–62; Saunt, *New Order of Things,* 170n.

29. Pedro Olivier to Baron de Carondelet, Mongulacha, June 11, 1793, in *SMV,* 4, pt. 3, 167–73, esp. 168.

30. Ibid., 173.

31. Manuel Gayoso de Lemos to the Chiefs and Warriors of the Chickasaw Nation, Natchez, June 20, 1793, AGI, PC, *leg.* 2353, trans. in *PETHS* 33 (1961), 75–76.

32. Manuel Gayoso de Lemos to Baron de Carondelet, Natchez, Sept. 12, 1793, AGI, PC, *leg.* 178, trans. in *PETHS* 35 (1963), 93.

33. Manuel Gayoso de Lemos to Baron de Carondelet, Walnut Hills, July 18, 1793, AGI, PC, *leg.* 2353, trans. in *PETHS* 34 (1962), 89; Manuel Gayoso de Lemos to Baron de Carondelet, Walnut Hills, July 19, 1793, AGI, PC, *leg.* 42, trans. in *PETHS* 34 (1962), 90–91.

34. Manuel Gayoso de Lemos to Baron de Carondelet, Natchez, Sept. 12, 1793, AGI, PC, *leg.* 178, trans. in *PETHS* 35 (1963), 93.

35. Ougolayackabee [*sic*] to Mr. Gayoso, Boukfouka, July 9, 1793, AGI, PC, *leg.* 2353, in *PETHS* 34 (1962), 87; Manuel Gayoso de Lemos to Baron de Carondelet, Walnut Hills, July 25, 1793, AGI, PC, *leg.* 178, trans. in *PETHS* 34 (1962), 94–95.

36. Juan de la Villebeuvre to Manuel Gayoso de Lemos, Boukfouka, Aug. 30, 1793, AGI, PC, *leg.* 2353, trans. in *PETHS* 35 (1963), 85–87; Juan de la Villebeuvre to Elías Beauregard, Boukfouka, Aug. 30, 1793, AGI, PC, *leg.* 2353, trans. from the French by Robert L. Smith.

37. Manuel Gayoso de Lemos to Baron de Carondelet, Natchez, September 12, 1793, AGI, PC, *leg.* 178, trans. in *PETHS* 35 (1963), 94.

38. Manuel Gayoso de Lemos to William Blount, Walnut Hills, July 21, 1793, AGI, PC, *leg.* 208, in *PETHS* 34 (1962), 91–94.

39. Juan de la Villebeuvre to Manuel Gayoso de Lemos, Boukfouka, May 25, 1793, AGI, PC, *leg.* 2353, trans. in *PETHS* 32 (1960), 92; Juan de la Villebeuvre to Manuel Gayoso de Lemos, Boukfouka, June 8, 1793, AGI, PC, *leg.* 2353, trans. in *PETHS* 33 (1961), 65–66.

40. Oguoulayacabé to Manuel Gayoso de Lemos, Boukfouka, July 9, 1793, AGI, PC, *leg.* 2353, in *PETHS* 34 (1962), 87–88.

41. Manuel Gayoso de Lemos to Baron de Carondelet, Walnut Hills, July 25, 1793, AGI, PC, *leg.* 178, trans. in *PETHS* 34 (1962), 96; Manuel Gayoso de Lemos to Baron de Carondelet, Natchez, Sept. 12, 1793, AGI, PC, *leg.* 178, trans. in *PETHS* 35 (1963), 95.

42. Manuel Gayoso de Lemos to Baron de Carondelet, Walnut Hills, July 25, 1793, AGI, PC, *leg.* 178, trans. in *PETHS*, 34 (1962), 95.

CHAPTER 8. THE NOGALES ASSEMBLY

1. Piomingo to Mr. [James] Seagrove, Cherokees, Sept. 12, 1793, AGI, PC, *leg.* 211, in *PETHS* 35 (1963), 90–91.

2. Jennings, ed., *The History and Culture of Iroquois Diplomacy*, esp. 24–28, 121; Document 14.

3. Document 14; Juan de la Villebeuvre to Manuel Gayoso de Lemos, Boukfouka, May 25, 1793, AGI, PC, *leg.* 2353, trans. in *PETHS* 32 (1960), 89–90.

4. Document 14; Manuel Gayoso de Lemos to Baron de Carondelet, Walnut Hills, Oct. 18, 1793, AGI, PC, *leg.* 41, trans. in *PETHS* 36 (1964), 70–71; Manuel Gayoso de Lemos to Baron de Carondelet, Walnut Hills, July 25, 1793, AGI, PC, *leg.* 178, trans. in *PETHS* 34 (1962), 96. Paul's first letter to the Corinthians (Cor. 12:12), for example, contains the following: "For just as the body is one and has many members, and all the members of the body, though many, are one body, so it is with Christ."

5. Document 14; Manuel Gayoso de Lemos to Baron de Carondelet, Walnut Hills, Oct. 18, 1793, AGI, PC, *leg.* 41.

6. Document 14. Richard White discusses the redistribution function of chiefs for both this region and that of the Great Lakes in *Roots of Dependency*, 40, 42, 73–82, and *The Middle Ground*, 173–80.

7. Document 14. Gayoso had earlier told Carondelet that he did not think any chiefs

would come from the Six Villages "because they must go to see Your Lordship to excuse themselves for the killing and the robberies they committed recently, which has caused Mistichico, their principal chief, to take all the party with him to that Capital, fearing that before they had given satisfaction they would not be well received here." Manuel Gayoso de Lemos to Baron de Carondelet, Walnut Hills, Oct. 18, 1793, AGI, PC, *leg.* 42, trans. in *PETHS* 36 (1964), 70.

8. Document 14.

9. Ibid.

10. Ibid.

11. Ibid.; Jennings, ed. *The History and Culture of Iroquois Diplomacy,* 121–22; Swanton, *Indians of the Southeastern United States,* 381–86.

12. Document 14; Williams, *Linking Arms Together,* 73.

13. Document 15.

14. Manuel Gayoso de Lemos to Baron de Carondelet, Natchez, Nov. 10, 1793, AGI, PC, *leg.* 42, trans. in *PETHS* 36 (1964), 72–73.

15. Ibid.; Manuel Gayoso de Lemos to Elías Beauregard, Natchez, Nov. 11, 1793, AGI, PC, *leg.* 42, trans. in *PETHS* 36 (1964), 74–75; Hoig, *The Cherokees and Their Chiefs,* 80.

16. Manuel Gayoso de Lemos to Baron de Carondelet, Natchez, Nov. 12, 1793, AGI, PC, *leg.* 42, trans. in *PETHS* 36 (1964), 75.

17. [Baron de Carondelet to Manuel Gayoso de Lemos], New Orleans, [Nov.], 1793, ibid.

CHAPTER 9. PATHS FROM NOGALES TO SAN FERNANDO DE LAS BARRANCAS

1. Document 15.

2. Jack D. L. Holmes, "Spanish-American Rivalry Over the Chickasaw Bluffs," *PETHS* 34 (1962), 26–57; Pedro Rousseau, "Diary," trans. in Nasatir, *Spanish War Vessels on the Mississippi,* 107, 185; [Carondelet to Casas], New Orleans, May 22, 1793, N.° 79, *Reservado,* AGI, PC, *leg.* 15-B.

3. Atkinson, *Splendid Land, Splendid People,* 102–3.

4. Calloway, *American Revolution in Indian Country,* 221, 229; Atkinson, *Splendid Land, Splendid People,* 112–15, 124; *SMV,* 3, pt. 2, xii, "Declaration of Labadie," July 5, 1782, in *SMV,* 3, pt. 2, 21–34; "Robberies on the Mississippi—Madame Cruzat Captured—Her Account—1782," in Houck, *The Spanish Regime in Missouri,* 1: 211–34.

5. Atkinson, *Splendid Land, Splendid People,* 125; Alexander Frazer to Arturo O'Neill, Yazoo, June 12, 1787, enclosed with Arturo O'Neill to Estevan Miró, Pensacola, July 20, 1787, AGI, PC, *leg.* 37, in *PETHS* 11 (1939), 85; Holmes, "Spanish-American Rivalry Over the Chickasaw Bluffs, 1780–1795," 32–33; Benjamin James to Mather and Strother, Choctaw Nation, July 23, 1787, AGI, PC, *leg.* 200, in *PETHS* 11 (1939), 85–87; Cotterill, *The Southern Indians,* 74.

6. Baron de Carondelet to Manuel Gayoso de Lemos, New Orleans, Dec. 18, 1792, in *SMV,* 4, pt. 3, 103–6.

7. The Baron de Carondelet to Luis de Las Casas, New Orleans, May 22, 1793, AGI, PC, *leg.* 1447, trans. in *PETHS* 32 (1960), 88.

8. Ben James to Governor Blount, Choctaw Nation, June 30, 1792, repr. in *ASP: IA,* 284; Atkinson, *Splendid Land, Splendid People,* 124.

9. Harry Ammon, *The Genêt Mission* (New York: W. W. Norton, 1973), 10–20., esp. 19; Crane Brinton, *A Decade of Revolution, 1789–1799* (New York: Harper and Row, 1934), 164.

10. Baron de Carondelet to Luis de las Casas, New Orleans, Feb. 15, 1793, in *SMV*, 4, pt. 3, 137.

11. "Proclamation by Carondelet," New Orleans, Feb. 15, 1793, in ibid., 139.

12. Ammon, *The Genêt Mission*, 26.

13. Ibid., 44–56, 65–79; François Barbé-Marbois, *The History of Louisiana, Particularly the Cession of That Colony to the United States of America*, edited, with an introduction, by Wilson Eugene Lyon (Baton Rouge: Louisiana State University Press, 1977), 153–60.

14. *SMV*, 4, pt. 3, xxxii.

15. Ammon, *The Genêt Mission*, 147–70.

16. Whitaker, *Spanish-American Frontier*, 19, 32, 187.

17. Ammon, *The Genêt Mission*, 81–82; Frederick Jackson Turner, "The Origin of Genêt's Projected Attack on Louisiana and the Floridas," *American Historical Review*, 3 (1897), 650–71.

18. Whitaker, *Spanish-American Frontier*, 187–88, 190–92; Manuel Gayoso de Lemos to Elías Beauregard, Natchez, Nov. 4, 1793, *Muy Reservada*, AGI, PC, *leg*. 41; Manuel Gayoso de Lemos to Baron de Carondelet, Natchez, Dec. 23, 1793, AGI, PC, *leg*. 178, trans. in *PETHS* 36 (1964), 77–80.

19. Ougelayackabee to Govr. Gayoso or Chactamathaha, Thisatera, Mar. 15, 1794, AGI, PC, *leg*. 126, in *PETHS* 38 (1966), 79.

20. Carl J. Ekberg, *Colonial Ste. Genevieve: An Adventure on the Mississippi Frontier* (Tuscon: The Patrice Press, copyright, Carl J. Ekberg, 1996), 78; Ammon, *The Genêt Mission*, 86.

21. James Robertson to Manuel Gayoso de Lemos, Mero District Nashville, Feb. 1, 1794, in *SMV*, 4, pt. 3, 253; Abernethy, *The South in the New Nation*, 49.

22. Baron de Carondelet to the Duque de Alcudia, New Orleans, June 10, 1795, transcript copy in MDAH, MPA, SPT, ledger 5, 882–86; Gwendolyn Midlo Hall, *Africans in Colonial Louisiana: The Development of Afro-Creole Culture in the Eighteenth Century* (Baton Rouge: Louisiana State University Press, 1992), 343–74; Gilbert C. Din, *Spaniards, Planters, and Slaves: The Spanish Regulation of Slavery in Louisiana, 1763–1803* (College Park: Texas A&M University Press, 1999), 154–77.

23. Baron de Carondelet to Manuel Gayoso de Lemos, New Orleans, Dec. 18, 1792, in *SMV*, 4, pt. 3, 105. See also Baron de Carondelet to William Panton, New Orleans, Dec. (?), 1792, AGI, PC, *leg*. 122-A, in PL, reel 7.

24. Document 16.

25. William Panton to Baron de Carondelet, Pensacola, Nov. 6, 1792, AGI, PC, *leg*. 177, in *PETHS* 28 (1955), 132–33; Baron de Carondelet to Manuel Gayoso de Lemos, New Orleans, Mar. 5, 1793, AGI, PC, *leg*. 2353, trans. in *PETHS* 31 (1959), 65; Baron de Carondelet to Luis de las Casas, New Orleans, Aug. 27, 1793, AGI, PC, *leg*. 1447, trans. in *PETHS* 34 (1962), 104

26. Juan de la Villebeuvre to Baron de Carondelet, Boukfouka, Mar. 8, 1793, AGI, PC, *leg*. 208, trans. in *PETHS* 30 (1958), 97.

27. Taskihatoka and Others to Delavillebeuvre, Chickasaw Nation, Mar. 10, 1793, ibid.

28. William Panton to Baron de Carondelet, Pensacola, June 7, 1793, repr. in *Georgia Historical Quarterly* 23 (Sept. 1939), 301–2; "Contract between John Joyce and Panton Leslie, & Company," New Orleans, Jan. 30, 1795, AGI, PC, *leg*. 203, trans. in *PETHS* 43 (1971), 97–98; Document 13.

29. Juan de la Villebeuvre to Baron de Carondelet, Boukfouka, Feb. 7, 1793, AGI, PC, *leg*. 208, trans. in *PETHS* 29 (1957), 151.

30. Baron de Carondelet to Luis de las Casas, New Orleans, Mar. 30, 1795, AGI, PC, *leg*. 354, trans. in *PETHS* 45 (1973), 84; Document 16.

31. Nasatir, *Spanish War Vessels on the Mississippi*, 9–21, 59–73, 73n.30.

32. Ibid., 63–65; Pedro Rousseau, "Diary," in ibid., 153–88, esp. 186.

33. Ibid., 85–92, 89n.7.

34. Abernethy in *The South in the New Nation*, 136–68.

35. Nasatir, *Spanish War Vessels on the Mississippi*, 107–8.

36. Manuel Gayoso de Lemos to Baron de Carondelet, Natchez, Jan. 8, 1795, AGI, PC, *leg.* 2354, trans. in *PETHS* 42 (1970), 99–106; John Forbes to [William Panton], Mobile, March 29, 1795, AGI, PC, *leg.* 31, in *PETHS* 45 (1975), 82.

37. Manuel Gayoso de Lemos to Baron de Carondelet, Natchez, Jan. 8, 1795, AGI, PC, *leg.* 2354, trans. in *PETHS* 42 (1970), 100; Atkinson, *Splendid Land, Splendid People*, 164–65.

38. Manuel Gayoso de Lemos to Baron de Carondelet, Natchez, Jan. 8, 1795, AGI, PC, *leg.* 2354, trans. in *PETHS* 42 (1970), 101–4.

39. Ibid., 106.

40. Nasatir, *Spanish War Vessels on the Mississippi*, 100–101, 108; Atkinson, *Splendid Land, Splendid People*, 167.

41. Atkinson, *Splendid Land, Splendid People*, 108.

42. Ougoulayacabe to Manuel Gayoso de Lemos, Chickasaws, Feb. 17, 1795, AGI, PC, leg. 211, in *PETHS* 43 (1971), 105–6.

43. Manuel Gayoso de Lemos to Benjamin Fooy, Natchez, Mar. 14, 1795, AGI, PC, *leg.* 211, trans. in *PETHS* 44 (1972), 109.

44. Manuel Gayoso de Lemos to Ugulayacabé, Natchez, Mar. 14, 1795, ibid., repr. in *PETHS* 44 (1972), 109–11.

45. Nasatir, *Spanish War Vessels on the Mississippi*, 108–11; Pierre Rousseau to Manuel Gayoso de Lemos, Chickasaw Bluffs, Apr. 24, 1795, AGI, PC, *leg.* 211, trans. in *PETHS* 46 (1974), 112.

46. Rousseau to Gayoso, Chickasaw Bluffs, Apr. 24, 1795, AGI, PC, leg. 211, trans. in *PETHS* 46 (1974), 114.

47. Pierre Rousseau to Manuel Gayoso de Lemos, Chickasaw Bluffs, Apr. 25, 1795, ibid., trans. in *PETHS*, ibid.; Nasatir, *Spanish War Vessels*, 111.

48. Pierre Rousseau to Manuel Gayoso de Lemos, Chickasaw Bluffs, Apr. 25, 1795, ibid., trans. in *PETHS*, ibid., 115.

49. Baron de Carondelet to Luis de las Casas, New Orleans, May 1, 1795, AGI, PC, *leg.* 2354, trans. in *PETHS* 47 (1975), 145.

50. Manuel Gayoso de Lemos to Baron de Carondelet, Roadstead of Esperanza, May 23, 1795, AGI, PC, *leg.* 31, trans. in *PETHS* 48 (1976), 135–36; "Diary of Gayoso de Lemos' Expedition on La Vigilante, Part I: April 16, 1795–[September 7, 1797]," trans. in Nasatir, *Spanish War Vessels on the Mississippi*, 238–87, esp. 252–78.

51. Gayoso to Carondelet, ibid., 137.

52. Manuel Gayoso de Lemos to Baron de Carondelet, Roadstead of Esperanza. On Board the Vigilante, May 26, 1795, AGI, PC, *leg.* 31, trans. in *PETHS*, 48 (1976), 137–38; Document 16.

53. Copy of a letter from Payemingo to Manuel Gayoso de Lemos, Chickasaw Nation, June 8, 1795, enclosed with Manuel Gayoso de Lemos to Baron de Carondelet, San Fernando de las Barrancas, June 17, 1795, *Reservado*, N.° 11, Louisiana Papers, Bancroft Library, Box 3, folder 317.

54. Manuel Gayoso de Lemos to Baron de Carondelet, San Fernando de las Barrancas, July 18, 1795, *Reservado*, N.° 14, AGI, PC, *leg.* 25 B.

55. Document 16.

56. Document 17; Atkinson, *Splendid Land, Splendid People*, 171–72.

57. Whitaker in *The Spanish-American Frontier,* 171–222; Weber, *The Spanish Frontier in North America,* 289; José Antonio Armillas Vicente, *Mississippi, frontera de España y los E. U. ante el Tratado de San Lorenzo* (Zaragoza: Institución Fernando el Católico, 1977).

58. Document 3.

59. Josef Deville de Goutin to Juan Ventura Morales, San Fernando de las Barrrancas, Dec. 18, 1796, n.° 39, a portion of which Juan Ventura Morales attached to a letter to Diego de Gardoqui, New Orleans, Mar. 3, 1797, AGI, PC, SD, *leg.* 2614.

60. Calloway, *One Vast Winter Count,* 375.

61. On Jackson and the Indians, see Anthony F. C. Wallace, *The Long, Bitter Trail: Andrew Jackson and the Indians* (New York: Hill and Wang, 1993), and Robert V. Remini, *Andrew Jackson and His Indian Wars* (Robert V. Remini, 2001; New York: Viking Penguin), esp. "The Making of an Indian Fighter," 1–20; and on Indian fighters as part of an American frontier mythology, see Slotkin, *Regeneration Through Violence,* 4–24.

Notes to Documents

DOCUMENT 1

1. An old French measure of length, equal to one meter, 949 millimeters.

2. The *galeota* (galiot) was a smaller version of the galley, a vessel powered by both sails and oars. See Nasatir, *Spanish War Vessels on the Mississipppi 1792–1796*, 38–40.

3. Girault was born in London. He served with George Rogers Clark in his western expedition of 1778 during the American Revolution and settled in the Natchez district in the 1780s, where he became a major landowner. He knew both French and Spanish and served as "the King's translator" until 1794. See *Biographical and Historical Memoirs of Mississippi* (Chicago: Goodspeed Publishing Company, 1981), 2 vols., 1: 672.

4. Hutchins describes this site in some detail in his *Historical Narrative and Topographical Description of Louisiana and West Florida* (1784), 53–54. He writes, "the water of the Mississippi, when the river is high, runs up the Yazu several miles and empties itself by a number of channels, which direct their course across the country, and fall in above the Walnut Hills." Victor Collot records the same phenomenon; see Georges-Henri-Victor Collot, *A Journey in North America*, 3 vols., trans. J. Christian Bay (Firenze: O. Lange, 1924; repr. New York: AMS Press, 1974), 2: 44.

5. The French had built a fort in 1718 and named it St. Pierre, about eight miles north-northeast of Nogales near a town of the Yazu Indians along the Yazu River. It was destroyed at the time of the massacre at Natchez in 1729. The site has been conclusively identified and is located just north of Redwood, Mississippi, in Warren County on State Highway 3. See Jack D. Elliott, Jr., "Comprehensive Plan for Historical Preservation for the Period of European Colonization in Mississippi," draft (Jackson: MDAH, Division of Historical Preservation, 1989), 39–42.

DOCUMENT 4

1. Ebenezer Fulson (Fulsom, Folsom) was one of three brothers who migrated with their parents from North Carolina to Mississippi before the American Revolution. See Wells, "Choctaw Mixed Bloods and the Advent of Removal," 73; H. B. Cushman, *History of the Choctaw, Chickasaw, and Natchez Indians* (Greenville, Texas, 1899), 326–27. Richard King served as captain of the militia in the Natchez district during the Spanish period. See May

Wilson McBee, *The Natchez Court Records, 1767–1813: Abstracts of Early Records* (Ann Arbor, 1953), 484.

2. A rather remarkable number of miles to travel in one day. With reference to New England, David Hackett Fischer writes that "thirty miles was a long day's journey in that era [1770s]" See his *Paul Revere's Ride* (New York: Oxford University Press, 1994), 139. In the introduction to their translation of Minor's account of his second mission to the Choctaws, Ross and Phelps suggest that Minor's estimates of distance in the Indian country were less accurate than those for the area closer to Natchez. See Edward Hunter Ross and Dawson A. Phelps, trans. and eds., "A Journey over the Natchez Trace in 1792: A Document from the Archives of Spain," *Journal of Mississippi History* 15 (Oct. 1953), 254.

3. Carlos de Grand-Pré identified a Sulusmastabé as a nephew of Franchimastabé and probably in line to succeed his uncle as chief of all the Chactas; Carlos de Grand-Pré to Estevan Miró, Natchez, Apr. 13, 1791, AGI, PC, *leg.* 41, N.° 101.

4. Sulusmastabé is a title, not a name, as in the case of "Franchimastabé" and other Indian Chiefs. "Sulusmastabé," as it is spelled here, was known to the French as "Soulier Rouge." The Spanish translated it "Zapatos Colorados," or "Red Shoes" in English. The French transcription of the Choctaw is "Soulouche Oumastabé," which was part of a war chief's title. There were a number of Choctaw and other chiefs who bore this title. See MPA, FD, IV, n. 16–17. The suffix *abe* means roughly "he who kills another man," according to Byington, *A Dictionary of the Choctaw Language*, 5. Hence, one translation of "Franchimastabé" might be "he who kills or killed a Frenchman." It does fit somewhat the present Franchimastabé, given his English proclivities while the British sustained a presence in the region. Franchimastabé was the principal leader of the Choctaw warriors who helped the British defend Natchez from rebellious Americans after James Willing's 1778 raid. See Greg O'Brien, "'We are behind you': The Choctaw Occupation of Natchez in 1778," *Journal of Mississippi History* 54 (Summer 2002), 107–24.

5. The Mississippi-Louisiana Almanac of 1815 records a Philip Hayes Stand along the Natchez Trace twenty-six miles from the Choctaw line. These stands provided places to lodge. See Dawson A. Phelps, "Stands as Travel Accommodations on the Natchez Trace," *Journal of Mississippi History* 11 (1949), 1–54. In an appendix to the journal submitted to Governor Miró in 1787 to report his mission to the Choctaw Nation, Juan Delavillebeuvre listed a Philip Hayes as a trader identified with the village of Oka Opoulou of the Large Party. See Charles A. Weeks, "Politics and Trade: Delavillebeuvre's 1787 Mission to the Choctaws and Journal," *Journal of Mississippi History* 65 (Spring 2003), 70.

DOCUMENT 7

1. A published Spanish text of Minor's diary can be found in [Serrano y Sanz], *Documentos históricos de la Florida y la Luisiana*, 418–36. Another English translation of this diary is by Edward Hunter and Dawson A. Phelps, "A Journey over the Natchez Trace in 1792: A Document from the Archives of Spain," *Journal of Mississippi History* 15 (October 1953), 252–73.

2. The manuscript omits a number.

DOCUMENT 10

1. Charles Louis Boucher de Grand Pré (Carlos de Grand Pré) played a major role in the history of the Natchez district during the Spanish period. He had served as a comman-

dant before the arrival of Gayoso and was active in the reorganization of government and the laying out of a town of Natchez. See Holmes, *Gayoso,* 17, 18, 20, 39 41, 166. His father, Joseph Louis Boucher de Grandpré, served in Canada for twenty years before coming to French Louisiana. He played a major role in ending the Choctaw civil war of the 1740s. See *MPA:FD,* IV: 96, n. 12.

2. On Dr. James O'Fallon, the general agent of the South Carolina Yazoo Company, see John C. Parish, "The Intrigues of Doctor James O'Fallon," *Mississippi Valley Historical Review* 17 (1930–31), 230–63; Abernethy, *The South in the New Nation,* 78–84; Holmes, *Gayoso,* 145; Coker and Watson, *Indian Traders,* 141–42.

3. See Document 9 for Gayoso's March 21 letter to Taskietoka, the king of the Chickasaws.

4. The third of the enclosures to which Gayoso refers lists goods purchased for the royal store from Manuel Texada, a resident of Natchez.

5. The fourth enclosure lists Stonahuma as a candidate to receive a large medal. Two others are listed, Nochamumaacho and Anchalimastabé, both for large medals.

6. The people listed for these gifts are the king of the Chickasaws, Franchimastabé, Itelegana, Taboca, Sulemastabé, Stonahuma, Nocjahumaacho, Tapanahuma, and Red Ground.

7. Born in Galicia, Joseph Vidal served as secretary to Gayoso. He remained in Natchez as Spanish "consul" after its transfer to the United States in 1798. He is noted as the founder of Concordia on the other side of the Mississippi River (present-day Vidalia, Louisiana). See Holmes, *Gayoso,* 50.

8. White was one of five priests chosen for the Natchez mission by the bishop of Salamanca. William Savage served as parish priest in Natchez until his death in 1793 at which time he was succeeded by Gregorio White, who had been serving as priest in Coles Creek. See ibid, 69–71.

9. From Alicante, Spain, Candel was one of three people to hold the important office of supervisor of Indian gifts and finances during the Gayoso years. See ibid., 51.

10. There are a total of six numbered attachments to Gayoso's letter N.°86 in AHN, Estado, *leg.* 3898, *exp.* 5.

11. This request was granted in the royal order accepting the treaty and approving expenses associated with it. See Duque de Alcudia to Baron de Carondelet, Madrid, December 26, 1792. AGI, PC, *leg.* 2317B.

DOCUMENT 17

1. Described as a mestizo chief and identified with the pro-American faction, although with a Spanish commission (captain); William Glover to Mr. Lavillebeuvre, Chickasaws, April 8, 1793, *PETHS* 31 (1959), 78n. Gayoso saw him and his town as "good Spaniards" in early 1795; Manuel Gayoso de Lemos to William Glover, Natchez, March 14, 1795, AGI, PC, *leg.* 211, in *PETHS* 44 (1972), 112–13. A Chickasaw name or title he carried was Olacta opaye.

2. The deceased king, Taskietoka, was succeeded by Chinubee (also identified as Chenumbee or Chinibe or Tinabe-Mingo). He was, according to Gayoso, a brother and succeeded "by right of blood"; Manuel Gayoso de Lemos to Baron de Carondelet, Natchez, Oct. 10, 1792, *PETHS* 41, 110. Another source identifies him as a nephew; see Atkinson, *Splendid Land, Splendid People,* 167, 348.

3. Gayoso had news of a sale by March 1795. Manuel Gayoso de Lemos to Juan de la Villebeuvre, Natchez, March 18, 1795, AGI, PC, *leg.* 31, copy in *leg.* 211, trans. in *PETHS* 45

(1973), 78; Manuel Gayoso de Lemos to the Baron de Carondelet, Natchez, March 30, 1795, AGI, PC, *leg.* 31, trans. in ibid, 83. The Georgia legislature passed and the governor signed into law the Yazoo Act in early January 1795. See Abernethy, *The South in the New Nation,* 136–68, esp. 146.

4. The Spanish reads "solo les llene al pie de ciento."

Essay on Sources

This short essay offers some observations about the sources from which both the narrative and document portions of this book derive. I have tried to use the sources in a way to allow the many voices they represent to be heard but obviously in a way that advances an argument about a dimension of political life in the lower Mississippi valley and Gulf South toward the end of the eighteenth century. Full bibliographical information can be found in the notes.

The documents, both Spanish and English, represent, of course, the perspective of their authors and, through them, the voices of Native Americans, filtered additionally through interpreters and recorders. The book places primary emphasis, however, on Spanish sources and their perspectives. Those sources are abundant and of course can best be encountered in Spain in such major holdings as the Archivo General de Indias (AGI) in Sevilla, the Archivo Histórico Nacional (AHN) in Madrid, and the Archivo General de Simancas (AGS) near Valladolid. Within those holdings, the most valuable were the archive collections of the Captaincy General of Cuba or the Cuban papers, the papers of the Audiencia of Santo Domingo in the AGI, and the State papers in the AHN. Other Spanish institutions hold important maps and documents for the lower Mississippi valley and Gulf South; these include the Biblioteca Nacional, the Servicio Histórico Militar, and the Museo Naval, all in Madrid. Many of these Spanish sources have been transcribed or copied and can be accessed in the United States in such state archives as the Mississippi Department of Archives and History in Jackson and in the Library of Congress, the Historic New Orleans Collection and various university libraries.

Important sources of American and British documents useful for the period or its antecedents were consulted. The Draper Collection in the State Historical Society of Wisconsin contains papers of Americans who played important roles in the region as private entrepreneurs and public officials, such as William Blount, James Robertson, and James Wilkinson; it also has other documents of relevance in its "Frontier Wars" section. This collection has been microfilmed and is available in many locations. A particularly important source of contemporary American documents for this project was the first of the two-volume *American State Papers, Class II: Indian Affairs,* published first in the early 1830s and reprinted later as part of the *New American State Papers* series. Of the British documents, the most useful for background to the 1790s were those in "Colonial Office Records: America and the West Indies" of the Public Record Office in Kew, England. Those records exist in the form of transcripts or microfilmed copies and can be consulted in a number of locations in the United States.

Many of these documents have been translated and published in the following collections: the three volumes titled *Spain in the Mississippi Valley* (*SMV*), edited by Lawrence Kinnaird, that formed part of the *Annual Report of the American Historical Society for 1945*; "Papers from the Spanish Archives Relating to Tennessee and the Old Southwest, 1783–1800," translated and edited by D. C. Corbitt and Roberta Corbitt for the annual *East Tennessee Historical Society Publications* (*PETHS*) from 1939 through 1977; and the two-volume *Spanish Regime in Missouri,* edited by Louis Houck (1909). The Kinnaird volumes contain only part of the Louisiana Papers in the Bancroft Library of the University of California at Berkeley; the entire collection, however, may be consulted there or by means of microfilm copies.

My article, "Voices from Mississippi's Past: The Spanish Provincial Archives in the Mississippi Department of Archives and History," *Journal of Mississippi History* 66 (August 1999), discusses in more detail these repositories and collections.

Of the American secondary sources that can be regarded as making up an older borderland's historiography, one should begin with the writings of Herbert Eugene Bolton, who is credited with expanding Frederick Jackson Turner's concept of the frontier to include a notion of "Spanish borderlands"; see Bolton, *The Spanish Borderlands: A Chronicle of Old Florida and the Southwest* (1921) and his other writings. Justin Winsor's late nineteenth-century books should be noted for what they contain on the lower Mississippi valley and the Gulf South in the eighteenth century: *The Westward Movement: The Colonies and the Republic West of the Alleghenies, 1763–1798* (1897) and *The Mississippi Basin: The Struggle Between England and France, 1697–1763* (1898).

Yet for this period, and for this book, Arthur Whitaker's *The Spanish-American Frontier, 1783–1795: The Westward Movement and the Spanish Retreat from the Mississippi Valley* (1927) was the most important. Its focus, however, is conflict between Americans and Spaniards in the region with a decided bias on the American side and with no recognition of the major population of the region, Native Americans, and their participation. Because of its major exploitation of both Spanish and American sources, its emphasis is much broader than Jane M. Berry's article "The Indian Policy of Spain in the Southwest 1783–1795," *Mississippi Valley Historical Review* (March 1917). Other works from the period written by Americans sustain this emphasis. Randolph Downes's articles "Creek-American Relations, 1782–1790," *Georgia Historical Quarterly* 11 (January 1971), and "Indian Affairs in the Southwest Territory, 1790–1796," *Tennessee Historical Magazine* (January 1937), do better by the Indians but still with a kind of patronizing tone. The many writings of Jack D. L. Holmes, using Spanish sources, endeavored to present a Spanish view of this region's late eighteenth-century past in an effort to lay to rest the nefarious black legend but, in so doing, did not pay much attention to that past's Indian component. He wrote a biography of Manuel Gayoso de Lemos, the Spanish governor in Natchez and later governor general for Louisiana in New Orleans—*Gayoso: The Life of a Spanish Governor in the Mississippi Valley 1789–1799* (1965)—and characterized him well as "the Indian diplomat." More recent literature in this tradition include Thomas Abernethy's contribution to a multivolume history of the South, *The South in the New Nation (1789–1819)* (1961), which assigns minimal importance to the Spanish, African, and Indian peoples of the region.

Of these older histories, albeit for earlier periods, some attach more importance to the participation of Native Americans and, in so doing, suggest ways to look at the last quarter of the eighteenth century when Native Americans remained the major population of the region. Of particular value were Verner W. Crane's *The Southern Frontier, 1670–1732* (1929) and John R. Alden's *John Stuart and the Southern Colonial Frontier* (1944).

Spanish writing in this tradition does a better job of treating Native Americans seriously and describing their role in the politics of the encounter period. Manuel Serrrano y Sanz, writing early in the twentieth century, perhaps led the way with his *España y los indios Cherokís y Chactas en la segunda mitad del siglo XVIII* (1916), a book that has now been translated by Samuel Doris Dickinson as *Spain and the Cherokee and Choctaw Indians in the Second Half of the Eighteenth Century* and published by the Potsherd Press (1995). Written in the context of the recent defeat of Spain in the so-called Spanish-American War of 1898 and in the context of World War I, the author in a very explicit way addresses himself to what he saw as perpetrators of the black legend, who in 1916 found themselves with a new enemy to demonize. A doctoral thesis by Frank De Fina done at the University of Madrid in the early 1960s exploited Spanish documentation extensively to produce "Rivalidades y contactos entre España, Norte América y las Naciones Indias Chacta, Chicasas, Cherokís y Criks en la segunda mitad del Siglo XVIII," a detailed study of Americans, Spaniards, and Indians and their roles in defining a dimension of the region's political life. Had it been revised and published I would not have undertaken this book. Elena Sánchez-Fabrés Mirat's *Situación histórica de las Floridas en la segunda mitad del siglo XVIII (1783–1819)* (1977) exploits fully the State Papers in the Archivo Histórico Nacional on the same subject but with less emphasis on the topic's Indian dimension. Again, with more focus on Indians than much of American writing, José Antonio Armillas Vicente's essay "La gran confederación India: Interacción Hispano-Angloamericana del Sudeste norteamericano a fines del S. XVIII," found in the second volume of *Estudios sobre política indigenista española en América* (Valladolid, 1976), discusses attempts to create an Indian confederation with Spanish participation. F. de Borja Medina Rojas's *José de Ezpeleta: Gobernador de la Mobila, 1780–1781* (1980) devotes a significant amount of attention to the role of the Choctaws, Chickasaws, and Creeks in the conflict between Britain and Spain during the American Revolution.

Native Americans maintained an awareness of their identity and importance and eventually gained allies among archaeologists and anthropologists. Together these groups made it possible for practitioners of written history to begin to revise in a major way the older histories that portrayed the region as one of the many where European powers competed for empire through most of the late seventeenth and eighteenth centuries. What has now emerged is a view of the area as one less of conflict and more of collaboration, interaction, and exchange involving Native Americans, Africans, and Euro-Americans. With a focus on Native Americans, many of these perspectives on the American Southeast find expression in the essays that make up Peter H. Wood, Gregory A. Waselkov, and M. Thomas Hatley, eds., *Powhatan's Mantle: Indians in the Southeast* (1989).

Of the anthropologists who stand out in this regard and have been of value and importance for this book, John Swanton should be noted. His volumes on the Southeast continue to be of value, and two in particular were used for this project: *The Indians of the Southeastern United States* (1946) and *Source Material for the Social and Ceremonial Life of the Choctaw Indians* (repr., University of Alabama Press, 2001). In addition to Swanton, Charles M. Hudson's authored or edited work, particularly *Southeastern American Indians (1976)* and *Four Centuries of Southern Indians* (1975), has been of value. One of his students, Robbie Ethridge, has now written *Creek Country: The Creek Indians and Their World* (2003), which—despite its emphasis on Creek country as portrayed at the end of the eighteenth century in the writings of the American agent to the Creeks, Benjamin Hawkins—contains much of value on the landscape and culture of the Creek for the earlier eighteenth century.

Since World War II the distinction between anthropology and history has blurred considerably to the benefit of all who seek a more complete and balanced understanding of this region's past. The mixing of the two has produced a new field of history known as ethnohistory, which has focused on Native Americans in an attempt to understand them as distinctive groups but also as participants with newcomers from Europe and Africa during the encounter period of 1500–1800. Historical interests have also shifted away from past politics and in the direction of the economic and social lives of peoples and have also come to attach importance to communication and language. The result has been a greater variety of histories and a more ample understanding of the past.

Ethnohistory has produced already a number of excellent historical studies of individual Indian groups and their interactions with European newcomers. They have made possible a better understanding of the politics and diplomacy related to that interaction. Those important for this work include Patricia K. Galloway, *Choctaw Genesis, 1500–1700* (1995); James Taylor Carson, *Searching for the Bright Path: The Mississippi Choctaws from Prehistory to Removal* (1999); Greg O'Brien, *Choctaws in a Revolutionary Age, 1750–1830* (2002); James H. Merrell, *The Indians' New World: Catawbas and Their Neighbors From European Contact Through the Era of Removal* (1989); Claudio Saunt, *A New Order of Things: Property, Power, and the Transformation of the Creek Indians, 1733–1816* (1999); Duane Champagne, *Social Order and Political Change: Constitutional Governments among the Cherokee, the Choctaw, the Chickasaw, and the Creek* (1992).

The writings of other anthropologists and historians, while sometimes focused on other periods or regions, contain chapters on or useful insights into the Gulf South. They include Colin G. Calloway, *Crown and Calumet: British-Indian Relations, 1783–1815* (1987), *The American Revolution in Indian Country: Crisis and Diversity in Native-American Communities* (1995), and *One Vast Winter Count: The Native American West before Lewis and Clark* (2003); Anthony F. C. Wallace, *Death and Life of the Seneca* (1969) and *Jefferson and the Indians: The Tragic Fate of the First Americans* (1999); Richard White, *The Roots of Dependence: Subsistence, Environment, and Social Change among the Choctaws, Pawnees, and Navajos* (1983) and *The Middle Ground: Indians, empires, and republics in the Great Lakes region, 1650–1815;* Morris Arnold, *The Rumble of a Distant Drum: The Quapaws and Old World Newcomers, 1673–1804* (2000). Gregory Evans Dowd's *A Spiritual Resistance: The North American Indian Struggle for Unity, 1745–1815* (1991) provided me an important source of insight into Native Americans as active historical participants. Dowd and White, for example, discuss efforts on the part of Indians to confederate as a way to preserve themselves from challenges emanating from Anglo-America.

More specialized studies on such topics as trade, diplomacy, and language should be noted. Some take an ethnohistorical approach; others do not. On the role of trade and traders in the Gulf South, see William S. Coker and Thomas D. Watson, *Indian Traders of the Spanish Borderlands: Panton Leslie & Company and John Forbes & Company, 1783–1847* (1986); Michael Morris, *The Bringing of Wonder: Trade and the Indians of the Southeast, 1700–1783* (2002); Kathryn E. Holland Braund, *Deerskins & Duffels: The Creek Indian Trade with Anglo-America, 1685–1815* (1993). On diplomacy, see Francis Jennings et al., eds., *The History and Culture of Iroquois Diplomacy: An Interdisciplinary Guide to the Treaties of the Six Nations and Their League* (1985); Robert A. Wilson, Jr., *The American West in American Legal Thought: The Discourses of Conquest* (1990), and *Linking Arms Together: American Treaty Visions of Law and Peace, 1600–1800* (1997). Wilson analyzes the language of written discourse to show how it functioned as a tool of conquest. David Murray offers some valuable insights into the nature of Native-American talk in *Forked Tongues: Speech, Writing & Representation in*

North American Indian Texts (1991). I found his essay on "Indian Speech and Speeches" in that book especially pertinent. Daniel H. Usner, Jr.'s *Indians, Settlers, & Slaves in a Frontier Exchange Economy: The Lower Mississippi Valley Before 1783* (1992) deals with both trade and diplomacy, with a valuable chapter on "The Indian Alliance Network," although the analysis is not carried through the Spanish period after 1783. Again, on an earlier period but with useful insight for understanding the trade, politics, and diplomacy of later times, see Allan Gallay, *The Indian Slave Trade: The Rise of the English Empire in the American South, 1670–1717* (2002).

David J. Weber sought in *The Spanish Frontier in North America* (New Haven: Yale University Press, 1992) to revise and update Bolton in light of the newer literature and its more varied perspectives, and he provides an extensive bibliography of that literature as of the early 1990s.

Index